NATIONAL SELF-DETERMINATION AND SECESSION

National Self-Determination and Secession

edited by

MARGARET MOORE

OXFORD UNIVERSITY PRESS
1998

Oxford University Press, Great Clarendon Street, Oxford OX2 6DP
Oxford New York
Athens Auckland Bangkok Bogotá Buenos Aires Calcutta
Cape Town Chennai Dar es Salaam Delhi Florence Hong Kong Istanbul
Karachi Kuala Lumpur Madrid Melbourne Mexico City Mumbai
Nairobi Paris São Paolo Singapore Taipei Tokyo Toronto Warsaw
and associated companies in
Berlin Ibadan

Oxford is a registered trade mark of Oxford University Press

Published in the United States
by Oxford University Press Inc., New York

First published 1998

British Library Cataloguing in Publication Data
Data available

Library of Congress Cataloging in Publication Data
National self-determination and secession / edited by Margaret Moore.
Includes bibliographical references and index.
1. State succession. 2. Self-determination, National. I. Moore, Margaret, Ph.D., London School of Econ.
KZ4024.N38 1998 341.26—dc21 98–18236
ISBN 0–19–829384–4

1 3 5 7 9 10 8 6 4 2

Typeset by Graphicraft Limited, Hong Kong
Printed in Great Britain
on acid-free paper by
Bookcraft (Bath) Ltd
Midsomer Norton, Somerset

ACKNOWLEDGEMENTS

As with all edited volumes, this collection would not be possible without the co-operation of all the authors. With ten busy and often-travelling authors, it was not easy to co-ordinate a work of this sort. I am therefore grateful to the authors for their co-operation in this matter, and especially for sending me chapters and revisions without having to be hounded and harassed. I would like to thank Wayne Norman, particularly. Our debates on various questions connected to self-determination and secession via e-mail encouraged me to embark on this collaborative enterprise.

I am also grateful to Joanne Voisin, my secretary at the University of Waterloo, who performed wizardry on this document to transform it from ten chapters written with various softwares, with different referencing systems, and numerous idiosyncracies, to a manuscript ready to be sent to the publisher.

I would also like to thank Dominic Byatt, the Commissioning Editor at Oxford University Press, who encouraged this project from the beginning, and was wonderfully helpful in answering my queries to the end.

I would also like to thank my children, Sean and Paul, for their (not entirely voluntary) co-operation. They both suspected that I was playing interesting games on the computer after putting them to bed, when, in fact, I was reading and commenting on chapters, sending e-mails, and doing other tasks connected to this collection.

Stratford, Ontario
October 1997 M. M.

CONTENTS

Notes on Contributors viii

1. Introduction: The Self-Determination Principle and the Ethics of Secession 1
MARGARET MOORE
2. Democracy and Secession 14
ALLEN BUCHANAN
3. The Ethics of Secession as the Regulation of Secessionist Politics 34
WAYNE NORMAN
4. Secession and the Principle of Nationality 62
DAVID MILLER
5. Self-Determination in Practice 79
DANIEL PHILPOTT
6. Liberal Nationalism and Secession 103
KAI NIELSEN
7. The Territorial Dimension of Self-Determination 134
MARGARET MOORE
8. National Self-Determination: Some Cautionary Remarks Concerning the Rhetoric of Rights 158
RONALD S. BEINER
9. Self-Determination: Politics, Philosophy, and Law 181
DONALD L. HOROWITZ
10. 'Orphans of Secession': National Pluralism in Secessionist Regions and Post-Secession States 215
JOHN MCGARRY
11. Myths and Misconceptions in the Study of Nationalism 233
ROGERS BRUBAKER

Select Bibliography 266
Index 277

NOTES ON CONTRIBUTORS

Ronald S. Beiner is Professor of Political Science at the University of Toronto. His books include *Political Judgment* (1983), *What's the Matter With Liberalism?* (1992), and, most recently, *Philosophy in a Time of Lost Spirit: Essays on Contemporary Theory* (1997). He is also editor of *Theorizing Citizenship* (1995) and *Theorizing Nationalism* (forthcoming).

Rogers Brubaker is Professor of Sociology at the University of California, Los Angeles. His books include *The Limits of Rationality: An Essay on the Social and Moral Thought of Max Weber* (1984), *Citizenship and Nationhood in France and Germany* (1992), and *Nationalism Reframed: Nationhood and the National Question in the New Europe* (1996). He is currently working on an ethnographic study of ethnicity in everyday life in the ethnically mixed Transylvanian city of Cluj/Kolozsvar.

Allen Buchanan is Professor of Philosophy at the University of Arizona (Tucson). He is the author of numerous articles in ethics, political philosophy, and bioethics and of the following books: *Marx and Justice: The Radical Critique of Liberalism* (1982); *Ethics, Efficiency, and the Market* (1985); *Deciding for Others: The Ethics of Surrogate Decision-Making* (with Dan W. Brock) (1989); and *Secession: The Morality of Political Divorce From Fort Sumter to Lithuania and Quebec* (1991).

Donald L. Horowitz is James B. Duke Professor of Law and Political Science at Duke University (Durham, NC). He is the author of *The Jurocracy* (1977), a book about government lawyers and *The Courts and Social Policy* (1977), for which he was awarded the Louis Brownlow Prize of the National Academy of Public Administration. Among his books on comparative politics and ethnic group conflict are *Coup Theories and Officers' Motives* (1980); *Ethnic Groups in Conflict* (1985); and *A Democratic South Africa? Constitutional Engineering in a Divided Society* (1991), which won the Ralph J. Bunche Prize of the American Political Science Association for the best book in ethnic and cultural pluralism. His most recent book, *The Deadly Ethnic Riot* will be published in 1998.

John McGarry is Professor of Political Science at the University of Waterloo (Canada). He is the co-author of *The Politics of Antagonism* (1993) and *Explaining Northern Ireland* (1995), the co-editor of *The Future of Northern Ireland* (1990) and *The Politics of Ethnic Conflict Regulation* (1993), and the author of several articles on ethnic conflict and nationalism.

David Miller is Official Fellow in Social and Political Theory at Nuffield College, Oxford. His interests in this field are wide-ranging, including theories of justice and equality, the ethics of market economies, and problems of nationality and citizenship. Among his books are *Market, State and Community* (ed. with Michael Walzer) (1989), *Pluralism, Justice and Equality* (1995), and *On Nationality* (1995). He is currently completing a new book on social justice, and exploring in a series of papers some of the wider ramifications on the principle of nationality expounded in *On Nationality*.

Margaret Moore is Associate Professor of Political Science at the University of Waterloo (Canada). She is the author of *Foundations of Liberalism* (1993) and several articles on liberal theory, citizenship, national identity, and self-determination.

Kai Nielsen is Professor Emeritus, Department of Philosophy, the University of Calgary and adjunct Professor Concordia University. His two most recent books are: *Naturalism without Foundations* (1996) and *Transforming Philosophy* (1993).

Wayne Norman is Chair in Business Ethics in the Centre for Applied Ethics at the University of British Columbia. He taught previously in the philosophy departments of the University of Ottawa and the University of Western Ontario. In recent years he has written widely in political theory on the tensions between citizenship and nationality, and on institutional solutions like federalism and secession. He is currently completing a book on these themes, tentatively entitled *Playing the Nationalist Card: Political Morality in the Multiethnic State.*

Daniel Philpott is assistant professor of Political Science, University of California, Santa Barbara. He specializes in ethnic and international relations, and is currently writing a book about the evolution of sovereignty since the Middle Ages.

1

Introduction: The Self-Determination Principle and the Ethics of Secession

MARGARET MOORE

Unlike the extensive and challenging debates about the history and sociology of nationalism, there has been, until very recently, a dearth of serious philosophical reflection on the normative implications of nationalism. Benedict Anderson, in *Imagined Communities*, contrasts the political power and appeal of nationalism with its 'philosophical poverty and even incoherence . . . Unlike other "isms", nationalism has never produced its own grand thinker: no Hobbeses, no Tocquevilles, Marxes, or Webers'.[1]

This volume is concerned with one of the most important normative issues at the heart of nationalism. This is the issue whether nations have a right to collective self-determination. If they do, what is it about nations that entitles them to this right? If not, are there any conditions in which a group can justifiably secede from a state?

This issue is of pressing importance. Between 1947 and 1991, only one instance of secession occurred (Bangladesh). In that period, the superpowers were committed to upholding existing state boundaries, and they encouraged the development of international law and practice in which borders were viewed as permanent—not negotiable—features of the international state system. Since 1991, however, numerous multinational states have disintegrated along national lines—the Soviet Union, Yugoslavia, Czechoslovakia, Ethiopia—and the process may not have exhausted itself yet, as many of the successor states are as multinational as the states they left behind. Nor is this limited to former communist countries. There are numerous secessionist struggles across the globe: in the First World (e.g. Quebec, Northern Ireland, Flanders, Catalonia, the Spanish Basque country, Israel/Palestine); and in the Third World (e.g. Sudan, Sri Lanka, Kashmir and Punjab, and the Kurdish regions of Iraq and Turkey).

This volume explores the issue of collective self-determination from two distinct, but related, perspectives. First, it analyses the various normative theories of secession, which elaborate the conditions in which a right to self-determination, including a right to secession, may be justified. Second, it analyses self-determination claims from the perspective of the nationalist dynamics which fuel these struggles. The first kind of argument typically applies existing liberal values such as autonomy or liberal theories of justice to the issue of secession; whereas the second type of argument tends to discuss the phenomena of nationalism directly, and to assess the extent to which granting self-determination, including secession, is consistent with basic values such as equal respect for minorities, whether it is consistent with the identities that the groups have, and will provide a stable solution to national conflicts.

Underlying the philosophical question of whether nations have a right to collective self-determination, and the conditions in which this right can be exercised, is the relationship between liberalism and nationalism, and the possibility of reconciling them, at least at the level of theoretical principles.[2] The two issues are, of course, related, since many of the discussions of a right to secession confine themselves to recognizing this right for groups that are prepared to abide by democratic norms, respect liberal rules of justice and equal rights under the law.

THE PRINCIPLE OF NATIONAL SELF-DETERMINATION

There are three questions that are often thought to be begged by the principle of national self-determination:[3]

1. Who are the people?
2. What is the relevant territorial unit in which they should exercise self-determination?
3. Does secession have a demonstration effect?

The issues of territorial units and the peoples that constitute a majority for self-determination are complexly interrelated. Most of the discussions of the problem of indeterminacy have approached this issue by focusing on the problem as it applies to peoples. As Ivor Jennings pointed out,

> On the surface, it [the principle of self-determination] seemed reasonable: let the people decide. It was in fact ridiculous because the people cannot decide until somebody decides who are the people.[4]

There are two distinct conceptions of who 'the people' are, which have predominated in international law in different historical periods, but both are very much alive in popular conceptions of self-determination. These different conceptions have different implications for the drawing of boundaries and have potentially explosive consequences when they conflict.

Throughout the nineteenth century until the end of the First World War, 'the peoples' who were entitled to be self-determining were conceived of in ethnic terms. As US President Woodrow Wilson said in his famous Fourteen Points speech, the USA aimed to secure a 'fair and just peace' by employing the 'principle of national self-determination'.[5] The 'peoples' entitled to exercise the right to self-determination, according to the Paris Peace Accord of 1919, were ethnic groups which had become nationally mobilized, and numerous states were carved out of the ruins of the Russian, German, Austro-Hungarian, and Ottoman empires along broadly ethnic lines.[6]

Whereas self-determination in the Wilsonian period was conceived of as the political independence of ethnic or national communities—a conception that still has force today—the principle has been elaborated in international law in the post-Second World War period to make clear that the 'peoples' in question are not ethnic or national groups, but, rather, multi-ethnic people under colonial rule. Self-determination has been conceived in international law as the 'right of the majority within an accepted political unit to exercise power' and boundaries have been drawn without regard for the linguistic or cultural composition of the state.[7]

On the ethnic conception of 'peoples' entitled to exercise the right to self-determination, the 'self' is the ethnic group residing on its historic or ancestral territory. On most interpretations, the ethnic principle is used to ensure that all members of a particular ethnic group are encapsulated in a single state, although, as Moore points out in Chapter 7, many ethnic or national groups also appeal to the particular nation's historical or religious or ethical conceptions to justify rights to territory (because the idea that a group has a homeland that is its own is important in the group's conception of itself as a nation, and they usually have arguments to justify this belief that the territory rightfully belongs to them).

On the conception of 'peoples' as majorities within accepted political units, the issue of the relevant territorial units in which self-determination is to be exercised is crucial, with different results depending on what is regarded as the area of the plebiscite.

On the Wilsonian conception of who the 'peoples' are that are entitled to be self-determining, the ethnic identity of the 'people' defines where the boundaries should be drawn; on the civic conception of peoples as majorities within accepted political units, the answer to the territorial question (what is the relevant territorial unit?) defines who counts as 'the people'. In many cases, the two conceptions do not coincide and the possibility of conflict is very real. Indeed, the principle of national self-determination is unproblematic only in the ideal case that the administrative boundary coincides with the ethnic or national group; the group is territorially concentrated, with no significant minorities; and the members of the groups are strongly mobilized in favour of self-determination. Most cases, however, fall far short of that ideal, although Iceland is the rare exception, in which both definitions of 'people' (those resident in the administrative boundaries of the unit, and those who are members of the nation) happen to coincide.[8] But in most cases, the definitions of 'the people' and territorial units in which self-determination is to occur are contested, and the possibility of alienated minorities within the state, stranded minorities on the other side of the border, contested homelands, and mobilized unionist groups against the possible secession are very real indeed, as McGarry outlines in Chapter 10.

Another criticism of the principle of national self-determination is that its demonstration effect would be destabilizing for the international state system. The source of concern is the destabilizing effects of a principle, which, it is alleged, could license a secessionist free-for-all and lead to the breakup of most of the world's states. This argument is expressed by Ernest Gellner, in *Nations and Nationalism*, who claimed that the principle of national self-determination is impractical because there are many potential nations (on his linguistic criterion for determining a potential nation) but only room for a small number of political units.

There are two distinct types of demonstration effects. One type has been empirically documented by Walker Connor in relation to the impact that the self-determination of one colony had on other colonies, particularly in the decolonization period.[9] He notes that the intensity of the effect was greater when the two colonies were closer in proximity and were ruled by the same imperial power. In this case, there is a parallel demonstration effect, whereby groups derive sustenance from the successes of other similar groups.

Another type of demonstration effect applies to minorities within secessionist regions. Here the self-determination of one group is viewed as compromising the self-determination of another group in the same territory. In this case, the minority within the seceding region demands self-determination on the grounds that they are a 'self', or a nation, similar to the nation that has achieved, or is striving to achieve, self-determination for itself. In this case of secessions within secession, there is the possibility of a sub-optimal outcome, namely, pockets or enclaves of unviable sovereign units over a territory. This topic is discussed in Moore's chapter on rival claims to territory, and McGarry's and Horowitz's chapters (10 and 9 respectively) on competing national identities and the difficult, if not impossible, task of drawing lines on a map that separate rival groups.

Normative theories about the right to secession deal with the demonstration effect mainly by restricting the right to secede to groups in unjust states (Buchanan, Chapter 2; Norman, Chapter 3). Another, not necessarily antagonistic, strategy is to erect hurdles to prevent the right from being exercised easily (Philpott, Chapter 5; Norman).

THEORIES OF THE MORALITY OF SECESSION

The philosophical questions that are begged by the principle of national self-determination are addressed indirectly by the various theories of justified secession. Most proceed by attempting to *apply* established liberal arguments or liberal values to the issue of secession. In 1991, when Allen Buchanan published *Secession: The Morality of Political Divorce from Fort Sumter to Lithuania and Quebec,* he began by pointing out that the issue of the morality of secession has received very little consideration from a normative standpoint and that he hoped to initiate a debate on the subject. Since then, writers in political philosophy, sociology, comparative politics, and other fields have taken up the challenge and there are now a number of diverse philosophical perspectives on this subject.

Most commentators on the philosophical argument concerning the ethics of secession organize their discussion by classifying the arguments, either for (or against) the right to secede into three types, each of which articulates the conditions under which there might be a right (or justified claim) to secede. These theories are: (1) choice theories; (2) just-cause theories; and (3) national self-determination theories.

(1) Choice theories of the right to secede, such as that advanced in his chapter by Daniel Philpott, typically require that a territorially concentrated majority express a desire to secede (in a referendum or plebiscite) for the secession to be legitimate, and do not require that the seceding group demonstrate that they are victims of injustice or that they have a special claim to the territory they intend to take with them. Different choice theorists pick different conditions that a group must satisfy in the absence of injustice, but, typically, the argument for a right to self-determination (including a right to secession) is based on an argument about the right of political association, thereby grounding the individualist right in a deeper argument about the value of autonomy. On this view, there is a close relation between democracy and a right to secession: both are legitimated by the importance of people making decisions about the institutional structure of the society in which they live (which state they live in).

This way of conceiving of secession ignores the fact that most secessionist movements are based on nationally mobilized groups. Because choice theorists tend to conceive of secession as justified in terms of individual voluntary choice, they ignore entirely the ethnic or ascriptive character of many of these secessionist movements. Moreover, as Moore and Horowitz argue, this understanding of secession as simply an extended form of individual freedom fails to explain the territorial claim that these groups make.

(2) Just-cause theories, such as Buchanan's and Norman's, place a heavier burden of proof on the secessionists. Underlying this presumption against secession is, typically, the view that national identities are mobilized by élites and that there is no (primary) right to national self-determination (even if this is couched in the individualist language of choice); or the view, expressed by Buchanan in his chapter, that choice or autonomy fails to ground a collective right to self-determination. Just-cause theorists typically argue that

the right to secession is in important respects analogous to Locke's theory of revolution: the right to secede is only legitimate if it is necessary to remedy an injustice (in Buchanan's terminology, it is a remedial right only). Different just-cause theorists focus on different kinds of injustices: some on prior occupation and seizure of territory; some on serious violations of human rights, including genocide; others view discriminatory injustice as sufficient to legitimate secession.

One advantage of this type of theory is that it suggests a strong internal connection between the right to resist tyranny (exploitation, oppression, genocide, wrongful seizure of territory) and the right to self-determination. By suggesting a strong link between the right to self-determination and human rights, this kind of argument grounds the right to self-determination within the generally accepted framework of human rights.

One disadvantage of this type of theory is suggested by Wayne Norman's own just-cause argument: because claims to justice are strongly contested, he ends up relying on procedural mechanisms which are easy to apply in order to approximate the relative justice or injustice of the seceding group's claims. In practice, then, his theory, like Philpott's, simply recognizes the secessionist groups's choices, although he has a different argument for placing restrictions, such as a requirement of a weighted majority, on the secessionists.

This difficulty also suggests a deeper problem with the just-cause approach. By assessing the legitimacy of secession according to the justice or otherwise of the states that face secessionist movements, just-cause theories of secession are aligned with the sentiment expressed by E. Kedourie in his scathing indictment of nationalism:

> The only criterion capable of public defence is whether the new rulers are less corrupt and grasping, or more just and merciful, or whether there is no change at all, but the corruption, the greed, and the tyranny merely find victims other than those of the departed rulers.[10]

The problem with this as an approach to secession is that many secessionist movements are not primarily about justice or injustice. This understanding of the legitimacy or otherwise of secessionist movements fails to capture the dynamic that is fuelling the movement in the first place. The political significance of cultural and especially national identity is ignored on this approach, because the argument appeals to a conception of fundamental human interests and erects liberal rights and rules and conceptions of legitimacy on that basis. Justice may be a good criterion for assessing government; but it does not seen to be the primary factor in understanding the quest to secede, or even making sense of the massive movement to decolonize in the 1960s; or the importance that the international community is currently placing on democratic legitimacy.

(3) The third type of argument for a right to secede flows from a theory of national self-determination. None of the recent philosophical defences of national self-determination adopt the normative nationalist principle, which Gellner, and, following Gellner, Buchanan criticize, according to which 'political and cultural (or ethnic) boundaries must, as a matter of right, coincide'.[11] On the weaker defence of national self-determination, the right to self-determination does not attach to individuals, as on the choice approach, but is held collectively, by nations. The justificatory argument for attributing a right to self-determination to nations does not lie in anything that nations as such have, but in terms of the importance of national identity and national membership to individuals.

In Miller's formulation of the nationality principle, the national attachments that people feel have intrinsic ethical significance and are also instrumentally valuable as a means to realizing other goods. Specifically, where a nation is politically autonomous, and where a state encompasses a nation, it is able to implement redistributive justice, protect a common culture, and collectively determine its own destiny (because people have a commitment to live together and are more likely to compromise). Nielsen (Chapter 6) defends a right to secession based on the principle of national self-determination on the grounds that nationality, which is the form that social identity takes under conditions of modernity, is instrumentally important to individual self-identity and self-definition and human flourishing.

These views are similar, in many ways, to the choice conception articulated by Philpott, since both writers seem to believe that national identity is largely (though not completely) *subjectively* defined. This conception has, however, the merit of acknowledging the nationalism underlying most secessionist movements and attempting to give ethical significance to a reiterative liberal nationalism.

One problem with this approach is that, to some extent at least, it either bases the right to secede on ascriptive, or, at least, not completely chosen criteria (like membership in a national community) or it identifies a national community with a certain territory (in Nielsen's case, Quebec) and so downplays the importance of cultural and national identities (which are part of the justification for the right to secede) in the case of minorities residing in the same territory.[12] This problem is discussed at some length by John McGarry (Chapter 10), who argues that secessions are based on nationally mobilized groups and are therefore rarely unproblematic.

A quite different kind of criticism is advanced by Horowitz (Chapter 9) and Brubaker (Chapter 11) who both imply that this thin conception of nationality fails to appreciate the dynamics of ethnic, or national, conflict. In his chapter, Brubaker argues that it is an illusion to believe that the right 'grand architecture', the right territorial and institutional framework, can resolve national conflict. Seeing secession as a possible method of conflict resolution is misguided, Brubaker contends, because nationalism takes many different forms and nationalist conflicts are, by their very nature, irresolvable. National self-determination theorists, Brubaker implies, may have acknowledged the national dimension underlying secessionist movements, but they have failed to understand the dynamics of nationalism.

This broad rubric of types of ethical theories of secession—choice theories, just-cause theories, and national self-determination theories—encompass most of the arguments to date, but this typology also obscures from view some of the different assumptions, or different methodological approaches or different contexts for ethical theorizing that underlie the different approach. Underlying the different type of theories of secession are: (1) different conceptions of the appropriate (institutional vs. non-institutional) forms of reasoning; (2) different views about the relationship between democracy and a right to self-determination; and (3) different understandings of the relevant comparisons for theorizing about secession.

INSTITUTIONAL VS. NON-INSTITUTIONAL REASONING

One of the questions that must be resolved prior to articulating a political morality of secession is the purpose that a theory of secession is intended to serve. This issue is so important, Wayne Norman argues in his chapter, that which question is asked goes a long way toward determining the kind of answer one gives to the issue of secession, for it affects the kinds of considerations that are seen as relevant to theorizing about secession.

Allen Buchanan, in his chapter in this collection and elsewhere,[13] argues that it is necessary to distinguish between two kinds of normative questions about secession. The questions are as follows:

(1) Under what conditions does a group have a moral right to secede, independently of any questions of institutional morality and in particular apart from any consideration of international legal institutions and their relationship to moral principles?

(2) Under what conditions should a group be recognized as having a right to secede as a matter of international institutional morality, including a morally defensible system of international law?

The first (non-institutional) question is the one that most philosophers have tried to answer and it is, Buchanan suggests, the wrong question, because it abstracts from many considerations that are relevant to secession. Buchanan argues that many treatments of secession possess cogency only when viewed in an institutional vacuum. His more restrictive right to secede follows from his definition of the kinds of considerations that ought to apply, and, specifically, from his concern about the incentive effects of different definitions of the right of secession and their consequences for developing a just international law regime for reasonably just democracies.

A similar charge is levelled by Donald Horowitz, in his chapter, who argues that many of the philosophical treatments of the issue of secession display ignorance of the complexities of ethnic interaction. Specifically, he contends that the incentive effect of any institutional right to secede combined with the likely possibility that dormant sub-ethnic cleavages will emerge in a new context and provide a new focus for secessionist demands is ignored by many of the philosophical treatments of secession that reason a priori from considerations of autonomy.

The challenge posed most directly by Allen Buchanan has been met in different ways by contributors who support a less restrictive approach to secession. In Chapter 4 in this volume, David Miller meets the challenge directly, by arguing that the proposal that a political morality of secession should seek to define a quasi-legal right of secession that might be formally codified, in the constitution of a state or the charter of the UN are very likely to be biased in favour of procedural criteria. He argues that this will mean that the criteria that will be supported will tend to be those whose application is relatively controversial, rather than substantive criteria whose application may depend on difficult and contested matters of judgement.

Daniel Philpott responds to the challenge posed by Buchanan by accepting that considering how to institutionalize right to secede in a state or an international body is an important goal in reasoning normatively about secession. However, he questions the dire consequences that Buchanan attributes to institutionalizing such a right. Implicitly, his method of proceeding suggests that we should establish basic principles first, and then try to implement them in such a way that they will not have negative effects on the behaviour of various actors.

And Kai Nielsen, in Chapter 6, questions the dichotomous nature of the two questions, as articulated by Buchanan. Those people who do not put international law and the situations and context of actual states at the forefront of their theory are not developing 'a morality that is free of all institutional constraints', as Buchanan argues. Rather, Nielsen claims, they are attempting to develop moral principles that should be incorporated into international legal regimes. On this view, all moral reasoning (since the collapse of foundationalism) is institutional in nature, although it tends to proceed at different levels. It is important that the principle that is implemented does not lead to counter-intuitive results. Nevertheless, there is a place for moral reasoning in abstraction (to some degree) from the existing interstate system, since part of the goal of moral reasoning is to allow one to assess the present institutions, and to challenge them, if they are deemed flawed or wanting.

THE RELATIONSHIP BETWEEN DEMOCRACY AND SELF-DETERMINATION

The precise nature of the relationship between democracy and self-determination movements is also an important underlying issue among some of the theorists of the morality of secession. This issue is raised partly by two dominant political processes since the late 1980s: (i) the wave toward democratization in Central and Eastern Europe, including the former Soviet Union, as well as parts of Latin America and sub-Saharan Africa; and (ii) the wave of self-determination movements which has resulted in the formation of more than twenty new states, particularly in Eastern and Central Europe. The fact that the two political processes have occurred roughly at the same time raises the question whether the spread of democracy and self-determination (secessionist) movements are discrete and unrelated phenomena, or whether there are important underlying links between the two.

There is also an apparent conceptual link between democracy and self-determination. Democracy is often viewed as *internal* self-determination, and secession as *external* self-determination, that is, as the right of a people to govern itself, rather than be governed by another people. On this view, democratization means that the people are to rule, and 'the people' can be interpreted either in statist terms, i.e. as the people who are resident within the boundaries of the political unit, or in ethnic terms, i.e. as the people who are members of the nation.

In Philpott's view, democracy and rights to self-determination (including secession) are very closely related: both are derived from the value of autonomy. On this conception, the value of autonomy grounds the case for democratic governance and for a plebiscitary right to secede.

In his chapter in this volume, Buchanan argues against this, in part because of the difficulty of moving from a principle giving value to *individual* autonomy to a collective (majoritarian) right such as democratic governance or a majoritarian plebiscite on secession. He also develops another argument based on Hirschmann's analysis in *Exit, Voice and Loyalty*, which suggests that too easy a right of exit (secession) would undermine voice and loyalty (democratic institutions). He concludes that the two ought to be treated in international law quite differently, because a right to secede by majority vote would deal a serious blow to reasonably just democracies.

The relationship between democracy and self-determination is also touched on in the following chapters by Horowitz and McGarry, both of whom suggest that democracy generally presupposes the legitimacy of majority rule, whereas in nationally divided societies, part of the difficulty is the majority–minority relations. This point is made by Horowitz to underline the fact democratization processes will not 'solve' the problem of national or ethnic divisions, and by McGarry to suggest that the real issue is not whether a majority (in a given area) seeks to secede, but *who* is the majority, *who* is the minority, and what is the relationship between them.

THE COMPARATIVE CONTEXT FOR THEORIZING

Since democracy is almost universally acknowledged to be a good thing, it is not surprising that the different views of the relationship between democracy and self-determination (including secession) correspond to different views—either positive or negative—of self-determination struggles, and different views—either restrictive or permissive—of the right to secede. Similarly, what is taken as the relevant comparative context for theorizing about secession helps to explain whether self-determination movements are viewed in a generally favourable or unfavourable light.

Many of the writers in this volume argue that thinking about self-determination should be contextual. Although Daniel Philpott articulates a generally permissive principle of self-determination, he does attempt to specify how that principle should be differently applied in different contexts, in his chapter. David Miller begins his chapter by objecting to a purely procedural theory about secession on the grounds that it will be insufficiently contextual. Ronald Beiner, in Chapter 8 on the problems attached to the language of rights in thinking about self-determination and secession, argues not simply that it tends to be polarizing and confrontational, but that it fails to capture the contextual considerations that should be weighed in making a judgement about secession.

These general claims about the importance of context in making decisions about self-determination and secession go some way to specifying the kinds of considerations that are important in evaluating self-determination claims, but do not explicitly articulate what kinds of comparisons might be relevant. This is tackled directly by Kai Nielsen in his chapter. He argues that not all secessionist movements can be compared with each other: self-determination, and secessionist, movements in liberal-democratic states should be assessed differently from such movements in states without strong liberal-democratic traditions. Thus, throughout his chapter, he argues that the secession of Quebec from Canada should not be compared with the experiences of the former Yugoslavia or the former Soviet Union, but would be much more similar to the (hypothetical) secession of Scotland from the United Kingdom (which, one would imagine, would be peaceful), or the secession of Iceland from Denmark, or Norway from Sweden.

Nielsen's claim that there is a sharp distinction between self-determination movements, based on civic nationalism, in liberal-democratic states and the kinds of self-determination movements typical of non-liberal-democratic states is criticized, implicitly and explicitly, by Brubaker and McGarry. One of the 'myths and misconceptions' that Brubaker outlines in his chapter is that of a sharp distinction between the good, civic Western kind of nationalism based on common citizenship and a bad, ethnic kind of nationalism based on common ethnicity. As Brubaker persuasively argues, the civic–ethnic distinction is problematic, since it is unclear how culture can be mapped onto this distinction. This is an implicit criticism of Nielsen's reliance on the civic–ethnic distinction in his argument. Nielsen characterizes ethnic nationalism in biological terms, as based on common descent or race, and so describes Quebec as a species of civic nationalism. However, as Brubaker notes, this manœuvre renders the category of 'civic nationalism' too heterogenous to be useful and the category of 'ethnic nationalism' seriously under-populated.

McGarry also takes issue with the distinction between self-determination movements in liberal-democratic states and in non-liberal-democratic states. He does not deny the importance of liberal-democratic traditions in providing principles and procedures to help negotiate the transition from a unified state to new (secessionist and remainder) states after a successful secessionist movement. However, he suggests that the key factor in predicting whether stability will result is the national divisions in the secessionist and remainder states, and, particularly, whether there are dissatisfied national minorities in the newly formed states who do not identify with the new state. On this view, the most important factor in assessing a self-determination movement is not the liberal-democratic traditions of the groups but the kind of national identity that the groups have, and therefore the relevant comparative context is other states with similar national divisions.

Of course, none of the authors in this volume crudely endorse a general principle of separation through national self-determination. In spite of their many differences and disagreements, all are careful to emphasize the many factors that must be taken into consideration in any normative assessment of a self-determination, as well as in particular cases. The themes touched on in this volume—the relationship between democracy and self-determination; the problem of different, contested versions of the principle of self-determination; the pattern of majority–minority relations characteristic of nationally divided communities and how these can be reconciled in liberal-democratic societies; the value of equal respect, autonomy, and liberal justice in assessing self-determination and secessionist movements; and the kinds of procedures that are likely to facilitate a peaceful transition from a unified state to new (secessionist and remainder) states or to prevent secessionist movements from occurring—all suggest the practical importance of normative inquiry into this aspect of nationalist theory, and into movements for collective self-determination.

NOTES

1. B. Anderson, *Imagined Communities* (London and New York: Verso, 1983), 5. For a criticism of this argument, see B. O'Leary, 'On the Nature of Nationalism', *British Journal of Political Science*, 27 (1997), 218, n. 78.
2. This is the project of Y. Tamir's book *Liberal Nationalism* (Princeton: Princeton University Press, 1993), D. Miller's defence of national identity in his book *On Nationality* (Oxford: Clarendon Press, 1995) and W. Kymlicka's appeal to collective rights for nations in *Multicultural Citizenship* (Oxford: Clarendon Press, 1995).
3. S. French and A. Gutmann, 'The Principle of National Self-Determination', in V. Held, S. Morgenbesser, and T. Nagel (eds.), *Philosophy, Morality and International Affairs* (New York: Oxford University Press, 1974), 138–53; J. McGarry and B. O'Leary, 'Introduction: The Macro-Political Regulation of Ethnic Conflict', in J. McGarry and B. O'Leary (eds.), *The Politics of Ethnic Conflict Regulation* (London and New York: Routledge, 1993), 10–16. McGarry and O'Leary argue that four problems are begged by the self-determination principle.
4. I. Jennings, *The Approach to Self-Government* (Cambridge: Cambridge University Press, 1956), 56.
5. Wilson's 'Fourteen Points' speech of 8 Jan. 1918 is quoted in part in A. de Zayas, *A Terrible Revenge: The Ethnic Cleansing of the East European Germans, 1944–1950* (New York: St Martin's Press, 1986), 14.
6. R. Emerson, 'Self-Determination', *American Journal of International Law*, 65 (1971), 463.
7. Emerson, 'Self-Determination', 464.
8. This example is from McGarry and O'Leary, 'Introduction: The Macro-Political Regulation of Ethnic Conflict', 15.
9. W. Connor, *Ethnonationalism: The Quest for Understanding* (Princeton: Princeton University Press, 1994), 172.
10. E. Kedourie, *Nationalism* (London: Hutchinson, 1960), 140.
11. A. Buchanan, *Secession: The Morality of Political Divorce from Fort Sumter to Lithuania and Quebec* (Boulder, Colo.: Westview, 1991), 48. On this page, Buchanan cites the relevant passage from Gellner.
12. This problem is avoided by Miller, who, aware of the many ethical considerations and the complexity of each individual situation, does not talk about a right to secede but about justified claims to self-determination, depending on the kind of identity in question, the problem of minorities residing in the same territory, and so on.
13. A. Buchanan, 'Theories of Secession', *Philosophy and Public Affairs*, 26/1 (1997), 30–61.

2

Democracy and Secession

ALLEN BUCHANAN

1. ENTHUSIASM FOR DEMOCRACY, ANXIETY ABOUT SECESSION

The world seems to have stumbled, almost inadvertently, into a new age of democracy. Democratization movements have sprung up in Central and Eastern Europe and in the fragments of the former Soviet Union. A great democratic revolution has won its first battles in South Africa. Political changes that hold some prospect of progress toward democracy are occurring in other states in sub-Saharan Africa and in parts of Latin America. These changes on the ground have both stimulated and been reinforced by significant developments in international law that go some distance toward the recognition of a right to democratic governance.[1]

This surge of democratic state-makings has been accompanied by a rash of state-breakings. Secession is not a new phenomenon, but the current pervasiveness of secession movements and, even more strikingly, of successful attempts at secession, is unprecedented. With the exception of the case of East Pakistan (Bangladesh) there were virtually no successful secession movements in the entire period from 1920 till the cataclysmic year of 1989. From 1989 there have been at least a dozen secessionist attempts and more than a twenty-five new states have been formed out of fragments of old ones.

Enthusiasm for democratization is almost universal; attitudes toward secession are often negative or ambivalent at best. And it is not just unregenerate statists or conservatives who shudder at the prospect of uncontrolled state-breaking. Secessionist attempts, and the efforts of states to resist them, have usually led to severe economic dislocations and massive violations of human rights. All too often, ethnic minorities have won their independence only to subject their own minorities to the same persecutions they formerly suffered.

I am indebted to Margaret Moore and David Schmidtz for their insightful comments on an earlier draft of this chapter. I would also like to thank Harry Brighouse for several discussions during his seminar on liberalism which helped clarify my thinking on the issues examined in this chapter.

International law has not provided coherent guidance for how to respond to the new wave of secessions. On the one hand, neither international legal doctrine nor practice recognize a right to secede, except in the case of the efforts of colonies to free themselves from metropolitan control; and this provision is of little practical relevance today, since the work of colonial liberation, which began in earnest in the 1960s, is virtually complete.[2] On the other hand, international law has not been invoked successfully to block secession either; nor has it provided a principled distinction between legitimate and illegitimate secession.

There is a tendency to view these two profound political changes—the spread of democracy and the surge of secessionist movements—as distinct and unrelated phenomena. The scholarly literature tends to concentrate on the one or the other, without attempting to provide a systematic analysis that links the two.

However, at least at a superficial level, democracy and secession are intimately related. Both are cases of self-determination—or so many have assumed. If democracy is popular sovereignty, government by the people, then secession might be seen simply as the effort of various peoples to govern themselves, to be politically self-determining in the most literal sense, by forming their own states. According to this view, the same values that justify democracy also support what may be called a *plebiscitary right to secede*, the right of a majority in any portion of the territory of a state to form its own independent state if it so chooses, even if the majority of the state as a whole opposes their bid for independence. If this is the correct view of the relationship between democracy and secession, then existing international legal doctrine and practice, which encourage democratization, but not secession, are starkly inconsistent.

However, there is a rival understanding of the relationship between democracy and secession that is consonant with enthusiastic support for the former and a much more guarded attitude toward the latter. On this second view, the *justifications* for democracy and for recognizing a group's right to secede are quite distinct. The right to democratic governance is seen as a general right which the citizens of every state have, while the right to secede is understood to be, like the right to revolution, a remedial right only—a right which groups come to have if seceding is the remedy of last resort for serious injustices perpetrated against them by the state.[3] These two opposing positions on the right to secede I will label 'the non-remedial, plebiscitary right view' (or 'plebiscitary right view' for short) and the 'remedial right only view'.

According to the first view, secession is the sibling of democracy; they are different shoots issuing from the same root. According to the second, secession and democracy have quite different justifications and a commitment to democracy is consistent with a rather constrained stance on secession. I shall argue that the second view of the relationship between democracy and secession not only renders existing international legal theory and practice more coherent; it is normatively preferable as well. Indeed, I shall argue that the recognition of a non-remedial right to secede by majority vote would deal a serious blow to the prospects for democratization.

Section 2 of this chapter sets out two arguments that purport to show that the same values that justify democracy justify a general, non-remedial plebiscitary right to secede, and shows that neither of these arguments is sound. Section 3 argues that such a right to secede would in fact be a serious obstacle to the development and maintenance of democratic institutions. Section 4 sketches a contrasting conception of the right to secede, as a remedial right. Building on this conception of the right to secede as a remedial right, Section 4 develops an account of the connection between democratic governance and state legitimacy that is suggested by recent international legal support for democratization. According to this account of legitimacy, democratic governance (along with respect for human rights) creates a presumption that secession is not justified.

2. DEMOCRATIC VALUES AND THE RIGHT TO SECEDE

Several recent writers on the morality of secession have assumed or suggested that a commitment to democracy requires recognition of a (non-remedial) plebiscitary right to secede, that is, that any group has the right to secede if it can muster a majority in favour of secession within a given part of the territory of an existing state.[4] Two in particular have explicitly argued for this claim by linking the alleged right to secede to the *justification of democracy*. Though both contend that the same values that justify democracy also justify a plebiscitary right to secede, they identify different values as those that justify democracy. Daniel Philpott contends that *individual autonomy* both grounds the case for democracy and requires a plebiscitary right of self-determination, which includes the right to independent statehood, and hence the right to secede. He concludes that if we are democrats, we must be plebiscitary secessionists: 'our [democratic] ideals commit us to it'.[5] David Copp, in contrast, assumes that the commitment to democracy rests on *equal respect* for persons, and claims that equal respect requires a plebiscitary right to secede. According to Copp to fail to recognize the right of the people in a region of the state to decide by majority rule whether or not to form their own independent state '. . . would indicate precisely the kind of disrespect for them that democratic decision procedures are supposed to foreclose'.[6]

Each of these attempts to found a right to secede on democratic values will be examined closely below, but at this juncture a preview of my strategy may prove useful. I will argue that while Philpott's position rests on an untenable account of the justification for democracy and a misunderstanding of the relationship between autonomy and the democratic values of participation and representation, Copps offers a more plausible justification for democracy but mistakenly assumes that the same considerations that justify democracy also establish a plebiscitary right to secede. Moreover, as I shall also argue, both Philpott and Copp overlook the fact that in several important respects the recognition of a plebiscitary right to secede would threaten democracy.

For our purposes a rough characterization of democracy and a simple taxonomy of types of justifications for democracy will suffice. At minimum, democracy consists of these elements: (1) popular legislative sovereignty with majoritarian voting rules (with each competent adult citizen having the right to vote in a process that issues, either directly or through a system of representation, in laws that are binding on all); (2) formally equal political participation (each citizen has an equal vote and has the right to run for office); and (3) a significant degree of freedom of expression and association so that citizens can exchange and form views about political decisions.[7]

Justifications for democracy are of two types: those that present democracy as being intrinsically valuable and those that appeal to its instrumental value. Of course, a comprehensive justification can argue that democracy is both intrinsically and instrumentally valuable.

To justify democracy by appeal to its instrumental value one must show that democratic processes produce better outcomes (overall and in the long-run at least) than any non-democratic methods. At least from the standpoint of a liberal political philosophy, the strongest instrumental argument for democracy is that democratic institutions tend to produce outcomes that better promote human rights (or at least are less threatening to them) than non-democratic ones. Since neither of the theorists who argue for a non-remedial plebiscitary right to secede appeal to the instrumental value of democracy, I will say no more at this point about that approach. However, my argument in Section 4. will show that instrumentalist considerations generally tell against a non-remedial plebiscitary right to secede rather than in favour of it.

According to Philpott, individuals are autonomous in a democratic state, not because democratic decision-making produces outcomes that promote autonomy (though this may also be true) but because being autonomous means being self-governing and democracy is simply the self-government of individuals: 'Democracy we may think of as the activity of governing oneself, of exercising one's autonomy in the political realm.'[8] There are two rather familiar and in my opinion conclusive objections against this particular intrinsic justification for democracy, neither of which Philpott considers.

First, it is simply false to say that an individual who participates in a democratic decision-making process is self-governing; he or she is governed by the majority. Unless one (unpersuasively) defines self-government as government by the majority (perhaps implausibly distinguishing between the individual's apparent will and her 'real' will, which the majority is said to express), an individual can be self-governing only if he or she dictates political decisions. Far from constituting self-government for individuals, majority rule, under conditions in which each individual's vote counts equally, excludes self-government for every individual.

The second problem with the attempt to show that democracy is intrinsically valuable from the standpoint of individual autonomy is betrayed by the qualifying phrase 'in the political realm' in the quote from Philpott above. Suppose Philpott were to acknowledge the foregoing objection—that democratic decision-making is not self-government for the individual. He might nevertheless contend that democratic politics gives scope for the exercise of individual autonomy in many ways, as individuals articulate their values, exchange views, and invest their energies in various political causes in an effort to sway the majority.

The difficulty with this suggestion is that one can exercise autonomy in many different areas of life; politics is only one area. For this reason, one could say, as Philpott does, that individual autonomy *requires* democracy only if it were true that individuals cannot exercise sufficient autonomy unless they participate in democratic politics. But this generalization appears to be quite false. Many people in democratic societies find numerous opportunities for the exercise of autonomy outside the realm of politics—in their work, in their personal relationships, in their religious communities, etc.[9]

Furthermore, even if it could be persuasively argued that adequate scope for autonomy requires that it be exercised in politics, politics can thrive in many arenas, from the governance of a social club to the running of a church congregation or participation in local public (state) school Parent Teacher Association meetings. There is no reason to believe that autonomy only has adequate scope when individuals can participate in the higher levels of *state* politics.

It might be true, none the less, that over the long-run and on average, a significant sphere for individual autonomy tends to be best protected in states that are governed democratically. This would be an instrumentalist argument for democracy, on the grounds that it is the most reliable means of ensuring individual autonomy. It is not the argument Philpott advances, however, and if it were, it would do nothing to show that a plebiscitary right to secede, as opposed to democratic governance within existing political boundaries, is instrumentally valuable for ensuring individual autonomy. In fact, apart from the confusion of majority rule and individual self-government, nothing Philpott says shows that having the opportunity to vote in a plebiscite on secession enhances autonomy, much less that there would be insufficient scope for autonomy in a state in which all the liberal individual rights were perfectly respected, but such an opportunity was lacking.

Before moving on to Copp's argument, it may be worthwhile to consider another link between democracy and a plebiscitary right to secede that Philpott attempts to forge. The idea is this: If territorially concentrated groups are allowed to secede by plebiscite from states in which they are in the minority on issues that matter to them, and to form their own states, then (assuming that they form democratic states) the states they form will maximize the virtues of democracy because politics in them will be 'more participatory' and the citizens in these states will be 'better represented'.[10]

It is not clear whether Philpott's point is (1) that a majoritarian right to secede is justified because it best serves democracy by enhancing representation and increasing participation, or (2) that a majoritarian right to secede is justified because it increases individual autonomy by enhancing representation and increasing participation. Let us consider each alternative.

The problem with (1) is not that it assumes that participation and representation are constituents of democracy, but that it assumes that participation and representation are enhanced by getting a smaller state with a more homogeneous citizenry. Other things being equal, a smaller state may provide more opportunities for participation at the highest levels of decision-making, but larger states, if they have considerable decentralization, with various levels of government, may in fact provide more opportunities for participation or for a greater variety of meaningful opportunities for participation. More importantly, better representation is not, as Philpott seems to assume, a matter of getting what you want—of being in the majority rather than the minority. (Note Philpott's remark that if a group has its own government it will be better represented because it will not find '. . . [its] political will diluted or hindered . . .' by others with different preferences).[11] It is simply misleading if not outright false to say that one is better represented when one is in a political unit in which one is (more often) in the majority than in one in which one is not.

Claim (2) is equally unconvincing. Smaller-scale, more homogeneous political units do not necessarily provide greater individual autonomy (for one thing, they may facilitate a repressive orthodoxy that stifles individual autonomy). And individual autonomy is not a matter of getting what you want more often (because your fellow citizens want what you want). Thus, the thesis that recognition of a plebiscitary right to secede would serve democracy or promote individual autonomy by enhancing participation and improving representation does little to support such a right, especially if, as I shall argue in Section 3, recognition of this right would pose a serious threat to democracy.

A number of recent theorists, including Copp, contend that the strongest justification, if not the only sound justification, for democracy is that it is required by the fundamental moral value of equal respect for persons. This equal respect argument is, in fact, only one variant of a type of approach to the justification of democracy: what I shall call the intrinsic equality approach. Other variants include the view that democracy is required by the principle that individuals' interests are to receive equal consideration and the view that resources are to be distributed equally (where influence over political decisions is counted as a resource).[12] I will concentrate only on Copp's variant of the intrinsic equality justification for democracy, but what I say about it will apply to the other variants as well.

Copp apparently thinks that it is intuitively obvious that it would show less than equal respect to the individuals comprising any territorially concentrated group capable of governing itself not to recognize that it has the right to secede by majority decision. He provides no argument to show why this is so.

However, we might construct an argument, albeit a rather simple one, on his behalf: equal respect requires equal influence over political decisions (that is, democratic decision-making); the decision to redraw political boundaries so as to form a new state is a political decision; therefore, equal respect requires that this decision be made democratically. This argument is suggested by Copp's statement that 'One reason for favouring democracy is that it treats citizens with equal consideration and respect by giving them equal authority over key political decisions.'[13] The idea would be that if one believes that equal respect and concern (or equality of resources or equal consideration of interests) requires equal influence over political decisions, then it is arbitrary to exclude this type of political decision—the decision concerning what the basic political units will be.

The first difficulty with this argument is that it gives us the conclusion that decisions concerning how the world is divided up into states ought to be decided democratically, not that they ought to be decided democratically by a vote only of those within a particular region. If equal respect requires an equal say over all political decisions and decisions about how to divide the world into states are political decisions, then why not have a vote of *all* the citizens of the state (not just those in the would-be secessionist area) or, better yet, have a world-wide referendum on boundaries, so that all people can be treated with equal concern and respect regarding the disposition of this 'key political decision'?

Even if this first objection can be met, the simple argument stated above would be a sound argument for a plebiscitary right to secede only if no meaningful distinctions could be drawn between political decisions made within a state and decisions to set the boundaries of states. For then it would be arbitrary to say that equal respect requires democracy for other political decisions but not for decisions to define political units.

We should be wary about this claim that there is no difference between the two types of decisions, however. After all, most proponents of democracy acknowledge that not all political decisions (in the sense of decisions that in some way affect the character of political units) ought to be made democratically. For example, it shows no disrespect to anyone that certain issues are excluded altogether from democratic decision-making by a doctrine of constitutional rights and that others are left to determination by market forces. So even if we concede to Copp that the same equal respect that grounds democracy creates a presumption that decisions defining political units ought to be made democratically by the people in the region in question, this is only a presumption and not a very strong one, since there are numerous cases in which it is overridden or does not apply. The real question is whether there are good reasons for distinguishing between decisions made within a defined political unit and decisions that define political units.

In the next section I will argue that there is a great difference. In particular, utilizing Hirschman's important distinction, I will show that democratic institutions are most likely to flourish when exit is not so easy as a majoritarian right to secede would make it.[14]

3. SECESSION, STRATEGIC BEHAVIOUR, AND DEMOCRACY

We have seen that some theorists have argued that the same values that justify democracy ground a majoritarian right to secede. If my analysis thus far is correct, these arguments are very weak. I now want to argue that democratic values tell *against* a majoritarian right to secede. Recognition of such a right would tend to undermine the conditions for a flourishing democracy, by stimulating destructive strategic behaviour and by weakening the incentives citizens have for principled political participation.[15]

If a plebiscitary right to secede were recognized (either as a matter of constitutional or international law or by a widespread moral consensus), a territorially concentrated minority could use the threat of secession as a strategic bargaining tool. If the threat of secession was credible and the majority viewed secession as a sufficiently high cost to themselves, the minority would in effect wield a veto over majority decisions. Under these conditions, democracy, understood as including majority rule, would not prevail, regardless of what the formal rules of voting and representation said. Even though a *de facto* minority veto is not strictly speaking a violation of majoritarian voting rules, it would restrict the range of decisions over which, according to democratic theory, the majority's will is supposed to be dispositive.

There is a second, more subtle way in which recognition of a plebiscitary right to secede can undermine democracy: by eroding the conditions that make it rational for citizens to sustain a commitment to practice the virtues of deliberative democracy.

In his deservedly famous book *Exit, Voice, and Loyalty*, Albert O. Hirschman emphasizes that where exit from an organization is too easy there will be insufficient incentives for voice—for constructive criticism and dialogue within the organization.[16] As I have argued elsewhere, this point has important implications for secession.[17]

In a state in which it is generally believed that a territorially concentrated minority has the right to secede if it votes to do so and that the exercise of this right will not be opposed, it will be less rational for individuals to invest themselves in the practice of principled debate and deliberation. A healthy democracy requires large numbers of citizens who are committed to rational dialogue—who feel obliged to become informed, and who are committed to agree to disagree rationally, to appeal to reasons backed by principles, rather than indulging in strategic behaviour that is designed to achieve their ends without the hard work of achieving principled, rational consensus. For it to be rational for citizens to make this investment they must have considerable confidence that two assumptions are well-founded: first, that their fellow citizens for the most part are committed to deciding issues by the weight of reasons, through appeal to principles, not by threats of exit; second, that the membership of the political community and the territorial jurisdiction of the state will remain relatively stable, so that those voting for or against proposals can be reasonably assured that they and their children will be subject to the laws they enact.

Unless they are confident in the first assumption, citizens may be unwillingly to cultivate and practice the demanding virtues of deliberative democracy—to restrict their own advocacy to participation in principled, rational dialogue and to support the institutions that facilitate rational dialogue. Unless they are confident in the second assumption, they will not consider what Rawls calls the strains of commitment as they evaluate competing legislative proposals, because they will be less certain that whatever decisions are made will actually affect them and their descendants. In a world in which states can be dismembered at any time and repeatedly, through the exercise of a plebiscitary right to secede, the results of democratic processes can be nullified simply by voting to change political boundaries. When new states can be formed whenever local majorities can be assembled, the significance of political decisions made within any given state is diminished and with it the rationality of investing in the political processes that generate those decisions.

There is, in fact, something very odd about a view that makes the determination of state boundaries procedurally indistinguishable from decisions made within states. It is perhaps not too much of an exaggeration to say that such a view betrays a desire to flee from politics altogether—an attempt to avoid the messiness of political disagreement by drawing a boundary around oneself and those who agree with one. Something very like this urge for apolitical harmony is suggested by the following passage from Philpott's defence of a majoritarian right to secede. In this passage Philpott uses the label 'Utopians' as a stand-in for any group with a shared identity and a shared preference to organize and direct society in the light of that identity.

> What self-determination [which includes the right to secede by plebiscite] does for the Utopian group is to redraw its political boundaries as tightly as possible. The ideal group's ideal borders encompass all those who share its identity and only those who share its identity.[18]

Now if one assumes that the best political society is the most homogeneous one—a society in which everybody agrees—then one will be tempted to think that the existence of political divisions is an imperfection to be remedied by an adjustment of political boundaries. But of course the democratic tradition emerges from a quite different picture of the conditions that make political institutions necessary in the first place—a vision of a world in which no one can or should expect to be governed by people like themselves. Justifications of democracy that appeal to its intrinsic value as an expression of the equality of persons rely on the assumption that in a free society the uniformity of identities Philpott celebrates is illusory, and that equal respect means learning to make decisions with others who are not like oneself, and who may deeply disagree with one. Instrumentalist justifications of democracy stress that a process that incorporates conflicting values and conflicting beliefs about the facts can produce better outcomes, and can sometimes produce a convergence of preferences where none existed before. In brief, democratic decision-making and the institutions they support take diversity as a given and are designed to use it constructively, not to banish diversity by reconfiguring the political map.

Philpott's dream of a politics of a single identity is not a dream of *politics* at all, and most assuredly not of democratic politics. Yet his fantasy of the Utopians gestures toward an important truth, and one which has a significant implication for an understanding of the relationship between secession and democracy. The point is not that political units should contain only those with shared preferences or a single identity and that the same values that justify democracy demand that this be so. Rather, the point is that if democracy is to function as it ought—that is, in such a way as to serve the values that ground it—the boundaries of a political unit must contain, for the most part, individuals who have *enough* in common to be able to engage in meaningful participation in rational, principled political decision-making.

Consider the most extreme and clear situation in which this fundamental condition is *not* met. Suppose that a state is composed of two groups, a minority N and a majority M. Suppose also that religious and cultural differences between the groups are so profound that it is simply not possible for them to co-operate in the practices of deliberative democracy. Their deepest values and their very ways of conceptualizing the social world are so unbridgeably disjoint that they cannot engage together in a rational, principled dialogue aimed at articulating even a minimal good that is common to both groups. In such a situation, democracy would not fail because the principle that each individual is to have an equal say over decision-making is violated; it would fail because the background conditions that make an equal distribution of political influence attractive are not satisfied.

In such a situation—call it the condition of *radical pluralism*—the minimal community that democratic decision-making requires if it is to be an attractive ideal is lacking, and there is no prospect of constructing it. Here the best option would be to try to redraw political boundaries to reflect the fact that there are two political communities, not one. But this is *not* to say that in general political boundaries should be drawn, by majority rule or any other way, so as to *maximize* homogeneity.[19]

I have *not* tried to show that there are no conditions under which recognition of a plebiscitary right to secede would be compatible with a well-functioning democracy. I have argued elsewhere, in fact, that if such a right were embedded in the right sort of constitution, with sufficient procedural hurdles and other exit costs, the dangers I have just articulated might be reduced to acceptable proportions.[20] My point, instead, is that recognition of a plebiscitary right to secede, far from being required by a commitment to democracy, is at least in tension with some of the most vital preconditions for a well-functioning democracy. Once the risks to democracy which such a right poses are appreciated, it is all the less plausible to rest the case for such a right, as Copp and others have done, on the unargued intuition that the same commitment to the moral equality of persons that justifies democracy also supports this right.

4. SECESSION, DEMOCRACY, AND POLITICAL LEGITIMACY

I now want to deepen the discussion of the relationship between secession and democracy by connecting both of these to the concept of political legitimacy and to sketch an account of how all three concepts would fit together in an *institutional* moral theory of international law. According to Philpott and Copp, democracy is not complete, or democratic values are not adequately honoured, unless the state recognizes a plebiscitary right to secede. Furthermore, both seem committed to the view that whatever the criteria for state legitimacy are, there is a right to secede by plebiscite from legitimate as well as illegitimate states. According to the contrasting view I shall now sketch, a state is *legitimate* only if it is democratic and legitimate states are generally immune to secessionist claims (unless those claims are based on considerations of rectificatory justice, as in the case of the secession of the Baltic republics from the USSR).

The view I am suggesting combines a *remedial right only theory of secession*, which I have developed and defended at length on other occasions, with a notion of legitimate statehood that is both morally attractive and increasingly approximated in international law.[21] The resulting account renders coherent the combination of attitudes noted at the outset of this chapter: enthusiasm for democratization with a more constrained response to secessionist demands.

The remedial right only theory holds that the right to secede, as a general right, rather than a special right established by negotiation or by explicit constitutional provisions, arises only in response to serious and persisting grievances. (In this respect, the right to secede is like the right to revolution.)

More specifically, a group has the right to secede (in the absence of any negotiations or constitutional provisions that establish a right) only as a remedy of last resort to escape serious injustices. On my version of the remedial right only position, injustices capable of generating a right to secede consist of persistent violations of human rights, including the right to participate in democratic governance, and the unjust taking of the territory in question, if that territory previously was a legitimate state or a portion of one (in which case secession is simply the taking back of what was unjustly taken).

The remedial right only position offers a constrained approach to secession, but not so constraining as it might first appear. It allows for secession by mutual consent of the state and the secessionist group and for a constitutional right to secede as well. What it does not allow is a right to secede from a *just* state (in the absence of a special right generated through negotiation or as included in the constitution). The remedial right only theory does preclude a plebiscitary right to secede of the sort endorsed by Philpott and Copp.

I have argued elsewhere that the remedial right only theory of secession is superior to alternative theories, including the plebiscitary right view, if what we are seeking is a theory of secession that can provide sound and practical guidance for developing an international legal response to secession.[22] I will not repeat those arguments here. Instead, I will only sketch an account of legitimacy that naturally goes with the remedial right only theory and which provides a quite different understanding of the relationship between secession and democracy than that offered by Philpott, Copp, and others who would link secession closely with democratic values.

The notion of political legitimacy is an ambiguous one. In classical and contemporary Western political philosophy the term is often used interchangeably with 'political authority': an entity is a legitimate political power only if it possesses political authority, where authority is understood to imply political obligation on the part of citizens to obey. A number of contemporary theorists, perhaps most prominently A. John Simmons, have argued persuasively that most existing states (perhaps all of them) lack political authority in this sense, though many or most of their citizens may have strong moral and prudential reasons for obeying the law.[23]

What is striking about this philosophical literature on political authority is that it is entirely disconnected from questions of political legitimacy in what might be called the *institutional recognitional* sense.[24] This latter sense of legitimacy is at issue in real world conflicts over secession, when governments of existing states must decide whether or not to recognize as sovereign states the new political entities that emerge from secessionist struggles. The question in such cases is whether or not to recognize an entity (say the ones that called themselves Katanga in 1962 or Bangladesh in 1971 or the Republic of Croatia in 1990) as a member of the system of states, with the rights, privileges, and responsibilities that this entails. For secessionists and for the states that must decide to recognize them or not, the issue is one of legitimacy in the institutional recognitional sense, not whether the population of these new entities have a special political obligation to obey the new entity's rules.

The institutional recognitional sense of 'legitimacy' has both a descriptive and a normative sense. Descriptively speaking, a state is legitimate if and only if it satisfies whatever the existing international legal criteria for legitimacy happen to be. Normatively speaking, a state is legitimate if and only if it ought to be recognized as legitimate, that is, if and only if it would be recognized as legitimate under an appropriate and morally defensible set of international legal criteria for recognition. So the distinction between the philosopher's and the international lawyer's concepts of legitimacy is not that between a normative concept and a descriptive concept. An adequate moral theory of international legal institutions would include a normative conception of legitimacy in the institutional recognitional sense.

On another occasion I have argued that this disregard for the political philosopher's sense of political legitimacy is neither an oversight nor a mistake.[25] From the standpoint of a morally justifiable theory of international relations, what matters is whether entities that act like states are justified in wielding coercive power to enforce rules within the boundaries of a territory, not whether those upon whom they attempt to enforce rules have a particular obligation to those entities to comply with their rules (as opposed to, say, a moral obligation to support just institutions or to refrain from the kinds of acts the state's rules prohibit, as with laws against theft and murder). And it simply begs all the important questions to assume that an entity is justified in wielding coercive power to enforce rules within a territory only if those within the territory have a particular political obligation to obey it.

In other words, according to my view we should distinguish sharply between whether the use of political power is *justified* and whether there is such a thing as political obligation. It is the former that matters from the standpoint of the ethics of political legitimacy in the institutional recognitional sense.

I am not claiming that whether citizens have a *moral* obligation to comply with the state's laws or policies is entirely irrelevant to whether the state should be recognized as legitimate in international law and political practice. According to my view, only those states that meet minimal standards of justice (including democratic governance and respect for human rights) ought to be recognized as legitimate, and in general citizens of such states will have a moral obligation to help support them and to make them more just. My point here, however, is simply that international law does not and need not concern itself with political authority in the philosophers' sense (which implies political obligation) but rather with political legitimacy in the institutional recognitional sense—with the conditions under which an entity ought to be recognized as a member of the state system.

That international lawyers and political philosophers should be interested in different notions of legitimacy is not surprising. For political philosophers the basic question has been: when are citizens justified in opposing state power? For international lawyers the basic question, at least so long as international law has been mainly the law of states, has been: which entities are states (and what are their rights, privileges, and responsibilities)?[26]

Issues of political legitimacy in the institutional recognitional sense (as distinct from the political authority/obligation sense) also arise in other contexts besides secession. For example, beginning in the 1970s several important international legal documents took the position that South Africa was not a legitimate state because of its massive human rights violations. What is at work in such pronouncements is a *normative* conception of statehood or of political legitimacy: only those political units that meet the most basic standards of human rights are to be recognized as members of the community of states; only those units that meet this fundamental normative standard are entitled to recognition by the state system. In the early part of this decade, especially in the Copenhagen Agreement of 1990 (which flowed from the earlier Helsinki Accords), this normative conception of statehood begins to be understood as including a requirement of *democratic governance*: if the right to democratic governance is among the basic human rights or is the best protection for other human rights, then democratic states deserve to be recognized and protected by the international legal community and non-democratic states ought to be branded and stigmatized as illegitimate.[27]

The Copenhagen Agreement extends protection to democratic states (if they also respect other basic human rights) by obligating the thirty-five signatories to the document (including the United States) to support democratic regimes against efforts to overthrow them.[28] The Agreement does not rule out the signatories' use of force to defend democratic governments. Taken at face value, this document is a rather radical authorization for intervention.

The Copenhagen Agreement does not explicitly address secession. However, it does explicitly obligate the signatories to support democratic governments whether they are threatened by external *or internal* forces. This provision is consistent with the idea that there is at least a presumption that there is no right to secede from a democratic state (so long as it also respects human rights).

A word of caution is in order at this juncture. As I have observed elsewhere, secession involves *opposition* to the government and may in practice result in the overthrow of the government; but the aim of secession as such is not to *overthrow* the government but only to remove part of the territory of the state from the control of the government.[29] It would, therefore, be logically consistent to make a commitment to defending democratic states from the actions of internal forces aiming to overthrow the government, yet to refrain from making any commitment to protecting them from secession.

My objective is not to engage in exegesis of the Copenhagen Agreement. Instead, my goal is twofold: first, to point out that this document appears to advance a conception of legitimacy based on democratic governance (and respect for human rights); and second, to exhibit the attractions of such a conception of legitimacy when it is understood to include protection for legitimate states against secession.

In authorizing intervention across state borders for the sake of protecting democratic governments, the Copenhagen Agreement appears to represent a major limitation on the most basic and entrenched principle of international law: the principle of the territorial integrity of existing states, understood as prohibiting not only forcible annexation of the territories of existing states, but also interventions across their borders. Thus, the Agreement appears to reject the principle that intervention is unlawful except for purposes of self-defence or to stop aggressions against innocent third-party states.

The Agreement's authorization of intervention to protect democratic governments can, however, be reconciled with a qualified and morally progressive understanding of the principle of territorial integrity. The Copenhagen Agreement can be read as implicitly identifying as *legitimate* states those that meet the criteria of being democratic and respecting other basic human rights, with the implicit understanding that *only legitimate states* are protected by the principle of territorial integrity.

Moreover, since the Copenhagen Agreement pledges support for states with democratic (and human rights-respecting) governments when they are threatened, it appears that the Agreement regards being democratic (and respecting human rights) as *sufficient* for legitimacy as well. Democratic, rights-respecting states are entitled to be recognized as legitimate and to the protections that go with legitimacy.

If this line of reasoning is accepted, it is only a small step to draw a momentous implication for the legitimacy of secession and to link strong support for democratization with a constrained approach to secession. If the justification for intervention to protect democratic governments is that democracy confers legitimacy on states (at least when other human rights are respected), and that forcible opposition to a legitimate state, including attempts to take portions of its territory, is *illegitimate*, then it appears that the attempt to secede from a democratic state would be impermissible (in the absence of a constitutional or negotiated right to do so).

Putting together the various strands of the argument we get a proposal for determining the legitimacy of secession and hence for the legitimacy of the new political entities that secessionists attempt to create.

1. (Except in cases where there is a negotiated secession agreement or a constitutional right to secede) secession from a legitimate state is impermissible.
2. A state is legitimate if and only if it is democratic (and respects human rights).
3. (Therefore) Secession from a democratic (human rights-respecting) state is impermissible (except in cases where there is a negotiated secession or secession as the result of the exercise of a constitutional right).

To be morally plausible, this position on secession and legitimacy would have to include the following qualification: a state's legitimacy can be compromised not only by serious and persistent violations of human rights and failure to govern democratically but also by unjust annexation of the territory of a legitimate state. Suppose, contrary to fact, that when the Soviet Union unjustly annexed the Baltic republics in 1940 it instituted democratic rule and strict respect for human rights. This would not suffice to defeat the claim that the Baltic republics had the right to secede from the Soviet Union to recover their lost sovereignty.[30]

Let me hasten to note that neither the Copenhagen Agreement, nor anything I have said in this chapter, provides an argument *for* the first premiss—the thesis that secession from a legitimate (that is, democratic, rights-respecting) state is impermissible. As I have already acknowledged, the Copenhagen Agreement is consistent with, but does not include a clear endorsement of the thesis that an attempt by a group within a legitimate state to deprive that state of part of its territory is impermissible, not just that attempts by internal forces to *overthrow* a legitimate government are impermissible.

In this chapter I have argued that certain arguments *against* premiss 1, are flawed, namely, those that try to show that a plebiscitary right to secede is based in democratic values; and I have shown that recognition of a plebiscitary right to secede would in fact threaten democracy. Elsewhere I have argued in detail for a remedial right only theory of the right to secede, and this position *does* entail that secession from a democratic, rights-respecting state is impermissible.[31] As noted earlier, my purpose here is not to repeat those arguments, but to criticize one type of rival to the remedial right only position, the plebiscitary right view and to explore rival accounts of the relationship between secession and democracy.

We have now arrived at an understanding of the connection between secession and democracy that is quite the opposite of that endorsed by theorists such as Philpott and Copp. Their view is that a consistent commitment to democracy and its underlying values requires a right to secede even from perfectly just and fully democratic states, and hence from legitimate states if democracy and respect for human rights are taken to confer legitimacy. In sharp contrast, the account just sketched, the democratic legitimacy account, holds that democratic institutions, when combined with protection for human rights, block secessionist claims (in the absence of a negotiated or constitutional right to secede).

I conclude by suggesting that the democratic legitimacy account is the more plausible one for several reasons. First, as we have seen, arguments to show that the same values that justify democracy require a (non-remedial) plebiscitary right to secede are unpersuasive; at most there is a very weak and rebuttable presumption that democratic decision-making should extend to the determination of political boundaries because equal respect for persons requires an equal say in political decisions generally. Moreover, it is not clear that this presumption even counts in favour of the plebiscitary right view, since it seems to support just as well the claim that all the citizens of the state, not just those of the would-be secessionist region, ought to have an equal say in the decision that determines boundaries. Second, by protecting democratic, rights-respecting states against dismemberment by exercise of a plebiscitary right to secede, the democratic legitimacy account actually promotes and protects democracy: by reducing the threat of secession as a strategic bargaining tool that gives minorities a *de facto* veto over majority decisions and by fostering the stability that is needed to make it rational for citizens to invest themselves in the demanding practices of deliberative democracy. Third, if implemented through the operation of international legal institutions, the democratic legitimacy conception would give states a strong incentive to respect human rights and to govern democratically, by offering them protection against secessionist attempts and by refusing recognition for secessionists.

NOTES

1. T. M. Franck, 'The Emerging Right to Democratic Governance', *American Journal of International Law,* 86 (1992), 46–91.
2. L. Buchheit, *Secession* (New Haven: Yale University Press, 1978); H. Hannum, *Autonomy, Sovereignty, and Self-Determination* (Philadelphia: University of

Pennsylvania Press, 1990); W. Ofuatey-Kodjoe, *The Principle of Self-Determination in International Law* (New York: Nellen, 1977). The work of decolonization is not entirely finished, as the cases of East Timor and Tibet show.

3. As a remedial right, the right to secede is a general right, as contrasted with a special right, which might be acquired through a negotiated settlement between secessionist and the state, or through a special constitutional provision for secession (as exists, for example in the Ethiopian Constitution and the Constitution of St. Kitts-Nevis, or as existed in the Soviet Constitution from 1917 until the demise of the Soviet Union).
4. D. Copp, 'Democracy and Communal Self-Determination', in J. McMahan and R. McKim (eds.), *The Morality of Nationalism* (New York: Oxford University Press, 1997); K. Nielsen, 'Secession: The Case of Quebec', *Journal of Applied Philosophy*, 10 (1993), 29–43; D. Philpott, 'In Defense of Self-Determination', *Ethics*, 105 (1995), 352–85.
5. Philpott, 'In Defense of Self-Determination', 352–3.
6. Copp, 'Democracy and Communal Self-Determination', 16. Copp qualifies the plebiscitary right to secede by limiting it to what he calls 'territorial political societies', but this qualification does not affect my argument in what follows.
7. My discussion of the elements of democracy borrows from T. Christiano, *The Rule of the Many* (Boulder, Colo.: Westview, 1996), 15–21.
8. Philpott, 'A Defense of Self-Determination', 357.
9. A. Buchanan, 'Assessing the Communitarian Critique of Liberalism', *Ethics,* 99 (1989), 852–82; Christiano, *The Rule of the Many*, 18–19.
10. Philpott, 'In Defense of Self-Determination', 359.
11. Ibid. 360.
12. R. Dworkin, 'What is Equality? pt. 1: Equality of Welfare', and 'What is Equality? pt. 2: Equality of Resources', *Philosophy and Public Affairs*, 10/3 and 10/4 (1981); J. Roemer, 'Equality of Talent', *Economics and Philosophy*, 1/2 (1985).
13. Copp, 'Democracy and Communal Self-Determination',16.
14. A. O. Hirschman, *Exit, Voice and Loyalty* (Cambridge, Mass.: Harvard University Press, 1970).
15. For a discussion of the pros and cons of a constitutional right to secede, see A. Buchanan, *Secession: The Morality of Political Divorce From Fort Sumter to Lithuania and Quebec* (Boulder, Colo.: Westview, 1991). For a somewhat later, but very similar discussion, see C. Sunstein, 'Consitutionalism and Secession', *University of Chicago Law Review*, 58 (1991), 633–70. As in my analysis in *Secession*, Sunstein utilizes the idea that rational self-binding (pre-commitment) strategies require serious restrictions on exit from democracy and would be designed to encourage voice (constructive criticism and deliberation). Sunstein concludes that these considerations show that a constitutional right to secede would virtually never be appropriate. My argument strikes a more cautious note, leaving open the possibility that a heavily proceduralized constitutional right to secede, perhaps with special exit costs, waiting periods, and super-majority requirements (as with the US Constitution's Amendment Clause), might be appropriate in certain special circumstances.
16. Hirschman, *Exit, Voice, and Loyalty*.
17. Buchanan, *Secession*, 127–49.

18. Philpott, 'In Defense of Self-Determination', 359.
19. It is not clear that the conditions of radical pluralism obtain anywhere in the world today. For one thing, the forces of international commerce have necessitated the bridging of many cultural divisions and created a common good, albeit a rather thin one, or at least a common legal framework of rights within which disparate groups may pursue their own conceptions of the good. Even in cases of large cultural differences, there are some commonalities in values (for example, the desire for physical security, and freedom from disease) and there is a growing consensus on the institutional arrangements needed to protect these common, minimal values. I speak here of what has been aptly called the growing global culture of human rights. See R. Howard, *Human Rights and the Search for Community* (Boulder, Colo.: Westview, 1995).

    It is a mistake to assume that because the global culture of human rights is to some extent Western in its origins that it is not valuable to people of other cultures, and that it cannot provide an effective means for building a common political culture across cultures. One of the best-documented and compelling instances of the ability of people of non-Western cultures to adapt to the so-called Western liberal democratic framework of legal concepts that dominates the global culture of human rights is that of the Cree of Northern Quebec. In a brilliantly argued book entitled *Sovereign Injustice*, the leadership of the Cree make a compelling case for their people's political autonomy, utilizing liberal-individualist moral arguments, Canadian Federal Constitutional arguments, and arguments based on the principles of international law. To assume that a group that is able to do this is *ipso facto* 'assimilated', not an 'authentically indigenous group', is to dismiss unfairly a simpler and more plausible explanation: the Cree are successfully utilizing the conceptual resources of the global culture of human rights in the service of their efforts to preserve their distinctive non-Western culture. See Grand Council of the Crees, *Sovereign Injustice: Forcible Inclusion of the James Bay Crees and Cree Territory Into A Sovereign Quebec* (1995).
20. Buchanan, *Secession*, 127–49.
21. A. Buchanan, 'Secession, Self-Determination, and the Rule of International Law', in J. McMahon and R. McKim (eds.), *The Morality of Nationalism* (New York: Oxford University Press, 1997); A. Buchanan, 'Theories of Secession', *Philosophy and Public Affairs*, 26/1 (1997), 30–61.
22. Buchanan, 'Theories of Secession'.
23. A. J. Simmons, *Moral Principles and Political Obligations* (Princeton: Princeton University Press, 1979).
24. In an unpublished paper, R. Sandler (1997) makes a similar distinction between 'internal' and 'external' legitimacy. Sandler assumes, however, that the former is subjective in nature—that a state is legitimate in the internal sense of legitimacy if most of its citizens regard it so. This view appears to me to be inadequate because, taken at face value, it provides no explanation of why citizens' regarding a state as legitimate makes their opinion true; or else it reduces to a somewhat misleading formulation of the consent theory of legitimacy (in the political philosophers', not the international lawyers' sense).
25. Allen Buchanan, 'Recognitional Legitimacy' (unpub.).

26. I would argue that legitimacy in the political philosophers' (correlative obligation) sense turns out to be of very limited significance even for the question of the justifiability of opposition to political power. On the one hand, even those who argue that most or many of the citizens of some existing states do have a political obligation to obey the laws of those states concede that it is only a *prima facie* obligation and a rather weak one at that. On the other hand, it is generally admitted that even if there is no such political obligation there can be and usually are good moral reasons to obey the law. So even if there is such an obligation, opposition to the state may often be justified; and even if no such obligation exists, opposition to the state may be wrong. In other words, it appears that a theory of legitimacy (in the political philosophers' sense) would shed little light on the one issue that was supposed to make it significant: the question of when it is justifiable to oppose the power of the state.
27. Franck, 'The Emerging Right to Democratic Self-Government'; 'Conference on Security and Co-operation in Europe: Document of the Copenhagen Meeting of the Conference on the Human Dimension', 29 June 1992, 29 I. L. M., 1305–24. Hereafter cited as 'Copenhagen Agreement'.
28. 'Copenhagen Agreement'. The document also adds two other conditions: the existence of a multi-party system and of the basic features of the rule of law.
29. Buchanan, *Secession*, 10.
30. Of course, any defensible institutional recognition of a right to recover unjustly taken territory must address what I have called elsewhere 'the moral statute of limitations problem'. A reasonable convention to set a time before which claims of unjust taking would not be regarded as justiciable would seem to be unavoidable. Here as in other areas of the law, some conventions are more reasonable than others, and being a convention is not equivalent to being arbitrary.
31. Buchanan, *Secession*, esp. 87–126, and 'Theories of Secession', 31–61.

3

The Ethics of Secession as the Regulation of Secessionist Politics

WAYNE NORMAN

When Allen Buchanan launched the current debate about the morality of secession a few years ago he felt it necessary to begin with a long section explaining why we needed such a debate.[1] First, there was the practical urgency of the topic: the world in 1991 was teeming with secessionist demands, some of which have since been granted. And second, he argued, the case of secession is not merely a problem of applied or non-ideal political theory: it challenges some of the most basic values and assumptions of liberal theory. 'A political philosophy [such as liberalism] that places a preeminent value on liberty and autonomy, that highly values diversity, or that holds that legitimate political authority in some sense rests on consent must either acknowledge a right to secede or supply weighty arguments to show why a presumption in favour of such a right is rebutted.'[2]

To my knowledge, nobody has challenged Buchanan on either of these claims. On the contrary, philosophers have enthusiastically taken up his project, usually by attacking Buchanan's own views, and have gone a long way toward filling the theoretical lacuna to which he drew attention. We now have a variety of competing moral theories of secession including some that place the burden of argument on the secessionists and some that place it on

This chapter would simply not exist in anything like its present form without persuasive criticisms from a number of colleagues, including Allen Buchanan, Will Kymlicka, Margaret Moore, Kai Nielsen, Hilliard Aronovitch, Pierre Laberge, Michael Freeman, David Miller, Attracta Ingram, John Baker, Daniel Philpott, Philippe Van Parijs, Jos De Beus, Adrian Favell, Filimon Peonidis, Dominique Leydet, Daniel Weinstock, Guy Laforest, Manuel Toscano, Ronnie Beiner, Geneviève Nootens, and Fred Bennett. I also owe many thanks to challenging audiences at the Université de Montréal; the Annual Meetings of the American Political Science Association, San Francisco; the Instituto de filosofía, CSIC, Madrid; the Institut de Ciències Politiques i Socials, Barcelona; European Forum at the European University Institute, Florence; the Nuffield Political Theory Seminar, Oxford; the Department of Politics, University College Dublin; the Centre universitaire de Luxembourg; and the Annual conference of the Société internationale des études kantiennes, Ottawa.

the state, some based on individual rights and others based on group rights where such rights are in turn derived, variously, from principles of individual autonomy, freedom of association, democracy, self-determination, distributive justice, property rights, consent, or consequentialist considerations. Indeed, what we have now are liberal theories of secession corresponding to most of the traditional justifications of liberalism itself.

It is unclear to what extent this exercise has, as Buchanan had hoped, *challenged* these traditional justifications or merely *reproduced* them. Rival positions, for the most part, are derived from rival starting points and there has been relatively little debate about these first principles. In some cases differences can be traced to very different contexts for normative theorizing: some philosophers take for granted a liberal-democratic *status quo* and are looking for principles to guide statesmen and citizens faced with secessionist movements; while others pose the question of secession in the context of a much more radical reconsideration of the system of states and the possibilities of cosmopolitanism. And underlying both of these types of divergence there seem to be very different implicit stands on a rarely discussed methodological question concerning the relation between institutional and non-institutional forms of moral reasoning. This issue arises acutely in the case of secession, as we shall see, because secession is a problem that seems to require an institutional response despite the fact that we find ourselves in a world which, for all intents and purposes, lacks the relevant institutional frameworks in constitutional and international law. I shall try to show the relevance of this methodological question after highlighting a number of problems with the three most common non-institutional moralities of secession.

All of the recent normative theories of secession that I have seen can be fit into three categories which I call (a) National Self-Determination theories, or *Nationalist* theories, for short; (b) *Choice theories*; and (c) *Just-cause* theories.[3] We will look briefly at each of these types of theories, highlighting the extent to which they seem to fall well short of grounding a justifiable institutional morality of secession in constitutional or international law.

1. NATIONAL SELF-DETERMINATION THEORIES OF SECESSION

A full-blooded nationalist theory of secession claims that nations have a right to self-determination, including a right to a state in which the members of the nation form a majority. For minority nations in a multination state, this implies a right to secede and form their own state (or join another). It is a curious fact that this theory provides the self-legitimization for just about every serious secessionist movement in the twentieth century; and yet, in its full-blooded form, it has virtually no defenders in the recent philosophical literature.

The reasons for the lack of philosophical defenders should be obvious. First of all, the internal logic of the nationalist principle seems to be a *non sequitur*. Several steps would be needed to get from the fact that a group believes itself (even if rightly) to be a nation to the normative conclusion that it should have its own state if it wants one. It is difficult to imagine what it is about specifically *national* difference that can *necessitate* such a strong conclusion. And secondly, as has been pointed out on numerous occasions, there are at least 5,000 groups in the world that—by virtue of distinctive languages, dialects, religions, or cultures—have developed or could develop a national consciousness, and hence, have a right to secede according to the nationalist theory.[4] If the nationalist theory were to be institutionally guaranteed, say, by a much more forceful United Nations, it would provide irresistible incentives to would-be nationalist leaders in a good many of these groups to mobilize a national self-identification within their groups in order to gain access to the right (if only, initially, to enhance their bargaining position within the larger state), even if such groups had neither felt like nations, nor felt unhappy within their larger state. It would also, on just about any scenario conceivable (and the idea of such an institutional guarantee is at the very margins of conceivability), result in civil strife and bloodshed on a vast scale. While the world and its people are probably not worse off by being divided into 200 states rather than 20, it is difficult to see the advantages of there being 2,000 states, let alone of fighting to bring this about. Among other things, multiplying the number of states is likely to increase exponentially—not to reduce—the number of minority groups within states. The peoples of the world rarely come in discrete territorial chunks.

There have been several recent philosophical attempts to ground a more moderate theory of national self-determination, one that does not necessarily imply a right of secession for national minorities. In the liberal tradition these theories explain why so-called ‘encompassing groups’, particularly national minorities with a different language from the majority in their state, have a special claim to a degree of political autonomy in which they can protect their language and culture. Among the more persuasive theories of this sort are those that show why political autonomy is conducive to improving the equality of opportunity and individual autonomy of members of the national minority.[5] On the plausible assumption that this degree of political autonomy and self-determination is possible within a federal structure, however, such theories cannot usually be used to ground a right for national minorities to secede unless the very possibility of federal accommodation is not on offer. Indeed, most theorists of this sort state explicitly that the existence of a sufficient degree of sub-state autonomy precludes a right to secede.[6]

It is also worth noting that if the nationalist principle were backed up in any significant way by international law it would probably erode the prospects of self-determination for many national minorities since it would give states an incentive to attempt to assimilate ethnic groups by depriving them of the political autonomy which their leaders could exploit in minority nation-building projects and for organizing a secessionist movement.[7]

The closest relative to national self-determination theories is also the most popular in the recent philosophical literature. I call these Choice Theories of Secession. I suspect that their popularity derives from the fact that they stand in stark contrast to the just-cause theory with which Buchanan launched the debate.

2. CHOICE THEORIES OF SECESSION

Choice theories of secession share the following features: (a) they require that the majority in a region express a desire to secede for a secession to be legitimate; (b) they do not require that the seceding group be culturally distinct or the victim of injustice, such as having had its territory illegally annexed or having been discriminated against or oppressed by the larger state; (c) they do not require that the seceding group establish some special claim to the territory they intend to take with them as they withdraw from the state; the fact that they occupy it and have a right to secede is sufficient in the normal case to allow them to take it if they choose to secede; hence (d), with certain caveats, the mere choice by a majority within a seceding region is sufficient to justify their right to secede and the duty of the state (and other states) to allow them to secede on fair terms (i.e. with compensation for state properties, etc, where appropriate).[8]

Choice theories are, in effect, nationalist theories shorn of the moral complications of ethnicity.[9] Groups do not have to prove they are nations in order to qualify for a right to secede, and this allows choice theorists to avoid entirely the problem of explaining why some often very apolitical cultural traits should take on such enormous moral weight in arguments for secession. Choice theorists derive the right of secession from supposedly fundamental principles of autonomy and democracy and hence, in theory, this right should be easier to reconcile with the other institutional features of a liberal-democratic state which are also justified by these principles. I believe that this perception is mistaken. In cleansing national self-determination theories of their national element, choice theories toss away the baby and leave the bath water. Again, as Kymlicka and others have urged, there are indeed very good liberal reasons for according political significance to certain elements of national identity—particularly where minority languages are concerned. While choosing to ignore these reasons along with the central motivating factor of virtually all actual secessionist movements, choice theorists end up merely multiplying, well beyond 5,000, the number of potential groups with the right to secede. This leaves them vulnerable to most of the principal objections to nationalist theories.

The analogy between secession and no-fault divorce is often alluded to by choice theorists, most elaborately by Kai Nielsen:

> The right of secession should be treated like the right to a no-fault divorce . . . No prior or imminent injustice need be shown in either case. If the parties want to split in either case they have the right to split provided certain harms (not all harms) do not accrue to the other party. If Mary wishes to split with Michael she should have the right to do so provided there is a fair settlement of their mutual properties, adequate provision and care of any children they may have is ensured, and the like. Similarly if Quebec wishes to split with Canada it should have the right to do so provided a fair settlement of mutual assets and debts is made and the like.[10]

For Nielsen and some others, the analogy seems to be the argument, or at least one of the arguments.[11] For most other choice theorists, the no-fault secession conclusion ((a) – (d)) is arrived at by trying to extend, variously, principles of consent, individual autonomy, freedom of association, political self-determination, or democracy.

There are now standard objections to all of these patterns of argument, many anticipated by Buchanan himself before sophisticated choice theories had even been proposed. The most serious and commonly recurring objections include the following: doubts about the usefulness of consent to justify the legitimacy or illegitimacy of states; doubts that the value of individual autonomy is necessarily enhanced by having sweeping powers to decide collectively with others the frontiers of one's state; concerns about the anti-democratic and unjust consequences of secession (i.e. that the right to secede would corrupt democratic politics by allowing pseudo-secessionists to make threats in order to receive preferential treatment); concerns about the fate of minorities within the seceding regions; and perhaps most importantly, concerns about secessionist anarchy in a world of legalized no-fault secession which would be to the detriment of liberal-democratic values.

These objections and others are now routinely addressed by the choice theorists themselves, most ingeniously and comprehensively by Daniel Philpott. While I believe that most of the standard objections have not, and will not, be overturned, I shall not try to prove this here by showing why particular replies are insufficient. Instead I will step back from the internal critique in order to develop a different (though not unrelated) set of objections that try instead to illustrate why the very basis of choice accounts seems misguided. Ironically, when I propose an institutional approach later it will bear many similarities to the no-fault conclusion, but from considerations drawn mainly from what I call just-cause theories.

The lack of an ethno-cultural dimension raises a number of problems for choice theories of secession. It is surely a significant fact that every serious secessionist movement this century has involved ethno-cultural minorities.[12] By failing to take this into account choice theories are unlikely to fit the problem of secession properly into the context of the much larger problem of ethnic conflict. Most choice theorists seem sincerely to believe that secession should be seen as a last-resort solution to ethnic conflicts, with minority rights and federal arrangements being preferred.[13] All the more peculiar, therefore, that their theory of secession is culture-blind, since surely those other proferred solutions will necessarily take the special circumstances of ethno-linguistic groups into account (e.g. in deciding which groups get minority rights, or what sovereign powers should go to federal subunits in which national minorities are the majority). Does it really make sense to treat the demands of ethno-cultural groups in terms of their distinctness as groups only until they demand secession, at which point we treat them merely as a collection of autonomous individuals who happen to have a desire for their own state?

The reflections of the dean of ethnic-conflict studies on these same choice and nationalist theories provide a sobering antidote. '[I]f interest [by philosophers] in the problem [of secession] is driven by events, the methodology is not, for much of the literature thus far often displays a thoroughgoing ignorance of the complexities of ethnic interactions. To say this is not to exhibit hostility to the efforts of philosophers on such issues in general—for moral reasoning is needed—but a priori methods that seem appropriate to other issues are utterly unsuitable to this problem.'[14] As an example of the relevance of ethnic politics, Donald Horowitz considers that 'it is sometimes, albeit rarely, noted [by philosophers] that secession could create a new set of minority problems in the secessionist region. The response is, as Margalit and Raz say, that this is a "risk [that] cannot be altogether avoided". This puts the problem rather mildly, since, nine times out of ten, the creation of a new set of minority problems is a "risk" that will come to pass.'[15] As Horowitz noted a little earlier in the same article, secessionist movements sometimes gain much of their energy from a desire to 'deal with' regional minorities, free from intrusion of the centre.[16]

Choice theories are derived from pure principles of democracy or freedom of association, as if choosing the frontiers of your state should naturally be subject to the same rules as choosing your member of parliament or choosing your friends. This makes for a peculiar conception of the state, one which bears a striking resemblance to that often held up by critics of liberalism: where the state is nothing but a collection of autonomous individuals. This conception of the state is certainly at odds with what now seems to be the mainstream view in post-Rawlsian liberal theory, as it was among most nineteenth-century liberal thinkers. It is now, once again, standard for liberals to take seriously the problems of identity and 'social cement' which make possible the sense of community and solidarity necessary for just and efficient liberal institutions.[17] I cannot defend this thicker conception of liberal citizenship here, but I would like to wind up this section by pointing to a set of problems with the thin conception of the state presupposed by choice theories.

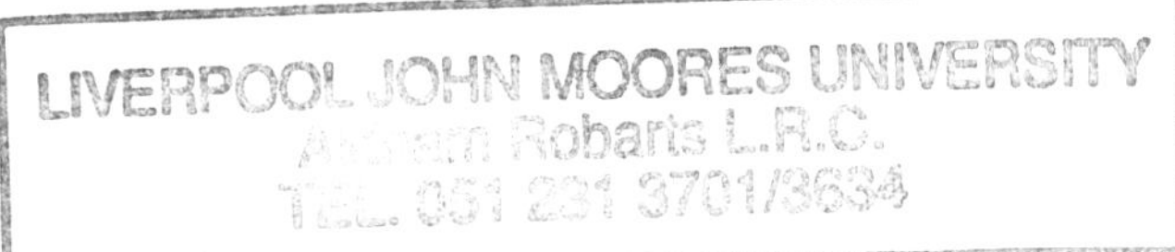

What do choice theorists think is the role of the state and of the system of states? The answer is not easy to discern. On the one hand, their theories, if current and in particular if supported by international and constitutional law (again, an unimaginably large 'if'), would almost certainly spell the end to the system of states as we know it.[18] Perhaps some of the great nation-states, which have experienced a century or more of successful nation-building projects, would remain without significant secessionist movements, at least at first. But most states, including the majority of currently undemocratic states, would likely be torn asunder by opportunistic secessionist movements —*including many for which there would have been no natural impetus in the absence of the currency and enforcement of the choice theory itself.* I think this would be so catastrophic in terms of human lives and well-being that the states making international law would never permit it; and not just out of cynical fears for their own dismemberment. But leaving this criticism aside, we see that choice theories, viewed in this way, look like a radical challenge to the authority of states and the system of states generally. And yet, at the same time, at the very heart of choice theories is a glorification of the state: statehood is so important that people are unjustly treated if they are not allowed to choose collectively what state they will be members of (even if they are not unjustly treated in any other respect). This profound contradiction can be squared only if one takes a very rosy picture of the consequences of the currency of a choice theory: namely, a view that it would lead to only a smallish number of secessions or attempted secessions and that these could be managed with a minimum of bloodshed.

Another way of thinking about these problems for choice theorists is that they are trying to work out a theory of political divorce without first having considered a theory of political marriage. They explain when states can be torn apart without first explaining or considering what states can do to keep themselves together and why unity and stability are often conducive to liberal goods and justice. Consider, for example, whether it would be democratically legitimate for the groups or subunits within a state to forswear their right to secede, or to adopt a constitutional secession clause which is more difficult to satisfy than the one demanded by a choice theory (say, by requiring two-thirds of the voters within a region to vote for secession). If not, then the choice theory stands in opposition to the entire tradition of constitutionalism and represents a much more radical challenge to mainstream conceptions of liberal democracy than any choice theorist has so far admitted. But if it is legitimate for states to make these sorts of pacts, it becomes difficult to see what normative standing choice theories have. Why should we not think that the appropriate morality of secession is one that would emerge out of free constitutional deliberations in a democratic state? (This, roughly, is what I shall argue for later.)

To get a hint of the appropriateness of peoples forswearing their right to a no-fault secession consider the following example. If the choice theory were current, then states would not take in refugees—particularly not those, who form the vast majority in the world today, from neighbouring countries. Why not? Because once settled, these refugees would acquire the right to secede and to take a portion of their host state with them. But obviously any conception of liberal justice requires that refugees be accommodated in a humanitarian fashion. We can suppose, therefore, that the choice theory would allow liberal states to demand that refugees (and presumably other immigrants) waive their right to secede. But if these kinds of deals can be made with foreigners, why can they not be made between the citizens of a liberal-democratic state? Assuming that they can be, then constitutionalism is back on, and I think it is pretty clear that no liberal state would adopt the recommendation of choice theories when considering what, if any, secession procedures to constitutionalize.[19]

3. JUST-CAUSE THEORIES[20]

If both national self-determination and choice theories of secession fail, then it would seem to follow that there is no *primary right* to secede. There are, however, good grounds for thinking that there must be a *remedial right* of secession, namely a general right for groups that have suffered certain kinds of injustices and for which secession is the most appropriate remedy.[21] Just-cause theories of secession vary depending on what sorts of injuries or threats to a group are considered to give just cause. Most of the just-cause theories in the recent philosophical literature were anticipated by Buchanan's initial contributions to the debate. Just-cause theorists insist that in addition to a majority (or supermajority) in favour of secession, a territorially concentrated group must be able to demonstrate one or more of the following: (i) that it has been the victim of systematic discrimination or exploitation, and that this situation will not end as long as the group remains in the state; (ii) that the group and its territory were illegally incorporated into the state within recent-enough memory; (iii) that the group has a valid claim to the territory it wants to withdraw from the state; (iv) that the group's culture is imperilled unless it gains access to all of the powers of a sovereign state; (v) that the group finds its constitutional rights grossly or systematically ignored by the central government or the supreme court.[22]

Just-cause theories attempt to find room for legitimate secessions while trying to avoid the negative consequences that would follow if secession was either too easy or too difficult. We have already noted a number of the dangers of too permissive a rule on secession. Secessionist politics can, over a protracted period, corrupt the democratic political culture of a state even if they are ultimately unsuccessful—e.g. by using secession as a threat to extract preferential treatment for a group within a state, or merely by having secession or the demands short of secession dominating the political agenda and distracting attention from the task of making the society more just and prosperous. Moreover, secession itself involves the alteration of international borders, the taking of territory from a sovereign state, the forced changing of the citizenship of unionists in the seceding region, and often, as Horowitz noted, the suppression of minorities within the newly created state. Finally, it goes without saying that in most parts of the world at most times attempted secessions have resulted in significant bloodshed. According to existing just-cause accounts of secession, these costs and potential costs of secession are high enough to warrant discouraging it in all but exceptional circumstances where these costs are in some sense outweighed by considerations of justice.

Of course, we cannot discount the injustice of too restrictive a view of secession. The fate of groups like the people of East Timor (and many other peoples in Indonesia who lack high-profile supporters in the West), the Tibetans, and the Iraqi and Turkish Kurds, are sufficient reminders of the injustice and violence that can befall minorities who are given no legal and peaceful means to exit a state that does not, to say the least, treat their interests equally. The famous principle of territorial integrity is morally progressive in so far as it forbids aggressive interstate wars; but it cannot be treated as legitimating *any* possible action of a government within its internationally secured frontiers.[23]

In effect, the just-cause theory of secession follows from, or points toward, a view of the legitimacy of states and of the system of states more generally: namely, that states exercise legitimate authority over a territory as long as they treat citizens and groups within that territory justly.[24] We can be tolerant about what counts as just treatment in different political traditions while still retaining an ability to note markedly unequal standards of treatment for different groups or regions within a state or the oppression of certain groups which cannot be defended by any conceivable standard of justice (e.g. nerve gas attacks on Kurdish villages). On this view the division of the world into sovereign states is itself legitimate in so far as this is the best way to maximize the number of individuals and groups throughout the world living under just regimes. (The comparison set will vary with feasibility and time-frame considerations.) A world in which the just-cause theory of secession was current and enforced would give states an incentive to treat their minorities justly, and perhaps more importantly, it would not give states an incentive to be stingy with minority rights and political autonomy, since they would not have to fear that groups would use this autonomy for nation-building exercises and the mobilization of secessionist movements.

That, at any rate, seems to be the intuition behind the theory. Choice theorists and nationalists may even be able to concede that there is some form of presumption in favour of existing states, but they believe that this presumption is nevertheless defeasible without having to demonstrate serious injustice. The presumption is based partly on the spectre of secessionist violence. But in many political cultures, notably in established liberal democracies, there is no reason to expect (or tolerate) violent opposition to secession, especially not from the central government. So at the very least, they could argue, the presumption against secession need not apply in these cases. And if it does not, choice theorists might add, it is difficult to see why it should be used as a ready-made moral justification for regimes, such as Iraq's, that are prepared to use extreme force to retain their reluctant minorities. In many parts of the world, including the world's most populous state, peaceful demonstrations for democracy can also elicit violent reactions from the regime; but surely this is no reason to say that there is a moral presumption against these people having or exercising a right to democratic representation. Moreover, critics of just-cause theories add, it is wrong to look at only one side of the ledger. In many cases there will be more violence in the long term by not allowing a minority to secede.[25]

So choice theorists need not deny the spectre of violence. But rather than grounding a moral presumption against a right of secession, they believe it serves as a fact that secessionists themselves will have to consider when deciding whether to try to exercise their alleged right. As Philpott suggests, 'A full moral account [of self-determination] . . . requires a counterpart to just-war theory's category of jus in bello, or the justice of means of fighting. A key tenet is proportionality: if the morally evil consequences of an otherwise just war (in this case, self-determination movement) outweigh the good achieved, then the action should be avoided. It is difficult to be systematic . . . Ethics here is baffling and situational.'[26]

Note that these criticisms, if sound, chip away at only *one* ground for the just-cause theorists' strong presumption against secession, namely, the spectre of violence, and state violence in particular. These arguments would not be as effective for negating the relevance of paramilitary violence which may be expected to arise more or less spontaneously in some regions where secession is hotly contested among the people themselves. But even in situations where this risk is minimal (it is never non-existent, not even in exemplary bastions of democratic tolerance such as the UK and Canada), just-cause theorists will still insist on the presumptive force provided by their arguments, sketched above, for the way a secessionist political culture can corrupt a state's democratic decision-making and system of distributive justice, and for how, in many cases, secession will create significant new minorities in the breakaway state who are likely to be as disgruntled as the secessionists. If minority rights within the new state are held up as the solution to the problems of post-secession minorities, why should they not be sufficient for the secessionist minorities themselves?

4. INSTITUTIONAL AND NON-INSTITUTIONAL MORAL REASONING ABOUT SECESSION

One way to sum up the above case for a just-cause theory of secession over the nationalist and choice rivals is to say that only the just-cause theory comes close to justifying a reasonable institutional response to secessionist politics. By this I mean that if constitutional and international law allowed only groups with just cause to secede and enforced their right to do so, then the world would be improved in a number of significant respects: many oppressed groups would find their oppressors easing off, and those that continued to be oppressed would be given a safe state of their own; states would lose their current incentives to deny their minorities basic rights and political autonomy, since these groups would not be able to use this autonomy to launch successful secessionist movements; similarly, states would lose much of their incentive to try (usually without much success) to assimilate ethno-cultural minorities; states would not have a special incentive to refuse to accept refugees or immigrants, and they would not have to worry about restricting the free circulation of minorities within the state in order to prevent them forming territorially concentrated majorities. All of this seems for the good. By contrast, the only benefit of codifying and enforcing nationalist and choice theories would be that they too would allow oppressed groups to seek a safe haven in their own states. But all of the other positive effects and incentives of institutionalizing just-cause theories would be reversed if we institutionalized choice or nationalist theories: oppression would be encouraged in cases where it could intimidate minorities from mounting a secessionist movement; and assimilationist policies would still look attractive to states, as would restrictions on mobility and the refusal to grant minority rights and to accept refugees.[27]

The arguments sketched in the preceding paragraph, and throughout much of the foregoing critique, could be classified as a form of *institutional moral reasoning*: they evaluate political principles in large part by evaluating the institutions they would justify, taking into consideration the dynamic effects of the institutions in society. In Rousseau's memorable phrase, this way of reasoning takes men as they are and laws as they might be. There are many forms of institutional reasoning depending on the criteria one uses to evaluate the institutions. In this case I have relied on general, widely accepted, conceptions of justice and (especially) injustice. The argument so far has been, roughly but not inaccurately, that there would be considerably less injustice —including less injustice to national minorities—in a world enforcing the just-cause theory of secession than in one enforcing the nationalist or choice theories. It is possible that nationalist and choice theorists would object on methodological grounds to the very idea that institutional moral reasoning is appropriate for the evaluation of a political morality of secession, at least in the first instance.

In order to consider the weight of such an objection we need some idea of what non-institutional moral reasoning would be like. For the purposes at hand we can simply refer back to the nationalist and choice theories themselves, since these have usually been defended in non-institutional ways: namely, by deriving them from more basic or general principles, for example, conceptions of pure democracy, autonomy, freedom of association, or nationalism. The idea is that if we accept these principles we must be prepared to accept the principles of secession that are their corollaries. It is prudent to consider practical problems with implementing an institution embodying such principles of secession because, for example, our world may be so imperfect that it is not yet feasible or would have undesirable or counter-productive consequences. Such problems, however, are regarded as problems not with the theory but with the world and its existing injustices.[28]

The case against using institutional reasoning—at least at early stages—in a political morality of secession relies on three interrelated claims. (1) We need to be able to identify ideal principles which institutions in the real world may only be able to approximate. To assume the limits of the institutionally possible right from the start is to give legitimacy to all sorts of injustices and imperfections in the world which makes ideals seem impractical. It is important that we identify ideals and keep them in sight in order to develop institutions that are themselves progressively more ideal. (2) The particular features of our world that make fair secession institutions difficult to realize are obvious. International law is made and enforced by states, and they each have an interest in never sanctioning any international institution that could encourage their dismemberment. At the domestic level, most of the multination states that might experience secessionist pressures are ruled by majority groups that also have no interest in sanctioning institutional means to allow minority groups to secede peacefully. The fact that state governments, individually and collectively, will not enact fair secession procedures, or would behave perversely if (counterfactually) such institutions were enacted, does not itself prove that such procedures are not fair or just. (3) Finally, there is something peculiar about using institutional reasoning for the morality of secession at this juncture in history since, for all intents and purposes, secession happens in a legal vacuum. Very few states have explicit secession clauses in their constitutions, and international law upholds the principle of territorial integrity over secession in virtually all cases that do not involve the liberation of overseas colonies.[29] Moreover it is unlikely that the legal vacuum will disappear in the foreseeable future. What we need in the meantime are clear moral theories based on sound principles (including liberal-democratic principles) in order to judge, in the absence of institutions, which groups have a right to secede.

Let us work through these objections in reverse order. While they are in some respects misplaced, they also raise important considerations that highlight some shortcomings of the just-cause theory as it has been developed thus far. Consider objection (3). It is true that our world, for the most part, leaves secessionist politics in a legal vacuum. In effect, secession is illegal without mutual consent (i.e. between the seceding region and the central government). In cases of contested secession—where the majority in a region wishes to secede but is denied permission by the state—there are no standing institutional mechanisms in international law or in most constitutions to settle the dispute.[30] (States have to be pressured into agreeing to negotiate with secessionists.) The question, then, is whether this legal vacuum presents a special problem for the use of institutional moral reasoning about a principle of secession. The answer, I think, is 'No' and 'Yes'. 'No', in the sense that it does not give us a reason to abandon institutional reasoning in favour of non-institutional reasoning. In states where divorce is illegal, or illegal without mutual consent, moral philosophers should not simply abandon an institutional approach to justifying an appropriate divorce law in favour of some non-institutional moral principles which couples could use to improve the intellectual quality of their arguments, or which their friends could use to decide whether the marriage should in fact be dissolved. Rather the appropriate response would be to show why a legal divorce procedure is necessary (and just), and to explain what the best divorce law should be, taking its social consequences into account. Something similar could be said about secession. We should argue (as I shall presently) for why an institutional mechanism for secessionist politics is necessary, and we should suggest what the best mechanisms would be in particular states or in international law.

But while the institutional vacuum does not justify abandoning institutional reasoning, it does nevertheless create problems for the role of a political morality of secession. As the non-institutionalists insist, we want such a moral theory not only to help us create just institutions, but also to make judgements about the legitimacy of various secessionist claims in the absence of institutions. For example, to know whether as citizens we should support the demands of a secessionist movement in our own state or elsewhere, and also for governments to know whether they should give international recognition to a breakaway region in some other state. In order to make such judgements with an institutional morality in the absence of institutions we must make a counterfactual claim, e.g. if reasonably just institutions were in place, then this group would (or would not) have a right to secede. Along with criticizing inferior principles for the right of secession (or for denying such a right), arguing for this kind of counterfactual claim is the best we can do. And yet we are well aware of the dangers of this form of reasoning. Institutions create rights and duties that do not necessarily exist otherwise. For example, from the fact that an ideal welfare state would give me certain benefits, it does not follow that I have a right to such benefits if I am not in such a state—or more to the point, it does not follow that I have a right to take such benefits (say, by theft). To sum up: the fact that our world happens not to have fair institutions regulating secession does make things awkward for a political morality of secession, but it does not in any way justify abandoning an institutional approach to such a moral theory.

The first and second objection to using institutional reasoning for a morality of secession are based on a misconception that institutional reasoning is constrained by *realpolitik*.[31] That is, that it limits itself to consideration of institutions that could be accepted by leaders of states with no interest in giving minorities fair terms to secede. This view of institutional reasoning, however, is simply false. Both Rousseau and Rawls are institutionalists *par excellence* about justice, but their theories will never be institutionalized in the actual world. My arguments in favour of the just-cause theory and against nationalist and choice theories did not in any way rely on the fact that just-cause theories would probably stand a higher (though not necessarily high) chance of being accepted in international or domestic law; although this is true and does provide an additional reason for supporting just-cause theories.[32]

So what is at stake, then, between those who use and those who reject the use of institutional reasoning for a morality of secession? Obviously there is not space here to hope to settle the general question about when it is appropriate to employ these two different forms of moral reasoning in political philosophy. (Among other things, this is not the sort of issue we should ever expect to see 'settled'. Philosophers will always have different casts of mind which favour one or the other of these approaches.) Nevertheless, whatever the virtues of non-institutional moral reasoning on some other questions in political philosophy, I do believe that there are good reasons for sticking with institutional reasoning for the issue of secession. I have presented a number of these reasons already, and will now add another general one.

There are some issues that are so conceptually bound up with the idea and the apparatus of the modern state or the system of states that it would be peculiar to try to address them outside the context of this network of institutions we have assembled so recently in human history. Consider, for example, the question of the principles that justify an appropriate amending formula for any given constitution. Such a formula would specify, among other things, who in society could veto changes, whether regions and their political authorities get a say, what qualified majorities are necessary in which legislative bodies, whether there should be national referendums, etc. Could anybody imagine there being any abstract principle of autonomy or democracy from which (with a minimal and specifiable amount of particular information) we could *deduce* the best amending formula for a given country? (This is not to deny that considerations of democracy and autonomy are relevant.[33]) The very idea seems absurd. On the other hand, we can see, more or less, how we would approach the question with institutional reasoning—roughly as Rawls does at the 'constitutional convention' stage of his four-stage sequence: by asking which amending formula would best ensure that the constitution was conducive to just government in the long run.[34] When we do this in actual states we can see that different political structures and political cultures require quite different amending formulas. To give just one obvious example, federal states will almost certainly see it as appropriate that the people or the governments of the subunits—and not just the central government or the people as a whole—should have a significant say over constitutional change; whereas a regional role may seem wholly unnecessary in many unitary states. My general point here is simply that some issues, such as the justification of amending formulas, are so bound up with the apparatus and nature of the state that they cannot be thought through with criteria that ignore the broader institutional context. Other such issues include whether a state should be federal or unitary, what the division of powers should be in a federal state, what form the electoral system should take, and, I would argue, whether there should be a constitutionalized secession procedure, and if so what conditions it should impose.

Why should we think of secession in terms of a procedure that is so closely tied to the institutional apparatus of the state that we should not expect to be able to evaluate it without using institutional moral reasoning? For one thing, in a democratic state, secessionist politics will be continuous with and closely resemble in form politics for winning elections or mounting movements for constitutional change, including, among other things, changes in the balance of powers in a federation or the entrenching of minority rights. This suggests that a secession clause in a constitution would serve a similar function to rules for elections or amending the constitution. It would regulate a form of politics by specifying clear criteria for success and failure. A secession clause could be thought to be continuous with these other constitutional features in so far as secession is like a special form of amendment of the constitution to write a region out; it will involve rules for referendum campaigns and votes; and seceding can be thought of as a massive transfer of powers from the federal government to the seceding region.[35] My basic point here is that it seems natural to think that the appropriate form of arguments for a fair secession clause (including the arguments for why one is or is not needed) would be like those used for these other constitutional features: i.e. institutional reasoning which takes into account the potential dynamic effects of a given proposed procedure, where such reasoning typically is concerned with identifying institutions that would promote justice (and deter injustice) in the long run. I will say more in the next section of what such a clause might look like.

Now it may be objected that in framing the normative problem of secession as the problem of justifying the best legal procedure for regulating secessionist politics I have simply begged the question in favour of an institutional approach. If we ask instead whether there is a right for certain kinds of groups to secede and form their own state (or join another) we are more likely to see it as a substantial moral question, rather than a procedural one. I think the point behind this objection is correct, although I do not see the approach I am defending as begging the question because reasons have already been adduced for thinking about the morality of secession in an institutional context. Two additional reasons seem decisive. First, secession just *is* a legal matter, the way divorce is. There is a difference between secession and merely having political autonomy, including the sort of *de facto* independence from central authorities, analogous to conjugal separation, that many substate territorial entities have carved out for themselves (or with the help of others) in countries like Iraq, Somalia, the former Zaire, and Israel and the territories it occupies. Secession is essentially the changing of a region's legal status within the constitutional law of its former state and the acceding to a new legal status in international law. It is hardly surprising, then, that we should think about the morality of secession as we do other legal arrangements (including divorce).

A second set of reasons for thinking about the morality of secession in a procedural context, rather than as a simple matter of substantive right, derives from the nature of secessionist politics. Most articles supporting choice and nationalist theories read as if secessionist desires were a kind of brute fact that calls for moral (and ultimately legal) recognition. Of course, it is easy to think this way if one suddenly pays attention to a full-blown secessionist conflict where desires are intense and opinions galvanized. But all such movements have a political history, even if that history is one of leaders and writers fighting the assimilationist pressures on behalf of the people of a conquered territory. In reasonably just democratic states nationalist politics may require generations of political effort and agitation to forge a minority national identity and to convince enough members of this minority nation that their destiny lies outside of their historic multination state. (This is certainly the pattern in Scotland, Flanders, Quebec, Corsica, Catalonia, and the Spanish Basque Country.) Secessionist politics will be very similar in form to other familiar long-term political projects, such as building a base for a political party (think of the long struggle of socialist and labour parties in Europe this century) or for movements, such as feminism or the pro-choice and anti-abortion coalitions in America. How odd, therefore, to think that at a moment when a secessionist movement is finally supported by a majority within a region we are suddenly asked to stop thinking of it as a political artefact, but rather as a group that happens to have a desire which gives it access to a moral right derived from abstract, non-political principles. The ultimate peculiarity of the non-institutional approach is that in ignoring the political formation of secessionist sentiments, it fails to take into account the fact that the institution of secession that is to be based on the principle will itself have an impact on the formation and development of secessionist movements. As I noted earlier in the critique of nationalist and choice theories, the institutionalization or even just the currency of these theories enables political leaders to create secessionist sentiments where none may have existed otherwise.[36]

5. FROM THE JUST-CAUSE THEORY TO A DEMOCRATIC SECESSION CLAUSE

The critique of non-institutional moralities of secession directly undermines most existing nationalist and choice theories. With theories of these two sorts in mind, Buchanan notes that, 'Although some writers pay lip-service to the distinction between arguments to justify a moral right to secede and arguments to justify prescriptions for how international law should deal with secession, they have not appreciated how great the gulf is between their moral justifications and any useful guidance for international law.'[37] He then goes on to demonstrate, persuasively to my mind, that the principles derived from the non-institutional approaches would not and should not be accepted into international law. While reinforcing a number of these arguments in my critique of nationalist and choice theories in Sections 1 and 2, I have also tried to explain why the very idea of a non-institutional morality of secession is suspect. This leaves just-cause theories as the most plausible candidates for justifying secession institutions in constitutional and international law. I would like to conclude now by pointing out that there is also something of a gap between the moral theory and the institution in this case. The upshot, ironically, is that the just-cause theory may end up grounding secession procedures that look similar to those favoured by some cautious choice theorists. (For the sake of space, I shall continue to concentrate on the justification of a secession procedure in constitutional law; Buchanan's recent paper stresses the implications for international law.)

According to just-cause theories, a group has a right to secede if and only if it has just cause (with the grounds for just cause varying from theory to theory). Institutionalizing such a theory, at first glance, would seem to require that we find a mechanism for determining whether secessionist movements do in fact have just cause. But any mechanism designed to do this too directly will be inappropriate in a democratic society for three interrelated reasons. First, there is the problem, raised by Buchanan in his early study, of the biased judge.[38] There are no philosopher monarchs, or at any rate, none that even philosophers would trust to make definitive judgements about whether some particular secessionist movement has just cause. It is also unlikely that secessionists would trust the judgments of a supreme court, since it is bound to have majority representation from outside the secessionist region and to be filled with 'small-c' conservative judges whose careers have unfolded within the institutions of the larger state. Even a special international tribunal would have to be selected by someone, and its judgments would be thought to be biased depending on who does the selecting. Questions about bias and perceptions of bias are important if we consider the nature of secessionist politics. Again we note that popular secessionist desires in just democratic states are typically the product of a generation or more of nationalist politics. Does anyone really believe that such a movement is going to fold up and die if it loses its day in court? If anything, the reverse is more likely: being stonewalled by a judgment from the supreme court would be held up by minority nationalists as yet another humiliating example of their people's internal colonization, and hence a further reason to secede.

A second reason against the direct institutionalization of the just-cause theory is that conceptions of justice and just cause are notoriously contested in cases of secession. Whether genuine or cynical, these contests can take place across several dimensions. Secessionists and unionists are likely to disagree about what kinds of incidents or events can give just cause to secede, about whether such events have occurred, about whether they have been or could be rectified by measures short of secession, about whether the particular violations were significant enough to justify secession, etc. We could never expect criteria for just cause to be spelled out in law, and this is yet another reason why we could not expect a tribunal or court to produce a decision that would not be open to doubt. Potential grounds for just cause are also omnipresent: what country does not contain regions, both rich and poor, that believe they have been historically exploited by the larger state? These grievances rarely give rise to secessionist politics where there is not also an overlapping ethnic cleavage; but where there is, they are magnified by nationalists looking for evidence for the justice of their cause.

A third reason against this way of applying the just-cause theory is implicit in the first two. It does not do what we would need a secession procedure to do, namely to regulate secessionist politics and allow contests to be decided one way or another. Secessionist politics can arise, as it does in many states today, no matter what secessionist procedure there is or is not in the political culture or the law. Not surprisingly, secessionists always believe their movement is legitimate, whether this is because they believe a version of the nationalist theory (or less often the choice theory), or because they think they do have just cause, or both. They will also insist that they have a democratic right to decide their fate, and if this right is denied (if they are prevented from organizing a referendum) that will only make the movement more popular. It would seem to follow that the only way ultimately to manage secessionist disputes in a democratic state is through the ballot box. One of Buchanan's most insightful remarks about secession is early in his first article on the subject (and repeated in his famous book published the same year).

> The question is not whether to recognize a right to secede but, rather, how to domesticate it. For many political actors in today's world, the issue is not so much, Shall we recognize a right to secede? as it is, Assuming that the notion of a right to secede is becoming a key force in practical political discourse and an inescapable item on the political agenda, how can we utilize clear moral thinking and wise institutional design to enable us to live with it?[39]

This sage advice has gone largely unheeded; the philosophical literature is still primarily concerned with *grounding* the right not domesticating it. But assuming, for reasons I have just given, that domesticating it requires a democratic institution, how can we continue to make use of the just-cause theory? After all, would not a referendum in the seceding region, perhaps organized by the secessionists themselves, merely reflect the choices of the local voters, and hence be nothing but a direct manifestation of the mistaken choice theory? Not necessarily.

Consider how most liberals have traditionally approached the question of deciding who should govern. From Rousseau and J. S. Mill to Rawls and Dworkin, they believe that the best government is that which governs most justly.[40] Yet for all of the standard reasons of bias and corruption, they would not trust a philosopher-monarch or a panel of experts to select the party or group of technocrats most likely to govern justly. (Mill is a little more trusting in this regard.) For these and other reasons there is no alternative to some form of democracy. Hence, they recommend an ensemble of institutions for electoral rules, parliamentary procedures, checks and balances, party financing, freedom of the press, etc., with the aim of increasing the likelihood that there will be just government (or decreasing the likelihood of unjust government) in the long run. I believe this is the core of the liberal approach to the justification of procedural institutions. The liberal tradition is of course pluralist, and many writers, including Rawls, mix various 'intrinsic' criteria of fairness with this basic consequentialist justification. My only concern here, though, is to note how natural it is for liberals concerned with promoting justice to opt for democratic procedures and to attempt to 'rig' them in a way that encourages just outcomes.

Since, as I have argued, secessionist politics can only be resolved democratically in a modern state, it follows that those supporting the just-cause theory must seek fair rules that will make it relatively easy for those with genuine just cause to secede, and relatively difficult for those without it to do so. Of course democrats must always accept that it is a feature of such 'imperfect procedural justice' that even the best rules will sometimes prevent a legitimate secession and permit a 'vanity' secession (i.e. one without just cause).

What would a reasonable secession clause look like? I think the answer to this question should form the substance of debates about the political morality of secession (as it has not thus far); but I shall give only a sketch here.

It goes without saying that specific secession clauses would vary from state to state, much as amending formulas and electoral systems legitimately do. Their general features, however, might include the following elements.[41]

First, they would have to specify which sorts of regions or groups would have access to the procedure. Assuming an otherwise just constitution, in a multination state the relevant units would most likely be federal subunits, since other considerations of justice would draw, or allow for the redrawing of, the boundaries of subunits to allow national minorities to be partially autonomous regional majorities.[42]

Second, a bold secession clause might actually specify the question, or strict guidelines for the question, that would have to be used; something like 'Do you want [your subunit] to secede from [the state] and become an independent state?'. Such a measure would discourage vanity secessions by preventing a secessionist government in the subunit from drawing up a 'soft' or misleading question.[43] As we saw in parts of the former Soviet Union, secessionist movements that have, or really believe they have, just cause do not need soft questions.

Third, authority must be given to some body to negotiate the terms of secession (e.g. the division of assets and debts, the terms of future trade) on behalf of the (soon to be) rump state. The central government would not be qualified, since it was elected to promote the interests of the country as a whole and some of its representation is likely to come from the seceding region. In the event of a vote in favour of secession, provisions for the democratic election of federal negotiators from outside the seceding region would seem fair. It would also make it more difficult for secessionists to increase their support in a referendum by promising that negotiations would be fair and amiable. One could predict that in an emotionally charged post-referendum election for federal negotiators, the tough talking would tend to win out over the conciliatory. Again, this factor would deter vanity secessions more than those inspired by a belief in the justice of their cause.

Fourth, the clause would seek fair ways of raising the threshold for referendum success to a level somewhat higher than a simple majority. Obviously if the requirement was a simple majority, then we would merely have an instantiation of the mistaken choice theory. A more substantial majority would make the task more difficult for vanity secessionists, while we could often assume that it would be easily attainable by secessionist movements among people who had been suffering substantial injustices.[44] In other words, strong support for secession is often a good proxy for just cause. What would be a fair way of raising the threshold? A qualified majority vote (say, two-thirds in favour) could be required. But this would be controversial (what if 63 per cent voted in favour of secession: could they really be stonewalled?). In fact, although qualified majorities are often required within parliaments and committees, they are very rarely demanded in referendums. A more acceptable measure, at least in some political cultures, seems to be the requirement for a majority of registered voters or citizens of voting age. In any case, the idea of a qualified-majority requirement is not a self-justifying principle. In some political communities it would make sense as a deterrent to vanity secessions, and it would embody the kind of caution appropriate given the irreversible nature of the change brought on by a secession. But we should not forget that in other political communities—consider, for example, Latvia, where ethnic Latvians had just cause to secede from the Soviet Union in 1989, yet constituted only about 52 per cent of the population—a qualified-majority requirement could permanently prevent the secession of a group with just cause.

Another mechanism for improving on a simple-majority requirement is to demand a series of affirmative votes over a period of two or three years.[45] The idea here is to prevent the possibility of secession due to temporary outrage over a political event which may appear somewhat less outrageous over time (i.e. due to a temporarily distorted sense of just cause). A clause could also specify in advance that an affirmative vote would be followed by another vote asking people whether they would like their county or electoral district to go with the seceding state or to stay with the original state. Such a vote might take place across the entire country to facilitate the possibility that communities outside the region holding the original vote might choose to be included in the secessionist state. (Typically, those in the seceding region wishing to stay, or those in the rump wishing to join the new state, would be in the border areas, or in ethnic enclaves that would be linked to their preferred state as West Berlin was to West Germany.) This would have three desirable effects. First, it would help minimize the number of people who would find themselves on the wrong side of the border,[46] and second, it would serve as a further deterrent to vanity secessionists who could often predict in advance that they would not be permitted to take as desirable a chunk of territory with them. (By contrast, groups with genuine just cause to secede will likely be happy to leave, even in a somewhat diminished territory—they may in fact have little interest in taking with them a substantial minority of unionists, probably of the ethnicity of the state they are quitting.) And third, this process would limit the sorts of fears of pre-emptive attack that can spark violence and civil war.[47]

It is worth pointing out a final dynamic effect of having an ensemble of such measures agreed to constitutionally in advance: it would deter some political leaders from even deciding to go the secessionist route in the first place. I emphasize again that a political morality of secession must treat secessionist desires as a political phenomenon. The implicit, default requirement of a simple majority in a referendum is already sufficient in many places to prevent cynical leaders from using threats of secession to enhance their (perhaps reasonable) demands for autonomy or a change in redistributive practices—especially when they represent a group that is not culturally distinct. But a higher threshold would make the secessionist project (or threat) unattractive to an even greater range of groups. As noted, I think this would generally affect potential vanity secessionists more than those with genuine grievances. And in discouraging vanity secessionist politics states would be spared the distortions to regular democratic politics that I discussed in the critique of choice theories.[48]

It is a freak of history, albeit an explicable one, that most democratic constitutions in multi-ethnic states—which were written in the eras of nationalism and 'nation-statism', often to the advantage of majority groups—do not contain secession clauses. If different nationalities were to decide voluntarily to form states these days they would almost certainly demand clear rules for exit; the way parties do even for international trade deals such as NAFTA.[49] If constitutions *did* typically have secession clauses, even unfair ones, we would almost certainly think of the morality of secession much as we now think of the morality of electoral systems or amending formulas. I have tried to argue that this historical accident should not prevent us from thinking of the morality of secession in institutional terms. All of the features of a secession clause grounded by the just-cause theory could also follow from the logic of constitutionalism: where rational founders of a just state (including leaders of different ethnic groups) would agree in advance to democratic procedures that would enable regions with just cause to secede and discourage those without it. All parties in such a situation would have an interest in minimizing vanity secessionist politics, not to mention vanity secessions. Of course, such parties would also agree to generous forms of autonomy and special representation in central institutions for minority groups; indeed, where secession is more difficult, minority autonomy should be less destabilizing. The longer such a secession clause existed, the more it would appear as one of the legitimate background rules of democratic politics in the state. Secessionist politics seems just as likely, if not more likely, to arise in multi-ethnic states without such a clause. And when it does, secessionists will press for the intrinsic democratic legitimacy of the institutional embodiment of a choice theory: namely, a simple majority on a secessionist referendum. Given the weakness of the normative case for choice theories, this is as good a reason as any why multi-ethnic states should have secession clauses based on the just-cause theory.[50]

But again we note that it is unlikely that states will be able to follow this advice in the foreseeable future: if they are not currently experiencing secessionist politics they are not going to tempt fate by opening up a national debate about fair terms for secession; and if a secessionist movement is under way, it would be difficult to get the secessionists' agreement to legitimize a clause based on anything but a choice or nationalist theory. So it seems we are in a position analogous to that of democratic theorists before the age of democracy—arguing for an institution as necessary as it is ahead of its time. In the meantime, our moral, political, and diplomatic responses to secessionist demands should track the standards of reasonable domestic and international institutions if we had them. Secession where necessary, and even in some cases where, regrettably, it is not. In the absence of the proper institutions, the currency of a just-cause theory in the appropriate democratic setting is the best we can hope for.

NOTES

1. A. Buchanan, 'Toward a Theory of Secession', *Ethics,* 101 (1991), 322–6; and *Secession: The Morality of Political Divorce from Fort Sumter to Lithuania and Quebec* (Boulder, Colo.: Westview, 1991), 1–9. Although A. Margalit's and J. Raz's 'National Self-Determination', *Journal of Philosophy,* 87 (1990), 439–61 appeared a year earlier, it is nevertheless true that most of the subsequent philosophical literature on secession is clearly a response to Buchanan. Among the very few earlier philosophical studies of the problem are H. Beran, 'A Liberal Theory of Secession', *Political Studies,* 32 (1984), 21–31, and A. H. Birch, 'Another Liberal Theory of Secession', *Political Studies,* 32 (1984), 596–602. L. Brilmayer's 'Secession and Self-Determination: A Territorial Interpretation', *Yale Journal of International Law,* 16 (1991), 177–202 overlaps in important ways with Buchanan's approach.
2. Buchanan, 'Toward a Theory', 323–4; *Secession*, 4.
3. The names I have selected for these three kinds of theories reflect something of the content of the respective theories. A. Buchanan distinguishes more or less the same three categories with labels based on the structure of the rights claimed. Nationalist and Choice theories attempt to justify what he calls a *primary* right to secede; the former for *ascriptive* groups, the latter for *associative* groups. What I am calling 'just-cause' theories are, in Buchanan's terminology, *Remedial Right Only Theories*. See A. Buchanan, 'Theories of Secession,' *Philosophy and Public Affairs* (1997), 37–41.
4. E. Gellner, *Nations and Nationalism* (Ithaca, NY: Cornell University, 1983), 44 ff.
5. See, A. Margalit and J. Raz, 'National Self-Determination'; M. Moore, 'On National Self-Determination', *Political Studies*, 45 (1997); D. Miller, *On Nationality* (Oxford: Clarendon Press, 1995); and W. Kymlicka, *Multicultural Citizenship* (Oxford: Clarendon Press, 1995).
6. See, e.g. Miller, *On Nationality*, 117, and Moore, 'On National Self-Determination'.
7. See Buchanan, 'Theories of Secession,' 52–4. W. Connor argues, famously, that 'No examples of significant assimilation are offered which have taken place since the advent of the age of nationalism and the propagation of the principle of self-determination of nations'. See his *Ethnonationalism: The Quest for Understanding* (Princeton: Princeton University Press, 1994), 54. This lack of success has not, of course, prevented central governments around the world, throughout this century, from *trying* to assimilate or otherwise suppress their minorities.

8. The most elaborately explained choice theory to date is D. Philpott, 'In Defense of Self-Determination', *Ethics*, 105 (1995), 352–85. See also C. Wellman, 'A Defence of Secession and Political Self-Determination', *Philosophy and Public Affairs*, 24/2 (1995), 142–71, which can be considered a choice theory with a caveat; D. Gauthier, 'Breaking Up: An Essay on Secession', *Canadian Journal of Philosophy*, 24 (1994), 357–72; K. Nielsen, 'Secession: The Case of Quebec', *Journal of Applied Philosophy*, 10 (1993), 29–43; and Beran, 'The Liberal Theory'. Among the caveats attached to the right to secession are: that fair terms are worked out for dividing debts, surpluses, properties, etc.; that the new state guarantees minority rights; that the new state is liberal; that the new status quo satisfies a Lockian Proviso; that the new state would allow secession on the same terms; that the new state is viable. It is not obvious that all of these caveats are consistent with the central intuitions of choice theories, but I shall not pursue this critique here.
9. Philpott thinks this is a virtue for his type of theory. See Philpott, 'A Defense', 365.
10. Nielsen, 'Secession', 35.
11. See also Moore, 'On National Self-Determination', which highlights the similar autonomy-based considerations that she believes should drive liberal intuitions about both secession and divorce.
12. I am ignoring the comic-opera-*attempted* secession in Western Australia in the 1930s. We can also say that the Northern League movement in Italy cannot yet, in terms of popular support, be considered a serious secessionist movement. It is significant none the less that the leaders of this movement have made frequent efforts to highlight alleged ethnic differences between northern and southern Italians.
13. See, e.g. Philpott, 'A Defense', 382; Gauthier, 'Breaking Up', 372.
14. D. L. Horowitz, 'Self-Determination: Politics, Philosophy, and Law', Ch. 9 of this volume.
15. Ibid.
16. Ibid.
17. See Kymlicka, *Multicultural Citizenship*, ch. 11; Miller, *On Nationality*; Y. Tamir, *Liberal Nationalism* (Princeton: Princeton University Press, 1993); W. Norman, 'The Ideology of Shared Values', in J. Carens (ed.), *Is Quebec Nationalism Just?* (Montreal and Kingston: McGill-Queen's University Press, 1995).
18. Some choice theorists, such as C. Wellman and T. W. Pogge, 'Cosmopolitanism and Sovereignty', *Ethics*, 103 (1992), would seem to welcome this prospect.
19. For an argument against constitutionalizing a secession procedure see C. Sunstein, 'Constitutionalism and Secession', *University of Chicago Law Review*, 58 (1991), 633–70. I criticize these arguments directly in my 'Démocratie et sécession', in J.-P. Harpes (ed.), *Nouvelles voies de la démocratie* (Luxembourg: Presses du parlement européen), forthcoming.
20. The term 'Just-Cause' is not meant to imply that choice accounts cannot be grounded in considerations of justice, as, for example, Gauthier, Philpott and Wellman say theirs are.
21. On the distinction between primary and remedial rights of secession, and for a defence of the latter, see Buchanan, 'Theories of Secession', 34–5.

22. Typical representatives of a what I am calling a just-cause theory include Buchanan and Brilmayer, as well J. Berg, 'The Right to Self-Determination', *Public Affairs Quarterly*, 5 (1991), 211–25; R. Howse and K. Knop, 'Federalism, Secession, and the Limits of Ethnic Accommodation: A Canadian Perspective', *New Europe Law Review*, 1 (1993), 269–320; G. Laforest, *De l'Urgence* (Montreal: Boréal, 1995); and Kymlicka, *Multicultural Citizenship*.
23. See Buchanan, 'Theories of Secession', 49.
24. This idea is weaker than the teleological account criticized by Wellman in 'A Defense of Secession', 156–60, and is obviously not intended to legitimize annexations. It represents the limits on the principle of territorial integrity incorporated into international law since the 'human rights revolution', but was already present in the 1970 UN Declaration on Friendly Relations, quoted below.
25. See Nielsen, 'Secession', 37.
26. Philpott, 381. See also Nielsen, 'Secession', 37 for general support for the choice theorist's response to the just-cause theorists' presumption in favour of the state. Just-cause theorists need not disagree with Wellman when he argues that 'the costs of altering international borders may only limit the number, rather than completely preclude the possibility, of permissible secessions'. Wellman, 'A Defense of Secession', 159.
27. For the clearest and most thorough discussion of the healthy and perverse incentives of different theories of secession, see Buchanan, 'Theories of Secession', 52–5.
28. I am grateful to D. Philpott and M. Freeman for convincing me of the need to respond to this and some of the following criticisms of the use of institutional moral reasoning in the case of secession.
29. The United Nations Charter, Article 1(2), states that a central purpose of the organization is to 'develop friendly relations among nations based on respect for the principle of equal rights and self-determination of peoples . . .' Articles 55, 73, and 76(1) confirm this principle as do a number of subsequent UN resolutions. While this principle was invoked during the period of decolonization, most experts agree that it does not imply a legal right of secession. The 1970 Declaration on Friendly Relations makes clear that it shall not 'be construed as authorizing or encouraging any action which would dismember or impair, totally or in part, the territorial integrity or political unity of sovereign and independent States', so long as they have governments 'representing the whole people belonging to the territory without distinction as to race, creed or colour'. See L. Buchheit, *Secession: the Legitimacy of Self-Determination* (New Haven: Yale University Press, 1978); L. S. Eastwood, Jr., 'Secession: State Practice and International Law After the Dissolution of the Soviet Union and Yugoslavia', *Duke Journal of Comparative and International Law*, 3 (1993), 299–349; Patrick Thornberry, 'Self-Determination, Minorities, Human Rights: A Review of International Instruments', *International and Comparative Law Quarterly*, 38 (1989), 867–89.
30. Ethiopia and St. Kitts-Nevis are the only states I am aware of with explicit secession clauses in their constitutions. The United Kingdom committed itself to allowing Northern Ireland to secede and join the Republic of Ireland if a majority within Northern Ireland expresses such a desire in a vote.
31. See Buchanan, 'Theories of Secession', section VII, for a similar point.

32. Buchanan thinks that 'minimal realism' is a necessary condition for proposals for (international) law; and also that what I am calling the just-cause theory satisfies this condition while nationalist and choice theories do not. See his 'Theories of Secession', 42, 45–6.
33. See J. Elster, 'Introduction', and S. Holmes, 'Gag Rules or the Politics of Omission', both in J. Elster and R. Slagstad (eds.), *Constitutionalism and Democracy* (Cambridge: Cambridge University Press, 1988), 1–18, 19–58, for discussions of the way in which these notions figure in justifications or critiques of so-called 'gag rules'—of which onerous amendment formulas are a prime example—on democratic deliberation.
34. J. Rawls, *A Theory of Justice* (Cambridge, Mass.: Harvard University Press, 1971), ch. 3.
35. Indeed, secessionists in democratic states with integrated market economies are likely to be willing and even eager to share certain powers with the rump state in a confederal arrangement. This is a central feature of all of the Parti Québécois's proposals for sovereignty, for example.
36. Robert Lansing, then Secretary of State, rightly predicted that President Wilson's concept of the right to national self-determination would inspire countless secessionist movements. It is possible that in northern Italy we are now beginning to see the first non-ethnic secessionist movement inspired by the democratic, 'choice-theory' rhetoric of secession by majority votes in referendums in Eastern Europe, the former Soviet Union, and Quebec.
37. Buchanan, 'Theories of Secession', 32.
38. Buchanan, *Secession*, 138.
39. Buchanan, 'Toward a Theory', 339.
40. See, e.g. the sort of consequentialist reasoning that goes into procedural design throughout Books III and IV of Rousseau's *Social Contract*, to ensure that the will of the people will in fact track the general will. See also J. S. Mill, *Considerations of Representative Government*, and R. Dworkin, 'What is Equality? pt. 4: Political Equality', *University of San Francisco Law Review*, 22 (1987). For two concise surveys of theories of justification for political institutions see B. Barry, 'Political Systems, the Evaluation of', in L. Becker and C. Becker (eds.), *Encyclopedia of Ethics* (New York: Garland, 1992), and T. Christiano, 'Freedom, Consensus, and Equality in Collective Decision-Making', *Ethics*, 101 (1990), 151–81. For more detail see C. Beitz, *Political Equality* (Princeton: Princeton University Press, 1989).
41. I cannot emphasize strongly enough the point that a morality of secession cannot directly justify governments of secessionist movements acting as if the following sorts of procedural rules were in place when they are not. These features of a constitutional clause could be justified by rational founding partners, and they could have the effect of facilitating secessions with just cause, and discouraging those without it. But they are justified in the first place as background rules of the game. It is beyond the scope of this chapter to explain in detail how we might justify counterfactual moral judgements based on this sort of reasoning. The following procedural recommendations are designed to bring secessionist politics within the rule of law and to minimize the uncertainties (and hence risks of violence) that arise when clear and legitimate rules are not in place. But for a

central government simply to act as if these procedures were in place could, in some circumstances *increase* instability and uncertainty. Suffice it to say that I believe the rules for a legitimate secessionist procedure in situations where there are no constitutional guidelines would be closer to some of the following recommendations than they would be to those derived directly from choice or nationalist theories.

42. Switzerland, e.g., has democratic procedures to allow regional groups to secede from one canton and form their own. For an outline of a normative theory of federalism see my 'Toward a Philosophy of Federalism', in J. Baker (ed.), *Group Rights* (Toronto: University of Toronto Press, 1994).
43. Consider the question posed by the Parti Québécois government in the referendum of October 1995: 'Do you agree that Quebec should become sovereign, after having made a formal offer to Canada for a new economic and political partnership, within the scope of the bill respecting the future of Quebec and of the agreement signed on June 12, 1995?' Yes or No. Intense debate in the Quebec National Assembly could not add the word 'country' after the word 'sovereign', presumably because the majority PQ government knew full well that polls consistently show up to 20 per cent more Quebecers are in favour of Quebec being sovereign than in it becoming a sovereign country. The bill referred to is a long piece of legislation which calls for a declaration of independence if the offer of partnership is refused. And the agreement of 12 June is one between the leaders of the three nationalist parties in Quebec. Polls indicated that more than a quarter of 'Yes' voters believed that Quebec would remain in Canada and continue to send representatives to the Parliament in Ottawa after a 'Yes' victory. Given how soft this question is, even some leading secessionists have confessed relief that it was the 'No' side rather than the 'Yes' side that won by a narrow margin.
44. Obviously, matters are much more complicated with ethnically mixed populations, especially where a substantial ethnic minority is dead-set against secession.
45. See Pogge, 'Cosmopolitanism and Sovereignty', 71.
46. See J. Nickel, 'What is Wrong With Ethnic Cleansing?', *Journal of Social Philosophy*, 26/1 (1995), 5–15.
47. See R. Hardin, *One For All: The Logic of Group Conflict* (Princeton: Princeton University Press, 1995), especially ch. 6. For obvious reasons the stabilizing effect of such a clause could backfire if it were simply imposed by a central government when confronted with a passionate and popular secessionist movement.
48. The European Union is the international agency in the best position to have an impact on secessionist politics. It could put an end to vanity secessionist movements among its member states (which may number as many as thirty within a decade) with the addition of one simple clause in the Treaty of Rome: 'No region that secedes from a member state will be permitted to enter the European Union or the European Economic Area [the free-trade zone] for a period of seven years'. This would deprive secessionist leaders of the ability to convince their people that there would be no economic costs to secession. Indeed, it would ensure that there would be costs. It is safe to assume, in most cases, that a secessionist movement that would be deflated by such a prospect does not really have just cause to secede; yet this would be a relatively small price to pay for a region that was genuinely oppressed or exploited.

49. It is implicit in the European Union that member states can unilaterally withdraw, although the Treaty of Rome itself declares the union for an indefinite future.
50. In 'Constitutionalism and Secession', C. Sunstein argues that considerations of constitutionalism would not support the inclusion of a secession clause (and that the refounded states in Eastern Europe should not include one). I believe he is wrong on grounds of political psychology: i.e. in believing that an appropriate clause would encourage rather than discourage secessionist politics in most states. For this and other arguments against Sunstein's case see my 'Démocratie et sécession'.

4

Secession and the Principle of Nationality

DAVID MILLER

The secession issue appears to many contemporary thinkers to reveal a fatal flaw in the idea of national self-determination. The question is whether national minorities who come to want to be politically self-determining should be allowed to separate from the parent state and form one of their own. Here the idea of national self-determination may lead us in one of two opposing directions. If the minority group in question regards itself as a separate nation, then the principle seems to support its claims: if the Québécois or the Catalans come to think of themselves as having national identities distinct from those of the Canadians or the Spanish, and to seek political independence on that basis, then if we are committed to national self-determination we should support their claims. But then we face the challenge that once national identities begin to proliferate there is no feasible way of satisfying all such claims, given elementary facts of geography and population spread. As Allen Buchanan, citing Gellner, puts the point 'the normative nationalist principle is a recipe for limitless political fragmentation'.[1] And he rightly points out that this process may bring with it quite unacceptable moral costs, in the form for instance of the disruption, displacement, or even annihilation of communities that turn out to be territorially in the wrong place.

On the other hand, the idea of national self-determination may be appealed to in defence of the political *status quo*. The Canadians and the Spanish have a claim to be self-determining too, and a claim to determine the future of the territory that has historically been identified as Canada or Spain. If the principle is used in this more conservative way, it is subject to a different critical charge: that it turns out in practice to call for self-determination for

An earlier version of this chapter was presented to the Roundtable on National Self-Determination and Secession, American Political Science Association Annual Meeting, San Francisco, 28 Aug.–1 Sept. 1996. I am grateful to the participants in that meeting for their comments, and also to Michel Seymour for writing to me at some length about the case of Quebec. The present chapter was originally published in *Rethinking Nationalism*, *Canadian Journal of Philosophy*, supp. vol. 22, ed. Jocelyne Couture, Kai Nielsen, and Michel Seymour. It is reprinted by permission of the publisher.

states, not nations, or at least for states that are territorially compact.[2] Self-determination comes to mean the claim of a state to exercise sovereignty within its established borders, not to be invaded or coerced by its neighbours, for instance. But interpreted in this way the idea loses much of its original moral appeal, which came from the vision of a body of people sharing a common identity and wishing to be associated with one another deciding on their own future. The second reading collapses the crucial distinction between nations and states by treating 'the nation' simply as the set of people who fall *de facto* within the jurisdiction of a particular state.

The charge, then, is that the issue of secession reveals the idea of national self-determination either to be a recipe for political chaos and human bloodshed or to be a conservative defence of the rights of established states. My aim here is to see whether it is possible to develop a coherent position on the issue that avoids both extremes, starting out from the principle of nationality that I have defended elsewhere.[3]

WHY DO WE NEED A THEORY OF SECESSION?

Before we embark on matters of substance, it is worth pausing to ask what purpose we intend our theory of secession to serve. Some writers have proposed that we should be seeking to define a quasi-legal right of secession that might be inscribed in the constitution of a state, or in the charter of an international body such as the UN.[4] In other words, we should try to identify a set of conditions that might be formally codified, and that any group attempting to secede from an existing state might appeal to in order to justify its claim. This proposal has some obvious attractions. It holds out the promise that secessionist claims might be treated in a detached way by a constitutional or international court, rather than being fought over with words or guns. But this promise comes at a price. First the conditions justifying secession would need to be stated in a form that a judicial body could apply, and this immediately slants the discussion in favour of certain criteria and against others. For instance there is likely to be a bias in favour of procedural criteria (is there a majority in favour of secession in the territory in question?) whose application is relatively uncontroversial, and against substantive criteria whose application may depend upon difficult and contested matters of judgement (is the existing state suppressing or eroding the distinct culture of the minority applying to secede?). Secondly, as Buchanan points out, we have also to think about the incentive effects of different definitions of the right of secession; we have to ask how inscribing one or other version of such a right in a constitution would alter the behaviour either of the existing state or of the would-be secessionists.[5] For instance, would the effect be to make established states less willing to devolve power to regions that might subsequently foster secessionist demands? But it seems to me a mistake to allow our thinking about the secession issue to be dominated by such considerations. We should establish the basic principles first, then ask what effect the public promulgation of these principles might have on the behaviour of different political actors.

In contrast to the legalistic approach sketched in the last paragraph, I believe that a theory of secession should be seen as a political theory, meaning one that articulates principles that should guide us when thinking about secessionist claims. 'Us' here means the would-be secessionists, non-secessionist citizens of the relevant state, and members of the international community who may be called upon to intervene on one side or the other. We are looking for guidance when we have to decide (say in a referendum) whether to vote for secession or for remaining in association with a larger state. Equally we need guidance about how to respond, as British citizens say, to demands for Scottish or Welsh independence. We likewise need to know whether to recognize and support a Slovenia that has chosen to sever its ties with the rest of the Yugoslav federation. A theory of secession should tell us in broad terms when secession is justified and when it is not.

Some critics might argue that the questions I am raising here are insubstantial. If a referendum is being held on secession, then I should vote for secession if I want it, and against if I do not. The issue is settled procedurally, by a majority or a qualified majority, or however. It is irrelevant to ask about the principles that might guide me when casting my vote. But notice that this is not how we think about democratic decision-making in general. We agree, of course, that the party which wins an election should form the government, or that when a referendum is held the result should be adopted as policy, but that does not deter us from putting forward principles which we think voters ought to follow—principles of social justice for instance. Sometimes we will say that the voters got it wrong, that they supported the party whose policies were less just, or less in their interests, than the opposition's. We can say this while still thinking that the democratic procedure should be followed. How are things different when the issue is one of secession? Even if we come to believe that such questions should be resolved procedurally, there may still be good grounds and bad grounds for secession, and it is surely not irrelevant to try to spell these out.

It is in any case implausible to think that a purely procedural theory of secession could be satisfactory. If we say, for instance, that a majority vote to secede is sufficient to justify secession, this immediately raises the question of how the constituency for the vote is to be established, and how the territory which the seceding group would take with them is to be defined. In practice we are likely to think of regions like Quebec which are already administratively defined, and where we can pick out a 'people', the Québécois, among whom a referendum might be held. Here we are tacitly invoking a background theory about the circumstances that make a referendum on secession appropriate: whether on balance we think the secessionist claim justified or unjustified in this case, we can at least recognize it as a plausible candidate. If, by contrast, someone was to propose holding an independence ballot among the Jews of Montreal, we would immediately recognize this as a not-very-serious proposal and react accordingly.

A substantial theory of secession is not likely to be simple. To break up a state and create a new one is a serious matter. It raises questions about political authority, about historic identities, about economic justice, and about the rights of minorities. Any adequate theory must address all of these issues, and this means that it will have to be multicriterial. Instead of looking for a set of necessary and sufficient conditions to justify a secessionist claim, we must accept that the different criteria may pull in opposite directions, and so to reach a verdict on any concrete case we are likely to have to balance conflicting claims. Keeping that in mind, what guidance can an appeal to nationality offer us?

THE PRINCIPLE OF NATIONALITY

The principle of nationality I defend holds, as one of its three elements, that where the inhabitants of a territory form a national community, they have a good claim to political self-determination. Although a sovereign state is not the only possible vehicle of self-determination, both now and in the past it has been the main vehicle, and so this principle grounds a claim to secession made by a territorially compact nation which is currently subject to rule by outsiders. I say 'a claim' rather than 'a right' in order to signal that the claim in question is not necessarily an overriding one, but may be defeated by other considerations that we shall come to in due course. This is not the place to set out the reasons supporting self-determination; I want instead to consider some of the ramifications of this apparently simple principle.

As has often been pointed out, territories occupied by homogeneous nations are very much the exceptions in today's world. Let me say, very briefly, what I take a nation to be: a group of people who recognize one another as belonging to the same community, who acknowledge special obligations to one another, and who aspire to political autonomy—this by virtue of characteristics that they believe they share, typically a common history, attachment to a geographical place, and a public culture that differentiates them from their neighbours.[6] If, with this definition in mind, we look inside those entities popularly described as 'nation-states' we are likely to find some combination of the following: (a) minority groups (especially immigrants) who do not see themselves as sharing in the national identity of the majority (e.g. Turkish immigrants in Germany); (b) regionally gathered minorities who see themselves as forming a separate nation and who aspire to a greater or lesser degree of autonomy (e.g. Kurds in Turkey); (c) regions with intermingled populations identifying with different adjacent nations (e.g. Rumanians and Hungarians in Transylvania); (d) regions in which a substantial part of the population bear a dual or 'nested' identity, as members of a national minority within a larger nation (e.g. Catalans in Spain).

If we want to apply the principle of nationality to cases fitting one or more of these descriptions, our question must be: what structure of political authority will best fulfil the principle for each community, given that the simple solution (homogeneous nation/unitary state) is not available in these circumstances. This involves first of all making qualitative judgements about how people conceive of their identity, and how the identity of one group relates to that of others. Compare, for instance, the position of the Kurds in Turkey with that of the Catalans in Spain. Although the Catalans regard themselves as a distinct people, there is no deep-seated hostility between them and the Spanish people as a whole. There is a considerable cultural overlap (in religious belief, for instance), living standards are somewhat higher than the Spanish average (traditionally Catalonia has been one of the more prosperous regions of Spain), Catalans are not held in low esteem elsewhere in Spain, and so on. In these circumstances, it is not problematic for Catalans to regard themselves both as Catalan and as Spanish, as many of them do.[7] The Kurdish case is in many respects different: per capita income in the Kurdish region of Turkey is less than half the national average, Kurdish language and culture are vigorously repressed by the Turkish state, there is a long history of armed conflicts and massacres between the two communities.[8] Furthermore the Turkish leadership has for many years been committed to the ideal of a unified, homogeneous Turkish nation which leaves no space for cultural pluralism. Given these differences, the Kurds have a claim for independence that is qualitatively different from that held by the Catalans. Short of a dramatic reversal in mainstream Turkish attitudes, there is no chance of the Kurds achieving cultural recognition in a Turkish state, nor of Turks and Kurds working together to achieve political democracy and social justice. This is not to say that full secession would necessarily be the right solution for Turkish Kurdistan. Various practical considerations count heavily against this solution, and it seems that few Kurds themselves are actively seeking secession.[9] My point is that to apply the nationality principle to this problem, we have to begin by looking at the actual content of group identities, in order to discover whether group X has a distinct national identity whose substance places it at odds with that of group Y to whose political institutions it is presently subjected. To the extent that this is so, any claim that the group may make for political independence is strengthened—which is not to say that its claim is decisively vindicated for, as indicated above, it may eventually be defeated by countervailing factors.[10]

One such factor which we must now consider is the competing claim of group Y, the larger nation whose present territory would be broken up if the secession were to go ahead. Do they not have a claim which is at least as strong as that of the would-be secessionists? Here we need to take account of the following empirical fact: in most of the cases under discussion, there will be an asymmetry between the way the smaller group sees its relationship with the larger and the way that the larger group sees its relationship with the smaller. The larger group will play down the distinctness of the minority: rather than regarding them as a nation with a separate identity, they will tend to see them as one variation on a common theme: not as distinct Xs, but as Ys who speak a different language or have their own quaint folk culture. Thus whereas the Québécois tend to see themselves as belonging to a nation separate from the rest of Canada, Canadians at large are likely to regard the Québécois just as French-speaking Canadians, and parallels to this case can be found in many other places, for instance between the Scots and the English or the Macedonians and the Greeks.

There may be a temptation to think that in such instances, the majority has simply got it wrong—that if the Xs no longer identify themselves as Ys, then for the Ys to assert a common identity with the Xs amounts to ignorance or a refusal to face up to the facts. But the issue will very rarely be as clear-cut as this. Assuming that the Xs and the Ys share a single citizenship and have been associated politically for a substantial period of time, they do indeed have a good deal in common. And the Xs themselves are very likely to recognize this when not actively waving their nationalist banners—for instance by acknowledging the two-sidedness of their national identity, as do most Catalans and most Scots. So the issue is how best to interpret a complex state of affairs in which the minority group has both a distinct identity and a sense of belonging to the larger community. Members of the majority group are very likely to be unperceptive and to behave in ways that are insensitive to the minority, but this does not mean that they are simply in error when they invoke a shared identity in order to resist the Xs' claim to secede.

A second tempting error is to think that if the seceding group wants to break up the political union, the majority's sense of identity is irrelevant. Some authors draw a parallel with individuals divorcing: if Anne decides she no longer wants to be married to Brian, then Brian's belief that they are still a viable domestic unit is neither here nor there. The union must rest on the continuing consent of both parties.[11] This analogy cannot be sustained, however. Most obviously, nations are not individuals with a single will. They are likely to embrace a wide range of opinions about how national identity is best expressed—through union with a larger nation, through devolution, through an independent state, and so forth. This point hardly needs to be laboured: it raises issues that I return to in the following section. A bit less obviously, secession does not only involve a political separation, but also a partition of territory. Here we must address the difficult question of how best to understand the rights of peoples to the territory that they occupy.

We might think initially that what is at stake here is an aggregate of property rights: I own this plot, you own that, and so all of us together own the territory that we call Britain.[12] If that were the right way to think about the problem, then a secessionist group occupying a compact area would simply have to assert their joint property rights to establish a conclusive claim to the land they want to take with them. But, as Buchanan has argued, the relationship between a people and their territory cannot properly be understood in these terms.[13] When we say that Iceland belongs to the Icelanders (to take a simple case), we do not mean that they own it as property: we mean that they have a legitimate claim to exercise authority over Iceland, to determine what happens in that island, including what individual property rights there are going to be. (If they were to decide to leave it as common land, that would be their prerogative.) This authority is exercised in practice by the state on the people's behalf, but the Icelanders' claim to authority is not reducible to the authority of the Icelandic state, as we can see if (*per impossible*) we were to imagine a revolutionary upheaval in that country which established an entirely new set of political institutions. The Icelanders' claim to control Iceland would survive such a political cataclysm.

How are such claims established? The people who inhabit a certain territory form a political community. Through custom and practice as well as by explicit political decision they create laws, establish individual or collective property rights, engage in public works, shape the physical appearance of the territory. Over time this takes on symbolic significance as they bury their dead in certain places, establish shrines or secular monuments and so forth. All of these activities give them an attachment to the land that cannot be matched by any rival claimants. This in turn justifies their claim to exercise continuing political authority over that territory. It trumps the purely historical claim of a rival group who argue that their ancestors once ruled the land in question.[14]

If that is the right way to understand territorial claims, let us now return to the case of a divided community where a minority of Xs wish to secede (with the territory they occupy) from a majority of Ys. Can the Ys make a valid claim to continued control of the territory in question? The answer must depend on how the relationship between the two groups has developed historically. At one extreme we might have a case where the Xs were always the unwilling subjects of the Ys whom they regarded as an occupying force: the relationship between the native populations of the Baltic states and the Russian majority in the Soviet Union may have been close to this extreme. Here there has been no real political community between the Xs and the Ys, no freely undertaken collective projects, and it is hard to see the Ys having a legitimate claim to the territory occupied by the Xs except in so far as they have, say, invested physical capital in that territory (in which case some compensation may be due if the Xs secede).[15] At the other extreme we find the case where the Xs, although perhaps always having certain features that distinguished them from the Ys, have been free and equal partners in the building of the community. Their new-found nationalism is a result not of historic exploitation but of cultural developments that make them now want to have greater control over what happens in their particular territory (for instance their language is in danger of being eroded). Here I think the legitimate demand of the Xs does have to be set against the equally legitimate demand of the Ys not to be deprived of part of the territory which they and their ancestors have helped to shape, and which they quite naturally think of as theirs. In a non-economic sense, the Ys will be poorer if the Xs secede. If no compromise is possible the Xs' demand may finally prove the stronger, but in such a case there is a powerful reason to find a solution that gives the Xs a form of autonomy that falls short of independence. This argument applies, I believe, to groups such as the Scots and Welsh in Britain, the Catalans and Basques in Spain, and the French-speaking communities in Canada.

To conclude this part of the discussion, if we appeal to the principle of nationality to ground the case for self-determination, then we shall want to apply two criteria to any group of would-be secessionists. The first is that the group should form a nation with an identity that is clearly separate from that of the larger nation from which they wish to disengage.[16] The second is that the group should be able to validate its claim to exercise authority over the territory it wishes to occupy. These criteria can't be applied mechanically or by counting heads; their application requires judgement and a degree of historical understanding. But if both criteria are met, the group in question has a serious claim to be allowed to secede. This is still not a conclusive claim, however, for there may be other factors weighing in the opposite direction, but *prima facie* the group has a good case. Let me now turn to explore some of the other factors that may count in the final judgement.

MINORITIES AND NUMBERS

Up to this point I have been considering the artificially simple case of a nationally homogeneous group of Xs occupying a discrete piece of land, and attempting to secede from a state in which the Ys form a majority. In any real case that we might wish to consider, matters will not be so clear-cut. Within the territory that the Xs are claiming (a claim we are supposing to be legitimate by the criteria set out above) there are likely to be a number of Ys, and also members of other minorities who are neither Xs nor Ys. Within the borders of the remainder state, likewise, there may be found some Xs and also members of other groups. Secession does not simply mean shifting from a nationally heterogeneous community to one that is nationally homogeneous; it means replacing one heterogeneous pattern with two different (but still to some extent heterogeneous) patterns.

The assumption guiding our discussion is that there is a value to each member in being a citizen of a state that embraces your nation; to be part of a minority, although by no means always a disaster, is generally a worse option. So how should we compare the state of affairs prior to secession with that which would obtain afterwards, using this principle? One proposed criterion is that we should simply count up the numbers of people who live in a state in which they form a national majority.[17] In the case envisaged, this criterion will favour secession, on the assumption that the Xs form a majority in the territory that they are claiming. If the new state is formed, it will contain more Xs who now meet the criterion than Ys who now fail to meet it (they become a minority in the new state); the position of the Xs who remain in the Y state is unchanged; and so is that of the other minorities in both states.

But this proposal takes too little account of the political realities of secessionist movements. It assumes, in particular, that the treatment of national minorities in the new X-state will be no worse than their treatment in the original Y-state—for instance that whatever degree of autonomy was given to the Xs in the original state will be matched by the autonomy granted to the Ys in the new X-state. But in many cases this assumption is highly unrealistic. Donald Horowitz has argued that secession nearly always intensifies conflicts between groups.[18] The Xs, in order to justify their secessionist demand, may have to exaggerate the features that differentiate them from the Ys. If they are successful, they are likely to want to purge the new state of the baneful influence of the Ys by cultural repression or at the extreme ethnic cleansing. Furthermore a side-effect of secession may be the stimulation of new group conflicts: Horowitz points out how, in Africa and elsewhere, new ethnic cleavages have almost always developed following the breakup of larger states. Differences that had little salience in the bigger unit may come to loom large in the smaller one, so that the vision of a culturally homogeneous political community gives way to infighting between the subgroups.

It is also false to assume that there is no change in the position of those Xs who, as a result of living in the wrong place, find themselves citizens of the rump Y-state. Most obviously they now form a much smaller minority and will have less political influence than previously. There may no longer be any constituencies regularly electing members of X to parliament, for example. Special rights which may have been in place before, such as rights designed to protect the X-culture, may now be dismantled on the grounds that there are too few Xs left to bother about. Furthermore political leaders in the Y-state may argue that the very existence of the X-state provides ample protection for that culture. It is hard, for instance, to imagine a Canada shorn of Quebec accepting responsibility for preserving French language and culture in North America. Finally the creation of the X-state inevitably alters the political identity of those Xs who remain outside it. Although their sense of self-worth may in some ways be enhanced by its existence (as the self-esteem of many Jews has been bolstered by the creation of the state of Israel), they may also feel more estranged from the Ys, and this feeling may be reciprocated ('If you don't think you belong here, why don't you move out to X-land?'). On balance, therefore, the position of the stranded Xs is likely to worsen as a result of the secession.

For these reasons, the proposal to settle the minorities issue by counting heads seems to me seriously inadequate. Once again qualitative judgements about how the status and welfare of different groups would be altered by the creation of a new state must be made. How can the principle of nationality guide us here? Let me make it clear first of all that the principle as I understand it does not advocate the creation of states that are culturally or ethnically homogeneous through and through. To say that fellow-citizens should as far as possible share a common national identity leaves space for a rich pattern of social diversity along lines of religion, ethnicity, and so forth. So alongside the principle of nationality we may—and surely should—hold other principles that protect the rights of minorities—principles of human rights, of equality, and so forth. These principles must also be brought into play when judging a claim to secession. Looking at the facts of a particular case, we have to try to estimate whether minority rights are likely to be better or worse protected if the secession goes ahead.

Such estimates are clearly difficult to make. One thing we cannot do, however, is simply to take whatever reassurances the secessionists may give at face value. Political philosophers writing on this topic are prone to say, in effect 'let the secession go ahead provided that those who form the new state undertake to respect the rights of minorities within it'.[19] But how should we apply this conditional to an actual case? How are we to judge the real worth of such an undertaking? It is important to bear in mind here that once the new state is formed and recognized, powerful norms of international non-interference come into play. As the experience of former Yugoslavia demonstrates, it is very difficult to control from the outside even massive violations of the rights of minorities. So there is a serious risk that in permitting the secession to occur, we (as third parties to the conflict, say) may be tacitly condoning maltreatment of minorities in the newly formed state, which at a later stage we will be unable to do anything about.

The principle of nationality itself may guide our thinking in one further respect. Recall that the underlying vision is of a state whose citizens share an inclusive national identity that makes room for cultural differences. How far this ideal vision can be realized in any particular case will depend on the character of the identity in question—for instance, how far it includes elements that are tied to the culture of a particular ethnic group. If the national identity of the Ys is relatively amorphous whereas the identity of the Xs contains a much stronger ethnic or religious component, say, then there is clearly a much better chance of a common identity in which the Xs (and others) can share evolving in the Y-state than there is of the reverse happening in the X-state. This criterion does not necessarily tell in favour of the *status quo*, but in many cases it will, especially where the existing state is long-established, and over time has developed mechanisms for coping with cultural pluralism. If we consider the case of Quebec, for instance, it is reasonable to expect that an independent Quebec would protect the private rights of its English-speaking minority at least as effectively as Canada has so far protected the rights of French-speakers. On the other hand it is hard to imagine that it would evolve a national identity that was as hospitable to English-speakers in Quebec as Canadian identity has become to French-speakers throughout Canada, since the active promotion of French language and French culture would necessarily be a central component of that identity.

There will, however, be some tragic cases where the project of reconciliation is simply not feasible. These are cases where two physically intermingled communities cannot live together peacefully because of ingrained mutual hostility, and where there is no reason to believe that under any division of the territory the rights of the minority groups will be respected. Here I think it may be necessary to contemplate some exchange of populations so that two more or less nationally homogeneous entities can be created. Most liberals will baulk at this suggestion, because it brings to mind the horrifying spectre of forced ethnic cleansing, and indeed there is no doubt that historically most population shifts of this kind have taken place more or less under coercion. But it is at least possible to envisage an internationally supervised operation in which people are given financial incentives to exchange their homes and their land, and if the alternative to this is a continuation of events such as those we have witnessed in Bosnia, or indeed on a much smaller scale in Northern Ireland, we should be prepared to contemplate it.[20]

In tackling the minorities issue, therefore, the principle should not be to allow secession whenever a territorial majority favours it, but to judge which outcome offers the best chance of creating states with national identities which are relatively congenial to internal minorities, and which are likely to protect their cultural and other rights. Numbers should count to some extent, but in so far as they are predictable, overall consequences should count for more. Where the consequences for minorities look very bad wherever the boundaries are fixed, some people—as few as possible—may have to be encouraged to move their abode.

DISTRIBUTIVE JUSTICE

When secession occurs, it is likely over time to alter the pattern of economic distribution both between and within the new-formed and remainder states. So ought we to judge secessionist demands by applying principles of distributive justice to them—favouring secession when it seems likely to be justice-enhancing, and disfavouring it in the opposite case? Several recent discussions of the question have followed this strategy, giving principles of justice a more or less prominent place in the theory of legitimate secession.[21] How far, then, should we modify the conclusions already reached to take account of such considerations?

As Buchanan points out, the first issue that has to be settled here is the *scope* of the principles in question.[22] Should we see principles of distributive justice as applying globally (though no doubt given practical application through more local institutions) or do these principles themselves have a restricted scope? Buchanan analyses this issue by drawing a contrast between 'justice as reciprocity' and 'subject-centred justice', the former holding that obligations of justice hold only between the contributors to a co-operative scheme, the latter imposing no such restriction. I want to propose a somewhat different view. Principles of distributive justice, and especially *comparative* principles, such as principles of equality, need and desert, do indeed have a restricted scope, but the limits are not set by the bounds of a co-operative practice for mutual advantage; rather they are set by the bounds of a community whose members recognize one another as belonging to that community. This view avoids what Buchanan takes to be the major weakness of justice as reciprocity, namely that it cannot recognize obligations of justice towards those who are unable to contribute to a scheme of social co-operation, such as the seriously disabled. If instead the scope of principles of justice is determined by the boundaries of the relevant community, then these principles will embrace members of the community who for one reason or another cannot contribute to the social product; for instance principles of equality and need will apply to them. And I take it that although nations are not the only communities that will count from this perspective, they are arguably the most important.[23]

If that picture (which I state rather than defend here) is right, then how should we judge the justice of a claim to secession? We begin with a single political society whose institutions are governed more or less closely by principles of justice which citizens of that society—or perhaps some portion of them—endorse. If secession occurs, we now have two political communities within which, again, each set of members' sense of justice will be more or less closely embodied. It is impossible to say in general terms whether the cause of justice is likely to have been served by the secession. In favour of the secession, it can be argued that the discontented minority—the Xs, to return to earlier terminology—will probably have suffered injustice in the large state, either because the principles they subscribe to were not adequately reflected in the state's policies, or because principles which they share with the Ys were implemented in a discriminatory way.[24] Against the secession, it can be argued that the pooling of resources that the larger state made possible served to protect the members of both communities against hardship of various kinds. What cannot be argued, though, is that the bare fact that the Xs as a group and the Ys as a group receive different treatment from their governments and other institutions after the separation is a reason against it. This follows from the premiss that comparative principles of justice apply within communities rather than between them. Just as it is no injustice that the Germans enjoy on average higher incomes or better medical care than the Spanish, so if the Basques were to separate from Spain it would be no injustice if they proceeded to enjoy a higher (or lower) living standard than their erstwhile compatriots.

In general, this means that the argument from justice will tend to reinforce, rather than offset, the original argument from national self-determination. Where a state presently contains two communities whose collective identities are radically at odds with one another, this is very likely to mean that the minority community gets treated unjustly for one or both of the reasons set out above. Contrasting national identities are likely to mean contrasting public cultures, and therefore somewhat different understandings of what justice requires. Equally where there is a good deal of hostility between the communities, political leaders in the majority community will feel strongly tempted to practise discriminatory policies in favour of their fellow-members, as Protestant leaders in Northern Ireland did for many decades. Where, on the other hand, group identities converge more closely at national level, neither the principle of nationality nor distributive justice are likely to support a secessionist cause.[25]

So are there no circumstances in which justice can be appealed to in order to contest a secessionist case that otherwise seems well-founded? I can think of two such instances. First, as several other commentators have observed, a secession might be unjust if it deprived the remainder state of some valuable resource that had been created collectively—for instance if the pre-secessionist state had made a large capital investment in a power station built in the territory to which the secessionists lay claim. In principle this problem is soluble by a transfer payment from the X-state to the remainder Y-state, though it may prove hard to agree precise terms. It is possible that a similar argument might apply when the Ys have taken decisions premissed upon continued co-operation with the Xs, as Gauthier suggests.[26] If the Ys suffer as a result of the Xs' withdrawal in circumstances where they could legitimately expect the co-operation to continue, they may have some claim to compensation which tapers downwards over time. These, however, are best regarded as transitional issues of justice, and should not be conflated with the idea, rejected above, that the relative position of the two communities formed by secession can be judged by applying comparative principles such as equality across both.

Second, a secession might conceivably leave the remainder state so depleted of resources that it was unable to secure its members' basic interests, and so was forced to contract an alliance with some colonial power or other neighbouring state. This could happen if a rich secessionist region chose to cast off an impoverished fringe area—not a likely scenario, perhaps, but one that is worth contemplating briefly for the light it can shed on the general principle at stake. The principle here is that the pursuit of national self-determination and justice for the Xs should not lead to a state of affairs in which the Ys are so deprived that they cannot achieve justice among themselves, and as a result have to give up a large measure of self-determination as well. This is a bit like Wellman's condition that both secessionist and remainder states should be 'large, wealthy, cohesive and geographically contiguous enough to form a government that effectively performs the functions necessary to create a secure political environment',[27] though I do not think we can insist that each state should measure up to some pre-formed standard of liberal legitimacy. What matters is that both the Xs and the Ys should have territory and resources from which a viable political community can be created; how this is done in practice may depend upon the differing political cultures of the two groups.[28]

CONCLUSION

I have tried to show that the principle of nationality provides us with a perspective on the secession issue that can avoid us having to condone a secessionist free-for-all without forcing us to defend existing state boundaries regardless. Sometimes these boundaries need changing, but we can decide whether they do by applying relevant criteria, not simply by listening to how loud the clamour for independence has become. It is far too crude to suggest that any territorial majority that wants to secede has a right to do so. Instead we need to measure the strength of its claim by looking at how far different groups have or have not evolved separate national identities, at how minorities are likely to fare under various possible regimes, and so forth. Admittedly this is demanding in terms of the level of knowledge that outsiders may be called on to acquire. But only by getting to grips with the facts of each particular case in this way can we decide whether outright secession is justified, as opposed to the many other forms of partial autonomy—consociationalism, federalism, local autonomy, etc.—that a constitutional settlement within existing state borders may provide.

NOTES

1. A. Buchanan, *Secession; The Morality of Political Divorce from Fort Sumter to Lithuania and Quebec* (Boulder, Colo.: Westview Press, 1991), 49.
2. Under international law, regions within the main body of a state have for some time been regarded differently from geographically separate territories, such as colonies. The 'right of self-determination' that international bodies such as the UN sometimes proclaim has only been taken to support independence movements in the latter case. In the case of a territorially compact state, it does not imply a right of secession for any part of the state, but the right of the population as a whole to determine its form of government. See J. Crawford, *The Creation of States in International Law* (Oxford: Clarendon Press, 1979), esp. ch. 3.
3. Most fully in *On Nationality* (Oxford: Clarendon Press, 1995). See also D. Miller, 'In Defence of Nationality', *Journal of Applied Philosophy*, 10 (1993), 3–16, repr. in P. Gilbert and P. Gregory (eds.), *Nations, Cultures and Markets* (Aldershot: Avebury, 1994); D. Miller, 'On Nationality', *Nations and Nationalism,* 2/3 (1996), 409–21.
4. See Buchanan, *Secession*, ch. 4 and W. Norman, 'The Ethics of Secession as the Regulation of Secessionist Politics', Ch. 3 in this volume.
5. A. Buchanan, 'Theories of Secession', *Philosophy and Public Affairs*, 26/1 (1997), 30–61.
6. I have given a fuller account of nationality in *On Nationality*, ch. 2.
7. I have drawn here on the discussion of Catalonia in M. Keating, *Nations Against the State: The New Politics of Nationalism in Quebec, Catalonia and Scotland* (Basingstoke: Macmillan, 1996), ch. 5.
8. See D. McDowall, *The Kurds: A Nation Denied* (London: Minority Rights Group, 1992); P. G. Kreyenbroek and S. Sperl (eds.), *The Kurds: A Contemporary Overview* (London: Routledge, 1992).
9. It should also be said that some Kurds have chosen the route of assimilation, forgoing their Kurdish identity in favour of a Turkish one. The important contrast with the Catalan case is that a Kurd in Turkey is more or less forced to make a choice between these two identities, whereas for a Catalan in Spain a hyphenated identity is easily available, and indeed a large majority of Catalans describe themselves in these terms (for instance as ' Equally Spanish and Catalan', 'More Catalan than Spanish', etc.) (see Keating, *Nations Against the State*, 129–34).
10. Nor is it to say that secession is only justified when there is a sharp conflict of national identities: national groups may decide to separate by mutual consent, as the Norwegians and the Swedes did in 1905, and here the depth of the antagonism between them is largely irrelevant. I am considering the much more common case where the Xs wish to secede but the majority Ys oppose this.
11. See, for example, K. Nielsen, 'Secession: The Case of Quebec', *Journal of Applied Philosophy*, 10 (1993), 29–43; D. Gauthier, 'Breaking Up: An Essay on Secession', *Canadian Journal of Philosophy*, 24 (1994), 357–72.
12. According to Hillel Steiner, for instance, 'since nations' territories are aggregations of their members' real estate holdings, the validity of their territorial claims rests on the validity of those land titles'. H. Steiner, 'Territorial Justice',

in S. Cancy, D. George, and P. Jones (eds.), *National Rights, International Obligations* (Boulder, Colo. and Oxford: Westview Press, 1996), 146.

13. Buchanan, *Secession*, 107–14.
14. If one group occupies the territory previously held by another, then, *ceteris paribus*, the strength of its claim to exercise authority will increase with time. At a certain point—impossible to specify exactly—it will have a stronger title than the original inhabitants. This may sound uncomfortably like a version of 'might makes right', but I cannot see any reasonable alternative to the view that it is the occupation and transformation of territory which gives a people its title to that territory, from which it follows that the competing claims of the present and original inhabitants increase and diminish respectively with the passage of time.
15. This brings into play questions about distributive justice which I shall address later.
16. Though note the qualification recorded in n. 10 above.
17. Margaret Moore argues for the relevance of numbers in 'On National Self-Determination', *Political Studies*, 45/5 (1997), 900–15; and in 'Miller's Ode to National Homogeneity', *Nations and Nationalism*, 2/3 (1996), 423–9. I am not sure, however, that she would endorse the criterion I am discussing in its crude form because she also speaks about 'utilitarian calculations' which suggests taking into account intensities of feeling as well as the sheer numbers who are satisfied or dissatisfied with a proposed boundary redrawing.
18. D. L. Horowitz, ' Self-Determination: Politics, Philosophy, and Law', Ch. 9 in this volume.
19. See, for instancc, D. Philpott, 'In Defense of Self-Determination', *Ethics*, 105 (1994–5), 380. 'In a heterogeneous candidate territory, the decision [to secede] rests with the majority of the territory's inhabitants, with the qualification that under the new government, minority rights—including Kymlickan cultural rights—are guaranteed.'
20. Perhaps the most interesting example of an exchange of this kind occurred between Greece and Turkey in the 1920s. Under the terms of a formal agreement between the two states, some 200,000 people of Greek descent living in Turkey were required to emigrate to Greece, and about 350,000 Turks were required to move from Greece to Turkey. Alongside the formal exchange, however, much larger numbers of Greeks—perhaps about one million—emigrated to Greece either voluntarily or as a result of Turkish oppression, and a further 100,000 Turks moved in the opposite direction. There is not a great deal of hard evidence about the overall impact of the transfer on the people who experienced it, but, focusing on the Greek side, the following four statements appear to be true: (1) Materially speaking the infrastructure and investment provided by the internationally funded Refugee Settlement Commission allowed large numbers of immigrants to settle and flourish in their new places of residence; (2) the exchange appears also to have had a strongly positive effect on the overall economic prosperity and sense of national identity in Greece; (3) the refugees experienced psychological difficulties in adjusting to their forcible translation and continued to harbour hopes of a return to their birthplaces at least up until the Second World War; (4) over the same period there were significant social divisions between natives and refugees in Greek towns and villages. To arrive at a balanced assessment, these pluses

and minuses would need to be set against the likely fate of the minorities, particularly at the hands of the Turkish authorities, if the transfer had not occurred. For descriptions of the exchange, see S. P. Ladas, *The Exchange of Minorities: Bulgaria, Greece and Turkey* (New York: Macmillan, 1932); D. Pentzopoulos, *The Balkan Exchange of Minorities and its Impact upon Greece* (Paris: Mouton, 1962); J. A. Petropulos, 'The Compulsory Exchange of Populations: Greek-Turkish Peacemaking, 1922–1930', *Byzantine and Modern Greek Studies*, 2 (1976), 135–60.

21. Including Buchanan, *Secession*, ch. 3; Gauthier, 'Breaking Up: An Essay on Secession'; C. Wellman, 'A Defense of Secession and Political Self-Determination', *Philosophy and Public Affairs*, 24 (1995), 142–71.
22. Buchanan, *Secession*, 114 ff.
23. I have set this argument out more fully in 'The Limits of Cosmopolitan Justice', in D. R. Mapel and T. Nardin (eds.), *The Constitution of International Society: Diverse Ethical Perspectives* (Princeton: Princeton University Press, 1998) and in 'Justice and Global Inequality' in A. Hurrell and N. Woods (eds.), *Inequality in World Politics* (Oxford: Oxford University Press, forthcoming).
24. These two grounds do not necessarily coincide, as the Scottish case illustrates. In recent years many Scots have felt that their public culture and sense of social justice is increasingly at odds with the Thatcherite ideas that have infected some parts of British central government and administration. On the other hand, Scotland has for some while been a net beneficiary of the British system of public finance, so it would be hard for Scots to claim that they are victims of discriminatory treatment.
25. There may be cases—Blacks in America come to mind—in which groups suffer from injustice at the hands of the majority without having or developing a separate sense of national identity. But where a minority group is territorially concentrated, the experience of injustice has a strong tendency over time to foster such a separate identity, so that once again the cause of justice and the cause of national self-determination are fused.
26. Gauthier, 'Breaking Up: An Essay on Secession', section III.
27. Wellman, 'A Defense of Secession and Political Self-Determination', 161–2.
28. So, for example, I think that the Slovenian secession from Yugoslavia could not be condemned on the grounds that it made the achievement of liberal democracy in Yugoslavia as a whole less likely. We ought indeed to try to promote liberal and democratic ideals externally, but I don't think that our duty in this respect is so strong as to oblige us to remain in political association with groups whose culture or identity we find uncongenial.

5

Self-Determination in Practice

DANIEL PHILPOTT

If you want to see the problem with self-determination, drive through the Bosnian countryside and look at the villages. War's destruction there is checkered: houses of rubble and weeds lie next to wholly intact houses, ones with trimmed rows of bushes, lights inside, mothers and children walking in and out. The wrecked houses are the ones where the Muslims lived when the Serbs came to town, where the Croats lived when the Muslims came to town, or where the inhabitants were simply of the wrong ethnicity at the wrong time. The recent war's executions, rapes, tortures, deportations, market-place bombings, and battles, of course, did not always occur so neatly. A people's desire for political autonomy, even if intended peacefully, even if conceived according to the most ingenious federal scheme, nearly always leaves missed spots, swathes of stranded minorities, bringing war.

Self-determination movements are springing up in imitative abandon. In Europe alone more lives have been lost in independence struggles during the past five years than in all of its wars during the previous forty-five. Self-determination is resurgent—and violent—elsewhere, too. But the mimicry is not always bloody. Of the fifteen independent states that emerged from the former Soviet Union, most have remained at peace. Slovakia departed from the Czech republic without war, and Quebec's struggle over secession, despite its bitter words and messy procedures—that is, politics—has remained peaceful and relatively democratic. Elsewhere still, self-determination draws blood, but not so much in its pursuit as in its denial: witness Saddam Hussein's repression of the Iraqi Kurds' quest for autonomy. Today's self-determination movements splay our intuitions, leaving them tangled. The well-aware liberal democrat can only be conflicted.

For comments on this and earlier versions of the manuscript, I would like to thank Peter Digeser, Margaret Moore, as well as Nancy Kokaz and other participants in the conference 'Ethics and International Relations: Challenges to Sovereignty', Harvard University, 22–3 Nov. 1996. I presented an earlier version of this chapter at this conference as well as at the 'National Self-Determination and Secession' panel at the annual meeting of the American Political Science Association in San Francisco, 29 Aug.–1 Sep. 1996.

For the liberal democratic philosopher, knotted intuitions are grist, opportunities to elicit rigour, to plumb the intuitions, to elucidate when, where, and under what circumstances they ought to be applied. As self-determination has proliferated, indeed so have philosopher's arguments. This is welcome, for previously liberal democratic philosophers have only considered self-determination episodically—a Mill or a Walzer incorporates it into works on larger subjects.[1] But following Allen Buchanan's publication of *Secession* in 1991, a coterie of scholars, through their emendations and responses to Buchanan's thorough debut, has made it their common project to ask: Is self-determination just?

The answers fall into two sorts. At least in their initial, unqualified appearances, one is constrictive of the right to self-determination, the other permissive.[2] The first type, including Buchanan's theory, argues that a group attains a moral right to self-determination (to secession, in Buchanan's version) when it has suffered certain kinds of threats or grievances, including 'historical grievances', such as previous invasion or annexation, as well as threats to its cultural preservation, threats of genocide, and finally, 'discriminatory redistribution'—an economic grievance like the American South's protest against the North's high tariffs. This is the constrictive perspective. It denies that self-determination is a general right arising from liberal democratic commitments, and it burdens a claimant group to demonstrate an injustice that self-determination would remedy.[3]

The other answer argues the intuitions of John Stuart Mill and Woodrow Wilson, of the American Revolution and colonial independence movements: self-determination is a basic right, rooted in liberal democratic theory, available to any group the majority of whose members desire it. Threats and grievances are unnecessary to establish a claim. In a recent article, I sought to defend this approach—this more permissive approach—myself.[4] At least in my own version, though, the right to self-determination is also qualified, limited by the same liberal democratic commitments which ground it. Self-determining groups are required to be at least as liberal and democratic as the state from which they are separating, to demonstrate a majority preference for self-determination, to protect minority rights, and to meet distributive justice requirements. The constrictive perspective denies self-determination as a general right but permits the claim for groups that suffer injustices; my approach grants the general right but constricts the claim for groups which perform injustices.

A believer in democracy, then, ought to be a partisan of self-determination—this is the claim I sought to ground in political philosophy. Partisans and philosophers, though, may leave us chary. Even if convinced by their reasons, we may well wonder if they have sufficiently heeded self-determination's noisome particularities—the checkered violence, the rapes, the deportations. We hear more and more of these particularities, in Bosnia, Rwanda, and Zaire.

Now, my theory's qualifications do take into account these violent accompaniments to self-determination, restricting the exercise of the right whenever they surface. But some scholars question whether such qualifications could be secured in practice.[5] Indeed, however restricted a basic right to self-determination may be, it is not hard to envision spirited partisanship—set loose in speeches lauding the nation, in television and radio messages, in urban crowds, then in guerrilla warfare—drowning out the judicious pause of those cautious observers, within the movement or outside, who foresee the fate of minorities, refugees, civilians, and ethnically variegated neighbourhoods. Would the promotion of self-determination also encourage its perversities?

The question is really one about institutions—about the international law, the constitutional provisions, the foreign policy doctrines and procedures which might conceivably put into practice my theory of self-determination. Such institutions do not currently promote self-determination, at least not vigorously or systematically.[6] But if states or the international community gave them the requisite legal and political clout, as my moral argument appears to call for, could these institutions realistically promote the principle while discouraging the perversions? We must explore how self-determination movements would fare differently in a different institutional world. Of course, self-determination movements already exist, are already violent, and are growing. The question thus amounts to a difficult counterfactual, especially since we have little past experience with institutions that promote self-determination.[7] But if our theories are to have any practical implications, then we must confront the question, and that is what I propose to do in this essay. How would the qualified right to self-determination which I have advocated fare if it were put into practice by political institutions?

THE BASIS AND VALUE OF A MORAL RIGHT TO SELF-DETERMINATION

But first, what are the essentials of the right to self-determination for which I previously argued, and which now poses as a candidate for institutionalization? I defined self-determination as a legal arrangement that gives a group independent statehood or expanded powers within a federal state. The basis of the right, the fundamental good that it promotes, is individual moral autonomy. But how does self-determination further autonomy? I argued that it is a form of democracy, one that promotes the kind of individual autonomy that democracy promotes, and promotes it in the way that democracy promotes it. The sort of autonomy I have in mind is Rousseauian, the kind that is realized through governing oneself, shaping one's own political context and fate —directly, through participation, and indirectly, through representation. In this case, though, those who realize autonomy share a common identity, ethnic, linguistic, or cultural, have determined that this identity is important to their political fate, and desire to shape this fate, to participate and be represented, with the other members of their group. Sharing some sort of cultural trait, desiring to govern itself more directly, the group is almost always a 'nation' —that is, a group which conceives of itself as a nation (the definition is subjective) and aspires to political autonomy.[8] Self-determination is one of a family of institutions that promotes democratic autonomy for the members of this group. Its institutional siblings are local government, minority representation schemes, and the like. Self-determination is unique, though, in that the members of the group are united by an identity, not just geographic residency, and want to govern themselves in co-operation with others in their group, not just be represented in the larger whole. What self-determination does for this group is redraw its political borders to circumscribe its residents more locally, making them better able to shape the political identity that they value, making them more autonomous.[9]

What justifies self-determination is not the mere fact of the members' choice, but their realization of democratic autonomy, their increased ability to steer their fate. Autonomy, here, is a realized good. Theorists of self-determination often draw an analogy between self-determination and divorce, and which indeed usefully illustrates key features of the principle. But the analogy breaks down in so far as self-determination is a means to a realized good. In a divorce, spouses fail to realize the good of marriage and dissolve their bond, abjure the good. They are not seeking a positive good in itself—unless one conceives of 'reverting to singleness' as a realized good, a manner of speaking about divorce which few of us would share. But in self-determination, a group seeks not just the dissolution or relaxation of a bond, but a positive good in itself—self-government, realized autonomy—which amounts to much more than the choice to leave.

It is also important that in my argument, the good of the members' autonomy is alone sufficient to justify self-determination. The members may well seek goods besides intrinsic self-governance, and may harbour grievances which add to their desire to govern themselves, either of which may morally enhance their appeal for self-determination. They may want to strengthen their language, better educate their children, keep alive their religion, or deflect a threat to their cultural identity, economic livelihood, or even their lives. But the claim to self-government alone is adequate to establish their political claim to self-determination. Self-government intrinsically desired may seem abstract, but I believe it is at least an element in the alloy of motivations behind virtually every self-determination claim. In some cases, it is quite explicitly the central motivation. Consider the independence movements in many former British colonies. Certainly the colonists suffered grievances: slave labour or near slave labour, shootings into crowds of their protesters, suppression of dissent, all the absurdities of imperialism. Yet the leaders of many of the post-Second World War independence movements—in the British colonies more than in the French ones—did not make these grievances their central claim. Nor could they point to a historical conquering of their people—in virtually every case, no national 'people' existed prior to colonization. Instead, it was the inherent subordination entailed in colonialism, the mere governing of one people by another, that they decried. At least this is how Mohandas Gandhi, Jawaharlal Nehru, and Mohammed Jinnah argued in India, and how so many others argued throughout the rest of the colonial world.[10]

Democratic autonomy, then, is the ground of the right to self-determination, this legal arrangement that furthers autonomy by furthering a people's self-government. I also argued, though, that liberal democratic theory, along with grounding the right to self-determination, also demands restrictions upon it. A group need not suffer an injustice in order to warrant self-determination, but its own perpetration of injustice might limit or invalidate the prima-facie right. Here, I will only enumerate the relevant qualifications. Their rationales and details, I explore in the original argument.[11] They include liberal rights, including some minority rights, as well as some features of democracy besides self-determination—elections and representation, for instance—all of which derive from moral autonomy, just as self-determination does. A people seeking self-determination ought to guarantee these rights and features in its independence or enhanced federal status, at least to the same degree that the larger state guaranteed them prior to self-determination. Democracy also mandates that a majority, perhaps even a supermajority, of the group's members ought to approve of the self-determination claim in a plebiscite. A self-determining group that seeks economic independence might also be morally required to pay compensation or maintain a co-operative economic relationship with the larger state, according to the requirements of distributive justice. Finally, I pose a requirement that parallels just-war theory: that the means of obtaining self-determination, and the evil consequences of the struggle—war, refugees, disrupted lives—be proportionate to the amount of justice being sought. Recognizing that claims to full independence are most likely to bring such consequences, I argued for a presumption against secession, for a first resort to other forms of self-determination. Secession is most justifiable when claims to self-determination are in fact enhanced by grievances that are not likely to be remedied short of full independence—the treatment that the Bosnian Muslims feared if left alone with the Serbs in a unified Yugoslavia, the treatment of the Iraqi Kurds at the hands of Saddam Hussein.

A final important point about my argument: in no way does it imply the desirability of self-determination movements, particularly secession movements, nor the undesirability of multicultural democracy. The question of self-determination arises when, by definition, the unity of a political order has already been seriously ruptured. For one reason or another, a group of people within that order has developed a new identity or merely a separatist aspiration—as the Irish did, as the Basques have, as the American colonists did, as the American South did. We may hope that this never happens, but the question is what to do when it does, and specifically, whether separation is just. I have tried to answer yes, that at least some form of separation is just—if a group seeks it, and if it has not disqualified itself in any of the ways I have mentioned.

SELF-DETERMINATION INSTITUTIONALIZED?

A principle of self-determination does not have to be converted into law or policy. It could be that the world's political institutions, its international law and its domestic constitutions, are, at this stage in history, too blunt-edged, too bereft of judicial clout and enforcement capacity, to propound a law of self-determination that would, through its legitimation and its enforcement, effectively cull the just claims, sift out the harmful consequences, make the precious distinctions, qualify nimbly, issue the partial and truncated approvals that many imperfect claims will require, determine the extent and amount of settlements, and perform judgments that would be heeded and respected just as, say, the judgments of the United States Supreme Court are usually heeded and respected. It could be that to bolster any movement would be to goad all, even the worst.

The moral right to self-determination is institutionally open-ended. If no institution can promote both the principle and the qualifications satisfactorily, then it is perfectly acceptable for the right not to be legalized at all. Such a verdict would not mean that the right of self-determination is morally irrelevant, but only that the world's institutions are too unripe to have self-determination grafted onto them. The right would still be of concern, though, to all who care about what a just world ought to look like—statespersons, advocates, scholars, legislators, and citizens—and its validity stands or falls on its own terms, apart from whether it is institutionalized. But at this point I am not ready to concede the case against legalizing self-determination. The maturity of the world's institutions is still an open question.

It is also a speculative question. Institutionalized self-determination has scant historical precedent; we have little to go on. The case for it lies in our best guesses about the effects of international law and domestic constitutions on the incentives and decisions of nations and states. But we must guess anyway: almost any reform proposal is based at least partly upon judgements about future conditions of which we can only be uncertain. Perhaps the question is not entirely speculative, for self-determination was partially legalized though the United Nations' Declaration on the Granting of Independence to Colonial Countries and Peoples in 1960 and practised through the contagion of independence movements in Africa and Asia in the late 1950s and early 1960s.[12] But although the colonial experience may offer lessons about the effects of independence, it serves ill as a conceptual prototype. With some prominent exceptions, the colonial independence movements enjoyed an international and national consensus—about who was claiming self-determination, where their borders were, and the justice of their claim—that most present movements do not enjoy.

So the best we can do is systematically speculate. The effects of self-determination will depend firstly on the forum in which it becomes institutionalized. Given our current international system, I can imagine two possible forums. First, the right to self-determination might gain strength in international law, where it currently exists in United Nations agreements, but remains subordinate to sovereignty, allowing nations only paltry appeal to the outside in their demands for greater autonomy or independence. Second, the right might be incorporated into states' domestic constitutions, where they have rarely previously appeared, except farcically, as in the former Soviet Union's constitution. Self-determination might also find sponsorship from states themselves, who, acting either alone or through regional organizations like NATO, using military force, economic sanctions, and diplomatic pressure, can affect the incentives and prospects of self-determination movements within other states. But this is not a question of developing institutions, but of states becoming willing to use the political equipment they already possess on behalf of principles of self-determination. Less conceptually demanding, state foreign policy warrants briefer consideration.

In turn, there are three criteria by which we may evaluate how well these forums promote just self-determination. We can ask first about their capability to render impartial justice. Do they have the disinterested officials, the judicial status, the well-designed institutions, and the co-operation of enforcement powers needed to provide fair and heeded decisions? Second, we can ask whether a forum would be able to minimize self-determination's perverse effects while promoting its just outcomes. Finally, we can ask how utopian a forum is. Might we actually see it realized? Along these lines, I organize my speculation.

SELF-DETERMINATION IN INTERNATIONAL LAW

As self-determination's champions have long argued in the language of liberation, portraying the principle as a close relative, even inseparable brother, of liberal rights, democratic governance, and the rule of law, it unsurprisingly appears right along with human rights in several United Nations agreements.[13] Woodrow Wilson's public crusade after the First World War helped to weld self-determination to other liberal democratic principles, and it is partially his legacy that self-determination has been a rhetorical status symbol for any aspirant to liberal democratic legitimacy, whether one is a colonized or otherwise captive people, or a liberal democratic state trying to win such a people's favour. Self-determination's legal status, however, has advanced little beyond that of an inspired principle, enumerated with others in international covenants. In international legal consensus and state practice, there is no 'right' to self-determination (outside the colonial context) strong enough to elicit outside recognition for a people seeking federal autonomy or independence from a state. Self-determination has long lingered in the shadow of state sovereignty.[14]

Capability for Impartial Justice?

If self-determination were to attain the status of a genuine international right, then international law, and the bodies which enforce and interpret it, would grant recognition to peoples seeking federal autonomy or independence. Following the principles I have defended, a people claiming self-determination would be required to hold a plebiscite, approve their claim though a majority (or supermajority) vote, and meet qualifications of liberalism, democracy, distributive justice, and proportional consequences. Most of the time, it would be granted enhanced federal privileges; secession would be a last resort, accorded to peoples victimized by egregious threats or grievances. This law, with all of these provisions, would be enshrined in a UN covenant or some such international agreement.

But who would adjudicate, enforce, follow up? Liberalism, democracy, distributive justice, threats, grievances, and last resort are complex standards, subjective and situational, requiring a third party both disinterested and expert. We also desire strong and enduring enforcement. We can imagine the United Nations or a group of states recognizing and providing diplomatic, economic, and military assistance to a self-determination movement in its initial quest of independence or autonomy, but failing to oversee the movement's economic obligations or its long-term commitments to minorities. Such guarantees of future compliance are rare in our sovereign states system, for they require some states or institutions constantly to oversee other states' internal affairs and obligations.

At our contemporary level of political development, is there an institution that might guarantee principles of self-determination—all of them, evenly? A court, perhaps the World Court, would best meet the standard of disinterest and expertise. The World Court's sole, debilitating, weakness: it notoriously lacks an executive who will enforce its decrees. A UN Security Council willing to support judicial judgments through arms could fill this role, but only in a future, far more mature, UN system. More likely would be a Security

Council which itself judges when self-determination is warranted and when it is assisted, just as it is now coming to sanction intervention and other kinds of involvement in domestic affairs for delivering humanitarian aid, promoting human rights, state-building, and election monitoring. What the Security Council lacks, of course, is the disinterest of the World Court. Composed of Great Powers, it is more disinterested than a single state, but not as careful in weighing complex claims, and more swayed by the strategic interests of its members, than a judicial body would be. Just how disinterested, how capable of appraising complexity, the Security Council could be is difficult to say. In the several cases of intervention and domestic involvement since the end of the Cold War—in Iraqi Kurdistan, Somalia, Bosnia, Rwanda, Haiti, Cambodia, and elsewhere—UN involvement was, in fact, warranted on the merits of the case. Each case involved an injustice or humanitarian disaster that was not simply an excuse for great powers to pursue their interests. The Security Council may have chosen selectively, ignoring cases similar to the ones where it intervened, and was not always successful, but in many cases its proxy armies were at least partially successful in ending conflict or delivering relief.[15] The lesson for self-determination? The Security Council is significantly, if far from perfectly, able to enforce a just outcome to an internal conflict, and might well support—and refrain from supporting—self-determination according to just criteria.

Another judge and enforcer of international law is individual states; their tool of judgment and enforcement is their prerogative of diplomatically recognizing a new claimant to statehood. The question of recognition is a familiar one for international law. It arises when a larger state dissolves, as did Austria-Hungary at the end of the First World War and the Soviet Union at the end of the Cold War. In the context of self-determination debates, it applies mainly to secession: when should outside states recognize a nation seeking independence from a larger state? During the Cold War, states in their practice, international lawyers in their doctrines, answered: almost never. Outside the colonial context, the only secession sanctioned by the United Nations—the only successful secession at all, in fact—was Bangladesh from Pakistan in 1971.

If states were to adopt principles of just self-determination as their interest, we might well demand that they recognize secessionist claims more frequently, although we would insist that they acknowledge restrictions. Qualifications still apply; secession is still a last resort, reserved for the most beleaguered. But it is precisely the qualifications and last resort criterion that we most worry about in the matter of state recognition. It is difficult to tell how much a state's decision for recognition will actually help an independence movement. But recognition, whatever its effect—conferral of legitimacy, implied diplomatic, or military support—will likely be unilateral, and governed by the vicissitudes of the balance of power and domestic politics.

Impartiality, here, is most fragile. In 1991, the European Community set forth criteria for the recognition of Croatia and Slovenia, who had seceded from Yugoslavia against the will of Serbia. Respect for democracy and human rights were to be preconditions of recognition. In December 1991, Germany granted this recognition, unilaterally, before other EC states were ready to assent. Whether or not Germany's recognition contributed to the further dissolution of Yugoslavia, to the ensuing war in Bosnia, to the atrocities—a controversial question—it is apparent that Germany's decision was the product of its internal politics, not an assessment of the merits of the case. Internal politics and balance of power politics are likely to govern future recognition decisions as well.

These ancient political drives raise our general question about incorporating self-determination into international law, whether through the World Court, the Security Council, or state recognition policies. If we legalize claims to self-determination along with the qualifications and the last resort criterion, buttressing all these values with the enforcement capacities of institutions plus whatever legitimacy legalization may confer, might it happen that the claims would gain rampant recognition while the restraints would be ignored?

The danger is real, but also, I think, avoidable. Legalization alone would not seem to result in a bias for enforcing separatism over the restrictions. Human rights, including minority rights, and democracy are currently far more entrenched in international law and state foreign policies than is self-determination, and there is no reason to think that international bodies would abjure their enforcement, sacrificing them to an absolute value of self-determination.[16] What arouses more worry is the role of states in judging and enforcing international law. The Security Council, the most probable enforcer of law, is made up of states; recognition is granted by states; and states pursue primarily their traditional desiderata of security, position, and wealth, not legal rectitude. Here again, though, it is not clear that a general secessionist bias will result. Germany and Croatia was a single case; one can easily imagine other cases where great powers find it in their interests to oppose the breakup of a state. But if states' tendencies do not slant one way or the other in the aggregate, this hardly assures us that states will make the just decision in the single case of a Bosnia, a Quebec, or a Kashmir. Our hopes for impartial judgement and enforcement, in the end, depend on our confidence in the judgement of states, or of states acting in the Security Council, or, most speculatively, of states acting on behalf of an international judiciary body. Of these forums, we may have the most confidence in states as they act through the Security Council. Again, post-Cold War interventions sanctioned by the Security Council give us some reason to believe that the Council can act where justice demands it: imperfectly and selectively, to be sure, but also with some prospect for success.

Perverse Effects?

Thus far I have been discussing how well we might expect political and judicial bodies to judge and enforce particular self-determination claims. But self-determination might bring effects—perverse effects—that go beyond the goods and evils involved in particular claims, with which we must reckon. I want to consider two sorts of such perverse effects: first, those relating to the international system, and the fragile order on which it is based; and second, those relating to particular movements, to their minorities and to their populations that often straddle borders.

Our order of sovereign states dates roughly to the Peace of Westphalia of 1648, a settlement which ended the Thirty Years War, a war very much about self-determination, one in which Protestant and Catholic armies crossed borders again and again in order to alter the religious proportions of neighbouring territories, in the process wiping out perhaps a quarter of Germany's population. Westphalia was a *modus vivendi*, an agreement not upon common principles of religion or justice, but upon the mutual obligation of political authorities not to interfere in one another's territory. Westphalia state sovereignty became the most enduring, universal, and invoked, if not always respected, norm in international relations. Behind it is the moral intuition that whatever evils may occur within state borders, it is better to maintain the *modus vivendi* than to permit the manifold, self-multiplying claims that might justify—and more often, serve as a pretext for—widespread intervention.[17]

Would self-determination weaken our Westphalia order? In fact, self-determination does not challenge sovereign statehood as the basic, constitutive principle of international relations, for it does not propose an alternative political entity to the state. It is a state that a seceding people aspires to be; it is entirely within the state that a federal autonomy-seeking people hopes to remain. Self-determination often increases the number of states on the globe, but this is hardly a challenge to the Westphalian system.[18] Indeed, the self-determination of colonial peoples has globalized, not diminished, sovereign statehood.

What legalized self-determination would challenge is the absoluteness of legal sovereignty which states have generally enjoyed since the century of Westphalia. If self-determination claims of any sort gained recognition from outside states, Westphalian sovereignty would be notably loosened. It would not be the first such relaxation, for as I have mentioned, since the end of the Cold War, the UN Security Council has sanctioned curtailments to absolute sovereignty, often in the form of military intervention, for purposes of humanitarian relief, the promotion of human rights and democracy, state-building, and election monitoring. Enforcing self-determination would manifest this same trend. Thus far, there seems to be little evidence that these abridgements to sovereignty have entailed a general threat to the Westphalian *modus vivendi*. They have occurred under the auspices of the UN Security Council, and have not brought any noticeable swelling in unilateral interventions elsewhere. The Security Council itself has been reluctant to call its interventions by that name. In each case that it approved military force, it took pains to justify the action as a response to a threat to 'international peace and security', even though the target of intervention was primarily a domestic evil —a rhetorical strategy designed to limit the appearance of a departure from the Westphalian norm of non-intervention. Self-determination would certainly expand the justifications for intervention, whether military, diplomatic, or via recognition policies, but similar restraint and consensus in the Security Council ought to preserve the force of the Westphalian *modus vivendi*. This *modus vivendi* has real, but conditional, value. Along with helping to maintain order, sovereignty has served as a carapace for evil, as it did for Nazi Germany and many of its cousin troublesome regimes. If the *modus vivendi* is relaxed gradually, and only in cases where injustice is most consensually recognized, its beneficial function might be preserved while its absoluteness is curtailed.

Besides the undermining of sovereignty, another potential perverse effect of self-determination is the proliferation of separatist claims. Theorist of nationalism Ernest Gellner has written:

> To put it in simplest possible terms: there is a very large number of potential nations on earth. Our planet also contains room for a certain number of independent or autonomous political units. On any reasonable calculation, the former number (of potential nations) is probably much, *much* larger than that of possible viable states.[19]

Granting every nation statehood, Gellner concludes, is manifestly unrealistic. But would legalizing self-determination along the lines of the theory I have advocated provoke the rampant multiplication that Gellner fears? For several reasons, I do not think so. The qualifications to self-determination and the last resort status of secession greatly limit the number of nations entitled to statehood. The number of claims my own approach would allow probably does not greatly exceed those which threat and grievance theories like Buchanan's would allow. Of those self-determination movements which have not suffered serious threats or grievances—the sort which my own theory goes beyond Buchanan in allowing—many will be disqualified by their internal injustices. Quebec's francophones' case for independence, for instance, arguably does not rest upon serious threats or grievances *vis-à-vis* Canada, but is yet limited by questions about its prospective treatment of anglophone and aboriginal minorities. Indeed, I doubt that there are many cases to which my own theory would give a green light, but to which Buchanan's would grant a red or yellow light. The cases that most clearly fall into this category are those former colonies which had suffered relatively mild injustices apart from intrinsic colonial subordination, which seemed capable, at least at the time, of ruling themselves at least as justly as they were ruled as a colony, and were, in my view, entitled to independence. But today there are few colonies left captive, while most potential secessionist movements are more subject to qualification or fail to pass the test of last resort. Furiously breeding secessions, then, are not the inevitable product of a legalized right, at least in the qualified form that I have proposed.

Even if secessions did proliferate, though, which I do not advocate, we should be clear why it would be a problem. It is not necessarily a problem, for instance, for there to be small states. As I claimed in my original argument, there is no reason why even a city or tiny region cannot be self-determining. Andorra, Monaco, Liechtenstein, Singapore, and (up until this year) Hong Kong have all fared perfectly well as tiny sovereignties. There are some limits to how small a sovereign entity can be, but these arise from the necessity of providing certain public functions: maintaining roads and utilities, educating children, preserving minimal order, and providing basic public goods.[20] It is not necessarily a problem, either, for there to be a large number of states. International stability and peace has endured among the many and collapsed among the few. Compare Europe's fate with one Germany in the first half of the twentieth century with Europe's fate with 300 German states during the late seventeenth and eighteenth centuries.[21]

But Gellner goes on to claim:

> This argument is furthered and immeasurably strengthened by the fact that very many of the potential nations of this world live, or until recently have lived, not in compact territorial units but intermixed with each other in complex patterns. It follows that a territorial political unit can only become ethnically homogeneous, in such cases, if it either kills or expels, or assimilates all non-nationals.

Here is the most troubling, and most likely, problem with proliferating claims. It is not small states, many states, the demise of sovereign statehood, or the undermining of the international system. Rather, it is the fate of peoples within self-determination movements, whose populations are often mixed, and whose minorities often spill across declared borders. Quite often, a separatist group—a Croatia or a Bosnia—will have minorities of its own whose future in an independent state looms precarious—Serbs in Croatia, or Croats, Serbs, and Muslims in Bosnia. These minorities may eventually demand their own political separation; secession begets secession in a chaotic mitosis. Or they may form an irredentist group which seeks to join its brothers in a neighbouring state: Croats and Serbs in Bosnia want to unite with Croatia and Serbia. Secessions in one locale may also inspire and embolden secessionists elsewhere, empowering separation through their very demonstration. These predicaments lead further to the war, deportations, executions, and so on, with which we are becoming more familiar.[22]

The principles of self-determination I have proposed recognize this problem. Self-determination ought to be restricted and secession less favoured when minority rights are not likely to be respected, when a separatist minority within a larger separatist movement is unlikely to respect other minorities, and when war is likely to result. But if such likelihood approaches inevitability, if it is always the case that major fractures splinter into minor faults which then become major fractures themselves, and if any conceivable international institution is an impotent glue, then qualifying principles may be vain desiderata. Troublesome practice would suggest that we not institutionalize the principle at all.

My quarrel is with the inevitability—the always, the all, the everywhere—upon which the argument insists. Francophone Quebec, most of the former Soviet republics, Slovakia, Slovenia, and other movements, if they are not wholly irenic, just, and lacking in their own flaws, have avoided the atrocities of Bosnia, Croatia, Eritrea, and elsewhere. The atrocities are possible, but not inevitable. But if inevitability were the only false claim in the argument that warns us about minorities, we might still accept its conclusion: the widespread (if not universal) minority problems that an institutionalized right would allow might still far outweigh the cost of a few unrealized just aspirations to self-determination. But this ignores a different source of executions, deportations, and war—the denial of self-determination claims by oppressive larger states, which often strengthens separatist movements and leads them to take up arms in the first place. If the Soviet Union had not granted its constituent republics independence, instead seeking to perpetuate the empire, would not the war in Chechnya have been replicated several times over? The absence of institutions of self-determination may allow unionist evils, just as the presence of such institutions might admittedly promote the ill effects of self-determination. The difficult question is the magnitude of each effect, and this brings us back to the question of institutions—whether they can be efficacious, what potential for discriminating judgements they carry. As I have tried to argue, institutions capable of such judgements might not be out of the question.

Likely to be Realized?

Whether any of these issues of institutionalization will come to pass any time soon is another question. The final criterion for international law as an instrument of self-determination is whether it might develop in the conceivable future. The prospect appears unlikely. Conceptually, there is no lack of international legal grounds or bases for it. Several UN documents endorse self-determination along with human rights and minority rights.[23] But the same documents emphasize the value of non-interference as well. What would be needed is not the development of new legal doctrines or rights, but a recalibration of the priority of self-determination with respect to sovereignty. The will to abridge sovereignty, though, is precisely what the states of the UN are lacking. As I have mentioned, in approving interventions since the end of the Cold War, the UN Security Council has been loath to admit that its actions constituted intervention in domestic affairs on behalf of human rights, humanitarian relief, or state-building. Self-determination, far from rivalling any of these values in prestige, is even less likely to take priority over sovereignty in international law. Were self-determination to evolve into something like a 'right', it would probably happen first through the recognition policies of states who are sympathetic to the principle. This has not happened yet, not even in Germany's recognition of Croatia and Slovenia. Whether or not Germany's decision was impulsive, the European Community's concurrence hasty, there is little to suggest that Western European powers saw themselves as endorsing any sort of general right to self-determination, rather than merely recognizing the successor states to a dissolved federation. Nor do they seem likely to endorse a right to self-determination any time soon.

SELF-DETERMINATION IN DOMESTIC CONSTITUTIONS

Aside from international law, the main forum for a legal right to self-determination is the domestic constitutions of states. Usually, a constitutional right to self-determination is proposed in the form of the right to secede. A right to general self-determination, one that might include revisions to the terms of a federation but less than independence, is almost unheard of (although not wholly implausible, in my view, either). But even including a right to secede in a constitution—the version that I will discuss herein—might at first appear strange, somewhat like putting a divorce clause into a marriage. Would such a reservation not call into question the sincerity and legitimacy of the association? I have already suggested that the divorce analogy is not a perfect one. Here is another fault in the comparison: A political association may not depend upon the absolute commitment to permanence on which a healthy marriage depends. There may indeed be good reasons to allow a community within a state the future possibility of exit, even while it forms its bond with the state.

Capability for Impartial Justice?

Secession clauses are all but unprecedented in the world's constitutions, with a few exceptions such as the former Soviet Union, whose tanks stationed in Lithuania raised not a few questions about the possibility and legitimacy of the right of exit. Like an international legal right to self-determination, a constitutional right to self-determination is a practice at whose effects we can only guess. But also like an international legal right, we know what we expect from it: it ought to apply just self-determination's requirements—a plebiscite, the qualifications for liberalism and democracy, secession as a last resort, and so on. In a domestic constitution, this would involve a set of procedures specifying how these requirements would be achieved. The group that demands total independence would have to undertake some combination of petitions, legislative approval (if it has a regional legislature), and a plebiscite of its members that requires either a majority or some specified supermajority. The stringency of these requirements will depend on how difficult we desire that self-determination be in a particular state. This will, in turn, depend on the conditions of its founding: the difficulty of eliciting a people's assent, the prospect of a people oppressing their minorities in the act of separation, sundry other considerations of incentive and cost. In any case, these requirements, because of their procedural form, because they are an identifiable sequence of activities, are the easiest ones to specify, carry out, and verify, quite conceivably with impartiality.

More difficult to judge is whether a group meets standards of liberalism, democracy, and respect for minorities, what its distributive obligations are, and whether it merits the last resort of political independence. These are judgements about the substantive realization of goods, not merely the following of procedures, and given their subjective, contingent, and almost certainly contested nature, a court seems required to make them. But here, partiality is more questionable, dependent on the degree to which a domestic court could serve as an independent third party, rather than as a representative of the central government. Perhaps an international body could arbitrate, that is, if both parties could agree to abide by its judgement, but this would require even further institutional innovation, and is thus an even more distant possibility. The question of future enforcement also arises here, for once a region has seceded, the status of sovereignty makes it difficult to enforce compliance with commitments from the outside. Depending on the configuration of surrounding power, one possibility is for interested outside states or regional organizations of states to enforce the settlement, or at least provide incentives for compliance. For instance, one might imagine the United States using trade privileges or membership in NAFTA as a tool for pressuring an independent Quebec to live up to its commitments to the rights of anglophones and aboriginals.

Perverse Effects?

The most troubling implication of a constitutional right to secede, though, one that is raised frequently by its critics, is a particular perverse effect: it would undermine the stability of constitutional orders, especially democracies.[24] With a right to secede, any group whose members harbour a strong particular identity, even a moderately strong identity, one that might only potentially become the source of a separatist demand, would incur the ability to blackmail the rest of the state. In a democracy, where the region's consensus is needed for essential state decisions—raising troops for defence, taxes for common federal projects from building highways to providing national health care—the region could make every question a question of secession, constantly saying to the members of the larger state: 'Meet our demands or else the state will disintegrate; respond to our voice, or we will exit!' Any state-wide project would become all the more cumbersome in time and cost. Overcoming collective action problems in providing public goods, as difficult as it often already is, would become ever more difficult. The constant exercise of the threat of separation would also stunt the growth of civic unity, the collective cultural identity that a state's members need in order to co-operate in common projects.[25] The problem of unity would be especially acute at the birth of a state federation, where a right to secede might inhibit the formation of unity and cohesiveness. On this basis, Cass Sunstein has argued against including secessionist clauses in new Eastern European constitutions.[26] Over the course of a state's growth, a right to secede and its promise of potential independence might give the leaders of a nascent separatist group an incentive to deepen and radicalize their distinguishing identity. Worse still, a central state government, seeing this dynamic on the horizon, might pre-emptively seek to repress this identity formation by forbidding freedom of speech and worse.[27]

If these criticisms are correct, the problem of blackmail indeed seems formidable. But to assign to it inevitability or insurmountability may be too simple and hasty. Whether the separatist group's potential threat should even be called blackmail depends on one's perspective. Best fitting the description of blackmail are what Wayne Norman aptly calls 'vanity secessions', the exit threats of groups whose separatist desire is weak or ephemeral, but whose leaders use the desire to extract concessions. But what of the group which is in fact sincere, the solid majority of whose members consistently desire separation over time, who meet the criteria of liberalism, democracy, and minority treatment, and who may very well suffer mistreatment at the hands of their central government? If the moral criteria of the moral right to secede are correct, then this is just the sort of group whom we desire for the law to empower. Their advantaged negotiating position with the central government seems entirely appropriate; their leverage, we more accurately think of as 'empowerment', rather than 'blackmail'. Of course, most groups lie in between the cynical vanity secessionists and the morally pristine victims. But since they do, we ought to adjust our intuitions and not merely assume the subverter.

A right to secede would not necessarily undermine democracy, either. Indeed, one could imagine it helping a federal state to form, inducing a wary group to join in the first place.[28] If some or all of a region's inhabitants did develop a desire to secede over time, a constitutionally prescribed procedure might help to avoid bloodshed, or even to diffuse radicalism, perhaps even helping to dissipate popular support for secession. Consider the cases of Quebec and Slovakia, the first a region whose inhabitants narrowly voted down secession, the second a region which did secede, and both cases in which little blood was shed over the question. Although in neither case did a constitutional right to secede guide the way, in both cases the larger state's government and the separatist region's inhabitants were willing to abide by agreed-upon procedures. We may take these regions, then, as experimental proxies for constitutional secession. Now, there are admittedly grounds in both cases for scepticism. The procedures were messy and contested, the referenda presented the question of independence ambiguously to the voters, safeguards for minority rights were questionable, and depending on whom one asks, other flaws existed as well. But the crucial question to ask is: What if there had been no (approximation of a) right to secede at all? What if the Czechs and the Canadians had failed to brook even the possibility of secession in the first place?

I have little doubt that separatist sentiment would have been considerably more radical, that the process would have been considerably more contested, and that in all likelihood, considerable blood would have been shed. Of course, bloodshed might still occur in these places, even with procedures for secession. My point is only that the intransigency of central authorities, the absence of procedures, would likely have made the problem all the worse. In both cases, there is little evidence, either, that it was a right to secede that helped to form or radicalize separatist identities—after all, no right to secede existed, formally. Rather, these identities had their own roots in historical memories, perceived injustices, and common linguistic and cultural communities. Nor still is there evidence, in these cases or hypothetical cases, that a right to secede would induce a central government to quell separatists' identities pre-emptively and oppressively. Historically, in the nations of the Austro-Hungarian empire, in the American colonies, in place after place, again and again, centralized persecution has in fact contributed to nations forming and radicalizing their identities, only augmenting their separatist drive. Prosaic democratic procedure, by contrast, may well cool separatism.

This is not to deny that blackmail and destabilized democracy are possible results of a right to secede, but only to claim that salutary and unifying effects are possible, too. Which effects prevail will depend in important part on how the constitutional right to secede is designed. A constitution can best deter blackmail and assist justified secession if it raises high the procedural hurdles. Again, the moral right renders secession a last resort and most justifiable for victims of threats and grievances. Victimized groups are the most likely to be unified in favour of secession, and, appropriately, the most likely to straddle high procedural hurdles. The same hurdles, by contrast, would make life fittingly more difficult for an 'arbitrageur of separatism', the leader who banks on a shaky margin of support for secession to extract concessions from the larger state. To extract concessions, a threat of secession must be credible, which is only likely if it already has strong popular support. Otherwise, it fades into the background of the day-to-day affairs of the federation's politics, where it ideally belongs.

What would high procedural hurdles consist of? As constitutional design is intricate, voluminous, and highly contextual, I can only mention a few general ones here. Several of them I borrow from Wayne Norman, who has thought carefully about the matter.[29] First, a supermajority ought to be required. Exactly what the threshold ought to be—55 per cent? 67 per cent?—is impossible to determine in theory, but the need to deter blackmail along with the foundational nature of the decision together suggest the inadequacy of a simple 50 per cent. Second, the question ought to be worded clearly so that separatist leaders do not skew the question, and so voters know exactly what level of separation they are voting for. The liberal value of public justifiability demands this. A specification worded in the constitution itself or the approval of an international body might help to guarantee clarity. Third, Norman also suggests insightfully that multiple referenda spaced out over two to three years would prevent secession induced by the political passions of the moment. Fourth, also following Norman, for subregions which may not want to join the secessionists, a separate ballot asking which state they desire to join could help to represent choice more accurately, deter separatist leaders from defining their region to include the land of known dissenters, and ease the problem of new beleaguered minorities within new states. We may ask of this provision what we ask of the constitutional right to secede in general: Would it encourage fractiousness, war? What would have been the effect, for instance, of allowing the Bosnian Serbs to have voted upon their political membership at the same time as the Bosnians held their general referendum for independence? It is difficult to know, but also hard to imagine that the Bosnian Serbs would have been any more belligerent towards the Muslims and Croats than they already were. Like the general right to secede, how much a referendum for subregions would empower threatened minorities, how much it would strengthen blackmailers, how much it would restrain central governments, is highly circumstantial.

The most difficult problem with constitutional secession is the problem of agreeing upon the terms of the settlement—the economic obligations, for instance. What form of arbitration would representatives of both parties agree to, and prove capable of delivering a just settlement? The answer is hard to specify, and is likely to vary. The highest court of the larger state, if it is independent enough, an international arbitration board, an agreed upon third-party arbiter, or some forum which would satisfy both parties—any of these possibilities has potential. Many other features of an effectively just constitutional right to secede doubtless need to be mentioned as well as invented. In the matter of constitutional design, a moral theory mainly points to what constitutions ought to discourage, what they ought to allow.

Likely to be Realized?

Constitutional rights to secede do not seem any closer to realization than an international legal right; very few states in the world today have them. Yet, in places like Quebec and Slovakia, as I have argued, something like an implicit right to secede emerged, in that the separatists and the larger state were willing to abide by the outcome of some set of procedures, even if they did not like all of its terms or its manner of execution. It is cases like this in which the right of self-determination has come closest to being realized in the domestic sphere.

CONCLUSION

In our present world of institutions, the key arbiters of self-determination are going to be states. It is primarily states who recognize and assist self-determination movements. It is in the policies of states that moral principles of self-determination are most likely to be realized, to the degree that they are realized at all. We cannot generalize about what perverse effects might arise from states' attempts to promote self-determination, for unlike standing legal rights, which have a fixed character, the decisions of states are singular and adaptable to situations. The effects of states' decisions will depend on the quality of the decisions. What about impartiality? Because states are so centrally concerned with their security interests, we may doubt whether they would act to preserve the substance of a legal right. Often, though, the effect of a self-determination claim on a state's interests will be unclear, and to the degree that states look for rules of thumb to guide their pursuit of interests, theories about the moral principles and consequences of self-determination might have something to offer.

More speculative, less immediately relevant, are the effects of legalizing self-determination in international law or a domestic constitution. International law's provisions are currently weak and completely subordinate to sovereignty, while domestic constitutions rarely include provisions for a group to revise its political status. Nor does change seem in the offing. But in so far as philosophers' conclusions are heeded, perhaps it is better that theorists are taking up the question well in advance of the day when self-determination is institutionalized, if it ever comes. At least the problem will be well considered. The first step has been to determine the appropriate moral principles involved. I have proposed such principles in my argument that self-determination is a basic right, but also a qualified one. But here my question has been: What would be the effects of legalizing such a right? Should just self-determination be promoted through international law and domestic constitutions, or should it be confined to moral advocacy?

My answer, in the end, is an unsatisfying one: it depends. It depends on how effective a strengthened international legal right or a domestic constitution would be in bracing just self-determination claims while enforcing the qualifications and discouraging unjust claims. If these institutions are certain fiascos, then they ought not to be created. It depends, too, on the dynamics of self-determination movements. If it is the case that virtually all movements are likely to bring war, deportations of minorities, and other evil consequences that far outweigh the injustice which such movements suffer within their larger state, and if virtually all self-determination movements are purveyors of vanity secessions, then clearly we should not make self-determination any more possible.

I have tried to argue that this description is not accurate and that effective institutions are thinkable. I make no stronger claim, for we have little evidence about institutions to take us beyond educated speculation. Certainly, in an anarchic world of sovereign states, institutions to promote self-determination will be imperfect, far incapable of perfect enforcement. But the world of self-determination movements is imperfect, too. Apart from whether self-determination is legalized, there will be plenty of such movements, many of them violent, many of them resulting in new states which oppress new minorities, eliciting the familiar calamities. The question is whether, in a world in which self-determination does exist, might institutions on balance channel some of them in the direction of justice? Would institutions make the problem better or worse? The answer depends on just how effective the institutions are, and just how likely self-determination movements are to be affected by them.

Again, this answer is an unsatisfying one. But it does have a couple of important implications. First, legalizing a moral right to self-determination that does not depend on threats and grievances, but one that is amply qualified to be sure, is far from an inevitable moral disaster, and, quite possibly, could make the world more just than it otherwise would be. Second, whether a legal right is beneficial depends deeply on human choices. For instance, if the UN Security Council were to begin enforcing just self-determination, it would be wise to construct the right strictly, supporting only the clearest cases, shying from the ambiguous ones, so as to avoid encouraging movements whose claims are morally mixed. As I have argued, a constitution with high procedural hurdles would allow only the most popular separatist movements; such designs ought to be encouraged. At least initially, a legalized right ought to err on the side of making self-determination, especially secession, legally cumbersome.

There are limits to generalizing about international law or constitutional design. Political philosophers have the most to say about basic moral principles. These principles offer general insights for international law and domestic constitutions, but as the questions become more specific, dealing with the advantages of certain constitutional clauses, the good and ill effects of UN intervention, the dynamics of secessionist politics, and so on, the less the philosopher will have to say and the more we find ourselves turning to sociologists, political scientists, and constitutional lawyers, who can tell us better what sort of effects are likely to ensue from our proposed institutions. The debate over principles has been fruitful. Perhaps it is now time that the social scientists and lawyers take over.

NOTES

1. See J. S. Mill, 'A Few Words on Non-Intervention', in his *Dissertations and Discussions* (New York: Henry Holt, 1873), iii. 238–63; M. Walzer, *Just and Unjust Wars* (New York: Basic Books, 1977), 87–91. One of the major exceptions is H. Beran, 'A Liberal Theory of Secession', *Political Studies*, 32 (1984), 21–31.
2. My two-fold division is similar to A. Buchanan's in 'Theories of Secession', *Philosophy and Public Affairs*, 26/1 (1997), 30–61.
3. For Buchanan, a right to secede that does not require threats or grievances might be incorporated into positive law. See A. Buchanan, *Secession: The Morality of Political Divorce from Fort Sumter to Lithuania and Quebec* (Boulder, Colo.: Westview, 1991). L. Brilmayer's perspective also requires grievances; she focuses mainly on historical grievances. 'Secession and Self-Determination: A Territorial Interpretation', *Yale Journal of International Law*, 19 (1991), 177–202.
4. See D. Philpott, 'In Defense of Self-Determination', *Ethics*, 105/2 (1995), 352–85. Other perspectives falling into this category include T. Pogge, 'Cosmopolitanism and Sovereignty', *Ethics*, 103 (1992), 48–75; M. Walzer, 'The New Tribalism', *Dissent* (Spring, 1992), 164–71; Beran, 'A Liberal Theory of Secession'; Y. Tamir, *Liberal Nationalism* (Princeton: Princeton University Press, 1993), 73–4; and D. K. Donnelly, 'State and Substates in a Free World: A Theory of National Self-Determination', *Nationalism and Ethnic Politics*, 2/2, (1996), 286–311; C. Wellman, 'A Defence of Secession and Political Self-Determination', *Philosophy and Public Affairs*, 24/2 (1995), 142–71; D. Gauthier, 'Breaking Up: An Essay on Secession', *Canadian Journal of Philosophy*, 24 (1994), 357–72; and K. Nielsen, 'Secession: The Case of Quebec', *Journal of Applied Philosophy,* 10 (1993), 29–43.
5. See especially D. L. Horowitz, 'Self-Determination: Politics, Philosophy, and Law', Ch. 9 in this volume.

6. On the current status of self-determination in international law, see H. Hannum, *Autonomy, Sovereignty, and Self-Determination: The Accommodation of Conflicting Rights* (Philadelphia: University of Pennsylvania Press, 1990).
7. Although it is sometimes thought that the treatment of Eastern European peoples in the Versailles settlement of 1919 was an example of self-determination, in this case as part of the vision of Woodrow Wilson, self-determination was only realized to a limited extent. Plebiscites were held and borders drawn to accommodate the aspirations of minority peoples, but the settlement was largely one that recognized states that had already come into *de facto* existence, not peoples within already established states. More importantly, no lasting institutions to promote self-determination beyond the settlement itself were created.
8. On this definition and others who espouse it, see Philpott, 'In Defense of Self-Determination', 366, n. 28.
9. Ibid. 355–62.
10. Ibid. 360–2.
11. Ibid. 371–85.
12. Colonial self-determination was justified according to the 'salt-water rule', by which a region, to be considered a 'colony' entitled to independence, had to be separated from its mother country by an ocean. See L. Berat, *Walvis Bay: Decolonization and International Law* (New Haven, Conn.: Yale University Press, 1990).
13. On self-determination's legal status, see Hannum, *Autonomy, Sovereignty, and Self-Determination.*
14. Ibid. 49.
15. On humanitarian intervention, see A. C. Arend and R. Beck, *International Law and the Use of Force: Beyond the U.N. Charter* (New York: Routledge, 1993).
16. On international legal instruments for human rights, see Hannum, *Autonomy, Sovereignty, and Self-Determination*, 3–118.
17. A classic article on Westphalia and its significance for the international system is L. Gross, 'The Peace of Westphalia', *American Journal of International Law*, 42 (1948), 20–41
18. Self-determination does not always increase the number of states. It could take the form of fusion—witness the unification of Germany and Italy in the nineteenth century. Of course, this form of self-determination is hardly a challenge to the Westphalia system, either.
19. E. Gellner, *Nations and Nationalism* (Ithaca, NY: Cornell University Press, 1983), 2. Also quoted in Buchanan, *Secession*, 49.
20. Philpott, 'In Defense of Self-Determination', 366.
21. For this argument, see also M. Lind, 'In Defense of Liberal Nationalism', *Foreign Affairs*, 73/3 (1994), 87–99.
22. D. Horowitz emphasizes these problems in his 'Self-Determination: Politics, Philosophy, and Law'.
23. See Hannum, *Autonomy, Sovereignty, and Self-Determination*, 27–49.
24. Several critics raise the issue. See C. Sunstein, 'Constitutionalism and Secession', *University of Chicago Law Review*, 58/ 2 (1991), 633–70. See also Buchanan, 'Theories of Secession' and W. Norman, 'The Ethics of Secession as the Regulation of Secessionist Politics', Ch. 3 this volume.

25. On the importance of civic unity and shared identity for the functioning of democracy, see D. Miller, *On Nationality* (Oxford: Clarendon Press, 1995), 66–73, 81–8.
26. Sunstein, 'Constitutionalism and Secession'.
27. Buchanan, 'Theories of Secession'.
28. Buchanan mentions this possibility in his helpful discussion of a constitutional right to secede in *Secession*, 127–46.
29. See Norman, 'The Ethics of Secession as the Regulation of Secessionist Politics', Ch. 3 of this volume, pp. 53–5.

6

Liberal Nationalism and Secession

KAI NIELSEN

I

I want to explicate and defend the right of nations to some form of substantial political self-governance. This entails the right in certain circumstances (circumstances to be characterized in a moment) of nations to secession. I shall further argue that we should be more permissive about this than are many theoreticians (among them prominently Allen Buchanan).[1] The presumptive right to secession, where the majority of its citizens clearly express their preference for it, should generally be taken to be unproblematic. *Pace* Buchanan, *the burden of proof* will be to show that, in some particular circumstance or type of circumstance, this right (being defeasible as all rights are) should be overridden. There is, that is, a presumptive right of a nation to secede from a larger multinational state or centralized state should the majority of the members of that nation wish to do so. The burden of proof is not to establish that the right to secede is a general standing right, but, on the contrary, against this right to secede, that, for a particular case or range of cases, that this right can be justifiably overridden. I argue that this is the attitude to be taken in liberal democracies, particularly when both the remainder nations and the seceding nations are liberal democracies. In liberal democracies the right of a people to political self-governance is so deeply embedded that it cannot be easily overridden. Indeed the case for overriding it would have to be very strong. The step to secession, of course, should not be taken lightly, but a presumptive right to secession on the part of a people should always be acknowledged in a liberal democratic society. Such an acknowledgment is clearly tied to what it is to have a respect for democracy and (*pace* Buchanan) to the egalitarian belief in an equal respect for persons and for autonomy.

I proceed by first setting out my conception of a nation, of nationality and of liberal nationalism and why I believe that cultural-national membership is of deep significance to individuals and how this justifies their establishing some form of political self-governance for nations even when to do so involves the secession from a state, even a state that is not oppressive. Having set out my case I shall critically examine the powerful case made by Allen Buchanan that there should be no such strong presumption of the right to secession.[2]

II

I shall limit myself to what should be said concerning the liberal democracies of the rich capitalist democracies and whatever successor socialist liberal democracies that we might in time come to have. I do this not because I think these are the only societies worth talking about. That would be absurd. I do it because our thinking about nationalism, its justifiability or lack thereof, and of secession should be significantly different when we are talking about such societies than when we are talking about the nations of the former Soviet Union, the former Yugoslavia, or of much of Africa. Our thinking should be much more contextual than it usually is. We must be very cautious about grand scale generalizations. We should, of course, if such can be had, like an account ('theory' may be too grand a word) that we could generalize to cover all the world. But we need more humble beginnings. There is enough to be sorted out if we just stick to the rich liberal democracies. I shall resolutely so restrict myself.

III

There are myriads of definitions or characterizations of 'nation' and, for 'nation', its not being the name of a natural kind, there is no such thing as being the correct definition of 'nation'. But some definitions are more perspicuous and more useful than others. David Miller and Allen Buchanan give closely related conceptualizations (characterizations) that well bring out what a nation is. Miller takes a nation to be 'a group of people who recognize one another as belonging to the same community, who acknowledge special obligations to one another, and who aspire to political autonomy—this by virtue of characteristics they believe they share, typically a common history, attachment to a geographical place, and a public culture that differentiates them from their neighbours.'[3] Buchanan relatedly, but less fully, characterizes nations as 'encompassing cultural groups that associate themselves with a homeland, and in which there is a substantial (though not necessarily unanimous) aspiration for self-government of some kind (though not necessarily for independent statehood)'.[4]

Both authors stress the importance of a common culture. Miller speaks of a public culture and Buchanan of an encompassing culture and other authors with related characterizations of nation speak of an organizational culture or of a societal culture. They are all gesturing in the same direction. Often, though not invariably, that encompassing culture carries with it a distinctive language and where it does, that language becomes very important to that nation. This is plainly true for the Catalonian and Flemish nations. As well, for a group to constitute a nation, people in that group must generally have a sense of a common history and an historical attachment to a particular territory which they see, though sometimes only in aspiration, as their homeland in which they will practice some form of political self-governance. There must also be a mutual recognition between the members of a nation of their common membership and a recognition that they owe special obligations to each other that they do not owe to others. The members of any nation will aspire to in *some way* control a portion of the earth's surface. This makes the very idea of a nation, as distinct from some other cultural groups (an ethnic group, for example, made up of immigrants to a country) inherently political. They wish to be *maître chez nous*, to have political autonomy and some form of self-government. Again that distinguishes a nation from an ethnic group or even a national minority not in search of nationhood.

I spoke above of 'in some way' controlling a portion of the earth's surface or of having 'some form of self-government' because, given the extensive mix in many places of different peoples on the same territory—often different peoples long resident in the same territory—there are more nations than there are feasible nation-states and for some nations, the Samaritans, the Lapps, the Faeroese—and *perhaps*, as well, the Kurds, the Welsh, the Catalonians, and the Basques—their nations are too small or too scattered to be viable states. The First Nations in Canada, Quebec, and the United States are very good examples of nations that, while they can and should have some form of self-governance, they are arguably too small and too vulnerable to form states. They are plainly nations, but they are either too intermingled with other peoples on the same territory or are too small or too poor or too much without infrastructures to form viable states. But there are weaker forms of self-government short of statehood that could, and indeed should, be theirs.

So nations are inherently political *and* inherently cultural. The nationalism of a nation will give force to both of those aspirations. And these features will mark them off from other groups. Liberals, socialists, and communists, for example, will cut across cultures and across nations. And ethnic groups of immigrants living in a state will not aspire to a homeland or to a *political* community. As immigrants they will seek to adapt to, and in some considerable measure adopt, the public (encompassing or integrating) culture of the country to which they have immigrated. For them the issue is not to form a political community, to say nothing of seceding from the state to which they have immigrated. For them a crucial desideratum is to integrate successfully into their new adopted homeland while still preserving something of their ethnic identity. Only if they are for a long time oppressed will they sometimes move, if they are there in sufficient numbers, from being simply an ethnic group to becoming a nation seeking political autonomy. In such a circumstance they become a nation for they already have a common culture —a culture which is becoming more encompassing.

National minorities are distinct from both nations and ethnic groups. Like nations they are historically rooted in a state. They are groups whose historic homeland has been incorporated into a larger state through conquest, colonization, or voluntary federation. But unlike a nation they do not seek political autonomy; they do not seek a form of self-government. They do not see themselves as a *political* community, but seek to insure that their rights are protected and their common culture preserved and respected. The Lapps in Norway and Sweden are a good example, as are the Swedish-speaking Finns in Finland, the Alsatians in France, the German-speaking minorities in the south of Denmark, the Danish-speaking minorities in Flensburg and its surroundings, and the Tyroleans in Italy.

Sometimes the borderline between national minorities and aspiring nations is fragile as the struggles of Tyroleans in the first two decades after the end of the Second World War well illustrates. Still the distinction is an important one to make. In, for example, a sovereign Quebec the First Nations would remain nations and the immigrants ethnic groups, but the historically rooted anglophone community would become a national minority with the distinctive rights of a national minority. They would have rights that ethnic groups would not have, but also, as a national minority, they, without aspirations to nationhood, would not have rights to some form of self-government as, by contrast, the First Nations do. The same thing would obtain for the francophone minorities in the rest of Canada; they are national minorities in Canada in a way the Poles, Germans, and Italians are not. Similarly, the anglophone minority in a sovereign Quebec would become a national minority while the immigrant groups would not.

IV

I am now in a position to specify what is distinctive about liberal nationalism, principally, but not exclusively, by contrasting it with ethnic nationalism.[5] All nationalisms—liberal nationalisms, ethnic nationalisms, and authoritarian non-ethnic nationalisms (e.g. the nationalisms of Argentina, Brazil, and Chile under their dictatorships)—are cultural *and* political nationalisms. Those things just go with being nationalisms of *any kind*.[6] But pressing for the protection of their distinctive cultural institutions, including, where they have a distinct language, their language, does not turn a nationalism into an ethnic nationalism and, as well, seeking to form a state or some other form of political community to work to preserve and enhance their national and cultural identity does not make such nationalists into ethnic nationalists or make them chauvinistic. An ethnic nationalism will be rooted in an ethnic conception of the nation where membership in the nation and citizenship in a state will be rooted in *descent*. What determines membership or citizenship in an ethnic nation is who your ancestors were, not the language you speak, your cultural attunements; your conception of yourself, where you live, or what your loyalties are. This nationalism is exclusionist, xenophobic, backward-looking, and deeply anti-liberal. Where it, in some modified form, persists in some otherwise liberal states, e.g. Germany, it is an anachronism firmly to be condemned as running against what liberalism and democracy are all about. Where nationalism is rightly despised and condemned it is either this nationalism or the sometimes non-ethnic nationalism of some authoritarian states (e.g. Chile under Pinochet). But liberal nationalism, while remaining cultural and political as all nationalisms are, is none of these things. It is a nationalism which is non-exclusionist. Citizenship is open to anyone, with a landed immigrant status within the territories of these liberal democracies and immigration is at least reasonably open and is certainly not based on ethnic, racial, or religious grounds. It is, that is, quite independent of descent and ethnic background. Anyone who wishes to have full citizenship and be a part of the nation may, at least in principle, do so if they learn its language, history, and customs and are willing to abide by its laws. Perhaps in certain difficult circumstances they will have to as well meet certain educational or other work-skill requirements. Membership, with the recognition that goes with it, is defined in terms of participation in a common culture, in principle at least open to all, rather than on ethnic grounds. Both the Québécois and the Flemish stress open access to their nations and they protect the historic rights of their national minorities to have schools, hospitals, and other public services in their own languages and the right to use this language in parliament.

Where a nationalist movement prevails in a *liberal* democratic society, the state will, as will any state, in certain respects privilege the encompassing culture of the nation. But it will only do so in ways that will at the same time protect the rights of its minorities and indeed protect rights across the board. A central aim of a nationalist movement in a liberal democracy, as well as everywhere else, is to protect, and beyond that, if it can, to insure the flourishing of the culture of the nation that that nationalist movement represents. But, if it is a liberal nationalism, it will not seek to stamp out, or otherwise repress, other cultures and will actively work to preserve the culture and cultural institutions of the First Nations in its midst and of its national minorities. But it will also insist that there be a common cultural currency across society; it will insist that that common currency (that public culture) be learned by all the children in the society, *perhaps* very isolated native peoples apart. The children will learn, that is, the official language of that culture or, if (as in the United States) there is no official language the dominant (the *de facto* official language, if you will) of that culture as well as some reasonable bits of its history and customs and some knowledge of its political system and laws. There will through its educational system be this form of socialization. This is what a nation-state must do to preserve itself and to keep the society from being a Tower of Babel. If *per impossible*, liberalism gained such a neutrality, it would have gained something that would undermine any form of such socialization. But this socialization, into a culture, some form of which is inevitable, will not—indeed cannot if the state is a liberal democracy—be at the expense of minority rights and cannot turn either the people of its First Nations, its national minorities, or its immigrant citizens into second-class citizens. It cannot do those things and remain a liberal democracy. Its failure here is a measure of its failure as a liberal democracy.

There is one further thing that needs to be said about liberal nationalism before I turn to my argument for a strong right of secession for such nations, unencumbered by the strong restrictions that Buchanan would place on it. It is not only necessary that a liberal nationalism not be an ethnic nationalism; it must be a reiterated, generalizable nationalism and not a nationalism of the manifest destiny of a chosen people who can run roughshod over other peoples in terms of its allegedly privileged place in history as being the wisest and the best. It must not only be non-exclusionist; it must, as well, not be chauvinist or expansionist. There can be no favoured *Volk,* no single people destined to have a pre-eminent place in the sun, while the rest are judged in one degree or another, to be inferior and are placed in a subordinate position. (The nationalism of the white settlers in the former Rhodesia described so graphically by Doris Lessing is a paradigm case of such an ethnocentric nationalism.) Rather than a nationalism for God's chosen people, a liberal nationalism will be a reiterated nationalism which claims that *all* nations have a right to some form of self-government and the right, and indeed the same right, when certain generalizable conditions prevail, to justifiably secede from the state in which the nation exists in a multinational state or a centralized state which denies its multinational character and in which one nation dominates the other nation or nations in the society. A just social order will be a social order where all peoples—all nations and all national minorities—will have institutions which protect their culture and which will enhance and protect their national and cultural identities.

V

However, this just assumes that the preservation and enhancement of a national-cultural identity, which is also a conception fitting in with a liberal democracy, is something of great importance to human beings. But why should a liberal democracy or people in a liberal democracy care about preserving such an identity? Indeed should they care about preserving their cultural identities? Why not just think in terms of individuals and in terms of what would maximize their secure flourishing, including a commitment to equal respect for all people and, as well, to what would strengthen their self respect? What, as Buchanan asks, is so special about nations and having a robust sense of national identity? Why not, as Andrew Levine and Harry Brighouse ask, as well, just be cosmopolitans without any attention to such particularisms?[7]

First a red herring needs to be cleared out of the way. Cosmopolitanism and a caring about a more local identity (something that makes one a member of a particular and, for one, a cherished community) need not at all stand in conflict. One, for example, can be proud of being an Icelander and be very much committed to one's homeland, its traditions and distinctive culture and be committed to working to see it flourish without being chauvinist about it, thinking that 'the Icelanders are the best'. One can have such warm feelings about one's nation while also having cosmopolitan interests and commitments as well. There is, for most people at least, a place where one feels most at home, a place that one longs for after a long absence, and there is, in that particular culture, for many people, a reasonably definite answer—more accurately, an important part of an answer—to the question, 'Who am I?'. But that is perfectly compatible with valuing others and without feeling that their traditions are inferior to one's own and with taking an active interest in what goes on in the world. Moreover,[8] it is psychologically impossible for us to be 'free floating cosmopolitans' with no roots in a particular culture. If we are to be focused at all we must have roots in a particular culture. To the extent that we get extensively detached from those roots we will in one way or another suffer psychologically. But we should also not be ethnocentric, cooped up in our particular culture; we should both be cosmopolitans and have particular attachments. We should, that is, be cosmopolitans but *rooted* cosmopolitans.[9]

If we are not to be alienated and disconnected from our cultural environment we not only need to develop our powers, but to have an understanding of who we are. Self-definition is an indispensable condition for human flourishing.[10] But self-definition involves, though it, of course, involves much more than this, seeing ourselves as New Zealanders, Dutch, Irish, Ghanians, Canadians, or whatever. Or at least this sense of national identity has come into being with the establishment of industrial societies.[11]

When a Dane, for example, meets a fellow Dane abroad there is usually a spontaneous recognition of a common membership in a nation which is not the same when she meets, for example, a Chilean, though, if she is a liberal democrat, equal respect will go to the Chilean and, if she is reflective and cosmopolitan, she will take an interest in the different life experiences, conceptions of things, and cultural attunements of people with nationalities different than her own. But normally there will be a sense of at-homeness and an affinity with her fellow Danes that is rooted in their having a common culture: the songs they sing, the structure of jokes, the memories of places, a sense of a common history, literary references, political experiences, and the having of all kinds of common forms of intimate ways of living.

Nations, to summarize, are encompassing cultures associated with a particular territory where there is an aspiration on the part of at least a majority of the members of such encompassing cultures for a homeland. Encompassing cultural groups are cultures which pervade the whole range of an individual's major life activities and function as an indispensable source of self-identification and self-definition. Moreover, the very existence of such a culture requires social structures and a complex cluster of interdependent institutions. Without this being in place in the lives of human beings there can be no secure and stable sense of who they are and without that there will be little in the way of human flourishing. Instead people will experience anomie and alienation. These encompassing cultures—these nations—will have a fragile and insecure existence if they do not have a substantial degree of self-government. Moreover, in industrial societies such as our own—the rich capitalist, constitutional democracies—such a nation will be most secure when it has a sovereign state of its own. To achieve that may require it to secede from the multinational state or from some severely centralized state of which it is a part. In a liberal democracy there is a *presumption* that every nation has a right to its own sovereign state. This is a *presumption* which is always defeatable and sometimes defeated. I have discussed some of the considerations that could justify its defeat in a particular situation and I will return to this when I consider Buchanan's critique of such a claimed general right. But in arguing for the right of a nation to a state of its own I am not (*pace* Hegel) assuming that states are loveable institutions. They are not. But that unloveableness notwithstanding, we can see from what has been said above that for people to have such a nation-state is to have something which makes a very deep link with what is required (instrumentally required) to give sense to their lives. When, as sometimes must be the case, their nation, and for good reasons, cannot have a state of its own, there is, as a result, more fragility and anomie in their lives. That they can sustain a stable sense of identity is more at risk. This is why in liberal democracies—where human rights are protected and there is a general egalitarian ambience—I attach this strong form of political recognition to nations with the hope that circumstances will make it possible, without denying the conditions of a liberal social order, for nations to have nation-states of their own. We have here nationalism with a human face.

VI

Buchanan believes that sometimes nations have a right to secede. But his view of when this is so is much more restrictive than my own. He articulates and defends a particular version of what he calls a Remedial Right Only Theory of Secession.[12] For Buchanan, a group has the right to secede only if

1. The physical survival of its members is threatened by actions of the state (as with the policy of the Iraqi government toward Kurds in Iraq) or if it suffers violations of other basic human rights (as with the East Pakistanis who seceded to create Bangladesh in 1970); or
2. Its previously sovereign territory was unjustly taken by the state (as with the Baltic Republics).[13]

It must also be the case for the group to have the right to secede 'that there be credible guarantees that the new state will respect the human rights of all of its citizens and that it will co-operate in the project of securing other just terms of secession.'[14] This includes a fair division of federal properties in the old state, a fair apportioning of the national debt, a negotiated determination of new boundaries, agreed on arrangements for continuing, renegotiating, or terminating treaty obligations, and provisions for defence and security.[15] In his classification of types of theories of secession, my account, as distinct from his Remedial Right Only Theory, is a variant of a Primary Right Theory. It is an account which, as he rightly says, claims that a group constituting a nation 'can have a (general) right to secede even if it suffers no injustices, and hence it may have a (general) right to secede from a perfectly just state'.[16] Here 'just' must be construed in an uncontroversial and thus minimal sense, accepted by both theories, i.e. violation of uncontroversial individual moral rights and not engaging in 'uncontroversially discriminatory policies toward minorities'.[17] My account, as we have seen, also accepts the last set of conditions for the right to secede, e.g. credible guarantees that human rights will be respected, boundaries negotiated, a fair division of the national debt made, and the like. I would further add, where after protracted negotiations the seceding state and the remainder state cannot agree about borders, the fair distribution of the national debt or of federal properties and the like, the dispute should be settled in binding arbitration by an international tribunal. It is here where international law is very important. But my account differs from his Remedial Right Only Theory concerning his first two conditions. It need not be on my account that the physical survival of a nation is threatened. It may instead be the case, on the one hand, that only its cultural survival is threatened (say, the loss of its language) by the larger state in which it abides or, on the other, even that just the democratic will of the majority of the nation desiring to secede is not acknowledged by the state where secession is an issue. If either of these things obtain, then the state opposing the secession acts wrongly. There is here, I argue, (*pace* Buchanan) also a *general* right to secede that his account does not acknowledge. Put simply, the nation that would secede to form a state of its own need not have prior to that time been treated unjustly in the state in which it abides. It is sufficient on my account, provided the human rights of all people in the territory in question are protected, that the majority of the people of the nation want to secede and vote (in a simple majority) to secede. I would indeed bite what Buchanan regards as the bullet, and 'go so far as to recognize a right to secede even under conditions in which the state is effectively, indeed flawlessly, performing all of what are usually taken to be the *legitimating functions* of the state'.[18] (That a nation *has* such a right does not, of course, mean or entail that in such circumstances that it should *exercise* that right or even that in all instances it is reasonable to do so. I have the right to run for mayor in Montreal and it is important that I have that right, but I shall never do so. A people will not in fact secede without reason. So it is very unlikely that a nation will secede from a flawlessly just state. But it is important in a democratic ethos that it have the right to do so. So my view is very much more permissive than Buchanan's.)

Buchanan thinks such a permissive view is both dangerous and absurd—being in a very bad sense utopian. I think *au contraire* that it is entailed by a firm and clear commitment to the right, in a democratic society, of a people to be self-governed. That is something which is very central to democracy. The difference between us can be narrowed a bit by noting that Buchanan is giving a general theory of secession for all societies—democratic and undemocratic, liberal and illiberal—while I am only talking about the conditions under which secession is justified when the contending groups are both firmly and resolutely a part of liberal democratic societies and are committed to its values.

Consider in this context Buchanan's Minimal Realist argument for preferring Remedial Right Only Theories to Primary Right Theories. The former, as he puts it, 'places significant constraints on the right to secede, while not ruling out secession entirely. No group has a (general) right to secede unless that group suffers what are uncontroversially regarded as injustices and has no reasonable prospect of relief short of secession.'[19] Why accept such a very restrictive view which, Buchanan's intentions to the contrary notwithstanding, would *seem* at least to wed us to the *status quo*? Buchanan's reasons are realistic *realpolitik* ones. The majority of secessions, he reminds us, 'have resulted in considerable violence, with attendant large-scale violations of human rights and massive destruction of resources . . .'.[20] Given this experience we should move in the direction of secession with caution and reluctance. There is another realistic reason as well. When a national minority in a state forges itself into a nation and secedes, this will often, indeed typically, result in a *new* national minority within the new state. 'All too often,' as he puts it, 'the formerly persecuted become the persecutors.'[21] Moreover, frequently 'not all members of the seceding group lie within the seceding area, and the result is that those who do not become an even smaller minority and hence even more vulnerable to the discrimination and persecution that fueled the drive for secession in the first place'.[22]

However, it is just here that the restriction in scope concerning arguments for secession is crucial. I only argued about what should be said about secessionist movements in secure liberal democratic societies where all significant segments of the population, including the secessionists, are firmly committed to liberal democratic values. There, secession or not, the 'considerable violence', 'large-scale violations of human rights', 'destruction of resources' cannot obtain, nor could there, so long as the liberal state is functioning as a liberal state should, be persecution of or discrimination against minority groups new or old, large or small. These things are incompatible with *the very idea of liberal democracy*. And suffering from such injustices need not be the motive for secession in such societies. A society or cluster of societies, even in the severe strains of conflict over secession, cannot, if they are stable liberal democratic societies with both sides committed to such values, engage in wide-ranging violence or in massive violations of human rights, destruction of resources, persecution, or discrimination. This, if you will, is true by definition. Liberal democrats could not behave in this way and remain liberal democrats. So we lovers of democracy need not, and should not, have such a restrictive theory of secession for *such societies*, a theory which makes, if the recipe is followed, secession very difficult.

Buchanan could reply that I am engaging in a conventionalist's sulk by appealing to what is in effect an absurd ideal theory distant from the real world. It isn't what is entailed by the very idea of a liberal democracy that counts, but what happens in the real world of liberal democracies: the actually existing liberal democracies. But even there, the clash in Northern Ireland deeply involving Britain aside, liberal democracies have behaved in a manner that conforms rather closely, but not perfectly, to what the very idea of a liberal democracy requires. Consider Norway seceding from Sweden, Iceland from Denmark, the division of Belgium, the expected devolution of Scotland and Wales. Tensions were, and, where the struggle is ongoing, still are high and rhetoric and propaganda flowed or flows, as the case may be, freely, but there was (is) little or no violence, persecution, or human-rights violations and certainly no massive destruction of resources. Moreover, as things calmed (calm) down, relationships of reasonable co-operation came (will come) into being. There neither was nor will there be any undermining of the liberal social order or tearing apart of the liberal social fabric. There was arguably even a strengthening of it. The relationships between Ireland and Britain and Spain and the Basques, however, do not fit this model. But with the latter it is not clear that we have stable liberal democracies with the traditions that go with them. And in the case of the struggle in Northern Ireland, it is not at all clear that all the major players are committed to *liberal* democracy. There is indeed a Protestant majority in Northern Ireland, but what is not clear is that the Ulster Unionists are committed to *liberal* democracy and the same could be said for some of their adversaries. But, even *if* we take these to be cases of liberal democracies slipping into violence and fanaticism in the course of struggles for secession, it remains the case that secessions have peacefully taken place in societies where all the contending forces were more firmly liberal democratic than the ones slipping into violence. There—and they are the more common case in liberal democracies—none of the ill effects predicted by Buchanan followed during or in the wake of secession.

Of course, the existing states in the UN and in the international law establishment will stick together to seek to sustain the idea of the territorial integrity of states, i.e. of the existing states. They are pretty much, in this respect, like an old boys club. And, of course, we do not want a circus of anarchy, but, as a matter of historical fact, states come and go and it is not such a terrible thing if changes occur, particularly if the societies in question are liberal democratic ones with very distinct nations harnessed together rather artificially, and where the flourishing of these nations, or at least the smaller nations, within the umbrella state, could be enhanced by separation and no great harm would accrue to the remainder state by separation. A state should not, and indeed in most instances will not, break up without good reason. And when it does break up there will always be some dislocation and not all the after effects will be good. But some of them will be very good indeed. A nation or a people—which before had been treated as a national minority or worse still like an ethnic group—can now be in control of its own destiny as much (and as little) as any nation-state can be in the modern world.[23] States do come and go, and sometimes they break up, perhaps without the conditions that Remedial Right Only Theories could sanction obtaining, with no great harm resulting, and arguably sometimes with considerable gain, e.g. Iceland from Denmark and Norway from Sweden. If Quebec should secede from Canada, Scotland from Britain, and Wales from Britain, their thoroughly liberal democratic environments staying intact, it is anything but evident that that would not give more people more control over their lives and a fuller self-realization than the continuing of the *status quo*. Moreover, this could obtain without harming others in the remainder state. Quite possibly more good would obtain all around. At the very minimum, this idea should not be rejected out of hand. Perhaps in some of these cases—the case of Wales, for example—it would not be practically feasible. Here we should go case by case. But there are no good grounds for the rejection of the putative right to secession on high moral or legal principle. And, at the very least, none of the dire results that Buchanan believes must just go with secession seem at all to be in the cards in such cases. It looks at least like it is better to go in the more permissive direction of what Buchanan calls Primary Right Theories than in the direction of Remedial Right Only Theories.

Buchanan could respond that what I have said unfairly makes his account sound more statist and authoritarian than it actually is. 'Remedial Right Only Theories,' on his account, 'hold that a general right to secession exists only where the group in question has suffered injustices'—things that plainly and uncontroversially have been taken to be injustices.[24] But, Buchanan insists, the qualification '*general*' is critical here. Remedial Right Only Theory allows that there can be *special* rights to secede if the state from which a distinct nation would secede *grants* it the right to secede or if the constitution of the state includes a right to secede or if 'the agreement by which the state was initially created out of previously independent political units included the implicit or explicit assumption that secession at a later point was permissible'.[25] But this seems to me only marginally less restrictive than a Remedial Right Only Theory would be without such riders. It does not give a people even nearly strong enough rights to self-determination—rights that a liberal democratic society, fully respecting individual autonomy and the right of a people to govern themselves, would want to see instituted. For it is still, on Buchanan's account, the constitution or the authoritative will of the government of the state from which a people wish to secede or prior political arrangements of that state which determines whether the nation which wishes to secede can legitimately secede. It is *not sufficient*, on his account, for secession to be legitimate that a people (1) be genuinely a people (that is, a nation in the sense that Buchanan has defined and I have accepted); (2) in a fair democratic vote (as in a referendum with the issue clearly stated) have a majority of its members vote for secession; (3) for the various guarantees such as protection of minority rights to be firmly in place; and (4) for there to be a negotiated settlement on borders, on the division of the national debt, and on joint assets and the like. These are *necessary* conditions for justified secession and over them Buchanan and I are agreed. But Buchanan wants *additional conditions* as well. On Buchanan's account, the political arrangements of the state from which a nation wishes to secede call the tune. That state ultimately determines what can legitimately be done. That a nation can legitimately secede from it is a matter of *noblesse oblige* on the part of that state. But this runs too strongly against very deep considered judgements about democracy and the self-determination of peoples to be acceptable in a liberal democracy where everyone can be expected to play by the democratic rules of the game, e.g. no repression, violation of human rights, persecution, no negotiating in bad faith, and the like.

Buchanan, I am confident, would continue to resist by claiming that my account is too utopian and does not meet the conditions of *minimal realism* that any even nearly adequate substantive normative political account must meet. 'Primary Right theories', he has remarked, 'are not likely to be adopted by the makers of international law because they authorize the dismemberment [*sic*] of states even when those states are perfectly performing what are generally recognized as the legitimating functions of states.'[26] Because of this, Buchanan has it, Primary Right theories 'represent a direct and profound threat to the territorial integrity of states—even just states'.[27] Because states 'have a *morally legitimate* interest in maintaining their territorial integrity they should oppose Primary Right theory'.[28] I grant that liberal democratic states, including (when they come on stream) socialist liberal democratic states, have a morally legitimate interest in maintaining their territorial integrity. But I would certainly not generalize that to all states. Moreover, I think that Buchanan exaggerates when he says that Primary Right Theory represents a direct and profound threat to the territorial integrity of states. *Theories* seldom have such causal powers. But, even if they did, morally speaking, a people wanting to govern themselves, particularly when their very nationhood is at risk, is standardly, but not invariably, *a morally more stringent claim* than the claim to the territorial integrity of what, at least in effect, is a multinational state. And this is most prominently so when the nations making up the multinational state are not equal partners. This has typically been the case with secessions in liberal democratic societies. Transition has been, and can be expected to be, orderly though not without bitterness and, in both the seceding state and the remainder state, the generally recognized legitimating functions of the state have remained in place. A paradigmatic example is when Iceland seceded from Denmark. Protection of individuals' rights and the stability of their lives remained firmly in place in Iceland. And, after secession no partition took place and the two nations—the Danish and the Icelandic—now both nation-states maintained, without conflict, their respective territorial integrity. Or, more accurately, Iceland's territorial integrity was intact. The Icelandic nation had its homeland securely on the territory it claimed and territorial integrity returned to Denmark as well, as soon as the Nazi occupiers were driven out—something that was quite independent of the issue of Iceland's secession, though many Danes understandably resented that Iceland seceded when Denmark was under occupation. But that does not substantially touch the reasonableness or justifiability of the secession. Moreover, *pace* Buchanan, the 'incentive structure in which it is reasonable for individuals and groups to invest themselves in participating in the fundamental processes of government in a conscientious and cooperative fashion over time' were enhanced in the case of Iceland and not undermined in the case of Denmark.[29] And the case of Iceland and Denmark is not atypical of secession cases which have gone through the works or are in the offing in firmly liberal democratic societies.

Buchanan is right that in societies that are in the ball-park of being just societies, we want the rule of law and the effective enforcement of a legal order to remain intact. But he has his sociology and history wrong. There was no such breakdown with secession in such societies and it is not reasonable to expect it to happen if Scotland secedes from Britain or Quebec from Canada. After all Scotland/Britain and Quebec/Canada are not Serbia/Bosnia or Russia/Chechnya. Buchanan sees, wherever there is secession, the threat of anarchy, violence, and the stamping on people's rights. But this has not happened in firmly liberal democratic societies and it is not plausible to think that it will happen as new cases come on stream, though sometimes some extremist and sensationalist segments of the mass media make it sound as if it might. But that is just irresponsible sensationalist rhetoric. Territorial integrity is a desideratum, but, in liberal democratic societies, it does not have nearly the critical weight that Buchanan assigns to it. His account, his intentions notwithstanding, has a conservative *status quo* effect.

Buchanan has a further *realpolitik* argument against accounts of secession such as my own. Buchanan argues that such accounts 'would encourage even just states to act in ways that would prevent groups from becoming claimants to the right to secede, and this might lead to the perpetration of injustices'.[30] He adds 'Clearly, any state that seeks to avoid its own dissolution would have an incentive to implement policies designed to prevent groups from becoming prosperous enough and politically well-organized enough to satisfy this condition.'[31] A state, he has it, is justified in so acting even if it acts only from the morally legitimate interest of preserving its own territorial integrity.[32]

If we are doing ideal normative political theory, this contention of his is plainly mistaken. Recall we are talking about secession in liberal democracies where the seceding nation will remain a liberal democracy and in seceding it will be determined to play by liberal democracies' rules. The state from which it is seeking to secede indeed has a morally legitimate interest in preserving its own territory, but not at the expense of acting unjustly or in some other morally untoward way. A just state, as Buchanan takes it to be, particularly if it is a liberal democratic one, could not, while remaining just, so act as to perpetrate injustice by so treating a group so as to deliberately prevent them from becoming prosperous or politically organized. This is to treat them in an uncontroversially morally untoward way that runs flat against that for which a liberal democracy stands. In so treating them, there would be a manipulating of people and not even in any paternalistic manner for their own good. There would be with such behaviour no treating its citizens as moral equals, as ends in themselves, and there would be the deliberate harming of some for *reasons of state*. In this, the reasons of state come to a preserving the state's own territorial integrity at the *expense* of some of its citizens and at the expense of liberal values, e.g. autonomy and self-determination. Preserving their own territory is a morally legitimate state function, but not, in the case of a threatened peaceful secession, to do so at the expense of so harming its citizens and not treating them as having equal moral standing. Such behaviour is not morally acceptable in a liberal democracy. This is particularly starkly wrong when the seceding state would be a liberal democratic state respecting rights and the like and where no extensive harm, or in some instances no harm at all, would result to the remainder state as a result of the secession.

It might in turn be replied that while this may be well and good for purely ideal normative theory, it is not for a normative theory in touch with the real world. For such a normative theory, it could be claimed, Buchanan's argument remains intact. In *really existing* liberal democracies, as elsewhere, states will fiercely resist secession and will indeed play dirty pool with actual secessionist movements. And indeed the secessionist movements will respond in kind.

To this I have two responses. First, we still should for contexts such as this construct an ideal normative political theory in terms of what would obtain in a perfectly functioning liberal democracy. Thus, where we have a perspicuous constitution, we can clearly see what we should aim at in such an ideal world. With that clearly before us we can then see what accommodations we need to make to the actually existing political and social realities to get an account which here and now could guide policy while remaining the most morally adequate account available. Secondly, and quite differently, it is not clear that for the rich capitalist liberal democracies, the only firm democracies we have at present, that the Remedial Right Only Theory would be better, or even as good, at deterring such behaviour on the part of states as the Primary Right Theory. True, it would offer an incentive for the state to behave more justly, but, where there is a nation in its midst which wishes to run its own show, being treated as a national minority, or even worse as an ethnic group, there would remain, Remedial Right Only Theory or not, a creditable threat of secession. This being so, the incentive would remain on the part of the state to design policies to prevent those groups from becoming prosperous enough and politically well-organized enough successfully to take a road to secession. But, where secession is at all a threat to the existing state, there would, where the state in question is one of the rich capitalist democracies, be a sizeable number of people normally resident in a distinct territory of that state with a keen sense of nationality. Some of them would be well-educated and reasonably powerful. They, and others as well, would clearly see the state's actions as manipulative and repressive and they would respond by more forcefully struggling against it. And seeing the plain injustice of such repressive measures, some people in the existing state, with another nationality than those struggling to secure their nationhood, or with no sense of nationality (if such there be), will come, as well, to be critical of the state's behaviour. In the real world where nations are treated merely as national minorities or worse still just as ethnic groups, we will get struggle and strife and secessionist movements arising no matter what. We should at least know where the heart of the injustice lies. It lies—as ideal theory makes clear—in putting roadblocks on the way of a nation's right of self-determination when, in seeking self-determination, that nation does not violate the rights of others and is committed to not unfairly treating those it is seceding from or discriminating against its own minorities.

Buchanan also in effect argues that a view such as mine, as any variant of a Primary Right Theory, does not take the reasonable path, usually favoured in international law, of first trying to accommodate the aspirations for autonomy of a nation by urging, and seeking to put into place, arrangements *within* a state for it to become a decentralized federalized state: *a genuinely multinational, but still decentralized, state*. This way of proceeding might very well be able to protect a nation's aspirations for autonomy—remember that autonomy admits of degrees and of kinds—including the having of some form of self-governance, short of nation-state sovereignty, while still keeping the principle, so central in international law and so cherished by states, of the territorial integrity of the state.[33]

If the turn to decentralization, rather than secession, prevents nations from flourishing, and stably sustaining themselves in viable regions, then decentralized federalism is a farce: there is little in the way of a genuine self-governance there. However, if the decentralization is very deep—perhaps the cantonal system of Switzerland is an example—then the nations within such a decentralized federalized state would have a very considerable autonomy and a very considerable amount of self-determination. Then whether to go for decentralization or secession would be a real question and sometimes a decentralized federalism, with its resultant multinational state, could be the best option. But it would not have the obvious superiority that Buchanan thinks it has, for still, under the decentralized federation, a nation would not have as full a self-governance as it would have with outright secession. In making, or trying to make, judgements here, we need, as we do in most complex moral situations, to realize we will need to make trade-offs. In such situations we need to go very carefully case by case, attending to the details. Still, all that notwithstanding, if my previous arguments against Buchanan have even been near to the mark, namely my arguments that secession in liberal democratic societies would not produce the anarchy, instability, repression, and the weakening of the rule of law that Buchanan believes is very likely to go with secession, then it still seems that the scales are likely usually to be tipped in favour of secession. A nation, forming a nation-state, can have full self-governance—full sovereignty—while entering into co-operative arrangements with other nation-states. The Scandinavian Union is a good example. The key thing is that the ethos be stably liberal democratic. In such an ethos secession carries with it no terrors. Peoples will come to have the fullest form of self-governance possible while still being able to enter into co-operative arrangements with each other—arrangements which will enhance the flourishing of the members of each nation.

VII

In his 'What's So Special About Nations?' Buchanan, from a different angle, and even more deeply than in his 'Theories of Secession', attacks Primary

Right theories of secession.[34] If his arguments are sound they completely undermine the account of secession I gave in Sections 1–6. I think, however, perhaps not being able to see the mote in my own eye, that their soundness is very much in question. I shall try to show why.

I have argued that under conditions of modernity membership in a distinctive nation is critical for one's self-identification and self-definition. Where such local identities are not in place people will experience alienation and will not flourish. There is, if you will, that much truth in communitarian claims. Without nationhood involving necessarily self-governance in some form, people will be psychologically crippled or at least seriously disadvantaged. Questioning the wisdom of what he calls the new-found enthusiasm for national self-determination, Buchanan rejects root and branch such conceptions.

Again there are several red herrings to be disposed of. First I, and other Primary Right theorists, agree that the doctrine that every nation should have its own state is both impractical and dangerous. As I have made plain here, and as others have as well, including Buchanan, there are just too many nations for them all, given the territorial space that is available, to have nation-states of their own.[35] Sometimes nations must be part of a multinational state or be in some other way federated or confederated in a larger state and be content with a more limited form of self-governance than they would have if they had a nation-state of their own. But my point was, and is, that this is, in many circumstances at least, a *second best* that sometimes we must—including morally speaking 'must'—just accept. But it is, all the same, a second best and given the deep importance of nationality to people, it, where no harm to others ensues, or everything considered a lesser harm ensues, is usually better for each nation to have its own state. That will be an important ingredient in the maximizing of human flourishing all around and to seeing that the opportunities for it are as fairly distributed as possible. To illustrate, by translating into the concrete, it is too bad that the Israelis and Palestinians do not have separate uncontested territories on which to build their states and fulfil their aspirations for a homeland. But that is not the way things have turned out, so we must settle for something far more complicated and less satisfactory, but which still, given the circumstances, is the best thing to do. And where in other places, say, Lebanon or much of the territory that was once Yugoslavia, where people with distinct national identities are so mixed on the same territory, then the only reasonable and decent thing to do is to go for a genuinely multinational decentralized state. But these are second-best solutions determined by humanly inescapable social realities. Given the critical importance of nationality for people, where *possible without violating the human rights of minorities* or denying the genuine nationality of anyone in favour of another nationality, each nationality should have its own nation-state. Often this cannot be and then, to repeat, we must go for a second best.

There is a second red herring to be put in the fish disposal unit. In trying to counter this new-found enthusiasm for national self-determination, Buchanan rightly asserts that 'the basis for ascribing the right to secede has nothing to do with nationality *as such*'.[36] Sometimes nations have a remedial right to secede but never, he has it, do 'nations *as such* have a right' to secede.[37] What he is very concerned to deny—he returns again and again to his 'as such' conception in his 'What's So Special About Nations?'—is the claim that a nation *as such*—that is, *just in virtue of being a nation*—has a right to some substantial form of self-government. As he puts it in summarizing his position, 'I have not argued that nations do not have rights of self-determination; only that *as such* nations do not.'[38]

But his conception here is also a red herring; nations as such, nationalities as such, have no inherent or intrinsic value. Nationalists need not, and should not, flounder about with such murky notions. And a Primary Right theorist need not and indeed should not assume it or so argue. The thrust of my argument was to show the very crucial instrumental value, strategic instrumental value, of nations and nationality for human self-definition and self-identity and with that for human flourishing. I attach no independent value to nations and none to some *reification* 'a nation as such'—whatever that is—but rather I attach a central instrumental value to nations and nationality in the realization of human good. (This will be explicated in what follows.) Buchanan's arguments against nations *as such* having a right to secede have no critical force. They are diversionary, directed at a strawman.

Buchanan develops something he calls his *equal respect objection* to Primary Right theories. It is directed at the claim 'that nations *as* nations [*sic*] have the right to self-government (short of independent statehood)'.[39] The Primary Right Theory makes a stronger claim as well. But it also makes this weaker claim. I did just that when I argued that there are too many nations for them all to have states of their own so that the only thing nations have an unqualified general right to is *some form* of self-government. It is this weaker claim, which could be true even if the stronger claim is false, that Buchanan's equal respect objection is directed against. His objection is that the singling out of 'nations *as such* [*sic*] for such rights of self-government', while denying them 'to other groups, is morally arbitrary and this arbitrariness violates the principle that persons are to be accorded equal respect'.[40]

For starters, as I have already pointed out, we do not single out nations *as such* for rights of self-government, but we centre on nations because of their key—or, so as not to beg any questions, allegedly key—*instrumental* value in giving people a sense of themselves, something which is essential for their flourishing and their overcoming alienation. That claim *may* be false—something we will subsequently turn to—but, true or false, it is not morally arbitrary. It claims that every human being under conditions of modernity needs for her secure self-realization a sense of nationality and that everyone so situated should have a clear sense of nationality if she is to be able to live a good life. That is why we give such moral weight to considerations of nationality. Rather than a violation of the equal respect for persons principle, it is a consideration that is solidly in accordance with it. Equal respect for persons is one of the underlying deep moral motivations for our commitment to nationality.

However, Buchanan could abandon his nation *as such* talk and still forcefully argue that, only instrumental value or no, too much weight is being given in the Primary Right account to nations and nationality. Even in conditions of modernity, it is not for all people an indispensable part of their self-definition. In support of this, he brings forth a number of empirical considerations that certainly are deserving of careful consideration. Like Jeremy Waldron, he argues that there are many individuals, particularly in societies such as ours, for whom nationality is not nearly as important as defenders of nationality, including defenders of liberal nationalism, have alleged.[41] Why, Buchanan asks, should 'nations—among all the various sources of allegiance and identification—deserve . . . [the] very strong form of political recognition' that nationalists and Primary Right theoreticians accord to them? In facing this very forceful question, it is important, however, to keep in mind that my argument for a general non-remedial right of nations to some form of self-governance was limited in scope. While remaining, at least for the purposes of the present essay, agnostic about societies other than liberal democratic ones, I only argued for my Primary Right account for liberal democratic societies. But, and here is the sting of Buchanan's argument, it is precisely in such societies that claims like mine and David Miller's about the socio-psychological centrality of nationality become problematic. In such societies, Buchanan remarks, where

> there is substantial freedom of religion, of expression, and of association—pluralism will continue, with new groups and new conceptions of the good evolving over time. Some groups will attract or hold members, flourish for a time, then lose their grip on individuals' allegiances and identities, just as individuals will revise and in some cases abandon their initial conceptions of the good.[42]

Moreover, 'there is no uniformity as to the *priorities* persons attach to their multiple identifications. Some think of themselves first as fathers or mothers or members of a family, and second as Swiss, or Americans, or Blacks, or Hispanics, or Christians.'[43] Others have different priorities here. There is no even nearly uniform cultural pattern. And I would add, giving more fuel to Buchanan's fire, that some have these varied allegiances without having the foggiest idea of what priorities they have among them. Others *ambivalently* prioritize things in some contexts one way, and in other contexts prioritize them in another, without a sense of how more globally for themselves coherently to order their priorities. And there are still others, probably less frequent in our societies than the varied people I described above, but still there in considerable numbers, whose 'primary self-identification is religious or political-ideological'.[44] Finally there are some individuals for whom no *single* identification is more important than any other. Being a father, a professor, a socialist, or being French is no more or no less important than any other identification. How in such a world—a world that is our modern world (if you will, 'postmodern world')—can we reasonably privilege nationality? Indeed can we rightly privilege nationality?

The point is, I agree, that generally, special purposes apart, we cannot reasonably so privilege nationality or, for that matter, anything else. The crucial point to see about our modern societies, and perhaps other societies as well, is

> that in pluralistic societies nationality will be only one source of identification and allegiance among others, and for some people it will be of little or no importance relative to other sources of identification and allegiance, whether these are cultural or occupational or religious or political or familial.[45]

Given that cluster of sociological facts (and with Buchanan I take them to be facts), and given such a dynamically pluralistic society to single out nations as the group that is entitled, among the various groups, to self-government is to give, Buchanan has it,

> a public expression of the conviction that allegiances and identities have a single, true rank order of value, with nationality reposing at the summit. So to confer a special right of self-government on those groups that happen to be nations is to devalue all other allegiances and identifications.[46]

But this is incompatible, Buchanan asserts, with the fundamental liberal principle of equal respect for persons. Moreover, it is incompatible with the liberal assumption that governments are to act as the agent of its individual citizens. To give such priority to nations, Buchanan avers, 'is an insult to the equal status of every citizen whose primary identity and allegiance is other than national and to all who have no single primary identity or allegiance'.[47] It is a form of *discrimination* and as such it 'violates the principle of equal respect for persons'.[48] And, to move from individuals to groups, it is also the case that groups other than nations, i.e. other cultural associations, including prominently religious and political-ideological ones, are similarly disadvantaged and in effect discriminated against. Here we have a powerful cluster of considerations that must be soundly met if I am to make out my case for secession and for a liberal nationalism.

VIII

The cluster of considerations we have seen Buchanan raising in the last few pages constitutes, I believe, his strongest challenge to the type of liberal nationalist views on secession that I have articulated. It seems to me that it must be acknowledged that in modern societies, with their dynamic pluralisms, that not all people give that pride of place to the nation that *some* nationalists assume they do and that, as different as people are, it is not at all evident, to put it minimally, that without such strong nationalist identifications all people, or perhaps even most people, will suffer anomie.

Is there any kind of reasonable response that can be made to Buchanan? Buchanan suggests one himself only to set it aside after perfunctorily examining it. But I think there is more to be said for it than he acknowledges. So I shall examine it and extend it a bit. In speaking of a nation we spoke of an *encompassing culture*. What is special about a sense of national-identification is that it functions to encompass our other identities 'by integrating them and making them cohere together'.[49] It is in modern societies the integrating structure for our other identities. One's sense of family, say, is very strong. One's family life is the centre of one's life. But the kind of family that it is; the language it speaks; the practices that constitute its family life; the various roles and expectations that the members of the family have; the way the family makes social bonds; the way they see themselves in relation to others and the like is very much structured by their particular encompassing culture. And that difference is felt and appreciated by the members of these various encompassing cultures. One's encompassing culture is very much hooked up with a sense of who one is, and having a sense of who one is, is vitally important to everyone.

Encompassing culture does not, of course, *equal* language. The Québécois and the French have the same language, but they are different nations, i.e. their encompassing culture is not the same. The same is true for Americans and English-speaking Canadians and for the English and the Scots. But all the same Wittgenstein is on the mark when he says that the forms of language are the forms of life. Language is standardly very closely linked with an encompassing culture and an encompassing culture with language. This comes out very clearly when for a people their language is threatened or thought to be threatened with extinction, displacement, or devaluation. In such circumstances nationalist feelings and nationalist struggles come into being and broadly across the culture among people with various identifications and various more particular allegiances, and from different strata of the society. This seems to me to show how much of an integrating structure nationality (given its intimate, but not invariable, link with language) is in the lives of people. But it does not follow from this (*pace* Buchanan) that it must be, or even should be, at the *summit* of everyone's or even *anyone's* allegiances and identifications or that the nationalist need be claiming that it is. Being a good musician, being a gentle lover, being politically committed, being a kind and caring person, being a good Catholic, being a dedicated teacher, being an active member of one's local community, being a talented dry-fly fisherman, and a myriad of other things may be more important to one, sometimes vastly more important to one, than one's nationality, but, for most of these things at least, one's nationality provides the context of choice for these things and the integrating structure for them. How deeply important it is to one is revealed when one has a sense that one's language, and with that one's encompassing culture, is being threatened. That is too close to the bone—too close to what one is and what one can do—to be accepted with equanimity. But that does not mean that of all one's allegiances and identifications, one's highest one, and the most important one—the one one prizes the most—is one's nationality. Not at all. Sometimes that may be so but certainly not always or even usually. What it does mean is that in modern societies nationality as encompassing (integrating) culture presents the context for the secure realization of the others and that it is one that we would be at a loss to be without.

So there is no question (again *pace* Buchanan) that consistent liberal nationalists, while remaining consistent, can discriminate against people whose scheme of values is such that they do not place nationality on top. To do so would run against everything for which liberalism stands. People, for example, with a weak sense of national identity will not be regarded by liberal nationalists as less valuable members of the community. And it is not true that liberal nationalists just rather unwittingly assume that or that, to be consistent, they must assume it. In a liberal society people are not valued in that hierarchical way and a liberal nationalism far from requiring it repudiates it. But it does see, in most circumstances, the necessity of preserving the cultural life of the nation of which one is a member and, by generalization, liberal nationalists acknowledge that this holds for the people of other nations as well, for this (the having of such an encompassing culture) provides the context of choice where people, any and all people, can carry out their various life plans. In that way it is very like a Rawlsian primary good. Without an encompassing culture—without something which makes us a 'we' so that we can know who we are—we could do none of these things, could carry out none of our life plans; we could have very little, if anything, by way of a conception of the good. Being a good musician is indeed a very international thing, but an individual who is devoted to the task of coming to be a good musician comes to that in a particular culture, the very form it takes for her is not entirely free of that culture, and, more centrally, a person is not only a good musician but a certain kind of person and that carries with it the stamp of a particular encompassing culture. That stamp should not be seen, and standardly is not seen, as an infliction, but as an empowerment and something that gives us a sense of at-homeness in a very big, sometimes alienating, and amazingly diverse world. Each individual needs to have a sense of who she is and that sense carries with it, though that is not all that self-identification carries with it, a sense of being Dutch, Catalonian, Fijian, Faeroese, and the like. Moreover, nationality is politically important here for it provides the context of choice for people in realizing, and indeed in even being able to form, life plans. Thus nationality—people being members of a nation—is vital in politics without for a moment (*pace* Buchanan) implying or involving nation worship. There is no assumption at all for liberal nationalists that nationality is superior to other allegiances and identities. So liberal nationalism with its stress on the importance of nationality certainly does not involve 'an insult to the equal status of every citizen whose primary identity and allegiance is other than national . . .'.[50] A government, where it is decent, acts as the agent of the people: that is for *all* individuals under its jurisdiction. But to do so effectively it must, while continuing to respect individual rights, act to preserve the common encompassing culture of a people without which they, both as individuals and as groups, can do nothing, including, repairing the ship at sea. But in continuously repairing the ship at sea there will be a gradual changing of that encompassing culture. Modern societies will standardly be dynamic pluralisms, but that is perfectly compatible with liberal nationalist projects. Quebec before the quiet revolution was one thing: Quebec after it is something else again.

It is not that this sense of nationality (once more *pace* Buchanan) necessarily, or even typically, provides the primary source of self-identification for everyone. For some their religion will do that, integrating and rendering coherent their identifications and the like. But, as we have seen, religion, in the forms it takes, in its very possibility of arising and being sustainable, requires even more encompassing cultural structures, structures that go with nationality, e.g. we worship in a particular way, in a particular language, and with a whole battery of other practices.

There is no claim among liberal nationalists that nations are morally primary. The privilege that nations have in the political order is strategically instrumental. It is not that in a liberal society that the nation sets the moral order of the life of the people; that it tells them what conceptions of the good are legitimate or what life plans are acceptable. And, while I do argue, as Will Kymlicka does as well, that one's culture provides a meaningful context for choice and that without such a context autonomy is impossible, I do not deny that some people can over time, and usually with considerable effort, change their culture (even their encompassing culture), alter that is, what it is to have a certain nationality, and that with new cultural materials they will have a new, or partly new, meaningful context of choice. And it is a good thing, as Harry Brighouse has put it, that cultures become in that way permeable.[51] Liberal nationalism neither tells a tale of cultural imprisonment nor does it entail it. The (*pace* Jeremy Waldron) extensive changing of one's culture is very rare and for most people it is impossible, but the possibilities of such change are there for some few privileged people. Waldron and Buchanan are right that since this is so for some people there is no need for people to maintain their culture of origin. Indeed, by not doing so or completely doing so, we might even gain a certain kind of hybrid vigour here where people change—more realistically, partially change—their culture. But that does not mean we can be *rootless individuals shorn of all culture*. That is not even intelligible. What a few individuals might become is *polynational*. They could have an amalgam, stable or unstable, of several nationalities. I suspect that as a matter of fact the polynationalism that Waldron speaks of is very rare and so thinking of oneself may well be fraught with self-deception. But I need not, and do not, deny either that it can occur and that, if it occurs, it could be a good thing or that it could yield hybrid vigour. What I deny is that it is common and that it can be an option for anything more than a small élite. And I deny, as well, that it is a necessary condition for being a thoroughgoing cosmopolitan. Thus it seems to me of minor political and sociological significance.

What is so special about nations, among the various groups, that entitles them to political self-government and to a presumption, everything else being equal, to statehood, is that they, in contrast to the other groups, are encompassing (integrating) cultures, located historically on a territory which the people making up the nation regard as their homeland or, if they are in diaspora, aspire to make their homeland and furthermore, and distinctly, that they are of sufficient size and with sufficient infrastructure to be able to carry out the functions of a state. (There is no algorithm here for what constitutes 'sufficient size' or 'sufficient infrastructure'.) Such groups are (a) capable of self-government and (b) should, everything else being equal, be self-governing because that alone provides a thoroughly secure meaningful cultural context of choice which, in turn, is necessary for autonomy and human flourishing. No other group meets both conditions (a) and (b). The First Nations in Canada and the United States provide *problematic* cases. *Perhaps* they do not meet all these conditions, e.g. they *might* lack the size or infrastructure, and thus they might have a right to self-government but not to full self-government, and thus, not to complete sovereignty. Or perhaps in certain circumstances they might have that right, but it might be unwise for them to *exercise* that right. But it would have to be shown, to deny them full self-government, that the infrastructure could not in time be provided by the state in which they now exist or that they were too small or necessarily too weak to be self-governing or that they had no reasonable territorial claim.

IX

There is a final issue to which I shall now turn. It is the claim forcefully made by Buchanan in 'Theories of Secession' that Primary Right theories of secession operate in 'an institutional vacuum' and in doing so provide us with no guidance to the urgently practical question of what *institutional* responses are ethically appropriate to the secessionist challenges that actually face us. Theories, such as my own, the argument goes, are utopian in a bad sense for they can provide little in the way of moral guidance for the institutional reform of our international institutions, including the most formal of these, the international legal system.[52] Again we members of the chattering classes (of which philosophers are charter members) are constructing useless ideal theories that provide no guidance concerning actual questions concerning what is to be done.

In taking a more institutional approach to secession, Buchanan contends that we should distinguish between two questions and come to see that they require quite different answers. They are:

1. Under what conditions does a group have a moral right to secede, independently of any questions of *institutional* morality, and in particular apart from any consideration of international legal institutions and their relationship to moral principles?
2. Under what conditions should a group be recognized as having a right to secede as a matter of international institutional morality, including a morally defensible system of international law?[53]

His dichotomy, I think, like so many dichotomies, is more confusing than helpful. How, for example, is it possible—conceptually possible, if you will—to float free altogether from institutional morality? Morality, as one of our forms of life, is inescapably institutional such that 'a morality free of all institutional constraints' is an oxymoron. But to go on in this vein might be thought to be diversionary nit-picking. So, having registered a protest, I will let Buchanan's dichotomy stand. In doing so I will take him to be saying that persons centring on the first question give scant consideration to how international law works or to the situations and contexts of possibilities of actual states, while those concentrating on the second question put such matters front and centre. Buchanan's claim is that theories of the sort I have articulated, whatever their intuitive attractions, will not continue to remain attractive when serious attempts are made to institutionalize them.[54] 'Moral theorizing about secession', he argues, 'can provide significant guidance for international legal reform only if it coheres with and builds upon the most morally defensible elements of existing law . . .'[55] Primary Right theories, including my own, do not do that. Thus, even if all my previous criticisms of Buchanan's account were sound, still, as he sees it, my own positive account, since it does not meet this institutional constraint, must be woefully inadequate. A normative theory of secession, the argument goes, which does not take such institutional considerations into account from the very beginning, is just spitting into the wind. It is the idle speculations of some free-floating intellectuals.

Again I shall bite Buchanan's bullet and do precisely what Buchanan thinks I should not be doing. I have argued in this chapter for a general moral right to secede under certain conditions and I have spelled out what those conditions are. I have not considered how my normative argument could be incorporated into international legal regimes. And I am not proposing what I am proposing as an international legal right. Rather I am saying that if the general moral right I am claiming for liberal democratic societies is indeed such a moral right, then, whether it is actually incorporated into international legal regimes or not, it should be. As things stand, even if with a morally progressive understanding of the legal order, it cannot be taken as well to be an international legal right, then so be it. Then the international legal system should be altered so that it comes to be in accordance with that moral right. The moral tail should wag the legal dog. We should not tailor moral or normative political theory and our moral principles to square with the legal system.

It is just such a 'high-handed', if not 'high-minded', or, I expect Buchanan would think, 'light-minded', attitude that Buchanan believes to be thoroughly mistaken, and, if taken seriously, dangerously mistaken. It simply ignores, he has it, the decisive role of actually existing states as makers of international law and thus does not have even the minimal realism that any adequate normative theory of secession must have.[56] States, as we have seen Buchanan arguing, and as I have responded to, will stick to a principle of territorial integrity, in the teeth of secessionist challenges and the international legal order will, except over the most extreme cases, and sometimes not even then, where clear and extensive violations of human rights are involved, support the *status quo*, i.e. the firm territorial integrity of the existing system of nation-states. I have argued against the acceptance of this bit of *realpolitik*, as something which is morally acceptable, as something which is just to be taken as an institutional fact of life not to be subject to moral assessment. It yields, to put it minimally, a too restrictive account of the right to secession and, if accepted, firmly commits us to the *status quo*. Where we limit ourselves, as I have, to secession crises that emerge in liberal democratic societies, it makes secession in those societies too difficult in a way that works against or conflicts with the very deepest constitutive normative commitments of liberal democracies. In societies that are *actually such democracies* (if indeed there are any) Primary Right theories, if acted upon, will not create the perverse incentives of which Buchanan speaks and liberal democratic societies, to the extent they are actually genuinely liberal democratic, will not be so intransigently committed to actually existing borders. There will, of course, be a presumption in favour of these borders, not lightly to be set aside, but where secessionist issues come to the fore in such societies there will be no principle of territorial integrity *über alles* (excepting only the most extreme cases where states, against a people, commit extensive and repeated human-rights violations). I have resisted such territorial integrity *über alles*, arguing that it is a morally arbitrary statist conception.

Buchanan realizes such a response can be made and he faces it in the last two pages of his 'Theories of Secession'.[57] He imagines, and I believe rightly so, a Primary Right theorist responding to him by saying that they and Buchanan are simply engaged in two different enterprises. Buchanan, the argument goes, is offering a *non-ideal* institutional theory of the right to secede while the Primary Right theorist is 'offering an *ideal*, but none the less, institutional theory'.[58] Buchanan puts the following words into the Primary Right theorist's mouth. Primary Right theorists 'are thinking institutionally . . . but they are thinking about what international law concerning secession would look like under ideal conditions, where there is perfect compliance with all relevant principles of justice'.[59] In such an ideal world none of the untoward consequences Buchanan mentions concerning secession could arise and so there are no grounds in ideal theory for restricting the right to secede in the way Buchanan does. Ideal theory, being an ideal theory, depicts *counterfactual* conditions, but it does show us what *ideally* would be the best thing and that shows us what we should do our best to approximate in whatever ways are practicable under real life conditions.

Buchanan responds by saying that if Primary Right theories 'are only defensible under the assumption of perfect compliance with all relevant principles of justice, then they are even less useful for our world than my [that is Buchanan's] criticisms heretofore suggest—especially in the absence of a complete set of principles of justice for domestic and international relations'.[60]

This response only seems to have force because Buchanan makes his ideal theory more ideal than the ideal theory that the Primary Right theorist needs to deploy. Buchanan builds into his characterization of ideal theory the condition of 'perfect compliance with all relevant principles of justice' and then rightly points out that that kind of ideal theory is as useless as 'Christian Science' for providing any guidance in the real world at least in the context of theorizing about nationalism. But it is utterly gratuitous to foist that condition of perfect compliance onto the Primary Right theorists' conception of an ideal theory or perhaps onto any useful conception of an ideal theory. The proper characterization of ideal theory, without that dangler, is that we are articulating an ideal theory, for liberal democratic societies, which involves thinking institutionally about what international law concerning secession would look like under ideal conditions, i.e. under conditions in which states in such societies actually behaved in accordance with the moral principles embedded in the very idea of liberal democratic society, e.g. respected human rights, were committed to a principle of equal respect for all persons with its prohibitions on exploitation, manipulation, and the like and is, as well, a society committed to achieving and sustaining autonomy and indeed as much as possible equal autonomy. This is the counterfactual ideal conception of a liberal democratic society that ideal theory assumes. It says nothing about perfect compliance of individuals or about the invariant behaviour of individuals in that ideal conception of a liberal democratic society.

Setting aside for the purposes of ideal-theory construction questions of political sociology, I attempt to give a perspicuous characterization of what an ideal liberal democratic society would be without asking the question whether there is much likelihood that we could have an instantiation of such a society as distinct from something of an approximation of it. I try to give a characterization of what such a society would look like. But nothing need, or should, be said about perfect compliance of individuals or about having 'a complete set of principles of justice for domestic and international relations'. The former is 'Christian Science' and with the latter it is not evident that we even understand what we are asking for in asking for such a 'complete set' of principles of justice. The ideal theory that the Primary Right theorist needs, just as the ideal theory that Buchanan claims for his own, is open-ended and in various ways indeterminate as any reasonable normative account, ideal or non-ideal, must be. As in the body of my chapter my ideal account unfolded, I worked with articulating what it would be for our societies to be liberal democratic societies. With these ideas and ideals and on the assumption that this is the kind of society (deliberately idealized) we are talking about, we can come to say, where such liberal democratic principles are generally being adhered to, when secession would be justified and when it wouldn't be. In doing this we do not need to bring in anything about perfect compliance of individuals or about having a complete set of principles of justice both domestic and mondial.

The world we know is, of course, quite distant from the very idea of a liberal democratic society—our idealized picture. But by clearly seeing what should be done in a world (a counterfactual world) of well-functioning liberal democratic societies, we can, keeping this model firmly in mind, then, taking the hurly-burly real world into account, attend to determining what qualifications would need to be made for a non-ideal theory to articulate the best possible approximation in real life conditions to what is set out in the ideal theory. We would with the non-ideal theory have a theory saying something about what is to be done in real-life situations in the harsh, hard world that we know. There with such a non-ideal theory we would, as well as attending to the ideal theory, have also to consider what John Dewey called the means–ends continuum. That is, we would not only have to consider the ideal, but the probabilities and conditions for attaining or at least approximating what the ideal calls for and the costs of such an attainment. But without the ideal theory we would not know in what direction we should try to go in the correcting of our actually existing institutions. An analogy might help. We know that there cannot be such a thing as a frictionless plane, but understanding the idea of it, the conception itself, we gain some idea of in what direction we would have to go to get as little friction as possible. There is no good reason not to believe that Primary Right theories articulate an ideal theory which provides something to be approximated in real-life situations and in doing that provides something of a useful guide for real-life situations. Where we can see how we can, if we follow certain policies—policies that could actually be put into practice—we will be likely to come as close as possible to the ideals specified in a sound ideal theory, we will then have the best real world account we can gain. Our reach, as the old saw goes, must exceed our grasp—or what is heaven for?

NOTES

1. A. Buchanan *Secession: The Morality of Political Divorce from Fort Sumter to Lithuania and Quebec* (Boulder, Colo.: Westview 1991); id., 'What's So Special About Nations?' in J. Couture, K. Nielsen, and M. Seymour (eds.), *Rethinking Nationalism* (Calgary: University of Calgary Press, 1996), 283–310 and A. Buchanan, 'Theories of Secession', *Philosophy and Public Affairs*, 26/1 (1997), 31–61.
2. Buchanan, *Secession*; id., 'What's So Special About Nations?'; id., 'Theories of Secession'.
3. D. Miller, 'Secession and the Principle of Nationality', Ch. 4 of this volume.
4. Buchanan, 'What's So Special About Nations?'
5. K. Nielsen, 'Cultural Nationalism, Neither Ethnic nor Civic', *Philosophical Forum*, 28/1–2 (1996–7).
6. Ibid. *Purely* 'civic nationalism' is an oxymoron.
7. A. Levine, 'Just Nationalism: The Future of an Illusion', 345–64 and H. Brighouse, 'Against Nationalism', 365–406 in Couture, Nielsen, and Seymour (eds.), *Rethinking Nationalism*.
8. *Pace* M. Nussbaum, 'Patriotism and Cosmopolitanism' and 'Reply' in J. Cohen (ed.), *For Love of Country* (Boston: Beacon Press, 1996), 3–17, 131–44.
9. K. A. Appiah, 'Cosmopolitan Patriots', and B. R. Barber, 'Constitutional Faith', in Cohen (ed.), *For Love of Country*, 21–9, 30–7.
10. G. A. Cohen, *History, Labour and Freedom* (Oxford: Clarendon Press, 1988), 132–54.
11. E. Gellner, *Nations and Nationalism* (Ithaca, NY: Cornell University Press, 1983).
12. Buchanan, *Secession*, 27–80, and id., 'Theories of Secession', 37.
13. Ibid. 37.
14. Ibid.
15. Ibid.
16. Ibid. 40.
17. Ibid.
18. Ibid.
19. Ibid. 44.
20. Ibid. 45–6.

21. Ibid. 45.
22. Ibid.
23. E. J. Hobsbawm, *Nations and Nationalism Since 1780* (Cambridge: Cambridge University Press, 1990).
24. Buchanan, 'Theories of Secession', 36.
25. Ibid.
26. Ibid. 45.
27. Ibid.
28. Ibid. 46.
29. Ibid. 46–7.
30. Ibid. 52.
31. Ibid.
32. Ibid. 53.
33. Buchanan, *Secession*, 53.
34. Id., 'What's So Special About Nations?', 283–310.
35. Id., *Secession*, 48–50.
36. Id., 'What's So Special About Nations?', 298, italics mine.
37. Ibid.
38. Ibid., italics mine.
39. Ibid., italics mine.
40. Ibid.
41. J. Waldron, 'Minority Cultures and the Cosmopolitan Option', *University of Michigan Law Reform*, 25 (1992), 751–93.
42. Buchanan, 'What's So Special About Nations?', 293–4.
43. Ibid.
44. Ibid.
45. Ibid.
46. Ibid.
47. Ibid.
48. Ibid.
49. Ibid.; see also Buchanan, *Secession*, 53.
50. Buchanan, 'What's So Special About Nations?', 295.
51. Brighouse, 'Against Nationalism'.
52. Buchanan, 'Theories of Secession', 33.
53. Ibid. 31–3.
54. Ibid. 32.
55. Ibid.
56. Ibid. 59–60.
57. Ibid. 60–1.
58. Ibid. 60.
59. Ibid.
60. Ibid. 60–1.

7

The Territorial Dimension of Self-Determination

MARGARET MOORE

One of the most serious problems with the principle of self-determination is that this concept, in itself, does not tell us who the peoples are that are entitled to self-determination or the jurisdictional unit that they are entitled to.

There has been some philosophical debate about the problem of indeterminacy as it applies to peoples. Appealing to democratic criteria is not helpful, critics point out, because the idea that we should let the people decide is 'ridiculous because the people cannot decide until somebody decides who are the people'.[1] Some defenders of the idea of national self-determination have tried to define the idea of a people, appealing to a number of objective criteria for delimiting a national group or people. Others have argued that the quest to specify objective criteria is misguided, because there are good reasons to understand a 'nation' or 'people' as *subjectively* defined.[2]

This chapter does not focus on how to define national identity: indeed, like Philpott, I think that, in practice, it is not difficult to discern when there are rival national identities. This chapter focuses on the problem of indeterminacy as it applies to territory. It is concerned, that is, with specifying a jurisdictional unit in which a referendum can be held or in which self-determination can occur. Even if all groups agree on democratic procedures, and agree that there is a primary right to secede, in a fair referendum on secession, as argued for in both Philpott's and Nielsen's chapters, the jurisdictional unit in which a plebiscite is held may be essentially contested. As Brian Barry has argued, in a case where the majority of people in an area want the boundaries of that area to be the boundaries of the state and a minority do not, the 'issue is in effect decided by the choice of the area of the plebiscite'.[3]

The author wishes to thank John Charvet, Avigail Eisenberg, Ian Lustick, John McGarry, David Miller, Wayne Norman, Daniel Philpott, and Paul Viminitz for helpful written comments on an earlier version of this chapter. She also wishes to thank the participants at the Wilfrid Laurier University Critical Perspectives colloquium and the University of Waterloo Department of Philosophy colloquium series for their questions and comments.

The issue of jurisdictional unit first arose in terms of the secession of Ireland from the United Kingdom. Was the appropriate jurisdictional unit the whole of the United Kingdom? Or the island of Ireland? Or should majorities in the historic provinces or local government areas *within* Ireland be able to 'determine' their own destinies? In the contemporary case of Quebec, a referendum on secession may yield different results if the jurisdictional unit is taken to be the whole of Canada, or the province of Quebec, or only part of the province of Quebec.

Secessionist struggles are frequently assessed, from an ethical perspective, in terms of either justice-based or autonomy-based arguments. Justice theorists argue that there is a right to secede only when the secessionist group is a victim of injustice.[4] The right to secede is conceived as a remedial right only, as a right which a group may have to remedy an injustice done to them. Autonomy-based arguments, by contrast, typically ground the right to secede in an argument about the importance of collective identity to individual self-respect and the exercise of autonomy.[5] On this conception, the right to secede is a primary right, which a group has regardless of whether or not it can claim to be unjustly treated. However, both ways of framing the issue—and indeed, the focus on *self*-determination itself—ignore the vital *territorial* dimension of many secessionist claims.

On the autonomy-based argument, put forward by Philpott and others, secession involves the exercise of autonomy by members of a group. The problem with this is that self-rule does not attach itself to individuals, but applies to areas of the globe; the rules thus made govern all those people who reside within the *territory* of the state. Consequently, when a group aspires to self-determination, it is not merely making choices about its own life, or the lives of its members: it is also removing territory under the control of one state and placing it in another (new) state.

On the justice-based argument advanced by Buchanan, the territorial element of secession is at least acknowledged. The fact that secession involves the 'taking of territory' mainly functions as a presumption against secession. He argues that to establish a right to secession, one must demonstrate that the state has lost its right to carry out the agency/trusteeship function implicit in the notion of territorial sovereignty, and that the seceding group has to show that it has had or ought now to have territorial sovereignty. In this way, he grounds the right to secede in a deeper argument about the conditions under which territorial sovereignty can be forfeited or overridden.[6] This treatment of territory does not address the various claims that groups put forward to justify rights to territory, or the problem of indeterminacy as it applies to the unit which might secede. Some of the arguments that he considers, such as the right to protect a culture, suggests that he accepts that justified secession need not take place within existing administrative boundaries; however, most of his discussion seems to assume that secession will take place within the boundaries of a republic/province.

Scholars in international law have identified two distinct conceptions of the principle of self-determination, which are linked to distinct historical periods, and which have different implications for the drawing of boundaries and state control over territory.

Throughout the nineteenth century until the end of the First World War, or even, arguably, until the Second World War, self-determination of peoples was conceived of in ethnic terms. As US President Woodrow Wilson made clear in his famous Fourteen Points speech, he sought to secure 'a fair and just peace' by employing the 'principle of national self-determination'.[7] The 'peoples' entitled to exercise the right to self-determination, according to the Paris Peace Accord of 1919, were ethnic groups, which had become nationally mobilized, and numerous states were carved out of the ruins of the Russian, Ottoman, Austro-Hungarian, and German empires on broadly ethnic lines.

Since the Second World War, however, the self-determination of peoples has been conceived of in a non-ethnic or non-national way. Although the principle of 'self-determination of peoples' is endorsed in Article 1, par. 2 and Article 55 of the United Nations Charter, its elaboration by a whole series of resolutions passed by sovereign states concerned about the destructive effects (for them) of this principle makes it clear that self-determination is not national or ethnic in form: the 'peoples' in question are not ethno-national groups but, rather, (multi-ethnic) people under colonial rule. Whereas self-determination in the Wilsonian period was conceived of as the political independence of ethnic or national communities, in the post-Second World War period, self-determination has been conceived as 'the right of the majority within an accepted political unit to exercise power'[8] and boundaries have been drawn without regard for the linguistic or cultural composition of the state.

Part 1 of this chapter examines the dominant conception of self-determination in the decolonization period, which viewed self-determination as occurring within existing administrative units. I argue that this conception of self-determination is appropriate for multi-ethnic societies in which there is no dominant majority, but that, in other cases, where there is a national majority, it is not appropriate. Specifically, the idea falls to ground on three basic problems. First, in this kind of situation, the principle can be used by the dominant group to increase its territory: typically, the majority group prefers boundaries that include groups (and therefore territory) that do not wish to be included. Second, the boundaries may have initially been drawn haphazardly, or in accordance with a political or ethical conception which is now irrelevant, or drawn to frustrate the aspirations of the people living there. Finally, it does not address the most egregious cases of ethnic domination, namely, situations where minorities have been granted no measure of autonomy or political recognition of their identity by the central state.

Parts 2 and 3 are concerned with the principle of *national* self-determination, which can take many different forms. It can take the form of arguing that there is a religious or historic or cultural claim to territory, and that self-determination of the group should encompass the territory claimed. Part 2 is concerned with arguments of this kind. I argue that these historic or religious or cultural arguments are problematic because based on a biased, internal understanding of the particular group's tradition or history or religion.

These kinds of arguments, and my criticisms of them, can be conceived in the language of the liberal-communitarian debate. The liberal tradition tends to aim at general rules or general principles to adjudicate conflicts, and communitarians tend to argue that such neutral rules are impossible, and that any morality is specific to particular cultures and particular traditions. A dominant theme of this section is that when the conflict is between two national communities, each with its own history, it is not helpful to argue in terms internal to one's own understanding of one's history or tradition. The only alternative to a straightforward appeal to power relations, and the implicit threat of coercion, is to try to find some standpoint which is accessible to all points of view, and to arrive at general rules from this standpoint.

Finally, in Part 3, I consider arguments based on the principle of national self-determination, where that involves a straightforward appeal to democratic self-government along ethnic lines. I argue in favour of the ethnic and democratic understanding of the principle of self-determination in certain cases. This conception is less problematic than the other two, first, because it is generalizable (and the historic or religious or cultural claims to territory are not), and, second, because it is more morally defensible than the administrative boundaries conception of self-determination. This is a controversial result: most conceptions of citizenship reject the ethnic understanding of citizenship on the grounds that it is based on unchosen, ascriptive criteria. However, when ethnic identity is accepted by the people themselves—i.e. it is subjectively defined—and can be translated into democratic terms, it provides the potential for principled adjudication of national conflict. At the end of this section, I discuss the practical limitations of this principle. I argue that, in cases where communities overlap, or where a community has different, overlapping national identities, self-determination cannot take a secessionist form, and more imaginative mechanisms for realizing self-determination must be explored.

1. THE ADMINISTRATIVE BOUNDARY CONCEPTION OF SELF-DETERMINATION

The view that the borders within which self-determination should take place are those of previous administrative units, without regard for the cultural or ethnic identity of the people there, was dominant during the decolonization period in Africa and Asia.

In this part I argue that this principle may be appropriate in states where the linguistic or ethnic groups are so numerous that none can hope to have its own state, but is less compelling in states where there is a dominant national majority group.

As Horowitz has pointed out, in states such as Tanzania, where there are 120 different ethnic groups, it does not make sense to talk about minority rights in the sense in which that term is used in Europe.[9] There is no 'minority' which can be defined in relation to the majority: everyone is in a minority.

In cases where states can be conceived of as the political expression of a particular nation, the principle that self-determination should occur only within the confines of previous administrative boundaries is problematic. In these situations, there is a majority national community which can be said to be able to control the state, using standard democratic (majoritarian) principles. Appealing to the borders of previous administrative units may be a way for the dominant nationality to increase its territory, and yet still be a majority in the state.

This was the case with the German nationalist argument for including the duchy of Schleswig in the German empire in 1848.[10] The duchy of Schleswig had not been part of the Holy Roman Empire or the German Confederation of 1815. Therefore, the German case for its incorporation into Germany had to be based on the ethnic or national principle. But this jeopardized the German case for the entire duchy, because Danes occupied the northern parts. But here, German nationalists appealed to the idea of the duchy as a unified administrative unit, arguing that the territorial integrity of the duchy as a whole must be preserved. The simultaneous appeal to two contradictory principles was of course partly self-serving, but it also indicates genuine confusion as to the criteria for determining the nation that is supposed to be determining itself (is it the ethnic group? Is it shared history in a national homeland?) and therefore what principles should be followed in delimiting frontiers. In this case, it is clear that the German nationalist appeal to previous administrative boundaries helped to secure more territory than any other principle.

The issue at the heart of the 1991–5 conflicts in the former Yugoslavia was that of borders. The Slovenes wanted to redraw the borders of Yugoslavia, by seceding from it. The Croats also appealed to the principle of self-determination, arguing that they should be self-determining within the administrative borders of Croatia that they had inherited from Tito's Yugoslavia, which included a large and geographically concentrated Serb minority, but Croats in Bosnia appealed to the ethnic principle to argue for their inclusion in a Greater Croatia. The Serbs wanted to change the borders that had been drawn for administrative reasons at the end of the Second World War to ensure that all Serbs could be contained in one country. Serbs in the Slavonia and Krajina areas of Croatia and the eastern and northern regions of Bosnia-Hercegovina appealed to the principle of self-determination, defined in ethnic terms, to argue that they should determine their future and join the republic of Serbia.[11]

The question of whether the right to self-determination could be used to change republican boundaries, was posed by Serbia to the Badinter Arbitration Committee on the former Yugoslavia, a committee set up by the EU. Much of the international community—the UN and EU in particular—sought to recognize the self-determination of peoples as members of specific republics, but not as national groups. This view was also expressed by the Badinter Arbitration Committee, which argued that federations could disintegrate along the lines of their constituent units, but that there could be no reconsideration of borders, 'no secessions from secessions'.[12] This was so, even though it was evident that many people living within the republican borders of the former Yugoslavia did not share this view, and even though the dominant motivating force behind the secessions was nationalism, which inevitably created disaffected or alienated minorities which did not share the nationalism which mobilized the dominant ethnic community in the republic.

The justificatory argument for this decision, emphasized in the Badinter Arbitration Committee decision, and by many other critics of the idea of self-determination, was that the 'stability of frontiers' must be maintained. The Committee also justified its decision in terms of the principle of 'territorial integrity', which it described as 'this great principle of peace, indispensable to international stability'.[13] In the case of the former Yugoslavia, however, the external frontier was not disputed. There is also a significant moral distinction between insisting on the inviolability of territorial boundaries against external aggression and insisting on it against the people themselves.

The tension between the ethnic basis of the national movement and the territorial conception of citizenship is also evident in Quebec. The nationalist movement bases its claim to recognition on its distinct (ethnic) character and yet, claims that borders must be determined on the basis of the administrative unit (the province) in the Canadian federation.

The idea of Quebec as a 'distinct society' was adopted in two rounds of (failed) constitutional negotiations designed to accommodate Quebec nationalist aspirations within the Canadian federation. But the 'distinct society' clause referred to the French-speaking Québécois character of the dominant ethnic community in the province. The Greek immigrant in Montreal, the Cree native in northern Quebec, the anglophone in western Montreal or along the Ontario border, had no illusions that the 'distinct socicty' to be celebrated referred to their society. Québécois nationalism, which fuels the secessionist movement, and receives support only from the large community of francophone Québécois, nevertheless appeals to the idea that self-determination should only occur within administrative boundaries: this was the criteria for determining the jurisdictional unit in which a referendum on sovereignty was held, in October 1995, and the basis for drawing boundaries in the event of the secession of Quebec. What this meant, of course, was that the nationalist aspirations of natives in northern Quebec, among others, would be denied. Because natives had been denied political recognition of their distinct identity, had not held any devolved power or institutional recognition of their identity within the Canadian federation, they would now be denied the right to determine their own political future. This points to the first problem with this conception: it fails to address the most egregious cases of group injustices, where people have been denied any kind of recognition of their distinct identity.

In cases where there is a dominant national majority which can control the new state, the administrative boundaries principle does not have the moral force, the legitimating force, to persuade those people whose aspirations are denied by this conception. These are the people who are trapped as minorities in states with a particular dominant national group, a *Staatsvolk*. The territorial conception of citizenship is a means by which the dominant nationality can extend its control and encompass more territory. Furthermore, appealing to this principle in the case of determining boundaries is frequently in tension with the nationalist sentiment which underlies the original secession: secessionist movements are fuelled by nationalism, and are accompanied by rejection of the idea of equal citizenship in a state in which they are not a majority. It is therefore hypocritical that their own self-determination (combined with this idea of administrative boundaries) involves imposing this status on their own minorities.

Another problem with this principle is that previous administrative boundaries frequently have no moral force themselves: they were often drawn in accordance with a moral or political conception which is irrelevant in the current political situation, or they were drawn by the central state in order to facilitate assimilation of the minority or its control by the dominant group. It is therefore hard to see why these boundaries should be cast in stone, as the only unit in which self-determination can take place.

Much attention has been given to the idea of internal boundaries as a mechanism to recognize and grant political space to minorities, and some control over their destiny in a devolved federation. But, just as often, perhaps more often, internal boundaries are drawn either (1) haphazardly, and by ignorance or inattention the aspirations of people are denied; or (2) to deliberately frustrate the aspirations to collective self-government of people who share a sense of common national identity.

Internal boundaries in the former Soviet Union were often drawn in a way which ensured that many members of the titular nation were outside the boundaries of their (titular) republic. In Armenia, for example, Walker Connor argues that including the Nagorno-Karabakh Autonomous Region, with more than 80 per cent Armenian population, in the region of Azerbaijan was advantageous to the central authorities: it helped to ensure links between the Republic's titular ethnic group and the federation as a whole. Also, the resulting friction between ethnic groups—Azeris and Armenians—enabled the centre to more easily control events in these republics.[14]

In Romania, gerrymandering was used to control the Magyar minority, which predominated (1) along the Hungarian-Romanian border and (2) in the centre of the state where they were surrounded by Romanian-dominated territory. Along the border, no devolution of power or recognition was given to the Magyar character of the population. In 1952, the Magyar Autonomous Region was established to give some autonomy to this minority living in the centre of the state, but, following the pro-Budapest uprising in 1956 on the part of the Magyars, two districts with strong Magyar majorities (83.3 per cent and 90.2 per cent) were detached from the region and Romanian-dominated districts were added.[15]

In view of these practices, which are so numerous that only a few examples are mentioned here, it seems wrong that self-determination can take place only within previous administrative boundaries.

2. NATIONAL SELF-DETERMINATION; THE APPEAL TO HISTORICAL, RELIGIOUS, CULTURAL ARGUMENTS TO GROUND RIGHTS TO LAND

Because the idea of a 'nation' carries with it both the idea of membership in the nation and the territory or homeland of the nation, there are two distinct principles which nationalists appeal to in an attempt to draw boundaries: (1) the ethnic principle; and (2) principles based on the shared history, traditions, ethics, or religion of the national community.

This part of the paper examines the various arguments, based on shared history, traditions, or a particular ethical or religious conception, which groups use to claim superior entitlement to land. These kinds of arguments are sometimes used to justify the incorporation of territory by the group aspiring to be self-determining, and to deny the rights of other peoples living on the land to self-determination. They are particularly problematic, I argue, because the justificatory argument for the territory in question is internal to a specific tradition or culture and cannot provide the basis for a neutral adjudication of the conflict.

2.1. Indigenousness: Grounding Superior Entitlement to Land

One of the most widespread and generally recognized arguments for a right to territory is based on a claim to indigenousness. Many groups in all parts of the world claim to be indigenous: Australian Aborigines, New Zealand

Maoris, and native Cree, Ojibway, Cherokee, Mayan and many others in North, South, and Central America; Malays in Malaysia, Fijians in Fiji, Sinhalese in Sri Lanka, the Kannadigas of Karnataka state in India, the Bankonjo and Baamba of Western Uganda, the Kinshasa in Zaire, to name a few.[16] Rights which flow from indigenousness are also becoming generally recognized at the international level. The Draft Declaration on the Rights of Indigenous Peoples, for example, outlines numerous rights which attach, as it were, to indigenous people.

Some of the rights which are claimed by indigenous peoples, and which are recognized internationally, seem no different from minority rights. It does not seem that a special claim to *indigenousness* is necessary to ground the rights; rather, indigenous people are beneficiaries only because many indigenous people are also *minority* groups. For example, the UN Declaration grants rights to practise and transmit distinctive customs and to provide education in the indigenous language.[17] It is hard to see why this should apply solely to indigenous people and not other minorities, especially national minorities, in the state.

Other arguments made in support of rights of indigenous people are premised on considerations of justice. Many indigenous people, particularly in Australia and the Americas, are economically and socially marginalized, with lower literacy rates, lower socio-economic status, and higher mortality rates than the population as a whole. It is therefore an important issue of justice that these people are given rights which are designed to overcome their disadvantage. What is noteworthy is that these rights are based on an equality argument, and do not require any special claim to indigenousness, or first occupancy. They attach to indigenous people only because indigenous people are, in many cases, a disadvantaged group in society.

I do not wish to deny the cogency of various justice-related arguments concerning how modern people should interact with isolated groups of people, and/or people whose culture is threatened, or who have suffered various kinds of historical injustices, or who are economically and socially marginalized. However, the fact that the group in question is indigenous, in the sense of having first occupied the land, is not relevant to these kinds of arguments. The focus of this section of the chapter is on the more problematic claim that indigeneity, in the sense of first occupancy, confers a right to territory.

The claim to territory which flows from indigenousness is primarily a claim to prior, rightful ownership, based on first occupancy. Since the indigenous people are rightful owners of the land, the later arrivals were engaged in 'theft'. This is the suggestion behind the title of a recent book on American history, *Stolen Continents: The 'New World' Through Indian Eyes*[18] and it has intuitive plausibility in so far as everyone can understand the idea that I have a right to evict unwelcome guests from my home, or to set the terms under which guests can stay.

There are four kinds of problems with the argument that indigeneity confers superior entitlement to land, however: first, human migration is and has been extremely common, and it is difficult to argue for differential rights on the basis of descent; second, the actual history of migration is contested; third, the claim of indigenousness depends very much on which geographical context is taken as relevant; and, fourth, even if the argument from indigeneity is accepted, it is not clear that it is sufficient to overcome rival arguments based on equity or equal treatment.

The first problem stems from the fact that human migration is and has been extremely common: many people are descended from people who came from somewhere else and it would be very difficult and problematic to assign (general) rights to people based on where they originated. Where people originated may not bear any relation to where or who they are now. Non-indigenous people may feel a strong attachment to the place where they were born and not to the place where their ancestors came from. An alternative approach would be to give some people rights based on where the originated (indigenous people) but diminished rights to those people whose ancestors at one time migrated. If we take the view that any principle or policy should be capable of being justified to the person or group who does *worst* under it, then, it is not at all clear that it is straightforward to justify an inferior right to people born in a place but descended from one line of people, whereas others, who are descended from a different line of people and who are therefore indigenous may have a superior right.

Moreover, in many cases, the actual history of migrations is more complicated than the assertion of indigenousness might suggest. For example, in Sri Lanka, the Sinhalese claim to be indigenous, but in fact the Vedda people are aboriginal people whose time of arrival in Sri Lanka long preceded that of the Sinhalese. Similarly, in Malaysia, the Malays regard themselves as indigenous people—their name for themselves is Bumiputra (sons of the soil)—but in fact the Orang Asli people were in Malaysia long before the Malays. Indeed, many Chinese families have been in Malaysia longer than some 'Malaysian' families, who in fact arrived relatively recently from Indonesia and assimilated to the Malay identity.[19] Many Sri Lankan Tamils have been in Sri Lanka a thousand years and so are hardly recent immigrants, and sometimes claim to be indigenous to the north and eastern part of Sri Lanka, whereas the Sinhalese take as their relevant political context the whole of the island.[20]

Differing conceptions of the relevant geographical context are important in many cases of claimed indigeneity. In Durban, South Africa, many Africans settled on Indian-owned land after the Second World War. Although the Africans arrived later than the Indians, they regard themselves as indigenous and the Indians as the outsider, because they took the whole continent of Africa as the relevant political context.[21] Similarly in Ireland, some scholars claim that the problem in Northern Ireland is settler–native in origin, and implicit in that conception is the view that the Gaelic-speaking Irish people are indigenous (native) to Ireland, and that the Ulster Protestants, who form a majority in the north-east part of the island, are 'settler' people, who dispossessed the native Irish and oppressed them. However, the relevant geographical context is extremely important to the argument. It is generally accepted that waterways were a main mode of transportation in the past, that settlement tended to occur along waterways, and there was constant movement of people across waterways.[22] This generally accepted fact is used to support the claim that the 'settlers' from Scotland in the seventeenth century actually originated in Ireland, and were returning 'home' to their native land in the seventeenth century.[23] Here, the geographical context is politicized, with some viewing the island as a whole as the relevant (and static) geographical context, and others with a much more fluid conception of context. In this case, as in many others, the claim to indigeneity is subject to pseudo-historical and myth-making processes.

Considerations of equity pose a further complicating factor to claims to entitlement to land. Suppose that one group has a culture based on slash-and-burn agriculture or nomadic herding, which requires thousands of acres to support a small group of people. There are, it would seem, at least two kinds of argument for this group's right to territory. The first is a straightforward argument from indigeneity: this group has lived on this land for hundreds, perhaps thousands of years, and therefore are rightful owners of this land. Another, slightly more sophisticated argument would go like this: the group has a right to its distinctive culture and the culture requires access to and control over a large amount of territory. But even this argument, which in itself, might be valid, is surely subject to other considerations. Suppose, for example, that a non-indigenous group has been stripped of its territory, or its territory has become so degraded or is so resource-poor that it cannot support them, and the thousands of acres reserved for indigenous people is more than sufficient to feed and support all the people, especially if the land was used in a different way. This is not an argument from efficiency: the claim here is not a Lockian one that efficiency grants entitlement; it is merely suggesting that considerations of equity may override such land entitlement. This is particularly the case once the outsider group has lived on the territory for many years, perhaps even many generations; in this case, it does not seem fair to grant some people superior rights and others inferior rights to the territory on the basis of the line of descent of the two groups.

In conclusion, then, while the claim to indigeneity does suggest an historical attachment to the land, it does not generate a superior right to a particular territory that can be used, unproblematically, as the basis for defining the jurisdiction unit in which self-determination takes place. The four serious difficulties outlined above make this a very weak argument for denying the right of another (non-indigenous) group to self-determination, by denying them the territory within which self-determination can take place.

2.2. Historical Claims to Territory

A second, and closely related form of justification for a right to territory is based on *historic* entitlement. Thus, some Jews maintain their right to 'Eretz Yisrael' (pre-1967 Israel and the West Bank) on the grounds that their ancestors inhabited the territory two thousand years ago, although some also stress a continued Jewish presence in the area.[24] One of the justifications for Nazi Germany's *lebensraum* policies was the view that Germans had a 'mission' to 'resettle' territories once occupied by ancient Germanic tribes.[25] After the Second World War and the defeat of Germany, the Polish government argued that they were entitled not only to the area recently colonized by Germans since 1939, but also the provinces of Pomerania, Silesia, and East Prussia, all east of the Oder–Neisse line, on the grounds that these had originally been Slav lands (prior to the thirteenth century).[26]

One difficulty with this kind of justification for territory is that it is essentially contested, as is the claim to indigenousness, and subject to myth-making. However, the most serious problem is that it is impossible to develop an adequate principle or mechanism to adjudicate such rival claims to territory: it depends on where in history one starts, and whose history one accepts. Appealing to historical links can legitimize claims to vast areas and many different irredentist claims. In an absurd, but revealing, example, James A. Graff points out that 'one could press claim to all of the Levant, including the Holy Land and most of North Africa, in the name of the Greek Orthodox people, insisting on a "return" to territory that was the homeland for people of that faith community during centuries of Byzantine rule.'[27] Why should Jews (or Poles or Greeks) be given ownership rights to territory they occupied several centuries ago, rather than those whose ancestors were there before them, or after them?

This is an issue of contemporary importance. The Greek nationalist claim to the mainly Slavic-speaking Macedonia in the former Yugoslavia, and the Serb occupation of the Kosovo region, which has a 90 per cent Albanian population are both justified on historic grounds. Yet, on the view I've been arguing here, historic ties are insufficient to generate rights to control the territory. Historic monuments and national sites can, at best, legitimize a prima-facie case in favour of rights of *access* but not to control over the territory (and therefore the people) in which these national sites are located.

2.3. Chosen People and Divine Rights to Land

A quite different kind of claim to territory arises from a conception that a certain group of people is entrusted with a divine mission: they are God's chosen people; and they were granted the land by God.

The idea of a covenant between God and His chosen people is central to Judaism, and the idea that the terms of the covenant involved a divine right to land has been used, politically, by certain elements in Israel. A similar argument, based on the same passages in the Bible, but, of course, with a different view of who constituted the chosen people, was employed by early American colonists in the New World, Dutch settlers in South Africa, and Protestants in Ireland.[28]

There are some key passages in the Bible[29] which suggest that land is a crucial element in the covenant between God and His chosen people. At Genesis 17: 8 Abraham agrees to obey God's laws and worship him and in exchange he receives a promise of land. Specifically, God promises: 'And I will give unto Thee, and to thy seed after thee, the land wherein thou art a stranger, all the land of Canaan, for an everlasting possession.' The promise of land in exchange for the covenant is repeated to Moses, but it is explicitly extended not just to Abraham and his descendants, but to all people who worship God according to the ways God has outlined. God reminds Moses: 'And I am come down to deliver them out of the land of the Egyptians, and to bring them up out of that land unto a good land and a large, unto a land flowing with milk and honey' (Exodus 3: 8). There are many references pin-pointing the exact location of this land, references to Jerusalem as the centre of Judea, the centre of the earth, and as a sacred place.[30]

The importance of the territorial element in Judaism itself has been the subject of much dispute amongst Biblical scholars,[31] but there is little doubt of the *political* importance of the belief that the land is given to the Jews by divine right.

Israeli Jews in the militant Kach movement refer to these passages to justify Israeli settlement in Eretz Yisrael (pre-1967 Israel and the West Bank). The fact that the West Bank is 95 per cent Palestinian Arab, that these people overwhelmingly resist the settlement, that the rules surrounding the dispossession of Palestinians are biased and unjust, are not relevant if the land belongs to the Jews by divine right. On that conception, the Palestinians are trespassers anyway.

The colonization of the Americas, and the accompanying dispossession of native Indian tribes, was justified in a variety of ways, but one prominent form of justification involved the idea that it was God's will that Christian people tame the wilderness. Indeed, early colonists argued that God was making a place for his Christian children there by unleashing destructive plagues (of Biblical proportions) on the native peoples, and they noted that these pestilences seemed to afflict Indians selectively. Not all was left to divine action, however: the settlers occasionally helped God to secure His plan, by deliberately sending blankets infected by smallpox.[32]

The development of doctrine in the Presbyterian and Dutch Reformed Church by Ulster Scots in Northern Ireland and the Afrikaners, respectively, also drew on the idea of a chosen people with a divine mission. In both cases, the integrity and purity of the chosen people was maintained by endogamy, and the territory was justified in terms of divine sanction, with the Ulster Scots and Afrikaner Volk carrying the torch of Christian civilization to backward Catholics and heathens, respectively.[33]

The basic problem with all these justifications, of course, is that they establish the 'right' of a particular (chosen) people to particular pieces of land only in the eyes of those who accept (a) the authoritativeness of the text; and (b) the particular interpretation of the text being advanced. There are different authoritative texts and, even when all accept the same text as authoritative—the Bible, say, or the Koran—there are contested interpretations of the same text. Appeal to divine sanction, therefore, cannot provide a basis for a rule or mechanism to adjudicate conflicts between people over land, since all parties to the conflict could base their rights to the same piece of land on divine sanction. What is needed, therefore, is some impartial standpoint—impartial not in the sense of being outside all morality, but in the sense that the standpoint or basis of the argument is not acceptable from one position alone, but is comprehensible and accessible to all points of view.

2.4. The Argument from Efficiency; Superior Culture Claims

A fourth argument that has been employed, and is still sometimes employed, to justify rights to territory is based on the moral importance of efficiency. This argument was used to justify the taking of land in the New World and has been used, and is still used, to justify rights to land in Israel, and, implicitly, to deny rights to land and the right to self-determination within that territory to Palestinians.

In the sixteenth century, Sir Thomas More argued that land could justifiably be taken from 'any people [who] holdeth a piece of ground void and vacant to no good or profitable use'.[34] This conception was applied to the colonization of the Americas by John Winthrop, the first governor of Massachusetts Bay Colony, just prior to the Great Migration to Massachusetts in the 1630s. He anticipated the possible objection that 'we have noe warrant to enter upon that Land which hath beene soe longe possessed by others' with an argument appealing to efficiency, and which anticipated Locke's more famous justification of private property in the *Second Treatise of Government.* Winthrop wrote:

> That which lies common, and hath never beene replenished or subdued is free to any that possesse and improve it: For God hath given to the sonnes of men a double right to the earth; theire is a naturall right, and a Civill Right. The first right was naturall when men held the earth in common every man sowing and feeding where he pleased: then as men and theire Cattell encreased they appropriated certaine parcells of Grownde by inclosing and peculiar manuerance, and this in time gatte them a Civill

right . . . As for the Natives in New England, they inclose noe Land, neither have any settled habytation, nor any tame Cattell to improve the Land by, and soe have noe other but a Naturall Right to those Countries, soe if we leave them sufficient for their use, we may lawfully take the rest, there being more than enough for them and us.[35]

Locke, in *The Second Treatise of Government*, argued that the right to property was based on the person's right to his body; that the person can appropriate things in the external world through labour and that these became his goods as long as he leaves as much and as good for others. Like Winthrop, Locke justifies a certain form of (private) property-holding, for he goes on to argue that enclosure is more efficient than holding the land in common, and that, while it might seem to be taking land away from others (because others cannot use it), it is possible to produce more efficiently on private property and so, effectively, 'leave as much and as good for others'.

In these passages, the right to land, to territory was premised on a particular conception of land use, in which land is improved and transformed through private ownership. The native conception of the appropriate relationship between land and people, which involved communal holdings, and emphasized a sustainable relationship between people and resources, was not even seen as 'use'.

In the first half of the twentieth century, when early Zionists began to settle in Israel, the efficient use of the land argument was used to justify rights to land. Although some early Zionists claimed that there were few people or no people in Palestine, the evidence is that this wasn't meant literally—for the demographic reality was unavoidable and indeed of great concern to early Zionist leaders—but, rather, that there were no people using the land. Zangwill, a leading Zionist, made this point well:

If Lord Shaftesbury was literally inexact in describing Palestine as a country without people, he was essentially correct, for there is no Arab people living in intimate fusion with the country, utilising its resources and stamping it with characteristic impress: there is at best an Arab encampment.[36]

The same basic idea is still expressed today, even in doveish circles, although less crudely. In 1986, the then-Prime Minister of Israel, Shimon Peres, described the early period of Zionist settlement in an article in the *New York Times*:

The land to which they came, while indeed the Holy Land, was desolate and uninviting; a land that had been laid waste, thirsty for water, filled with swamps and malaria, lacking in natural resources. And in the land itself there lived another people; a people who neglected the land, but who lived on it.[37]

Implicit in this description is that the people who lived on the land, the unnamed Palestinians, were not attached to it: they had 'laid waste' the land, neglected it, and so it seems, they had no rights to it.

The basic idea here—that land should be allocated to those who use it most efficiently—has two basic problems: (1) lack of generalizability; and (2) that the consequences of implementing the rule would be disastrous. The first difficulty is that what counts as efficient use depends on the values of the people and their vision of desirable land use. It is impossible to assess one culture's 'efficiency' against another if they value different things, if one culture values low density and open spaces, for example, while another values a more intensive, transformative pattern of land use.[38]

The second, equally serious problem is that if this was adopted as a general principle or rule, it would not provide a secure basis for control over territory, but would lead to an unstable and counter-productive situation where borders are constantly being redrawn. If applied generally, this rule would seem to dictate that land rights should be conferred according to who is most effective in exploiting the resources. Because this would change over time, the rights to particular pieces of land would also shift. Changing technology, changing land-use patterns and demographic shifts would lead to a situation in which one area of land, previously best exploited by one group, now might be used more efficiently by another group; thus, one group would lose their rights to the land and another would gain rights. Because efficiency (or expected efficiency) is the foundation for rights, it would follow that the actual amount allotted to different groups would constantly change. Not only might this be undesirable in itself, causing instability and insecurity (and perhaps even less efficient use of the land because of this) but there would be a greater likelihood of conflict over the terms of the transfer, especially given that there are difficulties measuring efficiency across cultures.[39]

The problem with all these justifications for territory is that they only make sense for people who accept the particular version of history, the particular norms regarding efficiency or appropriate land use, or who accept the same sacred text, and the same interpretation of the sacred text. This is very unlikely to happen in cases where two national groups conflict, because, frequently, each has its own interpretation of history, its own shared memories, and culture, which define it as a distinct national group. Indigenousness is perhaps less contested, because the idea that prior ownership confers title to land is at least accessible to everyone. However, it is a difficult principle to generalize, because it will fail to confer rights on the vast majority of people, whose ancestors at one time migrated. It is also difficult to justify inferior rights to people who have lived for many generations in the territory, but whose ancestors may have, sometime in the past, migrated to the area.

Many of these claims to territory, of course, are intended only to confer special rights *within* a society. My concern in this section is to analyse these arguments in so far as they bear on claims to territory in self-determination cases. The issue of rightful ownership over territory is sometimes used in support of a definition of the appropriate jurisdictional unit for a referendum on secession, or territory within which self-determination can take place. The argument in this section suggests that these attempts to deny the rights of others on the basis of internal justifications are extremely problematic. Indeed, like the administrative boundaries conception (in the circumstances outlined in Part 1), these arguments are aggrandizing in the sense that they support an expansive definition of territory within which the people are to determine themselves, and fail to recognize the right of other (unchosen, non-indigenous, unhistoric) people to be self-determining.

3. NATIONAL SELF-DETERMINATION; THE ETHNIC AND DEMOCRATIC PRINCIPLE

In many cases, of course, the national group resides, as an overwhelming majority, on land which it claims or thinks of as its historic territory. In that case, there is no need for would-be secessionists to demonstrate a special claim to the seceding territory. Regulation of territory which they view as theirs is implicit in the status of a self-determining, self-governing people.

On this view, any territorially concentrated national group—any group of people who identify themselves as belonging to a particular nation—has a right to self-determination. This follows not only from the moral importance of autonomy, which underlies both democratic and liberal justice theories, but from the recognition that, in some cases, this is appropriate given that there are distinct political communities.

This approach applies best to self-determination for groups which accept democratic procedures. If it is clear, in a fair democratic plebiscite or series of plebiscites, that the vast majority of people in a particular national group aspire to be self-determining, then, this constitutes a compelling moral argument for rearranging the institutional structure of the state, or perhaps allowing the secession of part of the state, to satisfy this aspiration.

In some cases, the ethnic and democratic understanding of the principle of national self-determination enjoys distinct advantages over the others. Specifically, this principle is capable of being generalized. One important idea underlying the principle of national self-determination is the recognition of people's collective (national) identity, and this recognition as a nation is given by other nations. It can, of course, take an aggrandizing form, just as the individual liberty principle can take an aggrandizing form. I might think that the exercise of my individual freedom is more important than anyone else's freedom, and I might seek whatever I want, without regard for the interests of others. But liberals recognize that the unrestrained pursuit of individual liberty would be destabilizing, and could only be secured at the expense of other people's liberty. The solution to this problem has been the equal liberty principle: each person pursues his/her liberty as long as she respects the rights or legitimate interests of others. This is the essence of Mill's harm principle. Similarly, nationalism does not need to take an aggrandizing form: indeed, the only stable, coherent legitimate nationalism is one which recognizes, not only the rights of one's own nation to self-determination (whatever form that takes) but also the equal rights of other nations. This is a logical point: if my feelings of communal identity, and aspirations to have political institutions expressive of that identity are important to me, and justify my claims to self-determination, they might be important to others who belong to a different nation and seek rights to self-determination. And it is this logical, generalizable principle which is denied by the justificatory arguments internal to traditions, examined in Part 2, and denied also by the argument, examined in Part 1, that self-determination can only occur within the boundaries of existing administrative units. It is denied, more precisely, when nations, secure in their institutional identity, forming a majority in their boundaries, but encapsulating minorities whose identities are not recognized, appeal to the principle that self-determination can only occur within the boundaries of existing administrative units. That principle makes sense when there is political space but no conception of nationhood, as in Africa during the decolonization period: in that case, the state begins the process of nation-building. But when the nation is politically mobilized, this conception serves to deny institutional expression to that identity.

There are two serious practical limitations with this approach, however, and both bear on its general applicability as a mechanism to regulate national conflict. The first difficulty is that this approach presupposes a distinction between (1) dissenters and (2) minorities, which, in some cases, is problematic. In theory, the distinction is clear: dissenters are members of the national group who dissent from, or disagree with, the decision to secede, or seek self-determination; minorities are members of other national groups.[40]

In severely divided societies, voting tends to follow ethnic or national lines: members of group A seek self-determination; members of group B seek to repress it. Elections in Bosnia-Hercegovina and Croatia both reflected this kind of serious division. Serbs in Bosnia-Hercegovina overwhelmingly opposed the secession of Bosnia-Hercegovina from the Yugoslavian federation; Bosnian Muslims overwhelmingly supported it.[41] Similarly, in Northern Ireland, Catholics overwhelmingly vote for (Irish) nationalist parties; Protestants vote for (British) unionist parties. The non-sectarian Alliance Party rarely gets more than 10 per cent of the vote.[42] In these situations, taking national identity as the raw material from which to demarcate boundaries makes sense because each of the groups is relatively homogeneous in terms of national identity. Of course, there might be tactical differences about how to pursue self-determination or precisely what this involves (secession? devolved power within a federation?). Nevertheless, the distinction between dissenters and minorities is not problematic in this case, because the group identity which it presupposes is accepted by the people themselves.

In less seriously divided societies, such as Quebec, however, the situation is far more complex. Non-francophone Quebeckers are overwhelmingly opposed to Quebec secession: in the October, 1995 referendum on sovereignty, Cree, Inuit, and Montagnais voted against Quebec sovereignty in numbers suggestive of a very uniform attitude on this issue (96, 95, 99 per cent respectively);[43] anglophones and allophones in western Montreal, too, were united against sovereignty (90 per cent voted 'No').[44] But it does not follow from this that we can treat natives, anglophones, and francophones as distinct national groups, because some francophone Québécois do seem to have a Canadian national identity, or, at least, think that being Canadian is not incompatible with being Québécois. This was reflected in the referendum results: the francophone Québécois vote was 60 per cent in favour of sovereignty; 40 per cent against.[45]

In this situation, counting the francophone Québécois who votes 'No' as a dissenter means that his vote is treated differently from the 'No' votes of Quebec natives or anglophones. This is problematic, because it tends to treat ethnicity as co-extensive with nationality. Although they are obviously fluid, in the sense that ethnic groups, residing on their ethnic 'homeland', can usually be mobilized along national lines, they are not identical, as the case of the francophone Québécois who has a Canadian national identity makes clear.

Other groups also have ambivalent national identities. In a 1982 opinion survey, taken in Catalonia, 26 per cent of the population considered itself Catalan; 40 per cent felt dual Catalan-Spanish identity; and 30 per cent felt primarily Spanish.[46] Similar results have been found in Scotland, where many have dual (Scottish-British) identities. As in Quebec, the distinction between dissenters and minorities is problematic, because the national identity of the members of the group is ambivalent. In such a situation, the best solution is to find a constitutional arrangement—such as devolution of power or asymmetrical federalism—which gives both identities appropriate recognition and does not affirm one identity at the cost of denying the other.[47]

In seriously divided societies, while the ethnic principle might be conceptually unproblematic, it still faces an important practical obstacle. In many cases national groups are not territorially concentrated. Frequently, two national communities are intermingled and the self-determination of one national group may threaten to compromise the self-determination of another national group. Partitionist solutions are often inappropriate, because there is sometimes no way of drawing boundaries which would result in a homogeneous political community (at least not without massive ethnic cleansing).

But it is important to emphasize that this is not a conceptual problem with the idea of self-determination conceived in ethnic or national terms: it is a practical problem. It indicates the limits of partitionist or secessionist solutions to national conflict. In these cases, which are easy to identify, the equal recognition of different national identities must be achieved by different, and more imaginative means.

The secession of Slovenia from the former Yugoslavia, for example, was fairly straightforward: Slovenia was relatively homogeneous (about 90 per cent Slovenian) and its 10 per cent Croat/Serb/Yugoslav minority was not geographically concentrated. It made sense, therefore, to accommodate this minority through a system of minority rights within an independent Slovenia.

In Bosnia-Hercegovina, by contrast, the situation was quite different. According to the 1991 census, Bosnia-Hercegovina was comprised of 44 per cent Slav Muslim, 31 per cent Serb, 17 per cent Croat, and 5 per cent Yugoslav (in practice, people in, or children of, mixed marriages). It had no dominant national group and no neat dividing line to fragment along, because, with the exception of Croat-populated western Hercegovina, the different national groups were thoroughly mixed.[48] In Bosnia, then, there was no way of drawing boundaries which would have 'solved' the nationalities problem by separating antagonistic groups. Nevertheless, acceptance of the principle of national self-determination, defined in ethnic or national terms, has important practical and moral policy implications for such a situation. Recognition of (1) the importance and legitimacy of national ties, combined with (2) the view that internal borders are not inviolable, but must have demonstrated democratic legitimacy, would have led the international community to adopt a different policy with regard to Bosnia. The West would not have been eager to extend international recognition to a civic Bosnian state, in which all people have rights as individuals. The obvious route, following from acceptance of these two principles, would have been negotiations with all national groups to arrive at a solution which recognizes the equal right of all nationalities.

An application of the principle of national self-determination, according to which boundaries are delineated according to national groups, would have resulted in an unsatisfactory settlement, a patchwork of enclaves, or pockets of sovereign units throughout the republic. Where communities are intermingled in this way, and the domino threat is genuine, different mechanisms for realizing the fundamental principle of giving equal recognition to national identities are necessary. One possible arrangement, among others, would have been a confederal state, in which the constituent units are subject to a unifying treaty for certain purposes, but retain their individual sovereignty and international identity for other purposes.[49] This would have enabled the Serb and Croat national groups to develop links with their co-nationals in Serbia and Croatia, without violating the equal right of the Bosnian Muslims to determine their own group's future.

In short, territorial boundaries should be demarcated according to the national principle only in cases where (1) the group is nationally mobilized, and members overwhelmingly share the same national identity; and (2) the two national groups are not commingled on the same territory.[50] In cases where two national groups are interspersed in the same territory, self-determination cannot take a secessionist (territorial) form, but must be achieved by more complex arrangements.

4. CONCLUSION

In this chapter, I have examined three different principles for demarcating boundaries in which self-determination can occur, and, implicitly, analysing the arguments that groups deploy to justify rights over, or control over, territory.

I have argued that the principle that self-determination can occur only within existing administrative units is inappropriate if the unit in question is dominated by a particular ethno-national majority but also incorporates concentrated minorities who do not share this identity.

The principle of national self-determination is sufficiently vague that nationalists can appeal to two distinct principles under this rubric: they can appeal to the particular nation's history, or religion, or ethical conception to justify rights to territory; or they can appeal to a democratic majority amongst people who see themselves as belonging to a particular nation, if that group is territorially concentrated. I have argued that the first kind of justification is inadequate because it is only acceptable to people who accept that particular version of history, or religion, or ethical value, and so should not be used to deny the rights of other groups to exercise their right to self-determination. The appeal to democratic majorities within nations is less problematic, because it is, in principle, open to all nations. Sometimes, of course, the claim that nations make on their own behalf, to protect and determine their own culture and their political future, and have these recognized in political institutions, will fall short of independent statehood: not all nations seek outright independence (in cases where the group has ambivalent, or overlapping national identities); and, even for those who do, their claims cannot always be met, because doing so will compromise the (equally) good claims of another national group. But in the latter case, it is, at least in principle, open to everyone to recognize cases where the national group is not territorially concentrated, and more imaginative political forms are necessary to give the group control over its destiny, and to give expression to its shared national identity.

NOTES

1. I. Jennings, *The Approach to Self-Government* (Cambridge: Cambridge University Press, 1956), 56.
2. D. Philpott, 'In Defense of Self-Determination', *Ethics*, 105 (1995), 365.

3. B. Barry, 'Self-Government Revisited', *Democracy and Power* (Oxford: Clarendon Press, 1991), 162.
4. Examples of this approach are: A. Buchanan, *Secession: The Morality of Political Divorce from Fort Sumter to Lithuania and Quebec* (Boulder, Colo.: Westview, 1991); W. Norman, 'The Ethics of Secession as the Regulation of Secessionist Politics', Ch. 3 of this volume.
5. Examples of this approach are: Philpott, 'In Defence of Self-Determination'; K. Nielsen, 'Secession: The Case of Quebec', *Journal of Applied Philosophy*, 10 (1993).
6. Buchanan, *Secession*, 108–11, 113–14.
7. This was articulated in US President Woodrow Wilson's 'Fourteen Points' speech of 8 Jan. 1918. This is quoted in A. de Zayas, *A Terrible Revenge: The Ethnic Cleansing of the East European Germans, 1944–1950* (New York: St Martin's Press, 1986), 14.
8. R. Higgins, *The Development of International Law through the Political Organs of the United Nations* (Oxford: Oxford University Press, 1963), 103–5. Quoted in R. Emerson, 'Self-Determination', *American Journal of International Law*, 65/3 (1971), 464.
9. D. L. Horowitz, *Ethnic Groups in Conflict* (Berkeley: University of California, 1985), 37.
10. See O. Pflanze, 'Characteristics of Nationalism in Europe: 1848–1871', *Review of Politics*, 28 (1966), 129–43.
11. For an excellent discussion of this, see M. Crnobrnja, *The Yugoslav Drama* (Montreal and Kingston: McGill-Queen's University Press, 1994), 234.
12. D. L. Horowitz, 'Self-Determination: Politics, Philosophy, and Law', Ch. 9 of this volume.
13. A. Pellet, 'The Opinions of the Badinter Arbitration Committee: A Second Breath for the Self-Determination of Peoples', *European Journal of International Law*, 3 (1992), 184.
14. W. Connor, *The National Question in Marxist-Leninist Theory and Strategy* (Princeton: Princeton University Press, 1984), 368.
15. Connor, *The National Question*, 340.
16. Horowitz, *Ethnic Groups in Conflict*, 202.
17. Draft Declaration on the Rights of Indigenous Peoples, Articles 12–16. Quoted in D. Horowitz, 'Self-Determination: Politics, Philosophy and Law'.
18. R. Wright, *Stolen Continents: The 'New World' Through Indian Eyes* (Harmondsworth: Penguin, 1992).
19. Horowitz, *Ethnic Groups in Conflict*, 203.
20. Ibid.
21. Ibid.
22. This point is made in D. H. Akenson, *God's People: Covenant and Land in South Africa, Israel, and Ulster* (Montreal and Kingston: McGill-Queen's University Press, 1991), 105–6 for the period prior to the eighteenth century.
23. I. Adamson, *Cruthin: The Ancient Kindred* (Newtownards: Nos-mada Books, 1974).
24. J. McGarry, 'Ethnic Cleansing: Forced Expulsion as a Method of Ethnic Conflict Regulation', paper presented at the meeting of Canadian Political Science Association, 2 June 1996, 9.

25. M. Burleigh and W. Wippermann, *The Racial State: Germany 1933–1945* (Cambridge: Cambridge University Press, 1991), 62.
26. A. M. deZayas, *Nemesis At.Potsdam: The Expulsion of the Germans from the East* (Lincoln: University of Nebraska Press, 1989), 168–72. Quoted in McGarry, 'Ethnic Cleansing: Forced Expulsion as a Method of Ethnic Conflict Regulation', 9.
27. J. A. Graff, 'Human Rights, Peoples, and Self-Determination', in J. Baker (ed.), *Group Rights* (Toronto: University of Toronto Press, 1994), 211.
28. See generally Akenson, *God's Peoples.*
29. The first five books of the scriptures—the Torah, the Books of Moses—are nearly identical in both the Jewish and Christian religions, although arranged in slightly different order and with different titles.
30. See Ezekiel 38: 12. For a discussion of this, see W. D. Dawes, *The Territorial Dimension of Judaism* (Minneapolis: Fortress Press, 1991), 1–12.
31. Ibid. 14.
32. D. E. Stannard, *American Holocaust* (New York: Oxford University Press, 1993), 239.
33. See Akenson, *God's Peoples*, 120–1, 208–10.
34. Stannard, *American Holocaust*, 233.
35. J. Winthrop, 'Reasons to be Considered, and Objections with Answers', repr. in Edmund S. Morgan (ed.), *The Founding of Massachusetts: Historians and the Sources* (Indianapolis: Bobbs-Merrill, 1964). Quoted in Stannard, *American Holocaust*, 235–6.
36. Quoted in N. Masalha, *Expulsion of the Palestinians: The Concept of 'Transfer' in Zionist Political Thought 1882–1948* (Washington: Institute for Palestine Studies, 1992), 6.
37. Quoted in E. W. Said and C. Hitchens (eds.), *Blaming the Victims* (London: Verso, 1988), 5.
38. This point is made in Ian Lustick, 'What Gives a People Rights to a Land?', *Queen's Quarterly*, 102/ 4 (1995), 60.
39. This point is from Lustick, 'What Gives a People Rights to a Land?', 60.
40. This distinction is explored in Philpott, 'In Defense of Self-Determination', 378–9.
41. Crnobrnja, *The Yugoslav Drama*, 200–1. Crnobrnja makes the point that the Arbitration Commission's decision to recognize the secession of Bosnia-Hercegovina in the event that the majority sought it was extremely problematic, for a variety of reasons, one of which is that it merely confirmed how the different ethnic communities felt about sovereignty.
42. J. McGarry and B. O'Leary, *Explaining Northern Ireland* (Oxford: Blackwell, 1995), 287.
43. A. Derfel, 'The Message is Clear: We Won't Go': Coon Come has Warning after Vast Majority of Crees Reject Quebec Independence', *Montreal Gazette*, 26 Oct. 1995; T. Harper, 'Indian Leaders Vow to Fight Separation: 95% of Inuit Reject Yes Victory', *Toronto Star*, 27 Oct. 1995; A. Derfel, 'Montagnais Reject Quebec Independence: French-Speaking Aboriginals Vote 99% Against in Own Referendum', *Montreal Gazette*, 28 Oct. 1995. For an insightful analysis, see A. Cairns, 'The Legacy of the Referendum: Who are We Now?', paper prepared

for a post-referendum panel organized by the Centre for Constitutional Studies, University of Alberta, 9 Nov. 1995.

44. Cairns, 'Legacy', 5.
45. Ibid. 3.
46. Quoted in D. Miller, *On Nationality* (Oxford: Clarendon Press, 1995), 117–18.
47. This sensible suggestion is proposed by Miller, *On Nationality*, 117–18.
48. C. Bennet, *Yugoslavia's Bloody Collapse: Causes, Course and Consequences* (New York: New York University Press, 1995), 53.
49. For a discussion of these options, see D. Elazar, *Federalism and the Way to Peace* (Queen's University Institute of Intergovernmental Affairs, 1994).
50. Ian Lustick has pointed out that this would provide an incentive to engage in unjust policies such as ethnic cleansing. I do not wish to endorse a theory which offers a perverse structure of incentives, so I hasten to add the qualifier that these demographic facts would have had to obtain without prior injustice (subject to a statute of limitations, of course, since, if we go back far enough, probably all land was obtained through unjust means).

8

National Self-Determination: Some Cautionary Remarks Concerning the Rhetoric of Rights

RONALD S. BEINER

Unlike most of the other contributors to this volume, my purpose in this chapter is not to specify a set of theoretical criteria to help decide when national groups within a state seeking to renegotiate their citizenship are advancing just or unjust, or more just or less just, moral claims. Rather, my intention is to focus attention on the kind of moral language in which these moral claims are advanced and debated, and on how the character of different moral vocabularies makes a difference to the conduct of nationalist and anti-nationalist politics. In pursuing this argument, I will be drawing upon one strand of the so-called liberal–communitarian debate. It will be recalled that a notable feature of the so-called communitarian challenge to liberalism was the articulation of an anxiety about the hegemony of rights discourse within liberal society, along with an hostility towards, or at least scepticism about, the place occupied by 'rights' as the pre-eminent moral category within liberal theory. I want to make an analogous argument against the language of rights as applied to political-philosophical debates about nationality: whether one wants to opt for an expansive or restricted approach to the moral claims of politicized nationalities, affirming a general *right* to national self-determination, so I will be suggesting, is not a helpful way to deal with the complex predicaments that these nationalist claims invariably generate. But before I turn to this discussion of the language of rights, I want to offer a quick sketch of the general background to these theoretical issues, and some suggestions about why it is not realistic to postulate a general entitlement to self-determination that would in principle extend to all national groups.

I

I think it is beyond question that the legacy of European colonialism, and by consequence, the process of decolonization as one of the major political phenomena of this century, has done much to legitimize nationalist principles. When one reflects on the great movement of post-colonial independence in the middle of the twentieth century, it is impossible to think of nationalism as an ideology of the right, for left-nationalisms have been no less conspicuous, perhaps more conspicuous, in our century; just as the movements of national liberation from the dominant empires of nineteenth-century Europe make clear why liberal nationalism was a coherent and attractive creed for nineteenth-century figures like Mazzini, G. (and Mill). To make *no* concessions to the normative force of nationalist thought would entail not only embracing the nineteenth-century empires within Europe (as Lord Acton seems to do), but also denying the moral legitimacy of the politics of anti-colonialism in the twentieth century.[1] For this reason, one can applaud Elie Kedourie for the theoretical consistency of his critique of nationalism, for Kedourie suggests, at least implicitly, that anti-colonialism *is* theoretically dubious, to the extent that it rests upon nationalist principles. As he puts it in a crucial formulation: '[in judging whether a change of rulers is to be welcomed or regretted], the only criterion capable of public defence is whether the new rulers are less corrupt and grasping, or more just and merciful, or whether there is no change at all, but the corruption, the greed, and the tyranny merely find victims other than those of the departed rulers'.[2] By this he means: the nationality of the new rulers is *not* a legitimate criterion of moral-political judgement. Again, this way of thinking cannot be faulted for theoretical inconsistency, but I think it can be faulted for failing to take sufficient account of the kinds of moral intuition that have bestowed on this century's movements of post-colonial independence more-or-less-universal approbation. The kind of moral intuition to which I'm referring has been nicely expressed by Isaiah Berlin as follows: 'men prefer to be ordered about, even if this entails ill-treatment, by members of their own faith or nation or class, to tutelage, however benevolent, on the part of ultimately patronising superiors from a foreign land or alien class or milieu'.[3]

So I presume that we can agree with Berlin rather than Kedourie that in a world of colonial empires, the principle of self-determination has an undeniable normative force.[4] But what happens when we leave the world of empires behind?[5] Is it theoretically coherent to try to apply the self-determination principle to *all* multinational or multi-ethnic states? (Admittedly, any national-secessionist movement will portray its relation to the majority culture as quasi-colonial, and will therefore present its claims as being on a moral par with those of post-colonial independence movements.) Carried to the logical limit, the theoretical consequences are somewhat catastrophic; for hardly any states today would be immune from having their legitimacy normatively subverted. As many students of nationalism have highlighted, the 'nation-state' in any rigorous sense is not the norm today; the norm is multinationality.[6] As Gellner has put the point: we live in a world that 'has only space for something of the order of 200 or 300 national states'.[7] That leaves a vast number of potential nations, certainly many thousands, that could in principle claim statehood according to an ambitious application of self-determination principles.[8] If each of these potential nations put in its bid for full self-determination, only Iceland, South Korea, Japan, and perhaps a few others would be politically secure. Think of what a 'right' of national self-determination, rigorously applied, would do to states like India, China, and Russia (to say nothing of the various African states, with their colossal ethnic-tribal heterogeneity and arbitrary state boundaries)! One immediately conjures up the vision of a hundredfold multiplication of the kind of inter-ethnic chaos we witnessed with the fragmentation of the Soviet Union.[9]

Perhaps this problem would not be so intractable if one could at least determine clear criteria for establishing in principle the range of legitimate claimants to statehood. But this is impossible, as Eric Hobsbawm explains: 'To assume that the multiplication of independent states has an end is to assume that (1) the world can be subdivided into a finite number of homogeneous potential "nation-states" immune to further subdivision—i.e. (2) that these can be specified in advance. This is plainly not the case.'[10] The problem is further compounded by the fact that the open-ended character of national self-determination as a moral-political principle does nothing to constrain ambitious political élites, provided they have a sufficient degree of political creativity, from contriving new national identities (on the contrary, it virtually invites them to do so, by promising moral sanction): ' "ethnic" identities which had no political or even existential significance until yesterday (for instance being a "Lombard", which is now the title of the xenophobic leagues in North Italy) can acquire a genuine hold as badges of group identity overnight'.[11] There is little reason to think that Umberto Bossi's dream of a republic of Padania is anything other than a cynical fabrication. But nothing prevents Mr Bossi from invoking the morality of self-determination in pursuing his state-busting and state-inventing designs: all one has to do is invent a previously imaginary 'people', give it a flag, and stir it up with a suitable amount of demagoguery until it starts to believe that its national rights have been violated, and presto, a new 'nation' is born. In any case, even if we leave aside the most extreme cases of far-fetched appeals to and abuse of the idea of self-determination, it seems a strange kind of normative principle that relies for its coherence on the willingness of most national groups not to cash in the moral voucher that the principle gives them.

II

The discussion in the previous section has given us good reason to be wary of acknowledging a universal moral entitlement that it would be both difficult and hazardous to honour in practice. As we will examine in the remainder of this chapter, expression of these moral claims in the language of rights makes matters considerably worse, especially when one considers that nationalist political actors can be expected to make a sometimes cynical and opportunistic use of whatever legitimizing slogans one places at their disposal.

In order to pursue this argument, I will need to rehearse certain themes from what in the 1980s came to be called the communitarian critique of liberalism.[12] The appeal to rights as the central moral-political category is so familiar to us in contemporary liberal democracies, we are so thoroughly habituated to it, that we tend to take this moral language for granted, failing to see its distinctive features as one moral language among others and overlooking the ways it often expresses the social and political pathologies of contemporary liberal society. Therefore, critics of rights language (some more militant, some less militant) such as Alasdair MacIntyre, Charles Taylor, Michael Sandel, William Galston, and Mary Ann Glendon have performed an immense service in helping us to be more attentive to the deficiencies of this pervasive moral vocabulary. Common to all these critics is the idea that the more we find ourselves relying on rights discourse to articulate all of our social-political commitments, the more we know ourselves to be inhabiting a moral universe characterized by brittle relationships between individuals and groups, diminished social trust, a propensity to assert absolutist claims, stridency, a propensity to reduce complex social issues to simple slogans, and a constant proliferation of new supposed rights that demand satisfaction at whatever cost to society.[13] As Glendon summarizes this challenge to 'rights talk': 'A tendency to frame nearly every social controversy in terms of a clash of rights . . . impedes compromise, mutual understanding, and the discovery of common ground.'[14]

As theorists like Taylor and Sandel articulated very effectively, one has reason to feel deep anxiety about the quality of the moral bonds between citizens of modern liberal societies to the extent that our political relationships are founded exclusively on a procedural-juridical conception that finds its natural expression in the language of rights.[15] Although Sandel, in his first book, didn't present himself explicitly as a critic of the morality of rights, it's implicit in his general critique of the Rawlsian notion that justice is the first virtue of social institutions.[16] To quote an important Sandelian formulation of this critique: '[In the light of the Humean account of justice as a response to a condition of conflicting interests and aims], justice appears as a remedial virtue, whose moral advantage consists in the repair it works on fallen conditions . . . the virtue of justice [and the question of its primacy or non-primacy] is measured by the morally diminished conditions that are its prerequisite.'[17] But if Rawlsian justice is not the first virtue of social institutions but merely the response to our 'fallen conditions', this critical perspective applies with *much* greater force to a moral world in which the appeal to rights is the only currency to which citizens of a liberal society can resort in conducting their public discourse, and in which political community is defined by a compulsive insistence that our rights be protected. In line with Sandel's account of justice as a remedial virtue, rights are intended as a remedy to the deformations of a social condition that is assumed to be less than ideal.[18] The language of rights is never a language of shared projects or collective co-involvement (the language of friends or fellow citizens engaged in joint deliberation concerning a common good); instead, rights are always a means of enforcing inviolable boundaries against those (strangers, anonymous officials of the state, or estranged spouses) one has some reason to distrust—a protection against encroachment. As Glendon rightly points out, 'the assertion of rights is usually a sign of breakdown in a relationship'.[19] Or, as another famous critic of rights discourse has put the point: 'since in modern society the accommodation of one set of wills to the purpose of another continually requires the frustration of one group's purposes by those of another, it is unsurprising that the concept of rights, understood as claims against the inroads of marauding others in situations where shared allegiances to goods that are goods of the whole community have been attenuated or abandoned, should become a socially central concept.'[20]

For many theorists, the real problem is the *individualism* of rights language, with the presumption that discourse about rights necessarily privileges the claims of individuals over against other individuals. I think this is a serious misconception. If critics of rights talk are right about the infirmities of this moral language, then the same critique of individual rights applies with equal force to group rights.[21] The simple fact of calling one's moral claim (whether on behalf of oneself *or* on behalf of one's group) a *right* automatically renders one less inclined to compromise this claim or submit it to a process of mutual accommodation. To illustrate, I will borrow an example I have used elsewhere: 'consider an argument between two individuals of differing political persuasions concerning whether it would be *good* for the society as a whole if the state were to make available a certain social service (say, universal state-funded daycare). Now imagine how the tone of the debate would be altered if it suddenly turned into a contest between the *right* of one of the parties to receive the service in question and the *right* of the other party not to be burdened by the higher taxes necessary to supply the service.'[22] What the example illustrates is that the very fact that each side phrases its claims in the language of rights indicates that the barricades have already been erected by the two rival positions. Exactly the same point applies to group rights: it makes a difference, socially and politically, when one translates a set of claims about political good into the language of rights, which presupposes a social universe where individuals or groups are subject to the unjust depredations of other individuals and groups, and require binding protections or absolute guarantees against these violations of their rights, hence an implication of the non-negotiability of these protections or guarantees.

III

To summarize the argument thus far: contrary to what may be suggested by some of those who criticize the centrality of rights discourse within contemporary politics, the fundamental problem with rights discourse is not its individualism. Rather, the deeper problem with this discourse is its absolutism: that is, the notion that a right, if genuine, cannot be trumped or compromised. If so, the critique of rights discourse can be applied to collective rights, not just individual rights. This in turn suggests that the critique of rights language presents an important challenge to nationalism, with its foundational appeal to a universal *right* to self-determination. The purpose of our inquiry is to consider the possibility that a political philosophy that feels driven to articulate its social vision in the language of rights is for that very reason theoretically unattractive, and if we are right, this thesis has direct application to the philosophical problem of nationalism.

What's required here is a contrast between alternative forms of public rhetoric, and to make this as concrete as possible, imagine two different ways of conducting the argument for the secession of Quebec:

(1) We (Québécois) no longer feel allegiance to Canada. We appreciate the past benefits of the union, of how we have grown and matured as a nation during this period of national co-habitation, but we feel we have *out*grown this marriage of nations—we can flourish better on our own, without the constant constitutional squabbling, without the quarrelling over jurisdictions, without the feeling on the part of the other provinces that we are the spoiled brat of confederation. We go without rancour, even with some nostalgia for an interesting hundred and thirty years of this bi-national experiment. But we are ready for a new experiment.

(2) Give us our rights! We are a nation. We can determine our own fate. We have an inviolable *right* as a historical people to rule ourselves. You, as a separate nation, a separate people, have no right to involve yourselves in *our* national destiny.

It seems obvious that it makes a world of difference, practically speaking, whether one makes one's claim for nationhood in the first rhetoric or in the second. The second we might call: nationhood with a clenched fist. I think there is an intimation of this second rhetoric in the appeal to national *rights* as such. I also think it's fairly clear that the second rhetoric is the preferred rhetoric of Quebec nationalism as it presently exists (nor is it an accident—if the critique of rights talk is on the mark—that this is the dominant rhetoric).[23] However, nothing in principle precludes Quebec nationalists from switching to the first kind of rhetoric; and in fact Quebec nationalists in the past have sometimes used the first rhetoric with considerable effectiveness.[24] If nothing else, the choice of pre-secession rhetoric will make some difference to the quality of post-secession relations between the two divorced nations;

just as in a literal marriage between two spouses, one can be sure that one's in for a pretty nasty divorce as soon as both partners start demanding their rights.

'Rights talk' is a form of political discourse that is intended as the verbal equivalent of shaking one's fist in the direction of those with whom one is in a state of political disagreement. (That, at least, is its function in liberal societies; I allow that rights discourse serves a different function in non-liberal societies subject to regimes that persecute, torture, and otherwise oppress their citizens.) I don't want to suggest that nationalists are the only offenders here. In fact, it would be equally easy to illustrate the same point by looking at the other side of the barricades in Quebec. Consider the current (and never-ending) language debate. It is possible to make all sorts of plausible arguments about why it's reasonable and desirable to show respect for the anglophone minority by allowing a certain measure of English presence in the public face of Quebec. But anglophones at present insist on using the language of rights: they have a *right* to advertise in English—their fundamental human rights are being violated by Quebec language laws. Once again, this rights rhetoric is a form of fist-waving. It raises the political temperature, and inflames both sides, while doing little to advance the debate by tempering differences and locating means of mutual accommodation.

To formulate one's grievances in the language of rights (what one might call 'the juridification of political claims') is a politically familiar way of saying: 'To hell with you! Give me what I want or I'll sue you. I'll take you to the Supreme Court or the International Tribunal in the Hague if I have to.' The basic point here is that we *can* discuss these matters without waving the banner of rights and therefore making the agents of nationalist secessions (and perhaps their adversaries as well) more truculent and morally self-righteous. In place of the question, 'Do the Québécois have a *right* to exercise their national will by seceding from Canada?' one could substitute the questions: 'How far is it prudent to go in seeking to accommodate the national aspirations of the Québécois?' (stating the question in this form doesn't rule out secession as an appropriate answer); 'How is it good for Canada as a political community to constrain Quebeckers to remain a part of the federation if a majority of them declare in a clear way their determination to withdraw allegiance?'; 'What are the substantive gains and losses for *both* sides in the dispute?' In principle, it seems that one could address all the relevant moral-political issues while entirely avoiding reference to national rights; it must not be assumed that one *has to* formulate these issues in the language of rights. Above all, we want an accommodation of conflicting political purposes, and it seems unlikely that the idiom of national or group rights, any more than the idiom of individual rights, will be helpful in the attainment of a reasonable outcome.

IV

What concerns me in this discussion is not the 'logic' of rights language in any rigorous sense, but rather what one might call the 'grammar' of rights talk in something like a Wittgensteinian sense—that is, a mode of moral-political self-articulation rooted in particular forms of life, and expressive of social and political practices that naturally lend themselves to conceptualization in rights categories. I certainly don't rule out that sophisticated rights theorists in the academy can define rights in a way that avoids the pathologies I discuss (and philosophers who defend a 'right to secede' or 'right to self-determination', including those represented in this volume, are generally very careful to define these rights in a way that is far from unbounded or unqualified). On the other hand, I suspect that it is these very pathologies that contribute to the attractiveness of the appeal to rights within societies where rights are such a popular coin of public rhetoric (and my suspicion is shared by all those critics of rights talk referred to earlier).

To pursue this discussion, I want to identify what I will call various rhetorical functions of the language of rights. I will focus on three in particular: (1) the 'trumping function'; (2) the 'levelling function'; and (3) the 'short-circuiting function'. Again, what's being addressed here is not the idea of a right as we encounter it in the most refined versions of professional philosophers, but rather, what we might call the 'pragmatics' of rights rhetoric as it actually operates in real political life.

A 'right', according to its most modest definition, is simply a shorthand for a morally warranted political claim. But there is a price to be paid (rarely acknowledged by rights theorists) for the use of this shorthand. Ronald Dworkin made clearer the nature of this price with his famous image of 'rights as trumps'.[25] Just as in the realm of individual rights, one has a right to freedom of expression if the claims of free expression 'trump' whatever other social goods might be in conflict with the exercise of this right, so in the realm of collective rights, a group has a 'right' to national self-determination if the claim to self-determination 'trumps' other social goods that may be in conflict with the exercise of this right. The problem, from our point of view, is that this trumping function will become considerably more mischievous when we move from political philosophy to political practice. Someone who is the holder of a presumed right will say: 'Look, we're not just talking about any old moral claim here, we're talking about a *right*—the token of an essential moral guarantee, the boundary-marker of an inviolable moral space. It's non-negotiable.' Obviously, calling the moral claim a 'right' is intended to add extra force to the urgency of attending to the moral claim. Once everyone becomes habituated to talking in this way, we can easily find ourselves in a situation of political deadlock, where moral and political deliberation is stymied on all sides.

The choice of a moral vocabulary doesn't just condition substantive outcomes; more broadly, it structures possible lines of theoretical debate and moral deliberation. To take an absurd example: if, in response to my compulsive consumption of a hundred twinkies a day, someone puts the challenge, 'Don't you realize what you are doing to yourself by eating so many twinkies?', I can reply: 'It's my *right* as a free individual to eat as many twinkies as I desire.' In other words, I short-circuit the discussion of welfare or what's good for me by invoking my individual rights (as I suppose them to be). I'm certainly not trying to suggest that all appeals to rights are as frivolous as this. For the sake of balance, let's call to mind someone who invokes his or her right not to be deprived of regular physical exercise while incarcerated. The latter, unquestionably, embodies a legitimate moral claim. However, I also want to suggest that the absolutism of rights claims, as they operate within the common discourse of a rights-conscious society, tends to have a 'levelling' effect: that is, my right to consume twinkies free of moral scrutiny is asserted as if it were on the same moral level as any other right (such as the more morally weighty demand not to be incarcerated in a way detrimental to my basic welfare); or as if the questioning of the first 'right' would offend my humanity as grievously as the denial of the second. This levelling effect, I want to suggest, is central to how a rhetoric of rights operates in a society sensitive to that rhetoric.

Let's now transpose the discussion to the problem of putative rights to national self-determination. It is not hard to see how a similar set of considerations apply; how, here too, a sort of levelling effect is at work once one frames one's moral claims in a rhetoric of rights. Consider, first, the case of a national group like the East Timorese, who have been trampled on by their Indonesian captors, and have had to endure conditions that approach, or that actually constitute, systematic genocide (the plight of Kurds in Northern Iraq would be an equally apt example).[26] One would have to be morally obtuse to an extreme degree not to see the justice of the demand by the East Timorese for self-determination, since they have little or no reason to expect from the Indonesian state any respect for their cultural integrity or even their physical survival. The only way they can be assured of their cultural and physical security is by re-assuming control over their own fate. This example clearly corresponds to the case, in the domain of individual rights, of the prisoner who demands not to receive abusive treatment from his or her gaolers. In both cases, we have a set of claims that possess a profound moral seriousness. But if we grant a universal moral right to self-determination, then groups with a much more frivolous basis for their national claims will borrow the moral authority rightly granted to national groups that are genuinely oppressed. Hence the levelling of moral entitlements: nations that suffer merely symbolic slights from the majority culture; that aspire to what Wayne Norman has referred to as 'vanity secessions'[27]; that succumb to the demagogic promptings of nationalist entrepreneurs—all of these will presume that they have a moral entitlement no less sacred or inviolable than that of the most oppressed national minority. Here we have a group-rights equivalent to our twinkie glutton to whom the language of rights has yielded the moral high ground.

Part of the problem here is the essential universalism of rights claims. The whole point of asserting a rights claim is to identify an aspect of human existence that is so fundamental that its violation, anywhere, at any time, constitutes an affront to human dignity as such. For instance, if we have a right not to be tortured, *any* instance of torture, anywhere, at any time, is morally intolerable. Applying this logic to the problem of the moral status of nationalities raises a problem, for it puts a moralistic language at the disposal of nationalists everywhere, who, as such, are in the business of playing the ethnic grievances game. This isn't, of course, to suggest that there aren't, in various situations, ethnic grievances that are morally serious; in some cases, they are of the utmost moral seriousness. As I suggested above, no reasonable person, I think, could deny the moral claims of the East Timorese or the Iraqi Kurds. But phrasing these moral claims in the universalistic language of rights at the same time equips entrepreneurs of nationality politics whose moral claims are much more dubious—extending even to the absurd 'Padanian' project of opportunists in Northern Italy, as we mentioned earlier.

I want to say a little more about what I have called the short-circuiting function of rights discourse. What does an argument about nationalism look like when it's conducted in the language of good rather than the language of rights? It seems fairly obvious that judgements about the attractive or unattractive character of the nation-state project are shaped by competing conceptions of political good. For instance, with respect to my own political commitments, I support Canadian federalism, rather than Canada's partition into two states, each of which would be closer to the classic nation-state paradigm, because I am convinced that there are goods associated with bi-national partnership that override those to be found in the more simplified bonds of membership in the nation-state (in the narrower sense). It may be that political community founded on bi-national or multinational partnership is unobtainable in a particular case; it may be that the bi-national state that already exists in Canada turns out to be impossible to sustain; but what is in question here is not an issue of practicality but what is desirable as a matter of principle. Now it might be said that in the Canadian case, my judgements are hardly impartial; as a member of (not exactly the majority culture in Canada, but certainly) the majority linguistic community, I have some kind of vested interest in Quebec's continued subscription in the larger political community. I suppose this is true. But here I would like to think that if (a counterfactual, to be sure) I were a francophone Quebecker, I would have the same preference for bi-national political partnership that I do as an anglophone

Canadian.[28] And if (here the counterfactual involves less of an existential leap, and so my thought experiment has more credibility) I were once again an anglophone Quebecker in a Quebec that *did* decide to be an independent state, I would certainly oppose the 'partitionist' efforts of anglophone communities in Quebec, and *for exactly the same reason*: namely, allegiance to the idea that bi-national or multinational co-existence is a more noble political adventure than uni-national solidarity. But here the nationalist as such sees group-belonging or national togetherness as the overriding good, and correspondingly, is unmoved by what strikes me as the more attractive political ideal of bi-national partnership. The nationalist regards each nation as flourishing best on its own, and sees the strains of mutual accommodation within a political marriage of nations not as a noble (though sometimes unsustainable) cause, but rather, as a futile undertaking that's bound to cause more trouble than it's worth.[29]

Now it seems clear that one could have an interesting moral debate between these two opposing conceptions of political good. But once again, the appeal to rights has the effect of short-circuiting moral deliberation conducted within the discourse of good.[30] Instead of debating the alternative goods of political life shared with a co-national partner vs. those of a smaller and more exclusive national community that forgoes the challenge of federal or consociational partnership, as soon as one invokes the *right* to go one's own way as a nation with its own state, further deliberation about goods is beside the point. (Think again of the rights-claiming twinkie-eater. There's no point asking if it's *good* for my health or sanity to consume so many twinkies; it's my sovereign *right* as an autonomous individual to eat as many of them as I please.)

It's important to emphasize once again that if we eschew the language of rights, we don't necessarily wind up with different substantive moral outcomes. We may well conclude that the claims to secession on the part of oppressed East Timorese are morally warranted *whether or not* we see fit to express this moral claim in the language of universal rights. But the point is not simply whether we get this moral outcome or that moral outcome; the point is to appreciate the significance of the moral vocabulary by which we arrive at these outcomes.

V

I noted earlier that those political philosophers who treat the politics of nationalism within the horizon of the morality of rights tend to be careful not to define the rights in question in an absolutist or unqualified fashion, and are by and large quite sensitive to the risks of encouraging recklessness or of opening the floodgates to secessionist claims that would be likely to have destructive consequences. It might be helpful to conclude this discussion by considering how these rights theorists seek to qualify or hedge the moral rights they defend, and whether these theories succeed in staunching the anxieties about the rhetoric of rights that I have tried to identify.

To start with, let me survey various theoretical possibilities, so we have a better sense of the range of options.

(1) Needless to say, anyone who is hostile to nationalism will be correspondingly hostile to the idea of national self-determination. As we saw earlier, this is Kedourie's position, and it is a consistent view. No one can coherently think that nationalism is one of the plagues of the modern world while none the less believing that national self-determination stated as a universal moral principle is politically benign and philosophically defensible.

(2) One can be relatively sympathetic to (at least some kinds of) nationalism, but none the less think that national self-determination as a general principle is a misguided notion. Consider the following argument advanced by Bernard Yack:

> History has left us sufficient barriers to establishing broader political identities without multiplying them by using the concept of rights to erect and maintain new ones. Where past conflicts and injustices have erected such barriers, it may be wise, as a matter of political prudence, to offer special national rights . . . But introducing such cultural rights as a general principle would unnecessarily harden perceptions of cultural opposition and thereby promote greater mutual suspicion and contention within political communities. Translating nationalism into the liberal language of rights leads [one] to ignore the social and historical context of political problems.[31]

I take Yack to be suggesting here that it is one thing to try to cope with national conflicts as they arise; but declaring a universal *right* has the effect of egging people on to fight for the attainment of that right in situations where they might not otherwise have felt oppressed by the majority culture. Another political philosopher who has a large measure of sympathy for liberal versions of nationalism but who is nervous about applying the language of rights to these issues is David Miller.[32] Miller, too, recognizes that the notion of an across-the-board 'right' is a very blunt instrument in weighing up the complex and historically mediated considerations presented for moral judgement in any instance of national conflict, and therefore his preferred way of talking about these matters is not to say that a secessionist nation is the bearer of a right but merely to say '*prima facie* the group has a good case'.[33]

(3) One can support a just right to secede, provided that it is consistent with standard liberal principles, but be sceptical about, if not downright hostile towards, nationalist accounts of what renders secession justifiable. This is more or less Allen Buchanan's position. In Buchanan's book on *Secession*, the nationalist account of self-determination is only the eighth of twelve

pro-secession arguments that he considers (which in itself says quite a lot), and when he does finally get around to considering it, Buchanan finds it one of the weakest arguments for secession.[34] He concludes: 'the normative nationalist principle is a recipe for limitless political fragmentation'.[35]

(4) One can embrace a so-called right of national self-determination, but try to interpret it in a way that steers nationalism away from claims to statehood. This is a plausible description of Yael Tamir's project.[36]

(5) One can, of course, be a full-blown nationalist, and endorse a right to self-determination on standardly nationalist grounds.[37] Among the various liberal defenders of nationalism, Margalit and Raz come closest to defining self-determination on a characteristically nationalist basis.[38]

(6) Finally (although this hardly exhausts the possibilities), one can opt for a relatively ambitious right of self-determination, but see bonds of national identity as irrelevant to the issue: if a group of individuals wishes to opt out, national solidarity on the part of the seceders is not a necessary condition for the justice of their secessionist claims. This position deserves to be listed after the properly nationalist view, since it subsumes, and therefore is of wider scope than, a strictly nationalist justification of secession. A good example of this kind of theory is that of Harry Beran, who embraces a *more* expansive right of secession than would be entailed by a universal right of national self-determination.[39]

What emerges from this brief sketch of various theoretical positions is that there are three different indices at play here: (1) one's attitude towards nationalism in general; (2) one's acceptance or rejection of some notion of a right to national self-determination; and (3) one's acceptance or rejection of a just right to secede. There is no reason to assume that there will be a simple correspondence between one's positions along these three indices, or that each index will, as it were, 'line up' with the other two. To illustrate this lack of alignment, consider, for instance, my own position with respect to these three dimensions of the question: in general, I am not warmly disposed towards nationalism; I am a sceptic about rights claims in general and nationalist rights in particular; but I am none the less reasonably open to liberal-nationalist secessions (certainly more so than would be dictated by Buchanan's principles of rightful secession).[40] I am led to an acceptance (grudging, not enthusiastic) of secessionism not because I have any great sympathy for nationalism, and certainly not because I think every ethnic group and self-proclaimed 'people' has a right to its own state, but for a different reason altogether: because one is unlikely to have a happy and flourishing political community where a substantial and territorially concentrated minority has a minimal or less than minimal allegiance to the political community to which it happens to belong, and where the alienation is permanent, that is, where there is no prospect at all of wooing back their allegiance.[41] This way of thinking about the problem is deliberately phrased in the language of good (of what is choiceworthy) rather than the language of rights (of what is permissible).[42] Of course it would be vastly preferable to work out special constitutional arrangements, including federal institutions with sufficient authority to secure greater allegiance on the part of sub-communities with a distinctive identity. However, as Canadians already know and as Britons may come to find out as they move in a more federalist direction under the new Blair government, there is no guarantee that a highly decentralized federation with robust powers exercised by regional parliaments will solve the problem. It is always possible that giving nationalists their own parliament will simply furnish them with stronger instruments by which to pursue their more ambitious objectives. So in the end one might have little choice but to let them go their own way in the world (as the Czechs let their federal partners go), even if they are mistaken in thinking this will advance their own interests and mistaken in thinking that a uni-national political community is in principle normatively superior to a bi-national or multinational federation.

None of the theorists considered in our survey endorses rights without qualification; *all* of them want hedged rights—whether we're talking about rights to secede or rights of nations to determine their own political fate.[43] It would be perfectly easy for these defenders of the morality of rights to argue that my dire depiction of the language of rights at its worse has no application whatever to their own efforts as rights theorists. Buchanan, for instance, in a response to the communitarian critique of rights talk, made the point that it is unfair for communitarians to '[saddle] liberals with the implausible view that individual civil and political rights are absolute, that is, that they never may be justifiably infringed or restricted',[44] and he would no doubt make the same complaint against the present challenge to rights discourse. However, I don't think that this rejoinder gets liberal-nationalist rights theorists entirely off the hook, and I will try to explain why.

First, though, let me review once again a few of the theories that are on offer, some of which are rather complex. Buchanan, as we've already seen, forthrightly rejects any right of national self-determination, but he still uses the language of rights to characterize those claims to secede that he does accept. In fact, he's a strong defender of rights theory, although, interestingly enough, he intimates that he's only weakly committed to pursuing his theory of secession in the idiom of rights. In one noteworthy passage, he states that, although in his own view the advantages of rights talk outweigh the drawbacks, he recognizes that other theorists may be more averse to the language of rights, and he lets it be known that he 'would not protest too loudly if those who abhor the notion of a right wish to translate' his talk about rights into some other moral vocabulary.[45] As we've already seen, other theorists (such as Miller and Yack) are *more* sympathetic to nationalist claims than Buchanan is, but *less* inclined to formulate these claims in the language of rights.

Buchanan has a very restrictive view of the conditions of just secession (he says that his aim is to 'domesticate' the right to secede,[46] which surely implies making the conditions for permissible secession sufficiently stringent that the encouragement given to secessionists by moral philosophers will be minimized). But it is striking how hedged and full of qualifications are the theories of even those philosophers who embrace a much more expansive account of the scope of just secessions. For instance, Margalit and Raz, who *seem* to affirm a quite ambitious right of self-determination, say that 'the wish for a state must be shared *by an overwhelming majority*, reflecting deep-seated beliefs and feelings *of an enduring nature*, and not mere temporary popularity'.[47] (What will the institutional embodiment of this right look like? Will Quebec sovereigntists have to win three referenda in a row, with 80 per cent or more in each referendum?) Daniel Philpott, another defender of a moral right to self-determination, endorses 'high procedural hurdles',[48] and he says that while his theory is in principle more expansive than Buchanan's, 'I doubt that there are many cases to which my own theory would give a green light, but to which Buchanan's would grant a red or yellow light'.[49] This suggests that he would deny self-determination to the Québécois, since it's fairly clear that Québécois secessionism falls well short of satisfying Buchanan's principles. And Margaret Moore, who also appears to embrace an expansive right of self-determination, sees a compelling case for self-determination when 'the vast majority' of a national group expresses its will in a plebiscite.[50] Secessionists (sovereigntists in Quebec, for instance) could be expected to respond to these 'friends' of self-determination by saying, 'Who needs this? What's the point of granting us a right to self-determination if the conditions for the permissible exercise of the right are so narrow that our national rights are in effect voided? What you give us with the right hand, you take away with the left!'

If philosophical theories of national rights are so heavily qualified, why would one be left with any cause for concern that the philosophical defence of a right to self-determination would contribute to secessionist recklessness? There are several reasons to be anxious still:

(1) Most of the self-determination theorists state a strong preference for federalist accommodation of national distinctiveness over secession.[51] But, for reasons laid out by Margalit and Raz, it is not clear how the statement of this preference is consistent with self-determination in a strict sense. Margalit and Raz write that 'A group's right to self-determination is its right to determine that a territory be self-governing . . . the right to self-determination answers the question "who is to decide?", not "what is the best decision?" . . . [I]f it has the right to decide, its decision is binding even if it is wrong.'[52] If I have understood them correctly, Margalit and Raz are saying that what a right to self-determination serves to do is not to assert the wisdom or

advisability of governing oneself in this way or that way but simply to specify the morally relevant community that gets to decide this question. If we grant self-determination to the Québécois, *they* alone are authorized to decide their preferred form of self-governance. If so, then it is illegitimate to define self-determination in a way that privileges autonomy without secession over full secession: if granted self-determination, the group that aspires to secede gets to choose between autonomy and secession, otherwise self-determination isn't really self-determination. Philpott can speak of 'a presumption against secession', but if Margalit and Raz are right, self-determination means that *the group* gets to decide *for itself* what's appropriate, rather than have this dictated by some set of universal moral-political principles.

(2) Most self-determination theorists proceed by granting a general right but then qualifying it by requiring the secessionists to make various guarantees in advance, such as a pledge to institute a liberal regime of individual rights and the promise of protections for national minorities within the new state. But as critics of self-determination theory have pointed out, there is a problem here. David Miller, for instance, makes the important point that 'once the new state is formed and recognized, powerful norms of international non-interference come into play', so third-party states may have the power to grant recognition to seceding states but little power to regulate the consequences of having legitimized the secession (he cites the Yugoslavian mess).[53] Of course, *no* political movement with nationalist-secessionist aspirations is going to *say* that it intends to oppress its own national minorities after independence: if there are qualifications attached to the right to self-determination, the secessionists will have nothing to gain by admitting their intention to violate the qualifications and everything to gain by pledging their absolute fidelity to these qualifications. But surely the secession isn't revocable if all hell breaks loose after their claims to self-determination have been granted. It would make sense for the secessionists to agree to whatever conditions are laid down by the international community, and then, with recognition in their back pocket, conduct themselves pretty much as they please, as most existing states now do. As Miller says, 'we cannot [simply] take whatever reassurances the secessionists may give at face value'.[54] So the principle of national self-determination awards moral credentials to the nationalist group without being able to guarantee that the nationalists won't yield to the temptation to pocket the right while paying little attention to the 'fine print' (the hedges attached to the right).

(3) All the liberal defenders of self-determination want self-determination hedged by prudence. But once one lets the rhetoric of self-determination loose upon the world, prudence may be seriously handicapped. It is not hard to think of examples of how acknowledgement of a right of national self-determination would handcuff political prudence in coping with the challenges posed by nationalists.[55] Even if one thought that the Yugoslav federation was

doomed, the rhetoric of self-determination would encourage one to grant a more hasty recognition of the secessionist states than might be necessary, with severe injuries to the cause of prudence. It can be plausibly argued that the over-hasty recognition of Croatia and Slovenia by the EC (under German pressure) in fact contributed to the subsequent disaster in ex-Yugoslavia.[56] Or, to pick an example that is still playing itself out: speaking about self-determination in the idiom of rights helps nationalists in Quebec to convince themselves and other Quebeckers that the rest of Canada has no business meddling in Quebec's control over its own destiny (for instance, by becoming involved in the choice of a suitable referendum question); if, on the other hand, one rejects this rhetoric, one leaves more room for compromise and negotiation.[57]

(4) Finally, we can ask why, if philosophers like Margalit and Raz, Philpott, and Moore are as anxious about the right of self-determination getting out of hand as they say they are, they think it's reasonable or prudent to continue speaking of a 'right' of self-determination. If Philpott, for instance, thinks his principle of self-determination has very limited application (see the discussion above concerning red lights and green lights), why does he see fit to continue using the language of a 'right' of self-determination—with its universalistic-sounding associations—rather than a commitment to *ad hoc* consideration of the pros and cons of greater communal autonomy in this or that case?[58] Why start off with the presumption of legitimacy, which is what the 'right' announces, and *then* worry about how to limit and qualify exercise of the right (clawing back the right, so to speak), rather than, as seems more prudent, put the onus on nationalists and secessionists to make their case for the reasonableness, in their own situation, of sovereignty or self-determination? Donald Horowitz refers to the debate within international law 'over whether self-determination is still merely a principle or is now a right'.[59] This nicely captures the point that it *does* make a real difference whether we formulate a given moral claim in the language of rights.[60] If we hand this particular ball to partisans of nationalist politics, we can be sure they'll run with it, and the philosophers who hand them the ball may wind up being surprised at just how far they run.

As Donald Horowitz argues elsewhere in this volume, and for reasons that seem to me entirely persuasive, the politics of self-determination is full of perils; and the bolstering of this politics with the rhetoric of rights is likely to make these perils even more fearsome.

NOTES

1. According to Brian Barry ('Self-Government Revisited', in B. Barry, *Democracy, Power and Justice* (Oxford: Clarendon Press, 1989), 165–6, 167, 177, 180),

Acton's championing of multinationality is in the service of his more fundamental commitment to the cause of empire; this seems a rather deterministic and ungenerous interpretation. For another ungenerously reductionist interpretation of Lord Acton's argument against uni-national states, see D. Miller, *On Nationality* (Oxford: Clarendon Press, 1995), 85, n. 5.

2. E. Kedourie, *Nationalism*, 4th edn. (Oxford: Blackwell, 1993), 135. Cf. E. Gellner, 'Nationalism', in *Thought and Change* (Chicago: University of Chicago Press, 1965), 153: 'Life is a difficult and serious business. The protection from starvation and insecurity is not easily achieved. In the achievement of it, effective government is an important factor. Could one think of a sillier, more *frivolous* consideration than the question concerning the native vernacular of the governors?'
3. I. Berlin, 'The Bent Twig', in H. Hardy (ed.), *The Crooked Timber of Humanity* (New York: Vintage Books, 1992), 251.
4. However, as Walker Connor points out, calling this *national* self-determination is not unproblematic: 'Although [the African and Asian independence movements] had been conducted in the name of self-determination of nations, they were, in fact, demands for political independence not in accord with ethnic distributions, but along the essentially happenstance borders that delimited either the sovereignty or the administrative zones of former colonial powers. This fact combined with the incredibly complex ethnic map of Africa and Asia to create, in the name of self-determination of nations, a host of multinational states', W. Connor, *Ethnonationalism* (Princeton: Princeton University Press, 1994), 5. Cf. E. J. Hobsbawm, *Nations and Nationalism Since 1780*, 2nd edn. (Cambridge: Cambridge University Press, 1992), 169.
5. Cf. E. J. Hobsbawm, 'Some Reflections on "The Break-up of Britain"', *New Left Review*, 105 (Sept.–Oct., 1977), 11: 'The virtual disappearance of formal empires ("colonialism") has snapped the main link between anti-imperialism and the slogan of national self-determination . . . the struggle against [neocolonial dependence] simply cannot any longer be crystallized round the slogan of establishing independent political statehood, because most territories concerned already have it.'
6. See, for instance, W. Kymlicka, *Multicultural Citizenship* (Oxford: Clarendon Press, 1995), 1, 196, n. 1; Hobsbawm, *Nations and Nationalism Since 1780*, 66, 179, 186; Connor, *Ethnonationalism*, 77, 155, 166.
7. E. Gellner, 'Do Nations Have Navels?', *Nations and Nationalism*, 2/3 (1996), 369.
8. For Gellner's interesting reflections on potential nationalisms, see *Nations and Nationalism* (Ithaca, NY: Cornell University Press, 1983), 44–5.
9. Cf. S. Levinson, 'Is Liberal Nationalism an Oxymoron?', *Ethics*, 105 (1995), 631: 'there are far too many nations to make [a Wilsonian commitment to national self-determination] feasible, at least without bloodshed that would make Bosnia look almost mild. The phrase "self-determination", especially when it is interpreted as a call for political independence, is, as was said by Wilson's own secretary of state, "simply loaded with dynamite. It will raise hopes which can never be realized. It will, I fear, cost thousands of lives." Lansing's only error, of course, was the almost literally incredible underestimation of costs.'

10. Hobsbawm, 'Some Reflections on "The Break-up of Britain"', 12–13.
11. E. J. Hobsbawm, 'Ethnicity and Nationalism in Europe Today', in G. Balakrishnan (ed.), *Mapping the Nation* (London: Verso, 1996), 260.
12. In various places, I've tried to explain why I find the communitarian label more confusing than helpful: see, for instance, R. S. Beiner, *What's the Matter with Liberalism?* (Berkeley: University of California Press, 1992), ch. 2; and id., *Philosophy in a Time of Lost Spirit: Essays on Contemporary Theory* (Toronto: University of Toronto Press), ch. 1.
13. Cf. M. Glendon, *Rights Talk: The Impoverishment of Political Discourse* (New York: Free Press, 1991), pp. x–xi, 14, 16.
14. Ibid., p. xi.
15. See, for instance, C. Taylor, 'Alternative Futures', in G. Laforest (ed.), *Reconciling the Solitudes: Essays on Canadian Federalism and Nationalism* (Montreal and Kingston: McGill-Queen's University Press, 1993), 87–119. For my own version of this argument, see Beiner, *What's the Matter with Liberalism?*, ch. 4.
16. Sandel's criticisms of the culture of rights become more explicit in his later work on the 'procedural republic'.
17. M. J. Sandel, *Liberalism and the Limits of Justice* (Cambridge: Cambridge University Press, 1982), 31–2. Cf. A. Buchanan's characterization of the communitarian critique of justice: 'Assessing the Communitarian Critique of Liberalism', *Ethics*, 99 (1989), 853.
18. Cf. E. Andrew, *Shylock's Rights: A Grammar of Lockian Claims* (Toronto: University of Toronto Press, 1988), 17–20. '[It's not the case that] the more rights, the better the society. [On the contrary,] rights are to be understood as necessary evils, as claims against others that are necessary to societies based on conflict and competition. . . . to be conceived more as claims *against* others rather than as joint entitlements constituting a moral community. We have rights *against* others as we have duties *towards* one another.'
19. Glendon, *Rights Talk*, 175.
20. A. MacIntyre, 'Rights, Practices and Marxism', *Analyse und Kritik*, 7 (1985), 239.
21. Glendon implicitly accepts this point when she mentions that the rhetoric of rights serves to legitimate 'individual *and* group egoism', *Rights Talk*, 171, my italics.
22. Beiner, *What's the Matter with Liberalism?*, 42.
23. For a small but typical example, see S. Delacourt, 'Spectre of Split Spawned Plan B Strategy', *Globe and Mail*, 30 Oct. 1996, p. A10, referring to the 'angry Quebec commentary about [Ottawa's] alleged interference in the province's right to self-determination'. If there were indeed a national *right* to self-determination in a stringent sense, then it would be quite true that it would be illegitimate for the rest of the country to 'interfere' in Quebec's exercise of that right (including deciding for itself the conditions of its exercise). But it is worth mentioning that the political initiative that aroused this heated reaction, namely the federal government's attempt to clarify the conditions of a lawful secession, which as such presupposed an acknowledgement of the possibility of secession, would be considered as *exceeding* the requirements of justice by many of the philosophers who defend a right to secede!

24. For instance, there are certainly strong elements of the first rhetoric in R. Lévesque, *An Option for Quebec* (Toronto: McClelland and Stewart, 1968). In typical speeches of Lucien Bouchard, on the other hand, despite the fact that he is hardly the most immoderate among Quebec nationalists, the second rhetoric clearly tends to be predominant.
25. See R. Dworkin, 'Rights as Trumps', in J. Waldron (ed.), *Theories of Rights* (Oxford: Oxford University Press, 1984), 153–67.
26. See A. Buchanan, 'Theories of Secession', *Philosophy and Public Affairs*, 26/1 (1997), 31–61: 36, 37; more generally, see A. Buchanan, *Secession: The Morality of Political Divorce from Fort Sumter to Lithuania and Quebec* (Boulder, Colo.: Westview, 1991), 64–7.
27. W. Norman, 'The Ethics of Secession as the Regulation of Secessionist Politics', Ch. 3 of this volume, pp. 52–5.
28. When I speak of partnership, I mean shared citizenship in a full federation. Of course, Quebec sovereigntists also say they desire some kind of post-independence partnership with English Canada, but it remains very questionable whether anything would come of this promised partnership.
29. I don't mean to suggest that Quebec nationalists *welcome* partition along ethnic lines. Clearly, nothing infuriates them more than the claims made upon Quebec territory by non-francophone partitionists. On the other hand, whether these nationalists are willing to acknowledge it or not, the 'right' of non-francophone communities to secede from an independent Quebec corresponds to the logic of the nationalists' own project to partition the existing federation.
30. Cf. W. Galston, 'Political Economy and the Politics of Virtue: U.S. Public Philosophy at Century's End', MS, 25: 'There is a temptation to regard the language of rights, standing alone, as an adequate moral vocabulary. But of course it is not. The assertion "I have the right to do X", even if accurate, does not warrant the conclusion that "X is the right thing to do". The gap between rights and rightness can only be filled with a moral discourse that goes well beyond rights-talk.'
31. B. Yack, 'Reconciling Liberalism and Nationalism', *Political Theory*, 23/1 (1995), 174; the context is a criticism of Yael Tamir's theory of nationalism.
32. D. Miller, 'Secession and the Principle of Nationality', Ch. 4 of this volume, p. 65: 'I say "a claim" rather than "a right" in order to signal that the claim in question is not necessarily an overriding one, but may be defeated by other considerations'. The point here is that the implication of 'overridingness' is a familiar feature of the language of rights.
33. Ibid. 69. Cf. Miller, *On Nationality*, 81: 'it devalues the currency of rights to announce rights which in their nature are sometimes incapable of fulfilment . . . this applies to the alleged right of national self-determination. I have therefore couched the proposition that I wish to defend in terms of a "good claim" to political self-determination, recognizing that there will be cases where the claim cannot be met.'
34. Buchanan, *Secession* 48–52. Although Buchanan presents his book as a defence of *group* rights, it is somewhat astonishing to what extent he subordinates issues of nationality, ethnicity, and cultural identity to issues of distributive justice.
35. Ibid. 49. Also, ibid. 20: 'An unlimited right to secede for any and every ethnic group or "people" would be a dangerous thing indeed'; and 102: 'this principle

[the right of self-determination as a normative nationalist principle], and hence its use as a justification for secession, must be resolutely rejected.' Cf. Buchanan's criticisms of 'the Nationalist Principle' (or what he calls the 'Ascriptive-Group variant of Primary Right Theory') in 'Theories of Secession', 44–61.

36. Y. Tamir, *Liberal Nationalism* (Princeton: Princeton University Press, 1993), 57: 'The right to national self-determination . . . stakes a cultural rather than a political claim, namely, it is the right to preserve the existence of a nation as a distinct cultural entity . . . national claims are not synonymous with demands for political sovereignty.' According to Tamir's self-description of the project, what she offers is 'a cultural interpretation of the right to national self-determination' (p. 58). Yack ('Reconciling Liberalism and Nationalism', 172) refers to Tamir's 'depoliticization' of national identity, which seems a fair characterization of Tamir's nationalism.
37. Philosophers will assume that the way to be a nationalist is to affirm a *universal* right to self-determination, but those with a more historical bent may be inclined to be rather sceptical about how reliably universalistic most nationalists in fact are. See, for instance, E. J. Hobsbawm, 'Identity Politics and the Left', *New Left Review*, 217 (1996), 43: 'Zionist Jewish nationalism, whether we sympathize with it or not, is exclusively about Jews, and hang—or rather bomb—the rest. All nationalisms are. The nationalist claim that they are for *everyone's* right to self-determination is bogus.' A good test of Hobsbawm's thesis is to see how Quebec nationalists react to the claims to national self-determination on the part of aboriginal groups in Quebec. See R. Cook, *Canada, Quebec, and the Uses of Nationalism*, 2nd edn. (Toronto: McClelland and Stewart, 1995), 81, 245, 264 n. 23, and 286 n. 20.
38. A. Margalit and J. Raz, 'National Self-Determination', *Journal of Philosophy*, 37/9 (1990), 439–61. See also K. Nielsen, 'Secession: The Case of Quebec', *Journal of Applied Philosophy*, 10/1 (1993), 29–43.
39. H. Beran, 'A Liberal Theory of Secession', *Political Studies*, 32/1 (1984), 21–31. See Buchanan's helpful typology of theories in 'Theories of Secession'; Buchanan labels Beran's theory an 'Associative-Group variant of Primary Right Theory'.
40. However, it should be noted that it is not Buchanan's purpose to *prohibit* secessions where these are agreed to by the parties involved. Presumably, he would not object to Quebec secession if it was accepted by the Canadian political community as a whole, but he would say that Quebeckers could not *insist* on their secession on grounds of justice if the rest of Canada said No (and I assume the same goes for the Czech–Slovak divorce); see Buchanan, 'Theories of Secession', 36: 'Remedial Right Only Theories are not as restrictive as they might first appear.'
41. I certainly don't mean to present this argument as the basis for a general right, for reasons offered in Yack's critique of Tamir, cited above. In agreement with Yack, it seems to me self-evident folly to make judgements of what is advisable or inadvisable in advance of knowing a great deal about the historical context shaping particular nationality conflicts.
42. Cf. Andrew, *Shylock's Rights*, 20: 'Rights . . . function to secure choice rather than direct us to what is choiceworthy.'

43. See for instance Margalit and Raz, 'National Self-Determination', 461: 'the right to self-determination is neither absolute nor unconditional'; D. Philpott, 'Self-Determination in Practice', Ch. 5 of this volume, p. 80: 'the right to self-determination is . . . qualified'.
44. Buchanan, 'Assessing the Communitarian Critique of Liberalism', 855.
45. Buchanan, *Secession*, 152.
46. Ibid. 20, 103–4.
47. Margalit and Raz, 'National Self-Determination', 458, my italics.
48. Philpott, 'Self-Determination in Practice', Ch. 5 of this volume, pp. 96–7.
49. Ibid. 90.
50. M. Moore, 'The Territorial Dimension of Self-Determination', Ch. 7 of this volume, p. 150.
51. Philpott, for instance, speaks of 'a presumption against secession' ('Self-Determination in Practice', p. 83); he also refers to secession as 'a last resort' (ibid. 86, 87, 90). This seems to be Moore's position as well: see 'The Territorial Dimension of Self-Determination', pp. 153–4.
52. Margalit and Raz, 'National Self-Determination', 454.
53. Miller, 'Secession and the Principle of Nationality', Ch. 4 of this volume, p. 7. Philpott, too, concedes that there is a legitimate worry that having won recognition of its independent statehood, the new state will be able to evade 'follow up' on the part of the states granting recognition (which *ought to* provide long-term oversight and enforcement of the new state's commitments but may fail to do so). As Philpott put it in the original version of his chapter: 'We face the prospect of enforcing the principle, but not the qualifications'.
54. Miller, 'Secession and the Principle of Nationality', p. 71. Cf. D. L. Horowitz, 'Self-Determination: Politics, Philosophy, and Law', Ch. 9 of this volume, p. 198: 'The inability to forecast the emergence of an illiberal regime with any degree of reliability renders [qualifications such as the insistence on minority rights] illusory.'
55. Margaret Moore has objected that this appeal to 'prudence' suggests a familiar morality/prudence dichotomy, which in turn seems to imply that the prudential considerations being invoked here are extraneous to morality or are somehow non-moral. If so, she argues, the morality of rights is untouched by 'merely' prudential concerns. I should therefore clarify that when I speak of prudence in this chapter, I have in mind as the relevant theoretical context the Aristotelian tradition of moral reflection according to which prudence (in the Aristotelian sense of context-sensitive practical judgement), far from being irrelevant to morality, is actually the very core of moral life. One might say that for a rights-theorist, the centre of the moral universe is the protection of autonomy, whereas for an Aristotelian like myself, the centre of the moral universe is making the right judgements.
56. See B. Denitch, *Ethnic Nationalism: The Tragic Death of Yugoslavia*, rev. edn. (Minneapolis: University of Minnesota Press, 1996), 12–13, 51–3. See also Horowitz, 'Self-Determination: Politics, Philosophy, and Law', p. 189; and Philpott, 'Self-Determination in Practice', p. 88.
57. Cf. A. D. Smith, *Theories of Nationalism* (London: Duckworth, 1971), 10: 'Nationalism confuses principles with interests. It makes conflicts that much

less amenable to a negotiated peace, because men will not compromise over principles.' Naturally, the main culprit here is precisely the principle of national self-determination.

58. Cf. Hobsbawm, 'Some Reflections', 13: 'any finite number of [sovereign] states must exclude some potential candidates from statehood. . . . the argument for the formation of any independent nation-state must always be an *ad hoc* argument, which undermines the case for *universal* self-determination by separatism. The irony of nationalism is that the argument for the separation of Scotland from England is exactly analogous to the argument for the separation of the Shetlands from Scotland; and so are the arguments against both separations.'
59. Horowitz, 'Self-Determination: Politics, Philosophy, and Law', p. 200.
60. As cited above (see n. 32), David Miller makes the same point when he explains his reluctance to apply the term 'rights' to this question.

9

Self-Determination: Politics, Philosophy, and Law

DONALD L. HOROWITZ

It has been said of Mikhail Gorbachev that he had the distinction of having lost three world wars. He lost the Cold War, of course. He also lost the Second World War, because he lost Eastern Europe. And he managed to lose the First World War, because he presided over the end of the Russian Empire. This triple defeat produced great changes in the relationship of ethnic groups to territory. Not only did Eastern Europe become free of the Soviet Union but steps were taken to free Slovaks from Czechs, as well as various Yugoslavs from each other, to unite (in various ways) East Germans, Volga Germans, and Romanian Germans with West Germans, and to create new relations between Bulgarians and Turks, between Albanians and Serbs, and between Hungarians, on the one hand, and Romanians, Ukrainians, Slovaks, and Serbs, on the other. Within the former Soviet Union, the Baltic, the Central Asian, the Caucasian, the Ukrainian, and some Middle Volga republics all sought to or did disengage their fate, to a greater or lesser degree, from that of the Russian Republic and often from that of their neighbours as well. These movements have generally been painful, and they have recurring, generalizable

Portions of this chapter were first presented at the Harvard-MIT Joint Seminar on Political Development, and various versions were then delivered as lectures at Colorado College, Emory University, the London School of Economics, Stetson University, the University of California at Santa Barbara, the University of Lund, Rutgers University, the University of Auckland, the University of Melbourne, the Massachusetts Institute of Technology, and the University of California at Berkeley. I am grateful to my hosts at these various institutions—respectively, Samuel P. Huntington and Lucian W. Pye, David Hendrickson, Juliette R. Stapanian-Apkarian, Anthony Smith, Eugene Huskey, Cynthia S. Kaplan, Kajsa Ekholm-Friedman and Jonathan Friedman, Robert R. Kaufman, Thomas Telfer, Andrew Christie, Brian Hehir and Stephen Van Evera, and Edward Walker—for their hospitality and for the occasion to think and rethink these issues. I am greatly indebted to Layna Mosley for research assistance. The present chapter was originally published in *Ethnicity and Group Rights, Nomos*, 39, ed. Will Kymlicka and Ian Shapiro, and is reprinted by permission of New York University Press.

implications for the relations of ethnic groups to territories, to other proximate ethnic groups, and to their territories in turn.

To be sure, not all ethnic conflict has a significant territorial side. In some countries, groups are territorially so intermixed that political claims reflect aspirations to power within the existing territory, rather than ripening into movements for a change of state boundaries. (Neighbourhood and electoral boundaries are another matter, of course.) Yet, in many parts of the world, groups make claims to homelands that produce demands for ethnically induced boundary alterations. The conflicts in Bosnia, Chechnya, and Nagorno-Karabagh—not to mention Georgia-Abkhazia, Moldova-Transniestria, or Crimea-Ukraine—all make these issues timely. Nevertheless, they have enduring features that easily transcend current controversies, raising important and, as I shall suggest, intertwined questions about patterns of ethno-territorial politics, about the status of ethnic self-determination in philosophy, and about rights to a territorially conceived ethnic self-determination in international law. In pursuing these related questions, my theme will be that a fuller understanding of the patterns of ethnic politics can—and assuredly should—inform emerging debates about self-determination in politics, philosophy, and law.

What a fuller understanding discloses, above all, are the limits of territorial solutions to ethnic conflicts. The limits to territorially based ethnic aspirations have often been obscured, because the world has just emerged, as I shall explain, from a period of unusual stability in state boundaries. Now that territorial boundaries seem more generally adjustable, it has become plausible to inquire into the purposes for which boundaries ought to be changed. Moral and legal theories have been laid on the table, and the norm of ethnic self-determination is being revitalized after a period of dormancy. The theories have been cascading more quickly than has understanding of patterns of ethnic conflict in general or of ethno-territorial movements in particular. As a result, the emerging norms risk being seriously out of joint with the phenomena that form their subject matter. The norms may even foster the acceleration of conflict, without the attenuation of ethnic domination to which they aspire.

IRREDENTAS, SECESSIONS, AND STATE BOUNDARIES

There are two main forms of ethnically induced territorial adjustment: irredentas and secessions.[1] Secession involves the withdrawal of a group and its territory from the authority of a state of which it is a part. Irredentism entails the retrieval of ethnically kindred people and their territory across an international boundary, joining them and it to the retrieving state. The difference is between subtracting alone and subtracting and then adding what has been taken away to an adjacent state.

From these differences follow others. Secession is a group-led movement. Irredentism, on the other hand, is state initiated, although groups, of course, lobby the retrieving state to take irredentist action. In the post-Second World War period, there have been few actively pursued irredentas but many attempted secessions, some of them eventuating in warfare lasting decades, as in Burma since 1949 or the Southern Sudan on and off since 1963.

Irredentism is inhibited by all the forces that prevent rash action by states. An irredentist movement can be deterred by displays of force. It can be requited by concessions made by the state that is the target of the irredenta, even by concessions on unrelated matters of interstate relations.

Moreover, irredentist states are unlikely to be ethnically homogeneous, so successful pursuit of the irredenta would change ethnic balances in the retrieving state. Pursuit of the Somali irredenta against the Ethiopian Ogaden would, if it resulted in a transfer of people and territory, greatly augment the proportion of Darood, already the largest group in Somalia. Not surprisingly, Hawiye and Isaq have been less enthusiastic about the movement. Successful irredentism might alter sub-ethnic or political balances within the kindred group in the retrieving state. An Albania that managed to add Kosovo to Albania would also turn the balance of Ghegs and Tosks upside down in Albania, for while Tosks are the leading subgroup in the home country, Ghegs predominate on the Yugoslav side of the border. A Malaysia that got seriously interested in transferring Malays and their territory in southern Thailand to Malaysia would soon find that the affinities of Malays in Thailand to Malays in the Malaysian state of Kelantan would likely produce a dramatically unsettling change in the balance of party politics, in favour of the opposition Pan-Malayan Islamic Party that runs the Kelantan state government. All of these apprehensions operate to inhibit active irredentism. There are others as well.

A separate question relates to whether the group to be retrieved will wish to be retrieved. Often the answer is negative, as the Taiwanese, among many others, have made clear. The retrieving state may be poorer, or more authoritarian, or otherwise undesirable. The group to be retrieved may be seen at the centre of the irredentist state as consisting of country bumpkins or people who lived too long under the corrupting cultural influences of an alien regime. The group to be retrieved is, by definition, peripheral, and it needs to be saved from the effects of being located in what is viewed as the wrong state. These characteristics often produce a stigma. Members of the peripheral group surely know the stigma exists and may have experienced it on visits to the irredentist state, where they perhaps displayed the wrong accent, the wrong manners, or an inadequate knowledge of the group's destiny and history. If they know they are patronized as rustics, their enthusiasm for reunion may be diminished.

Politicians in the region to be retrieved have their own reservations. They can easily imagine that their position will not improve if their constituents and territory are transferred to a new, larger state. They will have to break into an already crystallized political situation in the annexing state from a merely regional (and in many ways still foreign) base. Their existing clientele will be vulnerable to absorption in a larger political party that serves the whole ethnic group, particularly if overarching group sentiment—pan-whatever-it-is—rises before and during the transition, as it surely will. They, however, will have little ability to expand their influence outward; they will need to worry about keeping the support they have. These leaders are therefore small fish jumping from one big pond, in which their clientele is at least secure—since they act as representatives of the minority that their group constitutes in the existing state—into another big pond, in which that security is gone.

As a result of all of these inhibitions, there have been few active irredentas, compared to the many possibilities raised by the dissonance between territorial boundaries and ethnic boundaries. Yet there are some. Armenia's claim to Nagorno-Karabagh is one, and Pakistan's claim to Kashmir is another. Even those that have been active at some time in the past tend to be on back burners: Somalia and the Ogaden; Albania and Kosovo; Hungary and Romanian Transylvania, the south of Slovakia, and the Vojvodina region of Serbia; until recently, China and Taiwan. In virtually all, there are restraints. If Kashmir were, with Pakistani aid, to free itself from Indian rule, the result would likely be, not accession to Pakistan, but an independent Kashmir, with major disintegrative consequences within Pakistan itself. With Somalia and Albania, there are restraints deriving from composition that I referred to earlier. With Hungary and Romania, any serious Hungarian irredentism would quickly confront the facts that Transylvania is itself heterogeneous and that Romanians are generally closer to the Hungarian border than are the centres of Hungarian population in Romania. The frequent heterogeneity of the region to be retrieved creates yet another inhibition on irredentism.

Secession, by contrast, is usually a more precipitously undertaken decision. Many secessionist movements (but only many, not all) are begun by groups stigmatized as backward.[2] Convinced that they cannot compete in the undivided state of which they are a part, colonized by civil servants from other regions, and subjected to uncongenial policies on language, religion, or other symbols of state ownership, the patience of such groups is quickly exhausted. Many attempt independence, often heedless of economic costs, including the loss of subsidies from the centre.

One reason for the relative attractiveness of secession, compared to the *status quo* or to irredentism, resides in the position of ethnic group leaders. In contrast to what they can expect if their group and territory are annexed by their irredentist cousins, secessionist élites can expect to become big fish in a small pond. In a secessionist state, they can easily push aside the queue for civil service positions and for political leadership that exists in the undivided state. When the Sudan became independent and senior civil service positions were 'Sudanized', Southerners were, by dint of their relatively low educational standing and seniority, allocated only about six of the 800 positions vacated by the departing British. Other relatively poorly educated groups have had comparable experiences. Similarly, political party leaders who, in the undivided state, head an ethnic minority party that is likely to be shut out of power permanently, can expect, with secession and independence, to see their minority status transformed overnight. That is the very meaning of ethnic secession, after all. For ethnic élites, small is indeed beautiful; it provides them with the prerogatives, the perquisites, and the trappings of power. Better to be the president of Abkhazia or Transniestria than to be the leader of an ethnically differentiated, permanent opposition party in Georgia or Moldova.

A good many transborder groups have the potential choice to be retrieved by an irredentist neighbour or to secede.[3] The convertibility of claims means that, all else equal, the fewer the irredentas, the more the secessions.

Secessionist movements persist despite the many obstacles to their success. For nearly fifty years after the Second World War, only one state was created by a secessionist movement through force of arms: Bangladesh.[4] Bangladesh had crucial assistance from India, which acted out of two idiosyncratic motives.

First, quite obviously, by detaching East Bengal from Pakistan, India could achieve an important strategic objective: the breakup and reduction in power of a menacing neighbour. Few states in a position to aid separatists in adjacent territories have such an overwhelming motive.

Second, India acted to avert the growth of pan-Bengali sentiment that might have produced alternatives to a secessionist Bangladesh. At the time of the insurgency in East Bengal, pan-Bengali sentiment was growing. If, as it then seemed, religion was an inadequate basis for statehood in Pakistan, perhaps ethnic affinity and the strong cultural links that bind all Bengalis might provide a more durable foundation. Had this sentiment been allowed to grow, it might have produced a movement to reincorporate East Bengal into India or to create a separate pan-Bengali state out of Pakistani East Bengal and Indian West Bengal. Either possibility would have been enormously destabilizing for India. The first would have unbalanced India in religious and ethnic terms, by adding some 70 million more Muslims (most Hindus having already fled to India) and some 70 to 80 million Bengalis altogether to the population and political mix of India. The second would have created a precedent for other states to detach themselves from the Indian federation. Given these devastating possibilities, India did not wait for them to develop: it aided Bangladesh to achieve its independence by force.

Most secessionists, however, receive insufficient aid to do the same. Many neighbouring states will aid secessionists in order to achieve some gain by meddling in the affairs of their neighbours, but few will provide sufficient assistance over a period long enough to help the secessionists through a protracted war.[5] Most states have more limited motives for supporting secessionists than the secessionists do for fighting. An assisting state is vulnerable to the quid pro quo, to domestic pressure to end support, or to some weak spot (perhaps an ethnic-minority vulnerability of its own) that makes it recalculate the costs of involvement. Most long standing secessionist movements receive support from multiple sources. The support comes and goes; it is rarely enough. By contrast, the international system has a strong bias toward central governments; these are able to augment their own military resources with external assistance for which they are likely to be able to give more than separatists are in return. For all these reasons, secession is usually a long shot.

Most of the time, then, irredentism is unattractive, and secession is impossible. Nevertheless, no one could have anticipated the extraordinary degree of territorial stasis in the fifty years since the Second World War. Given the considerable incidence of peoples divided by existing boundaries, the prospects for irredentism seemed, a priori, to be enormous. The number of aggrieved groups willing to resort to secessionist warfare has been large. In Asia and Africa, colonialism, which created the boundaries of inherited states, was unequivocally repudiated as illegitimate, thus opening the question of boundaries.[6] In the end, however, irredentism was subdued, secessionists were unable to make good their claims despite their heroic willingness to sacrifice for them, and successor states accepted and even legitimated the inherited colonial boundaries. Together with the European *status quo* induced by the Cold War, the confluence of these forces produced the most remarkable stability in state boundaries during the past half-century—a half-century marked, paradoxically, by severe and growing ethnic conflict within states that might have been expected to spill over boundaries and contribute to the disintegration of many states. None of the entirely reasonable expectations for state disintegration and boundary change was fulfilled.

SEPARATISM: A NEW WATERSHED

Several recent developments enhance prospects for a proliferation of states arising out of ethnic movements. Underpinning these developments are changes in thinking about self-determination, but the developments have also precipitated the changes in thought, and so I shall deal with the events before turning to explicit theoretical justifications. This is not merely to satisfy a general curiosity about a changing landscape. Rather, I shall argue that any legal or moral response to these phenomena that elides some of their recurrent characteristics will be inapt, inadequate, or counter-productive.

Sequencing is an underrated explanatory factor in social life. Whether one event precedes another and whether several events are confluent often shapes outcomes and certainly has in this field. In the case of secession and state dissolution, critical events have been confluent and capriciously sequenced. They came thick and fast, and easy cases came first, setting precedents for what should have been seen as harder cases.

First there was the victory of the Eritrean secessionists by force of arms —a victory unprecedented in independent Africa. It was a victory won in fortuitous ways and at a fortuitous time. The Eritrean war against Ethiopia was fought in conjunction with other insurgent movements within Ethiopia proper and was probably won for this reason. The victory and the secession came at the same time as the fragmentation of Liberia and Somalia. North Somalia, the former British Somaliland, a predominantly Isaq region, has declared its independence. The confluence of these movements may ultimately produce increasing instability in African boundaries, which have been remarkably stable.

On the other hand, perhaps not. North Somalia is unrecognized. Liberia has experienced territorial stalemate rather than the emergence of new polities. Eritrea was, like the Baltic states, a case of illegitimate incorporation. Haile Selassie disregarded his promise to maintain a federal relationship with the former trust territory of Eritrea. Equally important, the Tigrean and Oromo movements, which also defeated Addis Ababa, actually agreed that Eritrea could have its independence. Central governments do not generally agree to regional secession.

Idiosyncratic or not, successful secessionist movements are likely to have demonstration effects. The unsuccessful Biafra movement catalysed separatists among the Agni and the Bété in the Ivory Coast. Bangladesh had a stronger effect, especially on the Baluch of Pakistan, on the Sri Lankan Tamils, and on the Mizo and Naga in north-east India. Africa has many weak states that might be vulnerable, although most African secessionists will be unable to call upon a strong neighbouring state with motives for assistance as powerful as India's in Bangladesh.

The second critical event, the dissolution of the Soviet Union, more or less by consent, proliferated new states. In the wake of this fragmentation, there are many actual and potential sub-secessions—within Moldova, Georgia, and Tajikistan, in Chechnya, perhaps in the north of Kazakhstan or in the Narve area of Estonia, among others. Some 25 million Russians reside outside Russia, where they are subject to discrimination and sometimes clustered in compact areas adjacent to a Russian border that is subject to dispute. In a number of autonomous republics of the Russian Federation, there are so-called titular nationalities that aspire to independence.[7] In turn, Russian minorities or majorities in these republics may nurse their own aspirations or will when they feel the brunt of the hostility against them.

The more or less peaceful and consensual parting of the ways in the former Soviet Union was remarkable. Again fortuitously, the Baltic states, with indisputably legitimate claims, led the way, and the Central Asian republics, at first reluctant, soon joined in. The domino effects of secessions within states are considerable, which is one major reason central governments almost universally fight them. In Russia, however, the central government did not fight. Instead, it acquiesced in the movement to break the Union.

Two changes underlay the assent of Moscow. The first involved sentiment at the bottom. The second was a function of rivalry at the top.

During the pre-dissolution period of the late 1980s and very early 1990s, many Russians were abandoning Soviet imperial pretensions and identification with the Soviet Union in favour of identification with Russia. This contraction in identity was coupled with and fostered by the growth of anti-Southern (especially anti-Caucasus) and anti-Muslim sentiment. Food markets in Moscow were dominated by migrants from the Caucasus, many of whom were later expelled from Moscow. Ethnic clashes in the South were regarded with extreme distaste, and the prevailing Russian view of Southerners—especially Chechens and Azeris—was of corrupt and criminal influences. The results of these prejudices was a demand to 'cast off ungrateful neighbours'.[8] Here is an unusual case in which ethnic antipathy was conducive to a peaceful outcome.

Such an outcome was also the unintended consequence of leadership rivalry in what was formally a federal system. When Boris Yeltsin ascended the presidency of the Russian Federation, he was able to use his office as a platform to pursue his conflict with Gorbachev. The means to do this was for Russia to oppose the Soviet Union.[9]

In the background to these developments lay the crumbling legitimacy and diminished capacity of the Soviet regime.[10] No longer able to steer a course, Moscow vacillated between attempting to keep the Union together by force and speaking a wholly new language of consent. The decline of the centre enabled people to act on their sentiments and politicians to pursue their rivalries. As a consequence, what might have been a series of cataclysmic secessionist wars became instead a dissolution by something close to mutual consent. This is, as I have said, highly unusual.

It is not unusual for more than one region in a political unit to entertain secessionist aspirations. Often these aspirations are conceived as embodying the desire to separate from another region, not merely from the undivided state. Reciprocal secessionist movements result.[11] A year before the attempted secession of Biafra, the Ibo-dominated Eastern Region of Nigeria, there was a serious possibility of a Northern secession, at a time when the Nigerian regime viewed itself as having been controlled by Ibo military officers. Only after these officers were overthrown by a Northern coup did the Biafra movement take shape. By then, Northerners became committed to and fought for an undivided Nigeria. Likewise, in the Indian state of Andhra Pradesh, there was a strong secessionist movement in the Telangana region in the 1960s. When policies were put in place to respond to the movement and keep the Telanganas attached, there was a secessionist reaction to those policies by people from the coastal region, who saw themselves disadvantaged by them. Reciprocal secession is part of the zero-sum game of ethnic conflict. It is therefore an alternating rather than a simultaneous phenomenon. The alternating character of the sentiment explains why secession so often produces warfare rather than amicable agreement to part. And that in turn is why the Soviet case is so truly exceptional.

The effect of a peaceful dissolution of the USSR was to create at a stroke an array of new states, as well as to pave the way for secessionist warfare within several of them. Had the Soviet dissolution not been consensual, it would have had much less profound, albeit much less peaceful, results. Perhaps some republics would have freed themselves, while others remained repressed. The Soviet Union would have reinforced rather than undermined existing boundaries.

The third event, the dissolution of Yugoslavia and the creation of independent Slovenia, Croatia, Macedonia, Montenegro, Bosnia, and Serbia, occurred along the more usual—that is to say, non-consensual, violent—lines. Although Bosnia is a state with no history of independence,[12] the disintegration of Yugoslavia was followed by international recognition of the new states. Led by Germany, European and American recognition of the former Yugoslav republics was accomplished in disregard of international-law doctrine forbidding recognition of secessionist units whose establishment is being resisted forcibly by a central government.[13]

The recognition of the Baltic states, which was inevitable, may have affected recognition practice when it came to Yugoslavia. It seems clear, however, that there has been a sharp change in the willingness of Western states to recognize secessionists. It is not a uniform change, as non-recognition of Northern Somalia makes clear, but it is palpable, and it can be sensed by contrasting Biafra. Biafra was a cause with great sympathy in the West, particularly in the United States. Many Ibo had studied in the United States, and Biafran propaganda about ethnic oppression, wartime suffering, and infant starvation was extremely skilful. In spite of this, not only did Western countries, excepting France, which aided Biafra militarily, refuse to recognize Biafra, but the United States, Britain, and the Soviet Union all assisted the Nigerian central government in its military efforts, despite its culpability in creating the conditions that led to war. Barely a glimmer of such Western central-government bias was in evidence in the Yugoslav case. As we shall soon see, this change in the willingness to recognize secessionists may slowly be felt in international law.

If Eritrean independence and the dissolution of the Soviet Union and Yugoslavia are watershed events shaping prospects for the proliferation of states—and, to that extent, for a territorially based doctrine of self-determination—it is none the less possible to draw too much from them. The Eritrean and Soviet experiences are, in some ways, special cases, even if major special cases. The recognition of the Yugoslav secessionists took place at an especially weak moment for Western diplomacy and will surely not be seen everywhere as a successful policy.

Even so, there are now new incentives to secession. Secessionists have defeated central governments, and one central government has recognized the legitimacy of multiple national separations. Even in the case of Yugoslavia, it could be said that the resulting war was not about secession *per se* but about the boundaries and the ethnic composition of the successor states.

All of this surely means that people who were resigned to living together, no matter how uncomfortably, may now think they no longer need to be so resigned. Secessionist movements did not need much encouragement before, when their prospects for success were very slim. Now they need less.

The background to this development is, as mentioned earlier, a surprising degree of firmness of inherited boundaries, an international law that countenanced no real departures from them, and an insistence by affected states—particularly strong in the Organization of African Unity[14]—that legal doctrine reinforce them by inhospitability to secession. International actors generally took a hard line against secession except in the rarest case (Bangladesh), and then only when it became a *fait accompli*. To put the point sharply, the former view was that international boundaries were fixed and regimes could do what they wished within them. This was the international framework for a good deal of tyranny.[15]

THE ILLUSION OF THE CLEAN BREAK

Although the incentives to secession may be changing, the demographic and political relations of ethnic groups within secessionist and rump regions are not changing. The assumption has usually been that secession produces homogeneous states. In point of fact, neither secessionist states nor rump states are homogeneous. They can be made more homogeneous only by the clumsiest and most unfair methods of population exchange or by policies of expulsion, always carried out with a massive dose of killing. Like Bosnia and Croatia, even after ethnic cleansing, the Southern Sudan, Eritrea, and areas claimed by the Tamil Tigers in Sri Lanka and countless other secessionist movements are ethnically heterogeneous, and so are the states they would leave behind. There used to be a tendency to think of secession as a form of 'divorce', a neat and clean separation of two antagonists who cannot get along. But if a crude household analogy could be applied to large collectivities, then, as in domestic divorces, there is nothing neat about it, and there are usually children (smaller groups that are victims of the split). Sometimes secession or partition is the least bad alternative, but it is rarely to be preferred. As I shall suggest, the opposite course, international regional integration and the amalgamation of states, is likely to produce far better results in many (though not all) cases of ethnic conflict. Unfortunately, it is a course unlikely to be pursued.

Secession or partition usually makes ethnic relations worse, because it simplifies intergroup confrontations. Instead of six groups, none of which could quite dominate the others—call this Yugoslavia—it is possible, by subtracting territory, to produce various bipolar alignments of one versus one or two versus one, together with the possibility, even the likelihood, that one side will emerge dominant. Simplification by secession reverses the benign complexity of states such as India or Tanzania that are fortunate enough to contain a multitude of dispersed groups, none with the power to control the others or to take possession of the state for its own ends.

Furthermore, not only are secessionist regions heterogeneous, but secession is often conceived as affording the means of 'dealing with' precisely that irritating heterogeneity. For if Group A, no longer in the undivided state, now holds power over the secessionist state, it can regulate the rights available to Group B, expel Group B if it is an immigrant group, oppress it, or even take genocidal measures against it. It is insufficiently appreciated that concern about demographic changes from in-migration to the secessionist region often motivates secessionist sentiment, as it has historically, for example, in the Basque country, in Catalonia, in the southern Philippines, and in the Shaba province of Zaire. None of this should surprise observers in the United States. The secession of 1861 in the United States South was, in part, designed to permit Group A to 'deal with' Group B, without impediments from the North. Theories that rest on the reduction of the incidence of domination by means of territorial separation need to be treated with utmost scepticism. There is no clean break.

The clean-break theorists have another problem that derives from an inadequate analysis of the character of ethnic affiliations. Ethnicity is a contextual and therefore mutable affiliation. As I shall show later, what looks homogeneous today in an undivided state in which large groups oppose each other can look quite different after a secessionist state establishes itself. The benefits of secession and partition for the reduction of ethnic conflict are very easy to exaggerate. Those writers who, with increasing frequency and decreasing caution, advocate partition as the 'solution' to ethnic conflict[16] neglect the contextual character of ethnic affiliations at their peril.[17]

THE CONSEQUENCES OF TERRITORIAL DIVISION

If the break is not clean, perhaps it can be cleaned up by further territorial adjustments incidental to secession. In the Biafra case, for example, severing the territory of the non-Ibo minorities would certainly have reduced heterogeneity within Biafra as well as in the severed territory (particularly after the massacre and flight of Ibo from Port Harcourt). Apart from the fact that populations are more intermixed than many people imagine, such possibilities encounter two major obstacles.

The first is the common desire to limit the damage done by a secession. If secession is unavoidable, if it becomes a *fait accompli*, the undivided state will not necessarily be interested in multiplying the effects of secession by encouraging further territorial division, except to reclaim for itself part of the secessionist region. Identifying those who get to opt out becomes a new source of conflict.

The second obstacle to realigning groups and territories after secession derives from the confusion buried in the concept of self-determination when the expression of self-determination takes a territorial form. While self-determination refers to people, secession refers to territory. (As I shall suggest, this confusion reflects a deeply rooted ambiguity in the Western political tradition.) Despite the ethnic sources of most secessions, secessionists themselves generally claim independence for the whole territory and for everyone in it, just as the undivided state did.

There is to be, then, no secession from secession. This matter was made as clear as any such confusion can be made by the Arbitration Committee attached to the International Conference on the Former Yugoslavia. The conference had asked the committee to determine the lawfulness of the secessions from Yugoslavia. The committee pronounced Yugoslavia to be a federation 'in the process of dissolution',[18] and it therefore concluded that new states could emerge within the previous republican boundaries (Croatia, Bosnia, Serbia, etc.) but not within any other boundaries.[19] Croatia and Bosnia may thus secede but only intact.

The permissibility of disintegration of federations along the lines of their constituent units is profoundly important. This new doctrine appears to legitimate the secession of Eritrea, which earlier had a federal relationship with Ethiopia, and it could conceivably justify secession of intact units from other federal states, such as India, Pakistan, Malaysia, Canada, Belgium, Nigeria, and the Russian Federation. To the extent that the newly articulated rule means that the cessation of participation of a constituent republic in a federal government sets in motion the process of disintegration, the committee's decision puts in place an enormous disincentive for the creation of federal arrangements to ameliorate ethnic conflict in the first place. Inadvertently, it confirms the otherwise unfounded but very common fears of central policy-makers that devolution to regional units constitutes the first step to secession. Confining the lines along which dissolution of federal states can take place to the boundaries of the constituent units limits the possibility of further secession within those constituent units.[20] '[W]hatever the circumstances,' pronounced the committee, 'the right to self-determination must not involve changes to existing frontiers at the time of independence', barring agreement to the contrary.[21] In short, the minorities in Croatia and Bosnia are entitled to minority rights,[22] but they may not lawfully alter the boundaries of the states in which they find themselves, either to secede or to accede to the adjacent republics. So a liberal rule legitimating secession of constituent federal units is matched by a strict prohibition on any further territorial change.

One of the most prominent effects of secession (or partition) is to place an international boundary between former domestic antagonists, thereby transforming their domestic conflicts into international conflicts, as partition did for India and Pakistan. Without further boundary change, warfare is made more likely, because kindred minorities, formerly within the same state, are placed beyond the reach of their cousins across the border, where their plight elicits sympathy and urgency. This applies to Croats in Bosnia as well as to Serbs in Bosnia and Croatia; it applies to Russians in Transniestria, Estonia, and Kazakhstan, and to Uzbeks in Kirghizia, among many others.

To be sure, irredentism will still be considered illegitimate. The prohibitions of Article 2 of the United Nations Charter on the acquisition of territory by force will still have some effect. Irredentism will thus be seen as different from withdrawal of a group and its territory from a state controlled by others. Consequently, the Serbian and Russian temptations will not be regarded with favour. But the Arbitration Committee rules and the generally growing receptivity to secession create the conditions that make irredentism tempting. While there have been surprisingly few active irredentas in the post-Second World War period, the secessions of heterogeneous regions will provide new reasons for irredentas to recapture territory lost as a result. Not only will there be more groups straddling boundaries (as there are more boundaries created), but, as these are fresh losses of people and territory, the usual inhibitions on pursuing irredentas will often be overcome. Irredentism thus can follow smoothly from secession.

THE BASES OF COMMUNITY AND THE PROBLEM OF PLURALISM

If new secessions are likely to produce lower-level ethnic tyrannies,[23] this is the result of pervasive ambivalence about principle. The international community seems to value simultaneously self-determination, increasingly defined in ethnic terms, and the sanctity of frontiers—principles that are in collision. Some people therefore get to determine the future of others.

Much of this problem comes from mixing two different ideas of social organization. In Western political thought, which has influenced political practice far beyond the West, there is, on the one hand, the familiar idea of the social contract between individuals, and there is, on the other, the contending idea that society grows out of the family. Writers like Sir Henry Sumner Maine, who superimposed on this duality an evolutionist bent, identified contract with progress and status (including, prominently, birth-derived status) with 'primitive society'.[24] Not all nineteenth-century writers, however, accepted Maine's teleology; some were influenced by German notions of *Volksgeist*, which were decidedly anti-contractarian. As organizing principles, territorial proximity and contract form only one part of the Western tradition. The other part, informed by German Romanticism, consists of concepts of community based on birth. Contemporary evidence of the alternative can be found in citizenship law and practice. Until very recently, citizenship in Germany was almost entirely based on *jus sanguinis*, or descent, and naturalization was exceedingly difficult.[25] Alternative ideas about the bases of community remain, and they show up in many places.

Self-determination is one of those places. The theory and practice of self-determination oscillate between the two conceptions. The post-First World War Wilsonian idea of the self-determination of nations was applied, albeit far from completely, to national—or, for present purposes, ethnic—groups. The post-Second World War version was applied to 'peoples' in colonial territories. Everyone in the territory was supposed to form part of the people, and the right or principle of self-determination (such as it was) was deemed to be spent upon the attainment of independence. In this phase, self-determination did not have an ethnic dimension.[26]

In fact, there are two kinds of states in the world as well as a good many hybrids. Often self-determination of the Wilsonian sort produces states that are supposed to belong to particular peoples, those whom the Russians call the titular nationality because their name is reflected in the name of the republic: the Tatars in Tatarstan, the Bashkirs in Bashkortostan, and so on, even if they are a minority in the republic, as they frequently are. And so Romania is said to belong to the Romanians, Fiji is said to belong to the Fijians, and Kazakhstan is said to belong to the Kazakhs. Such notions legitimize the status of one group that purports to be at the core of the state. The problem is that others also live within the bounds of such states, and their position is, more often than not, tenuous. Each of the new states of the former Yugoslavia is based on a constitutional structure that accorded sovereignty to one group and so quickly threatened the future of others in the territory.[27]

In states based ostensibly on territorial proximity—which includes, among others, virtually all African states—different problems arise. Some ethnic groups may have claims to priority in the state, notwithstanding and even in defiance of its inclusive character. The conflict between competing principles of community is likely to be sharp in such cases.[28] With or without such explicit claims, the territorial-proximity state still has the problem of majority rule. In severely divided societies, under free elections, ethnic conflict produces ethnically based parties, and eventually one or more of them typically come to dominate the rest. Those who are excluded sense that their exclusion is permanent, since it is based on ascriptive identity, and they may resort to violence.

To put it starkly, then, the self-determination view makes birth-based identity the cornerstone of political community and produces a state with ethnic characteristics and minority exclusion (or occasionally majority exclusion). The territorial-proximity view, based on undifferentiated majority rule, also produces an ethnically exclusionary state. In the first instance, elections in such a state (for example, Nigeria, Sri Lanka, or Bosnia) look as if they are textbook illustrations of democracy in action. On closer inspection, however, their purpose is to determine who will be included in the governing institutions of the polity and who will be excluded.

In the end, then, the results of the two views are not much different. In fact, the domination of the territorial-proximity state by a single ethnic group may lead to its transformation into a state that increasingly belongs to a single ethnic group, as, for example, Sri Lanka after 1956 began to assume characteristics of a state belonging to the Sinhalese.

Now, to this predicament of inclusion and exclusion, rarely articulated quite so explicitly, several answers are possible. The first is consociation, a prescription for treating the multi-ethnic state for some purposes as if it is more than one polity and for according to each of the subpolities a considerable degree of veto power and autonomy.[29] Few states outside Western Europe have gone in this direction, and some that have been coerced into following this course (such as Cyprus) have rapidly turned away from doing so.

There are some obvious and non-obvious reasons for the unpopularity of parcelling out sovereign power in divided societies. It seems plain enough that those who have all of state power within their reach have no incentive to take a large fraction of it and give it away. The most likely motive advanced, the awareness by leaders of the risk of mutual destruction,[30] is based on a time horizon not generally employed in the calculations of political leaders; and, in any case, it certainly is not clear to them in advance that disintegrative conflict is not best deterred by a system that keeps power in their own hands. Furthermore, the sentiments of leaders and followers in divided societies are hardly conducive to what are regarded as concessions to the other side. If statesmanship is required, then it needs to be pointed out that the assumption that élites are invariably less ethnocentric than their supporters is without foundation. Most studies do not show leaders to be less ethnocentric than their followers, and some studies show that ethnocentrism actually increases with education.[31] Whatever the dispositions of leaders may be, when leaders have tried to compromise, it has been shown repeatedly that leadership leeway is very narrow on issues of ethnic power in severely divided societies. Compromisers can readily be replaced by extremists on their flanks, once the latter are able to make the case that a sell-out of group interests is in progress.[32] In short, no mechanism can be adduced for the adoption or retention of consociational institutions, particularly no reason grounded in electoral politics.

A rather different approach is to make multi-ethnic participation at the centre of power rewarding to all the participants who espouse it. The approach is different, because it does not require that élites entertain and act on conciliatory feelings that may not exist but assumes only that they will follow their interests. Since such an approach is based on political incentives, it requires some institutions, particularly electoral institutions, that are specially tailored for severely divided societies.[33] In severely divided societies, parties typically break along ethnic lines. The identification of party with ethnic group eliminates any significant number of floating voters. Where there are few, if any, floating voters, democratic business-as-usual results in the bifurcation of the included and the excluded. Some multi-ethnic states have stumbled across apt institutions to mitigate polarization of this kind, but it will require coherent packages of institutions, not partial adoptions that can be neutralized by countervailing institutions,[34] to make such incentives to intergroup accommodation effective.

Because this approach is designed to reward political leaders for inter-ethnic moderation, sustaining the system, once it is adopted, will be much easier than sustaining consociational arrangements that are based merely on exhortations and constitutional constraints, devoid of political incentives. Still, the threshold problem of adoption remains. Rather than innovate with an explicit view to conciliation, most states, most of the time, have adhered to institutions associated with their former colonial power or to institutions that were otherwise familiar to them. Hardly any state has learned from the actual experience with ethnic conflict of any other state.

A third, neglected approach is territorial, entailing the opposite of secession: international regional integration, to build larger, more complex multi-ethnic states, for reasons familiar to readers of the *Federalist* papers and exemplified, for severely divided societies, by India. Scale, as Madison wrote in the *Federalist*, no. 10, proliferates interests and makes it more difficult for any single interest to dominate. India is a federal state with so many compartmentalized ethnic cleavages that no single group can be said to dominate the state at the centre.[35] Nevertheless, it is perfectly obvious that the prevailing world-wide trend is in the opposite direction, toward smaller states, for reasons already explored.

Had any of these three approaches gained widespread popularity and displayed significant efficacy in mitigating severe ethnic conflict, self-determination—especially ethno-territorial self-determination—would not be the genuinely burning issue it has become. Largely in response to disintegrative events, there is a revived interest among philosophers in the political significance of ethnicity and among international lawyers in the law of secession and minority rights. Philosophers and international lawyers have been engaged in a dialogue about self-determination, a subject on which the international lawyers and foreign policy-makers have also had exchanges. Here, then, is a case in which evolving ideas may soon matter in practice.

PHILOSOPHICAL ARGUMENTS ABOUT SECESSION

Recent philosophical writings on self-determination would provide more latitude for secession than state practice has customarily afforded.[36] While the philosophical arguments vary, many have a core of similarity in their starting assumptions. Self-determination is to important groups (mainly birth groups) what moral autonomy is to individuals. Just as individual autonomy is an important value, argues Neil MacCormick, so is 'some form of collective self-constitution'[37] for those groups that share a consciousness of kind. For Margalit and Raz, groups important to the well-being of their members have rights to political expression, because collective welfare and individual welfare are linked; hence there is 'an intrinsic value' to self-government on the part of groups as 'an extension of individual autonomy'.[38] For David Miller, the relation of individual and group autonomy is most direct; he speaks of exercising 'at the collective level the equivalent of autonomy at the individual level'.[39] In such starting points, the roots of contemporary thinking on this subject in Kantian conceptions of individual autonomy are apparent.[40]

Viewing ethnic self-determination as simply the collective equivalent of the moral autonomy of individuals produces some fairly sweeping presumptions that groups from which people derive satisfaction and self-esteem should be able to govern themselves. Almost by virtue of their existence, such groups entertain political aspirations that require recognition.[41] Group membership, if it is to be fruitful, requires 'full expression', which is best assured through self-government.[42] Morally autonomous beings should have their political preferences respected, and territory easily follows.[43]

A free-flowing right to secede is sometimes qualified by concerns deriving from respect for the interests of other groups. If, for example, an 'illiberal regime' were to result, then secession might not be sanctioned.[44] And if there are minorities in the secessionist regime—a matter rarely touched on in these treatments[45]—then minority rights must be guaranteed.[46]

It hardly needs to be said that many ethnic movements have illiberal aspects, for reasons that derive from their focus on ancestry, on blood and soil, and on the mystification of group identity that often accompanies ethnic conflict. As mentioned previously, secessionist movements sometimes gain much of their energy from a desire to 'deal with' regional minorities, free from the intrusion of the centre. Even movements that do not begin this way can, nevertheless, produce illiberal, intolerant regimes. The inability to forecast the emergence of an illiberal regime with any degree of reliability renders this qualification on the right to secession illusory.

Neither does the assurance of minority rights assure much. The historical experience with minority rights is not reassuring, as I shall soon show. Since secessions are fostered precisely by the difficulty of accommodating minorities, the presumption that the situation will be different in the new state cannot be accepted without substantial evidence that it will.

I noted earlier that much of the recent philosophical literature is based on projection of claims to individual autonomy onto a larger collective canvas, rather than on any sense of qualitative distinctiveness about ethnic groups. These are liberal, individualistic theories. It may seem curious that such a thin understanding of the nation as an extension of the individuals comprising it quickly gives rise to territorial claims on behalf of such collectivities. Even more curiously, thicker and generally more conventional understandings of nations as differentiated, culture-bearing units, with an interest in expressing and preserving their distinctiveness—rather than as groups simply pursuing an extended version of individual freedom—do not necessarily lead to territorial claims.[47] Curious or not, sharply individualistic justifications of a collective right to secede appear to be ascendant.[48]

A few liberal philosophers are more circumspect and less generous to secessionists. Will Kymlicka finds secession acceptable when it is voluntary and mutual, but he acknowledges that secession 'is not always possible or desirable', because some states might not be 'viable', some movements would produce warfare, and 'there are more nations in the world than possible states'.[49] Kymlicka's focus, however, is not on secession but on the problems of undivided multi-ethnic states, and his consideration of the issues is hardly plenary. Allen Buchanan, who is focused squarely on the morality of secession, argues that secession is justified only where the undivided state refuses to cease perpetrating serious injustices or where a group's survival is threatened.[50] Even in the latter case, he would inquire about the availability of lesser alternatives, such as a loose federalism.[51] Per Bauhn would not countenance secession in the absence of serious discrimination and, like Buchanan, would seek less drastic alternatives, unless the undivided state resorts to repression.[52] The caution of Buchanan and Bauhn underscores the incaution of others, including some influential philosophers, who would not require any such inquiry.

The renewed activity of philosophers in this field derives, of course, from events. The claims of oppressed ethnic groups to self-determination are bound to have considerable prima-facie appeal when ethnic warfare and genocide are recurrent. Added to this is the great failure of imagination in adapting democratic institutions to the predicament of severely divided societies. But if interest in the problem is driven by events, the methodology is not, for much of the literature thus far often displays a thoroughgoing ignorance of the complexities of ethnic interactions. To say this is not to exhibit hostility to the efforts of philosophers on such issues in general—for moral reasoning is needed—but a priori methods that seem appropriate to other issues are utterly unsuitable to this problem.

Consider a recurrent set of empirical assumptions. It is sometimes, albeit rarely, noted that secession could create a new set of minority problems in the secessionist region. The response is, as Margalit and Raz say, that this is a 'risk [that] cannot be altogether avoided'.[53] This puts the problem rather mildly, since, nine times out of ten, the creation of a new set of minority problems is a 'risk' that will come to pass. In Biafra, there were the Rivers and Cross River people who were understandably hostile to Biafran independence. Bosnia has minorities everywhere; Croatia has Serbs in Krajina; Serbia has Hungarians in Vojvodina and Albanians in Kosovo; Kosovo in turn has Serbs. Slovakia has a large minority of Hungarians. Even relatively homogeneous Bangladesh had the Biharis, who were victimized immediately upon independence, and the Chakma in the Chittagong Hills, who soon resorted to arms. Beyond this, ethnic identities are extraordinarily responsive to context. A new, lower-level context will stimulate the salience of dormant, subethnic cleavages, usually submerged while common struggles are being played out on a larger canvas. Eritrea has Christian Eritreans and Muslim Eritreans, who fought each other intermittently even as both were fighting Ethiopia. The secession of South Kasai in Zaire in 1960 immediately produced a prominent, polarizing cleavage between Tshibanda and Mukuna. Both were subgroups of the Luba, who had suffered at the hands of the Lulua and had hoped South Kasai would be 'an all-Luba polity,' only to discover that 'the constriction of a political field may . . . generate new fissiparous tendencies'.[54] The same was true of the Ibo, solidary in the all-Nigeria context but in their home region divided by subregion into Owerri, Onitsha, Aro, and other subgroups that sought power along ascriptive lines. Aside from the Efik, Ijaw, and other Eastern Region minorities that resisted Biafran independence, the Ibo themselves would have produced ethnic heterogeneity and conflict, merely on a smaller scale, just as Pakistanis have done, in an ever-more-bloody way, since the partition of India. Underestimating the continuing problems of pluralism following secession, philosophers end up on this question just about where the Arbitration Committee did in the Yugoslav secession case: they make no provision for subsequent secessions or, for that

matter, for thinking about the adjustment of interethnic rights and duties in the new state. They also accord no weight to the interests of those left in the rump state in having access to people, property, and opportunities now to be located in the secessionist state.

THE EMERGING INTERNATIONAL LAW OF SECESSION AND MINORITY RIGHTS

International lawyers have so far been generally more cautious than philosophers but hardly more helpful. The evolving standards of international law bear close watching, because the end of the Cold War has produced, among other things, an intersection of two different trends. First, there has been more ethnic conflict in the former Soviet Union and Eastern Europe. Second, there has been a great reduction in, if not an end to, the impasse that blocked so much international action. As a result, there is likely to be more rapid development of international law and a more rapid development of international law pertinent to ethnic conflict, particularly, of course, self-determination claims, which so often implicate international actors. As the experience of the Yugoslav arbitral decisions already suggests, this is hardly a guarantee that the emerging legal norms will be crafted or enforced appropriately.

Some states respect the rights of minorities, but this respect cannot be attributed to international legal protections. The international law of self-determination and of minority rights has done very little to afford effective protection to minorities in undivided states or minorities in states created out of undivided states. Nevertheless, the efforts of international bodies and international lawyers have been directed disproportionately toward the creation of rarefied versions of new rights, often with a self-determination component to them. To the extent the new rights take hold in the consciousness of those they are to benefit, they are likely to prove disintegrative influences within states, without providing protection for minorities or any incentives for groups to find ways to live together.

The starting point for any inquiry remains the law of self-determination. There is a lively and long-standing debate over whether self-determination is still merely a principle or is now a right.[55] If it is a right, that does not determine who holds the right or what the right entails when exercised, particularly whether it embraces a right to secede. United Nations instruments speak variously of both the right and the principle of self-determination,[56] but there remains a consensus that there is no general right of ethnic groups to secession.[57] Even the self-determination exercise at Versailles following the First World War did not produce a general acknowledgment of a right to secede. Thus far the emphasis has been on the need to ascertain the freely expressed will of peoples, particularly colonized peoples; and *peoples* include all those occupying a territory.[58]

There have been many efforts to undermine the prevailing consensus. For some, the case for a legal conception of self-determination that includes ethnic groups, with the attendant possibility of secession, rests on cultural preservation as a collective good that is insufficiently cultivated by the present doctrine.[59] For others, the argument turns on the illegitimacy of a set of boundaries in the light of a historic grievance connected to the territory and how it came to be defined.[60] For a number of writers, the difficulties encountered by groups in living together in multi-ethnic states, with resulting discrimination, deprivation of human rights, and even genocide, have made recognition of a right to self-determination, including the creation of separate states on an ethnic basis, a matter of urgency.[61] A new openness to secession among writers on international law is unmistakable.

In an international system that remains, for most purposes, state dominated,[62] however, no broadly based rights of ethnic groups to secession seem likely to be recognized. Much more likely are post facto rationalizations of territorial separation on the basis of whatever attributes seem to fit particular cases, such as insurgent control over territory and consequent entitlement to recognition, as in Bangladesh,[63] or the dissolution of federal units along the lines of constituent republics, as in Yugoslavia. Since no such decision will affect a majority of states, what can be expected is incremental change in the rules of self-determination, with attendant and growing inconsistency of application. That, after all, is the common fate of flat rules in the face of what are seen to be changing circumstances.

An example of the inconsistency relates to those groups living under 'alien' or 'racist' regimes. Such groups are said to have a right to self-determination,[64] but the category of people living under 'alien' or 'racist' regimes turns out to embrace only one case for each adjective: Palestinians living under Israeli occupation and non-white South Africans living under apartheid, respectively. Other peoples living in territory acquired in warfare—Tibetans, for example—or peoples living under analogously exclusive regimes—such as Hutu living under the more violent version of apartheid prevailing in Burundi—are not included. To be sure, changes in Israeli–Palestinian relations and in the South African regime may vitiate these particular exceptions, but others may replace them. The categories are there for future invocation, even if for the moment 'alien' and 'racist' regimes constitute a limited edition.

The same cannot be said for the Draft Declaration on the Rights of Indigenous Peoples,[65] which spells out rights expansively and has considerable possibility for widespread application to divided societies in which one group claims to be indigenous and claims that others are immigrants, even though none is a so-called tribal people of the sort the Declaration aims to protect.[66] The effects on claims to a territorially based self-determination will, again, be incremental, but the prospects are assuredly considerable. The rights conferred by the Declaration constitute a combination of minority rights, such as the rights to practise and transmit distinctive customs and to provide education in the indigenous group's language,[67] and rights to self-determination, most notably provisions limiting the authority of states to take measures affecting indigenous peoples except with their informed consent.[68] Their expressly recognized 'right of self-determination' includes the right to 'freely determine their political status'.[69] The Declaration stops short, however, of providing for independence.[70]

The Declaration purports to create dozens of new rights for an indeterminate category of beneficiary-group. The Declaration does not attempt to define the term 'indigenous people', and the work of a United Nations Sub-Commission's Special Rapporteur on the problem of discrimination against indigenous peoples provides a conception sufficiently elastic to permit many groups to claim indigenous status.[71] The impact of the Declaration will prove difficult to confine. Interpreters close to the drafting of the document have made very broad claims for it.[72] Since all groups ultimately have their origin somewhere else, indigenousness is a concept that eludes definition, unless it merely refers to earlier arrival. Many groups claim to have arrived before others, in the state as a whole or in a single region. Sinhalese have often claimed priority in Sri Lanka by virtue of their arrival before the Tamils, but Tamils make contrary claims with respect to the Northern and Eastern Regions. Both groups may find support in the Declaration for their mutually exclusive aspirations, Sinhalese in the whole of Sri Lanka, Tamils in the regions they inhabit. The same applies in many other countries in which such claims are made. The likely disintegrative effects on territorially based ethnic conflict are not difficult to anticipate.

Attempts to protect the rights of minorities in general are not likely to have such effects. Rather, they are likely to have few, if any, effects at all. At various times, going back to the Treaty of Westphalia (1648), with its provisions regarding the rights of religious minorities, efforts have been made to breathe life into the international law of minority rights. Because the Wilsonian exercise in self-determination in Eastern Europe was incomplete, minorities treaties were imposed on the remaining multi-ethnic states that found themselves on the losing side of the First World War. The treaties were accepted reluctantly, enforced poorly, and undermined quickly as the Versailles order declined and the Second World War approached.[73]

The assertion of philosophers that secession may have to be accompanied by the provision of minority rights *tout court* needs to be viewed against this experience. International regimes for minority rights have generally failed to achieve even minimal objectives, and the frequency of secessionist movements themselves suggests the common inefficacy of measures within states to protect minority rights.

Following the Second World War, several minorities treaties were concluded: the Austro-Italian Treaty on the South Tyrol, relating to Austrians in Italy; the Austrian State Treaty, providing guarantees for Slovenes and Croats; and the Aaland Islands Treaty, protecting Swedes in Finland. These special regimes often allow a generous measure of minority protection. Because the treaties were concluded voluntarily, it stands to reason that their provisions, more generous than those of customary international law,[74] have had far more benign results.

There is no shortage of formal provisions to protect minorities. United Nations conventions are frequently inclusive in their coverage. The Convention on the Elimination of All Forms of Racial Discrimination (1969) covers groups based on 'national or ethnic origin',[75] and the Genocide Convention (1951) applies to national, racial, ethnic, and religious groups.[76] The protections afforded are often framed in general terms and, as recent experience indicates, often honoured in the breach. Some conventions, however, withdraw in one phrase what they accord in another. The UNESCO Convention against Discrimination in Education (1960), for example, recognizes the rights of minorities to maintain their own schools and teach in their own languages, but subject to the educational policy of each state.[77] The minority rights philosophers have assumed into their schemes, if and as necessary, turn out to be contradictions in terms when they are specific and to be ineffective when they are general.

In 1992, the General Assembly adopted a Declaration on the Rights of Minorities.[78] It provides, simultaneously, too little and too much. Like the Convention against Discrimination in Education, the Minorities Declaration takes as it gives: it allows minorities 'the right to participate effectively in decisions on the national and, where appropriate, regional level' but 'in a manner not incompatible with national legislation'.[79] The Declaration also accords members of minority groups 'the right to establish and maintain their own associations'.[80] If the term *associations* is meant to include ethnically based political parties, that is more than some states—especially African states—have been willing to allow. The Declaration exhorts states to 'create favourable conditions' for minority cultures to flourish.[81] It reaffirms the territorial integrity of states[82] but is silent on methods of implementing the one 'right' that might help preserve territorial integrity from challenge: the right not to be shut out of political power permanently by virtue of the ethnic exclusion of minorities, whether that exclusion is accomplished by ordinary electoral processes meant to produce democratic outcomes or by authoritarian means. The Declaration is a hortatory document.

Undaunted by the inability to effectuate even rudimentary guarantees of non-discrimination, international bodies have crossed new frontiers. The Conference on Security and Cooperation in Europe, meeting in Copenhagen in 1990, adopted a final document that included a provision obliging participating states to 'respect the right of persons belonging to national minorities to effective participation in public affairs' and mentioning local autonomy as one 'possible means' for meeting the obligation.[83] Other European bodies, notably the Council of Europe, have been active on the same front.[84] Despite all this activity, it is difficult to disagree with Hurst Hannum's conclusion that 'the substantive development since 1945 of international law related to minorities has been minimal'.[85]

International law has always been much influenced by academic writing, and academic writing has now moved toward a new emphasis on popular sovereignty. Thomas M. Franck has suggested that there may be an emerging international 'entitlement' to democracy.[86] Among the sources of this 'entitlement', its 'first building block', is the principle of self-determination,[87] and among its most prominent features is 'the emerging normative requirement of a participatory electoral process'.[88] Earlier, Antonio Cassese, who in 1993 became chief judge of the Yugoslav War Crimes Tribunal, had argued that the emerging meaning of self-determination is to provide the 'possibility for a people to choose a new social and political regime'.[89] Non-democratic governments deny self-determination, conceived broadly 'as the right of peoples or minorities to be free from any form of authoritarian oppression'.[90]

With widespread movements of democratization, these formulations will undoubtedly be influential in international law. What needs emphasis, however, is exactly how unresponsive they are to the political problems of severely divided societies.[91] To begin with, Cassese's formulation opens the door to a territorial fulfilment of the right to be free of oppression and to choose a new regime, without any criteria justifying its exercise. Much more fundamentally, both the Cassese and Franck formulations, with their intuitive emphasis on democracy and elections, miss completely the electoral paradox in divided societies. What is usually thought of as ordinary democracy is inadequate in societies in which Group A, with 60 per cent of the voters and often at least 60 per cent of the seats, can, under most democratic systems, shut out Group B, with 40 per cent. In such conditions, democracy is more the problem than the answer to a problem.[92]

The new declarations of minority rights, numerous though they are, are unlikely to contribute to the recognition of minority rights and in many cases are likely to stimulate further conflict, with unfortunate effects on minority rights. The same is surely true for newly invented rights to democratic governance, which are conceived too broadly to cope with the institutional difficulties encountered by divided societies.[93] International law can hardly be expected to prescribe appropriate and exact solutions to what is really a complex problem of electoral engineering.

A final area of international law with a heavy bearing on self-determination relates to recognition practice. Morton H. Halperin and David J. Sheffer have argued that international recognition ought to be the hook on which to hang certain international norms that are otherwise unenforceable.[94] Halperin and Sheffer contend that, before a secessionist state is recognized, the United States and international organizations ought to secure commitments from that state to democracy, minority rights, the inviolability of borders, the renunciation of force, the peaceful settlement of disputes, a market economy, the freedom for transborder minorities in the new state to decide on their own citizenship, and provisions for local autonomy and shared sovereignty over regions inhabited by such minorities.[95] It is left unsaid by Halperin and Sheffer that nearly all such new states have minorities, often minorities they wish to 'deal with' in their own way; that nearly all such states come into being by force; that nearly all are dissatisfied with their borders—or else the rump state is—and see those borders as eminently violable; that the drawing of any new boundary invites further conflict rather than shared sovereignty; and that, as already mentioned, democracy in divided societies is part of the problem, the 60–40 problem.

In any case, recognition practice hardly responds to such questions and is difficult to turn in these directions. Yugoslavia provides a convenient example.[96] Britain and France, concerned, respectively, about separatism in Scotland and Wales and in Corsica, were reluctant to recognize the dissolution of Yugoslavia. The Federal Republic of Germany, with East German unification on its agenda (not to mention long-standing ties with Croatia), led the way to recognition. In each case, apprehensions about fission or aspirations to fusion, as well as various other considerations based on interest, drove recognition policies that had major effects for the future of post-Soviet Eastern Europe and potential effects on European security overall. Given the idiosyncratic determinants of recognition policy, even in the face of the magnitude of the consequences of warfare in Yugoslavia, it is difficult to imagine how recognition could be turned to Halperin and Sheffer's objectives when the general stakes are, as they usually will be, much lower.

Even if recognition does not respond to idiosyncratic national interests and if Yugoslavia has more general significance, then recognition practice is going the other way—toward fewer conditions and faster recognition of secessionists. (By 'Yugoslavia', I mean both state practice and the arbitral award.) Obviously, this augurs ill for the imposition of conditions.

It seems perverse to start at the rear end of the problem—with secession and the demand for recognition—rather than to encourage domestic measures of interethnic accommodation. Early, generous devolution, coupled with abundant opportunities for a regionally concentrated group outside its own region, is generally a considerable disincentive to secession, since departure from the undivided state would forfeit those opportunities or leave a large fraction of the group's extraregional population outside any new state. (To be sure, for reasons specified earlier, these are not guarantees against secession. There are no guarantees.) Autonomous regions, provinces, or states in a federation that group people together homogeneously typically foster sub-ethnic divisions, if some are already present, thereby serving a variety of functions in interethnic conciliation. Politicians who have self-interested incentives to work in a conciliatory way across group lines will ordinarily do so, regardless of personal prejudice. But most constitution-makers, and certainly most international bodies, have not been diligent in creating those incentives.

Hardly any aspect of international law, save perhaps emerging rights to autonomy, is any more attuned to these domestic problems than recognition doctrine is. The problems are not aptly captured by the concept of minority rights, they do not really respond to the category of discrimination, and they are assuredly not within the province of a general entitlement to democracy or a right to be free from authoritarian rule. Ethnic conflict within states has international consequences, but it is not principally a problem for international law.

SELF-DETERMINATION OR INTERETHNIC ACCOMMODATION?

Self-determination is a magnificently resonant term, especially in the United States, where it conjures up notions of popular sovereignty. But there is no blinking the fact that, as things now stand, some people have managed to determine the fate of others. As that recognition has dawned, various extensions of the attractive doctrine of self-determination seem tempting, but the temptation should be resisted. What is needed is to substitute interethnic accommodation within borders for a self-determination that either creates new borders or legitimates ethnic exclusion within old ones. No doctrine of minority rights can be adequate to the task, and no amount of self-determination can give territorial expression to more than a small fraction of dissatisfied groups.

Still, the invention of new rights proceeds apace, confirming that civilized declarations are uttered in direct proportion to the commission of brutal acts. Rights will form only a small part of the solution to the problems of ethnic conflict. Most people will have to find political techniques to enable them to live together within existing states, unless they are prepared to do so much ethnic cleansing that the world will soon run out of soap.

NOTES

1. There are many theories of secession. See, e.g., R. R. Premdas, 'Secessionist Movements in Comparative Perspective', in R. R. Premdas, S. W. R. de A.

Samarasinghe, and A. P. Anderson (eds.), *Secessionist Movements in Comparative Perspective* (London: Pinter, 1990), 12–29; J. Nagel, 'The Conditions of Ethnic Separatism', *Ethnicity*, 7 (1980), 279–97; J. Wood, 'Secession: A Comparative Analytic Framework', *Canadian Journal of Political Science*, 14 (1981), 107–34; A. Alesina and E. Spolaore, 'On the Number and Size of Nations', National Bureau of Economic Research, Working Paper No. 5050, Mar. 1995. There is much less theoretical literature on irredentism. But see Naomi Chazan (ed.), *Irredentism and International Politics* (Boulder, Colo.: Lynne Rienner, 1991). And there is even less on the interrelations of the two phenomena. I have dealt with secessions and irredenta, and with relations between them, in, respectively, D. L. Horowitz, *Ethnic Groups in Conflict* (Berkeley and Los Angeles: University of California Press, 1985), 229–88, and id., 'Irredentas and Secessions: Adjacent Phenomena, Neglected Connections', in Chazan (ed.), *Irredentism and International Politics*, 9–22. In this section and occasionally elsewhere, I am borrowing from my essay, 'A Harvest of Hostility: Ethnic Conflict and Self-Determination After the Cold War', *Defence Intelligence Journal*, 1 (1992), 137–63.

2. The evidence for this is presented in Horowitz, *Ethnic Groups in Conflict*, 233–62.
3. We shall see very shortly, in the case of India *vis-à-vis* the emergence of Bangladesh, that this can present a problem for a putative irredentist state that wishes to forswear irredentism. In India's case, it helped push India toward aiding the secessionist alternative to irredentism.
4. The Turkish invasion of Cyprus in 1974 was something else altogether and has not produced a state, certainly not a recognized one. The separation of Singapore in 1965 was peaceful and was the result of expulsion, not secession.
5. See A. Heraclides, 'Secessionist Minorities and External Involvement', *International Organization*, 44 (1990), 341–78.
6. See generally R. Emerson, *From Empire to Nation* (Cambridge, Mass.: Harvard University Press, 1960).
7. For a useful survey, see *Fact Sheet on Ethnic and Regional Conflicts in the Russian Federation* (Cambridge, Mass.: Strengthening Democratic Institutions Project, Harvard University, Sept. 1992).
8. This account follows that of V. Zaslavsky, 'The Evolution of Separatism in Soviet Society Under Gorbachev', in G. W. Lapidus, V. Zaslavsky, and P. Goldman (eds.), *From Union to Commonwealth: Nationalism and Separatism in the Soviet Republics* (Cambridge: Cambridge University Press, 1992), 71–97, at 83–5.
9. I am indebted to Gail Lapidus for a helpful conversation on this point.
10. I am grateful to Ian Shapiro for stressing this point to me.
11. For a discussion, see Horowitz, *Ethnic Groups in Conflict*, 278–9, 672–5.
12. See M. Djilas, *The Contested Country* (Cambridge, Mass.: Harvard University Press, 1991).
13. For a careful treatment, see H. Hannum, 'Self-Determination, Yugoslavia, and Europe: Old Wine in New Bottles?' unpub. paper, n.d. For a scathing critique of German diplomacy on this issue, see H. Huttenbach, 'Post-Factum Diplomacy: Bonn's Revisionist Apologia for Its Policy of Recognizing Croatia', Association for the Study of Nationalities, *Analysis of Current Events*, 5 (4 Sept. 1993), 1–3.

Again, a fortuitous confluence took place, for the German government, interested in the reunification of East and West Germany, had a momentary stake in fostering the instability of boundaries. In this, its interests were at odds with those of France (*re* Corsica), Spain (*re* the Basque Country and Catalonia), and Britain (*re* Scotland, Wales, and Northern Ireland).

14. Organization of African Unity, Resolution 16(1) of July 1964, cited in H. Hannum, *Autonomy, Sovereignty and Self-Determination* (Philadelphia: University of Pennsylvania Press, 1990), 23 n. 65, 47.
15. See, e.g., L. Kuper, *Genocide: Its Political Uses in the Twentieth Century* (New Haven, Conn.: Yale University Press, 1981), 183. J. B. Hehir, 'Intervention: From Theories to Cases', *Ethics and International Affairs*, 9 (1995), 1–13, at 4, traces the roots of non-intervention to the Treaty of Westphalia, designed to end the interventionism of the religious wars.
16. See, e.g., C. Kaufman, 'Possible and Impossible Solutions to Ethnic Civil Wars', *International Security*, 20 (1996), 136–75.
17. D. Laitin, 'Ethnic Cleansing, Liberal Style', MacArthur Foundation Program in Transnational Security, Working Paper Series, M.I.T. Center for International Studies and Harvard Center for International Affairs, 1995. Laitin points out that those who are rewarded with states for making claims to nationhood will perforce have reason to make such claims in order to benefit from what he calls 'Wilsonian ethnic cleansing'.
18. Opinions of the Arbitration Committee, reported by A. Pellet, 'The Opinions of the Badinter Arbitration Committee: A Second Breath for the Self-Determination of Peoples', *European Journal of International Law*, 3 (1992), 178, App. at 183.
19. Unless the republics agree otherwise, which obviously they did not. Ibid. 183–4.
20. As Hurst Hannum remarks, this is the first time that the domestic constitutional structure of a state was deemed relevant, as a matter of international law, to its continuing existence and to the lines of its possible dissolution. Hannum, 'Self-Determination, Yugoslavia, and Europe', 11.
21. Opinions of the Arbitration Committee, at 184.
22. Ibid.
23. The framers of the United States Constitution understood that lower-level tyranny was more difficult to control than higher-level. This is a reason they advanced for a large republic. See *The Federalist*, no. 10 (New York: G. P. Putnam, 1888).
24. Sir H. S. Maine, *Ancient Law* (London: Oxford University Press, 1931; originally pub. 1861).
25. See R. Brubaker, *Citizenship and Nationhood in France and Germany* (Cambridge, Mass.: Harvard University Press, 1992).
26. For helpful surveys, see H. Hannum, *Autonomy, Sovereignty, and Self-Determination*, 28–49; L. Buchheit, *Secession: The Legitimacy of Self-Determination* (New Haven: Yale University Press, 1978), 8–20; R. Emerson, *Self-Determination Revisited in an Era of Decolonization* (Harvard University Center for International Affairs, Occasional Papers in International Affairs, No. 9, 1964).

27. See R. M. Hayden, 'Constitutional Nationalism in the Formerly Yugoslav Republics', *Slavic Review*, 51, (1992), 654–73; id., 'Constitutional Nationalism and the Wars in Yugoslavia', paper prepared for the conference on 'Post-Communism and Ethnic Mobilization', Cornell University, 21–3 April 1995.
28. See, e.g., the interesting discussion in Mahathir Bin Mohamad, *The Malay Dilemma* (Singapore: Donald Moore, 1970), 115–53, lamenting the demise of 'Tanah Melayu' [the Malay land] in favour of Malaysia, which includes citizens of all ethnic origins.
29. For the argument, see A. Lijphart, *Democracy in Plural Societies* (New Haven, Conn.: Yale University Press, 1977).
30. Ibid. 165.
31. I have gathered much of the evidence in D. L. Horowitz, *A Democratic South Africa? Constitutional Engineering in a Divided Society* (Berkeley and Los Angeles: University of California Press, 1991), 140–1 nn. 44–50. There is, however, more. In Romania and in Moldova, university-educated people exhibit the strongest hostility to minorities; and in Moldova, hostility increases directly with level of education. W. Crowther, 'Exploring Political Culture: A Comparative Analysis of Romania and Moldova', unpub. paper, University of North Carolina at Greensboro, n.d. (1993), 16, figs. 1–3. For similar results for Eastern Europe in general, see Radio Free Europe/Radio Liberty, 'Stereotypes Projected to Jews, Blacks, and Gypsies by East Europeans and Austrians' (unpub. paper, July 1980). In the European republics of the former Soviet Union, on the other hand, education is negatively associated with anti-Semitism. J. L. Gibson and R. M. Duch, 'Attitudes toward Jews and the Soviet Political Culture', *Journal of Soviet Nationalities*, 2 (1991), 77–117, at 98–100. In Guyana, education mitigates Indian prejudice toward Africans but has no significant effect on African prejudice toward Indians. J. B. Landis, 'Racial Attitudes of Africans and Indians in Guyana', *Social and Economic Studies*, 22 (1973), 427–39, at 436. The United States cannot be regarded as typical. See generally P. M. Sniderman and T. Piazza, *The Scar of Race* (Cambridge, Mass.: Harvard University Press, 1993); H. Schuman, C. Steeh, and L. Bobo, *Racial Attitudes in America* (Cambridge, Mass.: Harvard University Press, 1985). Cf. F. D. Weil, 'The Variable Effects of Education on Liberal Attitudes: A Comparative-Historical Analysis of Anti-Semitism Using Public Opinion Survey Data', *American Sociological Review*, 50 (1985), 458–74.
32. Sri Lanka recurrently illustrates this pattern. Every time a Sinhalese-dominated government proposes compromise with the Tamils, a Sinhalese opposition party gathers support by opposing it. For examples, see C. R. de Silva, *Sri Lanka: A History* (New Delhi: Vikas Publishing House, 1987), 238–45.
33. See, e.g., Horowitz, *A Democratic South Africa?*, 154–60, 163–203; id. 'Making Moderation Pay: The Comparative Politics of Ethnic Conflict Management', in J. V. Montville (ed.), *Conflict and Peacemaking in Multiethnic States* (Lexington, Mass.: Lexington Books, 1990), 451–75.
34. In 1979, for example, the Nigerians returned to civilian rule under a constitution containing a presidential electoral system that made the president a conspicuously pan-ethnic, conciliatory figure. The legislature, however, was elected under a

formula that did nothing for ethnic conciliation and turned legislators into representatives of mutually exclusive ethnic interests. One institution more than cancelled the other out.

35. This remains true despite the disturbing growth of a great Hindu–Muslim cleavage that threatens to rend the whole society.
36. See P. Bauhn, *Nationalism and Morality* (Lund: Lund University Press, 1995), 104–13; A. Buchanan, *Secession: The Morality of Political Divorce from Fort Sumter to Lithuania and Quebec* (Boulder, Colo.: Westview, 1991); A. Buchanan, 'Self-Determination and the Right to Secede', *Journal of International Affairs*, 45 (1992), 347–65; M. Maxwell, 'Normative Aspects of Secession and Supranationalism', unpub. paper presented at the annual meeting of the American Political Science Association, 1992; D. Philpott, 'In Defense of Self-Determination', *Ethics*, 105 (1995), 352–85; N. MacCormick, 'Is Nationalism Philosophically Credible?', in W. Twining (ed.), *Issues of Self-Determination* (Aberdeen: Aberdeen University Press, 1991), 8–19; Y. Tamir, 'The Right to National Self-Determination', *Social Research*, 58 (1991), 565–90; A. Margalit and J. Raz, 'National Self-Determination', *Journal of Philosophy*, 87 (1990), 439–61; D. Miller, 'The Ethical Significance of Nationality', *Ethics*, 98 (1988), 647–62.
37. MacCormick, 'Is Nationalism Philosophically Credible?', 14.
38. Margalit and Raz, 'National Self-Determination', 451. For the foundations of such views in Raz's conceptions of collectivities as aggregates of individuals, see J. Raz, *The Morality of Freedom* (Oxford: Clarendon Press, 1986), 207–9.
39. Miller, 'The Ethical Significance of Nationality', 659.
40. Perhaps less obvious are the similarities to John Stuart Mill's sympathetic speculations on the same subject. At least with respect to what he called 'civilized' nations, Mill advocated sweeping support for the efforts of peoples to free themselves from foreign rule or from 'a native tyranny upheld by foreign arms'. Mill, 'A Few Words on Non-Intervention', in J. S. Mill, *Dissertations and Discussions*, (London: Savill and Edwards, 1867), iii. 153–78, at 176. For a helpful exposition, suggesting that the analogy of communities to individuals was also on Mill's mind, see M. Walzer, *Just and Unjust Wars* (New York: Basic Books, 1977), 87–91. Mill was extremely doubtful that democratic regimes could survive in what would be called today conditions of ethnic pluralism; he described the prospect as 'next to impossible', and this may have coloured his receptivity to collective opting out. J. S. Mill, 'Considerations on Representative Government', in Mill, *Utilitarianism, Liberty, and Representative Government* (New York: E. P. Dutton, 1951; originally pub. 1861), 486. For a critique of Mill's views on the prospects for plural societies, see S. French and A. Gutman, 'The Principle of National Self-Determination', in V. Held, S. Morgenbesser, and T. Nagel (eds.), *Philosophy, Morality, and International Affairs* (New York: Oxford University Press, 1974),138–53, at 142–4.
41. MacCormick, 'Is Nationalism Philosophically Credible?', 17.
42. Margalit and Raz, 'National Self-Determination', 451–4.
43. Philpott, 'In Defense of Self-Determination', 355–62.
44. Ibid. 371–5.
45. The matter is, for example, never mentioned in P. Bauhn's treatment (*Nationalism and Morality*) and in most others; it is passingly acknowledged in a few.

46. Ibid. 27.
47. Tamir, 'The Right to National Self-Determination'. Tamir explicitly rejects the reduction of self-determination to the quest for freedom or autonomy (p. 584), insisting that national self-determination is 'attained only when certain features, unique to the nation, find expression in the political sphere' (pp. 584, 586). Yet she finds it possible to achieve adequate expression of cultural identity through many political institutions that fall far short of territorial separation (p. 587).
48. In a striking reversal of the usual parlance, MacCormick states flatly that groups are 'constitutive' of individuals: 'Is Nationalism Philosophically Credible?', 17. One problem, at least, that is obviated by such an approach relates to the ascertainment of the will of an abstract entity, such as a nation. See the critique of French and Gutman, 'The Principle of National Self-Determination', 148–53; and compare the solution of Margalit and Raz, 'National Self-Determination', 458.
49. W. Kymlicka, *Multicultural Citizenship: A Liberal Theory of Minority Rights* (Oxford: Clarendon Press, 1995), 186.
50. Buchanan, *Secession*; id., 'Self-Determination and the Right to Secede'.
51. Buchanan, *Secession*, 61.
52. Bauhn, *Nationalism and Morality*, 111–13.
53. Margalit and Raz, 'National Self-Determination', 458.
54. R. Lemarchand, 'Ethnic Violence in Tropical Africa', in J. F. Stack, Jr. (ed.), *The Primordial Challenge: Ethnicity in the Contemporary World* (New York: Greenwood Press, 1986), 199–200. For further empirical cautions regarding secessionist solutions, see V. A. Tishkov, 'Nationalities and Conflicting Ethnicity in Post-Communist Russia', (Conflict Management Group, Working Papers on Ethnic Conflict Management in the Former Soviet Union, Cambridge, Mass., April 1993), 17–20.
55. See, e.g., R. T. DeGeorge, 'The Myth of the Right of Collective Self-Determination', 1–7, and A. Michalska, 'Rights of Peoples to Self-Determination in International Law', 71–90 in Twining (ed.), *Issues of Self-Determination*; P. Thornberry, *Minorities and Human Rights Law* (London: Minority Rights Group, 1991), 9–10.
56. See M. Halberstam, 'Self-Determination in the Arab–Israeli Conflict: Meaning, Myth, and Politics', *New York University Journal of International Law and Politics*, 21 (1989), 465–87, at 465 n. 3.
57. See Hannum, *Autonomy, Sovereignty, and Self-Determination*, 28–49; M. M. Kampelman, 'Secession and the Right of Self-Determination: An Urgent Need to Harmonize Principle with Pragmatism', *Washington Quarterly*, 16 (1993), 5–12; Michalska, 'Rights of Peoples to Self-Determination in International Law', 78–9; R. G. Steinhardt, 'International Law and Self-Determination', unpub. paper, Atlantic Council Project on Individual Rights, Group Rights, National Sovereignty, and International Law, n.d., 41–3. Buchheit, *Secession*, argues for a right to secede but concedes it does not yet exist.
58. See, e.g., Western Sahara (Advisory Opinion), 1975 I.C.J. 12, 80–1 (opinion of Nagendra Singh, J.).
59. G. Binder, 'The Case for Self-Determination', *Stanford Journal of International Law*, 29 (1993), 223–70. For an extreme and ill-considered version, see M. Kirby, 'The Peoples' Right to Self-Determination', *New Zealand Law Journal* (Sept.

1993), 341–4. Kirby suggests simply that 'peoples should ordinarily be allowed to live together in a group identity which is congenial to them', provided they are 'respectful' of minorities. Ibid. 343.

60. L. Brilmayer, 'Secession and Self-Determination: A Territorial Interpretation', *Yale Journal of International Law*, 16 (1991), 177–202.
61. For numerous ways of arriving at a similar destination, see R. McCorquodale, 'Self-Determination Beyond the Colonial Context and Its Potential Impact on Africa', *African Journal of International and Comparative Law*, 4 (1992), 592–608; J. E. Falkowski, 'Secessionary Self-Determination: A Jeffersonian Perspective', *Boston University International Law Journal*, 9 (1991), 209–42; L.-C. Chen, 'Self-Determination and World Public Order', *Notre Dame Law Review*, 66 (1991), 1287–97. Cf. E. Kolodner, 'The Future of the Right to Self-Determination', *Connecticut Journal of International Law*, 10 (1994), 153–67.
62. But see B. Kingsbury, 'Claims by Non-State Groups in International Law', *Cornell International Law Journal*, 25 (1992), 481–530.
63. For one such, badly strained effort, see S. Marks, 'Self-Determination and People's Rights', *King's College Law Journal*, 2 (1991–2), 79–94, at 91.
64. Hannum, *Autonomy, Sovereignty, and Self-Determination*, 97, 103; Michalska, 'Rights of Peoples to Self-Determination in International Law', 80.
65. UN Doc. E/CN.4/Sub. 2/1994/2/Add. 1 (Economic and Social Council, Commission on Human Rights, Subcommission on Prevention of Discrimination and Protection of Minorities, 20 April 1994).
66. See V. P. Nanda, 'Ethnic Conflict in Fiji and International Human Rights Law', *Cornell International Law Journal*, 25 (1992), 565–77.
67. Draft Declaration on the Rights of Indigenous Peoples, Articles 12–16.
68. Ibid., Article 20.
69. Ibid., Article 3. Other articles reinforce their political independence, e.g., Articles 4, 23, 31–3.
70. Article 31 refers instead to 'the right to autonomy or self-government'. After vigorous controversy, the language was chosen deliberately. I am indebted to Benedict Kingsbury for this background.
71. See B. Kingsbury, 'Self-Determination and "Indigenous Peoples"', in *Proceedings of the American Society of International Law*, 86th Annual Meeting (1992), 383–94, at 385–6. See also id., '"Indigenous Peoples" as an International Legal Concept', in R. H. Barnes *et al.* (eds.), *Indigenous Peoples of Asia* (Ann Arbor, Mich.: Association for Asian Studies, 1995), 13–34.
72. See E. A. Daes, 'Consideration on the Right of Indigenous Peoples to Self-Determination', *Transnational Law and Contemporary Problems*, 3 (1993), 1–11. Daes wrote as Chairperson and Special Rapporteur of the UN Working Group on Indigenous Populations. Ruth Lapidoth, 'Autonomy: Potential and Limitations', *International Journal on Group Rights*, 1 (1994), 269–90, at 274, noting the 'far-reaching claims' supported by the convention, suggests the need to limit its scope if it is to be acceptable to states. For a more circumspect view of the claims of indigenous peoples, see A. Buchanan, 'The Role of Collective Rights in the Theory of Indigenous Peoples' Rights', *Transnational Law and Contemporary Problems*, 3 (1993), 90–108.

73. Hannum, *Autonomy, Sovereignty, and Self-Determination*, 50–4; S. Baron, *Ethnic Minority Rights: Some Older and New Trends*, the Tenth Sacks Lecture, 26 May 1983 (Oxford: Oxford Centre for Postgraduate Hebrew Studies, 1985).
74. Which accords them, in principle, the rights to equality and non-discrimination. Hannum, *Autonomy, Sovereignty, and Self-Determination*, 69.
75. *United Nations Treaty Series*, 660 (1969), 195.
76. International Convention on the Prevention and Punishment of the Crime of Genocide (1951), *United Nations Treaty Series*, 277 (1951), 78.
77. UNESCO Convention against Discrimination in Education (1960), *United Nations Treaty Series*, 429 (1960), 93.
78. *Declaration on the Rights of Persons Belonging to National or Ethnic, Religious and Linguistic Minorities*, United Nations General Assembly, A/RES/47/135, 3 Feb. 1993 (adopted 18 Dec. 1992).
79. Ibid., Art. 2(3).
80. Ibid., Art. 2(4).
81. Ibid., Art. 4(2).
82. Ibid., Art. 8(4).
83. Document of the Copenhagen Meeting of the Conference on the Human Dimensions of the Conference on Security and Cooperation in Europe, June 29, 1990, Art. 35. The text of Article 35 can be found in Thornberry, *Minorities and Human Rights Law*, 29. For a commentary, see H. Hannum, 'Contemporary Developments in the International Protection of the Rights of Minorities', *Notre Dame Law Review*, 66 (1991), 1431–48, at 1439–43.
84. Hannum, 'Contemporary Developments in the International Protection of the Rights of Minorities', 1439–43. See also M. Halperin and D. J. Sheffer, *Self-Determination in the New World Order* (Washington: Carnegie Endowment for International Peace, 1992), 59.
85. Hannum, 'Contemporary Developments in the International Protection of the Rights of Minorities', 1444.
86. T. M. Franck, 'The Emerging Right to Democratic Governance', *American Journal of International Law*, 86 (1992), 46–91.
87. Ibid. 55–6.
88. Ibid. 63 (emphasis omitted).
89. A. Cassese, 'Political Self-Determination: Old Concepts and New Developments', in A. Cassese (ed.), *UN Law/Fundamental Rights: Two Topics in International Law* (Alphenaanden Rijn, Netherlands: Sijthoff and Noordhoff, 1979), 137–65, at 158.
90. Ibid. 160 (emphasis omitted). Cf. M. Halperin and K. Lomasney, 'Toward a Global "Guarantee Clause"', *Journal of Democracy*, 4 (July 1993), 60–9.
91. For a trenchant critique, based on an analysis of the international instruments relied on by Franck and Cassese, see Steinhardt, 'International Law and Self-Determination', 38–43.
92. Compare ibid. 43: 'Popular sovereignty, to the extent that it translates into majority rule, does not necessarily reflect any commitment to minority rights and may well work against them.'
93. The occasional international law treatment that descends to institutional particulars is typically far too imprecise and cavalier to be helpful. See, e.g. J. B. Attanasio,

'The Rights of Ethnic Minorities: The Emerging Mosaic', *Notre Dame Law Review*, 66 (1991), 1195–1217, at 1205-08, blithely proposing electoral arrangements deemed a priori to be favourable to minorities and a variety of protective arrangements for regional minorities in autonomous provinces.

94. Halperin and Sheffer, *Self-Determination in the New World Order*.
95. Ibid. 84–93.
96. See generally S. Kaufman, 'The Irresistible Force and the Imperceptible Object: The Yugoslav Breakup and Western Policy', *Security Studies*, 4 (1994–5), 281–329, at 311–14. See also n. 12, above.

10

'Orphans of Secession': National Pluralism in Secessionist Regions and Post-Secession States

JOHN MCGARRY

Liberal philosophers have generally avoided focusing on the problem of national diversity within states. Most contemporary liberal political philosophers view the 'nation' as everyone in the state and the just state as one which treats all individuals with equal respect. There are, then, two related tendencies: a tendency to abstract from the role of the state in promoting a particular national culture, language, and history, on the one hand; and to abstract from the multinational character of the society that most states encompass.[1] These tendencies have led many contemporary liberals to overlook the fact that many states, even while respecting individual rights, do not treat all national groups with equal respect. Rather, these states frequently favour the majority nation, and promote its culture, symbols, and identity, over minority nations. As a consequence, minorities in such states argue not just for individual rights but for recognition of their national and cultural rights, and for equal respect for nations as well as individuals.

The tendency to abstract from multinationalism flows, in part, from the dominance of the United States (and, to a lesser extent, Britain and France) in the development of contemporary liberal thought. The case of the United States, which, as an immigrant society, is largely multi-ethnic but not multinational, has led many theorists to generalize from the experience of a society that makes rules to integrate culturally distinct groups to the quite different case of societies with different national communities, i.e. historical communities on what they perceive to be their 'ancestral territory' who aspire to some form of political self-determination. However, there are good grounds for believing that the expectations of the two groups are profoundly different, and the problems posed by these different kinds of diversity are distinct, and require distinct solutions.[2]

The experience of the United States is not typical, for it is, by and large, a 'nation-state' with no sizeable minority nations.[3] That such states are not the rule is evident from the explosion of a large number of intrastate national conflicts in the 1990s. This outbreak of sub-state nationalism has led to a questioning of the traditional emphasis on individual rights, and several philosophers are currently engaged in revising or reinterpreting liberalism to make it better able to cope with national pluralism.[4] This 'new liberalism', while still founded on conceptions of individual interest, is much more likely than the old to seek to devise rules which ensure fairness among national groups and not simply among abstracted individuals.

Surprisingly, such liberal revisionism, with its greater awareness of the state as a site of national and not just individual conflict, has not yet extended to the debate on self-determination and secession. Despite the fact that the 1990s has produced more minority-based secessions and secessionist movements than at any time since the First World War, liberal philosophers still tend to interpret rights to self-determination in abstraction from the national dimensions involved. Thus Allen Buchanan, who offers a restrictive view of the right to secession, argues that a group has a right to secede only if it is a victim of injustice.[5] He outlines a number of different kinds of injustice: from serious violations of human rights and genocide to prior occupation and seizure of territory and discriminatory injustice. His work applies liberal-justice theory, which is initially designed to regulate relations between individuals and the relation of the state to individuals, to the particular problem of secession, but doesn't consider the nationalist basis of most secessionist movements.

At the same time, philosophers who recognize a broader right to self-determination, such as Daniel Philpott in this volume, tend to gloss over the heterogeneity of secessionist regions and fail to think adequately about national pluralism in post-secession states.[6] On Philpott's 'choice' theory of secession, he requires that the majority in a geographical area express a desire to secede for the secession to be legitimate, and does not require that the group be a victim of injustice or establish any special claim to territory. On this argument, the right to self-determination, including a right to secession, is grounded in a deeper argument about the value of autonomy; and, indeed, the plebiscite for/against secession that his theory requires is viewed as an expression of autonomy.[7] Philpott is aware of the difficulties of moving from an individual conception of autonomy to the political sphere, and grounding any collective institution in an argument about individual autonomy, but, in the first instance, he argues for his principle by considering a group called the Utopians, who are nationally homogeneous, territorially concentrated, with no differences of opinion. He then concedes, in a rather understated way, that this utopian state of affairs will probably not be realized in many actual cases of secession. It is, however, doubtful whether it makes sense to elaborate principles while abstracting from national diversity, for the kind of diversity in the seceding area, the relationship between majority and minority, the type of identity that the groups evince, are vitally important in knowing what, normatively, we should think about particular cases of secession.

The failure of political philosophers to take sufficient account of national diversity is repeated by political partisans. Thus unionist politicians (those who seek to hold multinational states together) often fail to recognize sufficiently the identity of national minorities. Sometimes, as in the case of Turkey (with respect to Kurds) or Greece (with respect to Slavs), they deny the very existence of such minorities, insisting that their state is nationally homogeneous and imposing penalties on any minority citizen who contests this.[8] Ironically, given that secessionist movements usually grow out of the failure of a multinational state to recognize its national minorities, secessionists often repeat the same sins. They downplay opposition to their project from local minorities and others, and when secession is achieved they are no more likely to accommodate minorities than the élites of the predecessor state.

This chapter looks at the problem of national pluralism in regions where there are secessionist movements and in states which have been formed recently as a result of secession. It begins by showing that regions with such movements are often seriously divided on the secession project. Opposition to secession comes most noticeably from local ethnic minorities, but also in some cases from a sizeable proportion of the local majority. Second, following from this, the chapter discusses the problems involved in governing post-secession states. These new states are often as heterogeneous as their predecessors, as likely to abuse minorities, and, subsequently, as prone to conflict. Finally, the chapter examines different ways to resolve problems of national pluralism. The chapter argues that the way to address the existence of national diversity within states (post-secessionist and others) is to move away from the model of a 'nation-state'—with its normal emphasis on a common culture, majority rule, and political centralization—towards that of a 'multinational state' in which all national groups are treated equally. In those cases where national communities spill over boundaries, the principle of equal treatment involves moving away from the idea of independent states and embracing trans-border or supra-state political institutions.

THE CONTESTED NATURE OF SECESSIONIST PROJECTS

Secession is a political game in which it makes sense to exaggerate support and to downplay division. A territory united in its desire to secede is much more likely to win support from the international community, the remainder of the state, and even from the group the secession movement is based on, than a territory which is seriously divided over the question and which is, consequently, likely to experience divisions after independence. Thus in their language, secessionists usually claim that it is the 'territory' that wants to secede, as in 'Quebec (or Ireland or Croatia) wants independence' or it is the people in the territory who want to secede, as in 'the people of Ireland (or of Quebec or of Croatia)'. In neither formulation is there any hint of division within the territory on the secessionist project.

Secessionists like to compare their projects with the anti-colonial movements which gave independence to much of Africa and Asia after the Second World War. There are several reasons for this. The analogy gives the secessionist project legitimacy, as it casts the existing state in the role of imperialist exploiter. It allows the secessionists to claim they have the same right to self-determination which colonized peoples possess under international law. Most relevant for present purposes, it conveys an impression that the secessionist regions are united, as most colonies were, behind the independence project.

However, despite the abstractions of philosophers such as Philpott, the rhetoric of secessionists and the comparisons with anti-colonial movements, secessionism is usually highly contested, and not just by the remainder state, but also, and sometimes especially, within the secessionist region. The most obvious source of opposition comes from local ethnic minorities. They oppose secession in part because, unlike decolonization projects, which were normally pan-ethnic or territorial in scope, secessionist projects are usually driven by the region's largest group. The secessionist project is aimed at breaking up the state with which these local minorities identify and within which they might be overall majorities. It is aimed at constructing a new state which, in many cases, will promote the culture and language of the region's largest group, and perhaps also its political and economic interests, at the expense of minorities.

Even when secessionist intellectuals and politicians try to reach out to local ethnic minorities, their appeals often fall flat. In Northern Ireland, despite the consistent calls of Irish Catholics to Protestants to join them in building an 'agreed Ireland', the calls go unheeded: in one survey, less than 1 per cent of Protestants identified with Irish nationalist parties.[9] Such a result might be expected, given the polarized nature of Northern Ireland, which has experienced serious violence for over a quarter of a century.[10] However, one finds a similar result even in Quebec, where there has been no such violence. Despite the repeated 'nation-building' efforts of Quebec's civic nationalist élite,[11] the secessionist project there is almost completely rejected by non-francophone minorities: in a referendum on sovereignty held in Quebec in October 1995, 90 per cent of the anglophone minority voted against, with even higher levels of opposition among native groups.[12] This pattern, where support for secession is rejected by local ethnic minorities, also applies to a large number of other cases, such as Palestine, Kashmir, Northern Cyprus, Croatia, Kurdistan, and Sri Lanka. It was also the pattern in a large number of historic secessions (or imperial breakups), such as that of Greece and Bulgaria from the Ottoman empire in the nineteenth and early twentieth centuries, and (western) Poland from Germany after 1918.

The tendency of support for/opposition to secession movements to break down along ethnic lines is not a problem in all cases. Some secessionist regions are ethnically homogeneous. Slovenia, which broke away from Yugoslavia in 1991, had only minuscule Serbian and Croatian minorities. The Irish Free State, which won self-government from the United Kingdom in 1921, was 89 per cent Catholic. Singapore, which seceded from Malaysia after a brief union in 1965, was predominantly Chinese. When Czechoslovakia broke apart in 1993, its Czech part was overwhelmingly Czech in population and its Slovak part had few Czechs, although it had a sizeable Hungarian minority.[13] The post-secession stability of many of these states is linked to this high degree of homogeneity.

Most secessionist regions are, however, ethnically heterogeneous. If we use language, and in some cases religion, as an admittedly imprecise marker of national diversity, fifteen of the twenty-three states formed after the breakup of the Soviet Union, Yugoslavia, and Czechoslovakia, had minority national populations larger than one-fifth of the new state's population,[14] and eight had minorities constituting over one-third of the population.[15] In two cases (Latvia and Kyrgyzstan) the states had bare national majorities (51.8 per cent and 52.4 per cent respectively), and in two others (Bosnia and Kazakhstan), there were no majorities at all.

National heterogeneity continues because secessions normally occur along administrative rather than national boundary lines. This is what happened in the case of the twenty-three states that were formed out of the Soviet Union, Yugoslavia, and Czechoslovakia, which together account for the lion's share of secessions since the First World War and its immediate aftermath. While the internal boundaries of these three states were drawn to give (limited) self-government to particular national groups, the subunits were hardly ever homogeneous and hardly ever contained all of the group in question. Nor was this always coincidental: rather, gerrymandering was an important tactic used by these states to control minority passions.[16]

It would be over-simplified to leave it here, with the impression that secessionist movements are always supported by local ethnic majorities and always opposed by local minorities. The reality is more complex, and support patterns depend on context. In some cases, where ethnic boundaries are fluid or where minorities within the secessionist region see an instrumental advantage in supporting the secession project, minorities may support secession. One of the important reasons why the breakup of the Soviet Union was peaceful in nature was because large percentages of the Russian minorities in the various republics outside Russia supported it. Significant numbers of Russians voted for independence in referendums in Estonia, Latvia, and Ukraine, and in several other Soviet Republics.[17] The ethnic Russians believed that independence was in their economic interests, or were not mobilized along Russian nationalist lines.[18] Such support from local national minorities is more likely to be conditional than support from majorities. In the case of Ukraine and the Baltic states, Russian support faded as economic miracles failed to materialize and/or as the new states took measures which were seen as prejudicial to Russian culture and interests.[19]

In other cases, secession may be opposed by important sections of the local ethnic majority as well as by minorities. Slovakia's secession from Czechoslovakia in 1993 is an especially clear example of this: it was largely an élite project, which the majority of Slovaks—quite apart from the Magyar minority—did not share. An opinion poll in 1990 indicated that only 8 per cent of Slovakia's population desired secession.[20] Support for independence—as opposed to some form of group autonomy—is also low in a number of regions where there are current secession campaigns. In Quebec, levels of support for independence traditionally hover around 30 to 35 per cent. In the referendum of 1995, in which the separatist government deliberately posed a soft question on 'sovereignty' rather than 'secession' or 'independence' and in which it promised to hold negotiations with the rest of Canada on a new partnership in the event of a 'Yes' vote, 40 per cent of francophones still answered 'No'.[21] In Scotland, surveys indicate that independence seldom receives support from more than one-third of the population.[22] These figures suggest two things: that the demands of these groups for autonomy can be satisfied short of secession, and that if secession is to occur, it is unlikely that there will be a consensus behind it, even among local majorities.

Relatively low levels of support for secession may be linked to its political feasibility.[23] But significant proportions of local majority groups may also identify with the larger political community as well as their local group. In many cases it is wrong to assume discrete forms of identity in which groups either identify with one national community or another. Outside of polarized conflict zones, individuals frequently have nested identities, and feel part of several communities simultaneously. Thus, many Scots identify with Scotland and the United Kingdom, many francophone Québécois identify with Canada and Quebec, and many Catalans feel an affinity to Spain and Catalonia. The problem with secession, from the perspective of these groups, is that it forces them to choose one identity at the expense of another.

In sum, secession rarely involves the unproblematic breakaway of a region in which all of its inhabitants are united on the secession project. Most secessionist areas have ethnic minorities which are strongly opposed to the secession project, and want to stay part of the united state or have their own state. Sometimes, individuals from local ethnic majorities identify with the larger state, or have nested or dual identities and do not want to have to choose between them.

GOVERNING POST-SECESSION STATES

Many new states which have been created as a result of secession (or the breakup of an empire) experience problems related to their heterogeneity.

In many cases these problems are similar to those which existed in the predecessor state, and which contributed to its breakup. In these cases, secession does not solve the problem of national diversity; it merely places it in a different state context. Moreover, the process of new-state formation can exacerbate intergroup conflict. The new state's dominant group, concerned about the loyalty of minorities, especially if the states' borders are contested, is often in no mood to accommodate them. Having gained their own state, new majorities may often want to use their power to promote their culture and political position at the expense of minorities. The minorities, who normally find themselves cut off from their co-ethnics in the rump state, and who may find their status transformed from dominant to dominated group overnight, cannot be expected to take this lightly. The result is frequently conflict, although the intensity of this varies greatly from place to place, depending on the respective sizes of the groups and whether there are traditions of violence or accommodation.

Majority–minority conflicts are evident in practically all of the new states formed in Eastern Europe since 1991. These states are all associated with dominant ethnic groups. In Brubaker's language, they are 'nationalizing' states which seek to promote the interests of national majorities over minorities, albeit with different degrees of enthusiasm.[24] At one extreme, Croatia began its independence by refusing to accommodate its Serbian minority, and by adopting the symbols of the wartime Croatian state which had committed genocide against Serbs. Eventually, after a protracted struggle, most of the Serbs were forced out of the country in 1995. Slovakia, despite reaching an agreement with Hungary in 1995 to protect the language rights of its Magyar minority, has moved since to narrow these rights. Slovakia's premier, Vladimir Meciar, has threatened the Magyars with expulsion.[25] After achieving independence in 1991, Estonia and Latvia made it extremely difficult for their large Russian minorities to acquire citizenship in the new states.

Other new states have refrained from such radical measures, and some, such as Ukraine and Russia, have decentralized in ways which are designed to accommodate national minorities.[26] The general trend, however, has been for new states to privilege national majorities over minorities by adopting the language, culture, and symbols of the former, and offering scant, if any, provision for the language, culture, and symbols of the latter.

Minorities in post-secession states have reacted in different ways. Some groups who identify with the predecessor state, and who resent their transformation from majority to minority status or who are traditional enemies of the new masters, have violently resisted the secession. Violent resistance is particularly likely to occur when the minority believes its physical security is jeopardized and when it, as a result of its strength or outside help, believes it can prevail. Croatia's Serb minority greeted Croatia's declaration of independence with a violent rebellion which was aimed at uniting its territory with Serbia. Bosnia's Serbian and Croatian minorities also rebelled as did the Ossetian minority in Georgia, the Armenian minority in Azerbaijan (Nagorno-Karabakh), and the Ukrainian and Russian minorities in Moldova (Transdniestria).

In some cases, minority rebellion is pursued, not to prevent secession or to link the rebel territory with the rump state, but to win an independent state. In this case, secession has a domino or demonstration-effect.[27] Georgia's Abkhazian minority followed Georgia's secession from the Soviet Union with a violent independence bid of its own. Similarly, the Chechens were unprepared to accept the view that the dissolution of the Soviet Union should stop at the borders of the various Union Republics, and launched a bitter secessionist war against Russia.

Such violent reactions have to be put in perspective, however. While they understandably attract attention, and are used by unionist groups to warn against the perils of state breakup, they are in fact relatively uncommon. Most minorities do not revolt, although this does not mean they support the state's breakup. A more frequent minority response is for its members to vote with their feet by migrating from the new state in which they are a minority to a state in which they are a majority. This behaviour pattern was common during new state formation in Eastern Europe and the Balkans in the 1920s, a phenomenon which Lord Curzon described as an 'unmixing of peoples'.[28] It has become an important minority response to secession again in the 1990s.[29] The breakup of the Soviet Union in particular has led to large numbers of people migrating to be on the 'right' side of new state frontiers.[30]

Despite the wishes of majority chauvinists, however, many members of minority groups remain *in situ.* Rather than accepting the nationalizing policies of new states without complaint however, a more typical response has been to mobilize to ensure that the new states address their need for individual and group rights. Thus Ukraine's Tatar and Russian minorities have both been involved in campaigns to improve their position, although at least in Crimea their aspirations compete with each other. Minority mobilization is also evident in every other Eastern European state, including among Russians in the Baltic states and Magyars in Slovakia. Such minority campaigns frequently involve appeals to international organizations and to neighbouring states dominated by co-ethnics.

Discontent in new states created by secession is not limited to ethnic minorities who want their own state, to be part of another state, or substantial political accommodation within the new state. In addition, there are those members of the majority group who have dual identities and who, while accepting the new state, regret the passing of the old. These situations of nested identity, however, rarely result in violent rebellion or pose challenges to the stability of the post-secessionist state.

This focus on the various patterns of majority–minority relations that may precede and follow secession, and should inform normative theorizing about secession, raises two questions, which bear on the possibility of reconciling aspirations to self-determination (nationally defined) with liberal values of equal respect and individual autonomy. The first issue focuses on whether the kind of dynamics discussed thus far—which have taken place largely in the context of Eastern Europe—are relevant to Western cases, such as Quebec, which have strong liberal democratic traditions. The second issue bears on the focus on the period immediately preceding and following a secession, and whether this is not an unfair context for theorizing, rather than a longer-term approach, in which identities have had a chance to adjust to the new state.

The first issue is the relevance of the experience of Eastern Europe to possible Western cases of secession such as Quebec. Not surprisingly, Quebec secessionists claim that analogies between Eastern Europe and Quebec are inappropriate. In this volume, Nielsen argues that Eastern Europe lacks liberal democratic traditions and that East European 'ethnic' nationalism is quite unlike the 'liberal' or 'civic variety' put forward by Quebec nationalists. Nielsen argues, correctly, that for comparisons to be valid they must be appropriate and contextual. In his view, an independent Quebec would be more like Western states formed by secession, such as Iceland, or Norway, or like would-be independent states, such as Scotland, than like the new states of Eastern Europe.

Nielsen's comparative enterprise, however, is itself insufficiently contextual. As argued in the preceding account there is no single East European experience with secession, but rather a range of differing experiences. Quebec's experience, while likely to be different from some East European states, may be more like other East European states than the Western states cited by Nielsen.

The argument of Quebec separatists that Quebec is *unlikely* to be like Croatia or Bosnia or Nagorno-Karabakh seems valid. In contrast to these latter three societies, there are no traditions of intense violence in Quebec. Quebec's minorities are unlikely to fear for their physical security in the same way minorities in these other states did, and are unlikely to respond to secession by all-out rebellion.[31] This does not mean that Quebec's experience will be like that of Western states, such as Norway or Iceland, or like the secession of Scotland if that was to occur. Indeed its prospects for a smooth secession and stable future may not be as good as those of some East European states such as Slovenia or the Czech Republic. This is because Quebec, unlike these states, has a number of minority groups who are resolutely opposed to secession. Quebec has an anglophone/allophone minority—equivalent to about one-fifth of its population—which is passionately committed to Canada, and, since the narrow defeat of separatism in the 1995 referendum, is increasingly mobilized.[32] As significant numbers from this community left Quebec after the election of a separatist government in 1976, it seems reasonable to assume that more will leave if the province separates.[33] The rest will campaign for protection of their language and other cultural rights. Quebec also has several indigenous minorities, which while small in number, are highly mobilized against secession, and adept at winning international support for their cause.

A more appropriate comparative analogy for Quebec than Iceland or Scotland may be a set of new states in Eastern Europe located—in terms of ethnic antagonisms and heterogeneity—in between the likes of Croatia and the Czech Republic. These states, such as Ukraine or Lithuania, have been the site of lengthy interethnic dialogue, with their minorities seeking various forms of constitutional recognition. Something similar could be expected in Quebec: not the catastrophe sometimes predicted by opponents of secession, but also not the sea of civic tranquillity predicted by Nielsen and others. The point is that while liberal traditions in a secessionist region matter, and work in Quebec's favour, the degree of ethnic heterogeneity and minority mobilization in the region also matters, and this is less in Quebec's favour than its secessionist intellectuals are prone to admit.

The second issue or possible objection to the line of argument advanced thus far is that it assesses secession according to the degree to which the secession accords with the identities of the people in the state around the moment of secession.[34] Some might argue that this focus on the period preceding and immediately following the formation of the new state tends to exaggerate the degree to which it will be engulfed in interethnic tensions and conflict, and therefore is unfair to the aspirant secessionists. On this view, the problems identified in the preceding account are primarily a feature of state formation which will pass as the state matures. The argument for this position is that a state with a more established existence is likely to be more generous towards minorities. With its dominant group's identity secure through state institutions, symbols, and language policy, the state can be more beneficent towards minorities, and minorities can become accustomed to their position in the new state.

The problem with this logic, however, is that the conditions which produce conflict during state formation may be durable. New states may continue to worry about minority revolts and the security of its frontiers; minorities may continue to withhold their loyalty; neighbouring states may continue irredentist claims for decades after the state is formed. The experience of Israel, Northern Ireland, Turkey, Romania, all formed some time ago, suggest that the factors which give rise to conflict and tension at the point of state formation can continue long beyond that time.

MINORITY PROBLEMS ALL ROUND AND HOW TO RESPOND TO THEM

So far, this chapter has emphasized the problems of national pluralism in regions which have secessionist movements or have seceded. This focus should not be taken to mean that only these regions have such problems.[35] In fact, secession usually occurs because there are similar problems in the predecessor state.

Similar problems can also exist in the rump (or remainder) state. Just as it is difficult to draw lines on a map which ensure the secessionist region contains only those who want to secede, it is also difficult to draw lines which ensure the rump state only includes those who do not want to secede. Just as a seceding state may include a minority which is cut off from its co-nationals in the rump state, so a minority in the rump state may be cut off from its co-nationals in the seceding state. Such rump minorities may be held responsible for the breakup of the state, (correctly) suspected of plotting further revisions to state boundaries, and be the targets of irredentist claims—in this case a claim by the seceded territory over part of the rump state rather than vice versa. As a result, they may be subject to the same kind of 'nationalizing' abuses which are sometimes directed against minorities in territories which have seceded.[36] The most serious minority problem caused by the departure from the United Kingdom of the Irish Free State was not the inclusion of a Protestant minority equal to 11 per cent of the population within the new state's borders—this minority, small and dispersed, largely came to accept an Irish national identity. Rather it was the fact that a large Catholic minority of around 35 per cent was left behind in Northern Ireland, a largely self-governing part of the rump United Kingdom.

In short, there may be problems of national pluralism and unrecognized national identities all round, not just in regions which have seceded, but in states facing secessionist movements, and in rump states. How should such problems be confronted?

The first approach should be for the state which is facing a secessionist movement to address the causes of minority discontent before support for exit reaches a point where continuing union is unfeasible. Support for secession among a national minority usually increases when the state in which it lives behaves like a nation-state, i.e. a state in which there is only one nation, centred on the state or on the state's largest ethnic group. Such a state may operate in one language only, adopt Jacobin forms of centralized government, allow unregulated migration into minority regions, or it may simply insist on treating all its citizens equally with inadequate provisions for the protection of cultural minorities. What is required to hold such states together justly will depend on context, but it will generally involve the establishment of (evolving) institutional arrangements based on the concept of multinational partnership. Such a partnership entails a substantial amount of decentralization.[37] As polls suggest that many people in regions which currently have secessionist movements would settle for less than independence, increased autonomy for the region may undermine the separatist campaign and reduce support for it to manageable levels.

While states are often reluctant to decentralize, for fear it will promote secession, there is evidence that timely and genuine decentralization achieves exactly the opposite effect. While Francoist centralization coincided with a significant increase in support for Basque separatism, the granting of autonomy to Basques in 1979 resulted in support for independence dropping from 36 per cent to 12 per cent.[38] The long-time existence of the Canadian and Swiss federations also show that extensive decentralization is consistent with state unity. Canada's current troubles do not undermine this argument. To a considerable extent, the rise in support for Quebec separatism since the 1970s can be traced to a move away from the concept of a bi-national partnership on the part of English-speaking Canadians towards a view of Canada as a nation-state in which all individuals and provinces should be treated equally.[39] Similarly, the breakup of several Communist multinational federations should not cast any doubt on decentralization as a strategy, as these states were in fact highly centralized.

Decentralization strategies should be supplemented by arrangements which ensure national minorities are represented in central government. These arrangements will be more or less important depending on the powers possessed by the centre. In a full-blown power-sharing regime, a minority, in addition to being self-governing within areas of jurisdiction important to it, would be adequately represented in the central government executive (the cabinet), judiciary, legislature, and bureaucracy. It would also be capable of vetoing decisions of the central government which affect its vital interests.[40]

The success of such 'partnership' strategies, like other strategies of conflict regulation, depends very much on timing. It will be more difficult to get support for accommodation from majorities, and less likely that it will satisfy minorities, if relations are allowed to polarize. Beyond a certain point, it will be impossible to hold the multinational state together, unless force is used. In this event, the question then becomes how should the successor states be governed? As many of these will be as 'multinational' as their predecessors, the appropriate lesson for their élites to draw from the secession experience is that nationalizing states—à la Brubaker—or even nation-states which treat all their citizens as undifferentiated equals—the American model—are not suitable frameworks. If new states are to avoid the same problems which led to the undoing of their predecessors, they should engage in developing institutions based on accommodating all national groups. This would rule out approaches like those of Estonia and Latvia, which have nationalized their states and blocked the integration of large Russian minorities. It also raises questions about the approach of Quebec separatists, who, as Nielsen's chapter suggests, seem even less prepared to accommodate national minorities than the Canadian state they seek to leave.[41]

Instead, breakaway states should endeavour to win support from all population groups by the decentralist and consociational strategies referred to earlier. While such accommodation is difficult to conceive of in many post-secession scenarios, there is evidence that some new states, including Russia (with regard to Tatarstan and other regions) and Ukraine (with regard to Crimea) have gone at least some way along the route of multinational partnership.

Decentralization and consociational strategies may not be sufficient in all circumstances. As has been indicated, the breakup of a state into a number of smaller independent states may wrench several groups away from co-nationals and territory they identify with. This is not only the case with many minorities in secessionist and rump states but also with local majorities who have dual or nested identities. In the case of Quebec, secession would not only cut off anglophones and Natives who identify with Canada rather than Quebec, it would also affect Quebec francophones who identify with Canada or with Canada and Quebec, as well as all those Canadians living outside Quebec who identify with Canada as a whole.

The appropriate way to address these problems of parallel and overlapping national loyalties is to move beyond the notion of traditional 'Westphalian-style' independent states and construct supra-state partnerships and institutions. Such supra-state co-operation not only makes sense in terms of accommodating a variety of national groups, it can also, in an era of globalization and increased economic competition, be sold on trading and economic grounds.[42] Such institutions need not be restricted to the territory of the predecessor state, but could, like the European Union, include many states. Nor need they cover all of the territory of the predecessor state: like the Anglo-Irish Agreement which involves Ireland-UK co-operation over Northern Ireland, supra-state institutions could be limited to a part of the state.[43]

What is normatively desirable, however, is not necessarily what will materialize, as the brief review of new states in Eastern Europe suggests. While the meaningful accommodation of minorities will make them less inclined to emigrate or rebel, external compatriots less willing to intervene, and international bodies less likely to treat new states as pariahs, the dominant groups in these states often show considerable reluctance to accommodate national minorities. Given the bitterness which is often attached to secessions, the breakaway (and the rump state) may also be unwilling to co-operate in establishing supra-state institutions.[44]

CONCLUSION

This chapter has been directed against those who imply or argue that secession by itself is the way to address problems of pluralism, and/or who understate or ignore the problems of pluralism that follow secession. I have argued that in order to assess normatively the merits of secession, the context is crucial. Ethical theorizing about secession cannot proceed in abstraction from the national sentiment that fuels the secession, or the majority–minority relations in the secessionist region, or without considering the kinds of identities that the groups have. We should not ignore the fact that secession is usually highly contested within secessionist regions, that, if successful, it often merely replaces one nationally heterogeneous state with two or more similar states, and that the ill treatment of minorities which gives rise to secession is often replicated in these offspring.

I have outlined institutional arrangements within states and between states, which, when combined with protection of individual rights, would go further towards meeting the liberal requirement that all individuals be treated with equal respect than the current liberal emphasis on individual rights in abstraction from national identities. Such accommodation of minority nations is, however, very much the ideal, and rarely the practice.

NOTES

1. It is not only liberal philosophers who fail to focus on national diversity within states, but also many political scientists. See W. Connor, *Ethnonationalism: The Quest for Understanding* (Princeton: Princeton University Press, 1994), especially ch. 2.
2. See W. Kymlicka, *Multicultural Citizenship* (Oxford: Oxford University Press, 1995), 11–26.
3. Prior to the 1970s, the same was said of Britain and France, the two other states which have most influenced liberal thinking. Britain currently has a powerful minority nationalist movement in Scotland, and a smaller one in Wales. France's minority movements are smaller still, but there are nationalist parties in Corsica and Brittany.
4. See Kymlicka, *Multicultural Citizenship*; C. Taylor, 'The Politics of Recognition', in A. Gutmann (ed.), *Multiculturalism and the 'Politics of Recognition'* (Princeton: Princeton University Press, 1992); Y. Tamir, *Liberal Nationalism* (Princeton: Princeton University Press, 1993); M. Moore, 'On National Self-Determination', *Political Studies*, 45/5 (1997), 900–13.
5. A. Buchanan, *Secession: The Morality of Political Divorce from Fort Sumter to Lithuania and Quebec* (Boulder, Colo.: Westview, 1991).
6. Don Horowitz makes a similar point to mine in his contribution to this collection.
7. See D. Philpott, 'In Defense of Self-Determination', *Ethics*, 105 (1995), 352–85; C. Wellman, 'A Defence of Secession and Political Self-Determination', *Philosophy and Public Affairs*, 24/2 (1995), 142–71; D. Gauthier, 'Breaking Up: An Essay on Secession', *Canadian Journal of Philosophy*, 24 (1994), 357–72.
8. Helsinki Watch, *Destroying Ethnic Identity: The Kurds of Turkey*, (New York: Helsinki Watch, 1988); Human Rights Watch/Helsinki, *Denying Ethnic Identity: The Macedonians of Greece* (New York: Human Rights Watch/Helsinki, 1994).
9. E. Moxon-Browne, *Nation, Class and Creed in Northern Ireland* (Aldershot: Gower, 1983), 183, 195. In divided societies, one should not take the inclusive appeals of civic nationalists at face value. While many such nationalists are perfectly sincere, and wish that everyone within the designated territory would embrace

their cause, others know very well that such appeals are a waste of time but use them more for their external propaganda value.

10. J. McGarry and B. O'Leary, *The Politics of Antagonism: Understanding Northern Ireland* (London: Athlone, 1993); *Explaining Northern Ireland: Broken Images* (Oxford: Blackwell, 1995).
11. See the contribution to this volume by Nielsen.
12. The Cree voted 96 per cent against, the Inuit 95 per cent against, and the (French-speaking) Montagnais 99 per cent against. Figures cited in A. Cairns, 'The Legacy of the Referendum: Who are we Now?', unpub. paper (1995), 3, 5.
13. Slovaks make up 3 per cent of the Czech Republic's population, while Czechs make up 1 per cent of Slovakia's population. Magyars make up 11 per cent of Slovakia's population. Figures from J. Bugajski, *Ethnic Politics in Eastern Europe* (London: M. E. Sharpe, 1995), 293, 321.
14. The fifteen are Estonia, Latvia, Belarus, Ukraine, Moldova, Georgia, Turkmenistan, Uzbekistan, Tajikistan, Kyrgyzstan, Kazakhstan, Bosnia-Herzegovina, Macedonia, Serbia, Montenegro. Figures from S. Woodward, *Balkan Tragedy* (Washington: The Brookings Institution, 1995), 33–4, and I. Bremmer and R. Taras, *New States, New Politics: Building the Post-Soviet Nations* (Cambridge: Cambridge University Press, 1997), 706–7.
15. The eight are Estonia, Latvia, Moldova, Tajikistan, Kyrgyzstan, Kazakhstan, Bosnia, and Macedonia. If Serbs are distinguished from Montenegrins, Montenegro can also be added to this list. Figures from Woodward, *Balkan Tragedy*, 33–4, and Bremmer and Taras, *New States*, 706–7.

    Ethnic heterogeneity is a feature of most of the world's states and not just those created as a result of recent state breakups. According to Walker Connor, of a total of 132 states in 1972 (and none were added between 1972 and 1991) 53 per cent of them had ethnic minorities equivalent to at least one quarter of the population (*Ethnonationalism*, 29–30).
16. See Moore's chapter in this volume; W. Connor, *The National Question in Marxist-Leninist Theory and Strategy* (Princeton: Princeton University Press, 1984).
17. Over half of Ukraine's Russian minority voted for independence in the referendum of December 1990. Estonian sources claim that 25 per cent of Russians supported independence. In Latvia, estimates vary from 15 per cent to over 50 per cent. The Russian minority vote in favour of independence varied throughout the Soviet Union from 20 per cent to 70 per cent where referendums were held. Figures from P. Kolstoe, *Russians in the Former Soviet Republics* (Bloomington, Ind.: Indiana University Press, 1995), 10, 118, 178.
18. One reason for not generalizing from the example of Ukraine is that ethnic and national identity there, particularly in its eastern zone, is not as fixed as it is elsewhere in Eastern Europe. In this ethnic 'borderland', Ukrainian ethnic identity merges with Russian ethnic identity, and some individuals who give their language as Russian identify more closely with an independent Ukraine than some who give their language as Ukrainian.
19. Kolstoe, *Russians*, 11, 186.
20. W. Connor, 'From a Theory of Relative Economic Deprivation Toward a Theory of Relative Political Deprivation', paper presented to a Conference on 'Minority Nationalism and the New State Order', London, Ontario, 7–8 Nov. 1997, 13.

21. The salient part of the referendum question is as follows: 'Do you agree that Quebec should become sovereign, after having made a formal offer to Canada for a new economic and political partnership. . . . Yes or No'. Federalists in the Quebec legislature insisted on an amendment inserting 'a sovereign country' instead of 'sovereign' but the separatist Parti Québécois government rejected this elaboration as unnecessary. As Norman argues elsewhere in this collection, polls consistently show that significantly more Quebeckers are in favour of Quebec being sovereign than in it becoming a sovereign country. Polls indicated that more than a quarter of 'Yes' voters believed that Quebec would remain in Canada and continue to send representatives to the Parliament in Ottawa after a 'Yes' victory.
22. Connor, 'From a Theory', 13.
23. Ibid. 14.
24. R. Brubaker, *Nationalism Reframed* (Cambridge: Cambridge University Press, 1995).
25. *The Economist*, 13 Sept. 1997, 54–6.
26. It remains to be seen, however, whether this limited decentralization will satisfy the national groups in Ukraine and Russia.
27. It is possible to distinguish between two types of secession demonstration-effect. On the one hand, secession may give rise to a further secession from the seceding territory. This is the type I am concerned with in this chapter. On the other hand, the secession of one part of a state may have demonstration-effects for another part of the rump state (or for a part of another state). For a discussion which centres on this type, see Connor, *Ethnonationalism*, 172–3.
28. M. Marrus, *The Unwanted: European Refugees in the Twentieth Century* (New York: Oxford University Press, 1985), 40–51.
29. See R. Brubaker, 'Aftermaths of Empire and the Unmixing of Peoples: Historical and Comparative Perspectives', *Ethnic and Racial Studies*, 18/2 (1995), 189–218.
30. The numbers involved in such migrations are in addition to those who are forced out of their homes as a result of 'ethnic cleansing' policies.
31. While one should not exaggerate the risks of violence, nor should one rule it out completely. There are a number of militant native groups in Quebec, particularly the Mohawks of the Akwesasne reserve near Montreal, who might use violence to prevent Quebec gaining control over their territory, and in an attempt to bring about an intervention from Canada on their behalf.
32. One result of the near victory of secessionists in the 1995 referendum is the growth of a vocal partitionist movement among Quebec's minorities. Several municipalities in minority regions have passed proclamations insisting on their right to remain part of Canada if Quebec separates.
33. It is impossible to predict with any degree of certainty the number of anglophones who will migrate from Quebec in the event of its secession from Canada. There is a tendency among some Quebec civic nationalists to downplay the possibility of a significant exodus, as this is incompatible with their optimism about constructing a civic nation in Quebec. However, some 30 per cent of all Quebec anglophones, and 40 per cent of those aged between 18 and 34, tell pollsters that they would like to be living somewhere else in five years, *The Economist*, 1 Sept. 1996, 46.

34. This issue is raised by J. Bernier, 'Liberalism, Secession, and the Problem of Internal Minorities', paper presented to the American Political Science Association, Washington, Aug. 1997, 10, and M. Moore, 'The Limits of Liberal Nationalism' in B. O'Leary and G. Schopflin (eds.), *Understanding Nationalism* (forthcoming).
35. This is a problem with Bernier's paper, 'Liberalism, Secession . . .'. It is written from a perspective critical of Quebec separatism, and focuses on the minority problems created by secession, without mentioning the minority problems which give rise to secession. Apart from this, Bernier's paper is a good account of problems encountered by minorities in post-secession states.

    When Bernier presented her paper at a recent conference, separatist philosopher Kai Nielsen, who contributes to this volume, reprimanded her for ignoring the problem of minorities in the pre-secession order. He, on the other hand, has little to say about minority problems post-secession.
36. This point, that rump states can also be nationalizing, is not at odds with Brubaker's work on 'nationalizing states', *Nationalism Reframed.* None the less, the impression created by his focus is that it is breakaway states—those states governed by national majorities which acquire a state for the first time—which are likely to be nationalizing.
37. Ideally, minority nations should not only have significant control over their own affairs but their self-government should not be subject to diminution or abolition at the hands of majority groups. Federation is, therefore, more suitable for multinational partnerships than devolution.
38. Connor, 'From a Theory', 16.
39. This move towards Canada as a nation-state rather than as a multinational partnership is most closely associated with Pierre Trudeau, ironically a francophone, who was Canadian Prime Minister almost continuously from 1968 to 1984 and who has continued to exercise tremendous influence in English Canada, though not, tellingly, in his native Quebec. Trudeau took several important steps: first, he introduced a Charter of Rights into the Canadian Constitution in 1982, which promoted the idea of equal citizenship and individual rights over the idea of Canada as a compact between two founding peoples; at the same time, Trudeau introduced a new amending formula which removed a veto which Quebec had enjoyed by convention; finally, he is widely believed—directly and through lieutenants like Newfoundland Premier Clyde Wells and New Brunswick Premier Frank McKenna—to have destroyed the Meech Lake Accord, a constitutional amendment which would have gone some way towards restoring Canada as a multinational partnership. Support for Quebec separatism soared in the period immediately after the collapse of the Meech Lake Accord, and has remained at historically high levels since.
40. See A. Lijphart, *Democracy in Plural Societies* (New Haven, Conn.: Yale University Press, 1977).
41. Canada is officially bilingual, and, with Switzerland, is one of the two most decentralized federations in the world. Nielsen's chapter suggests that Quebec will be officially unilingual and much more centralized than Canada. If Canada is unacceptable to its Québécois minority, an independent Quebec constructed according to Nielsen's vision should be even more unacceptable to its anglophone minority.

42. M. Keating, *Nations Against the State: The New Politics of Nationalism in Quebec, Catalonia and Scotland* (Basingstoke: Macmillan, 1996).
43. Since 1985, the United Kingdom and Ireland have had an agreement which allows the Republic of Ireland's government a limited role in the governance of a part of the United Kingdom inhabited by Irish nationalists, i.e. Northern Ireland. The governments of the rump of Canada and an independent Quebec could consider a similar supranational agreement to cover the large region of northern Quebec which is inhabited by Crees. The Canadian federal government is already committed by a tripartite agreement signed with the Crees and the province of Quebec to protecting Cree interests, and such supranational institutions would help it to meet its fiduciary obligations as well as going some way towards meeting the aspiration of Crees to remain part of Canada.

    Just as supra-state agreements of this sort can vary in the amount of territory they cover, they can also vary in terms of how wide-ranging the interstate co-operation is. It is possible, as in the case of the Anglo-Irish Agreement, for one state to allow another state (in this case, the Irish) a limited say in the governance of part of its territory. It is also possible to establish a full-blown condominium, so that the territory is jointly governed by both states as equals. In this case, the territory belongs to both states, and the people in it are citizens of both states. See B. O'Leary, T. Lyne, J. Marshall, and B. Rowthorn, *Northern Ireland: Sharing Authority* (London: Institute for Public Policy Research, 1993).

    While such supra-state arrangements are of most obvious benefit for trans-border groups—those straddling two states—they can benefit all minorities. Thus the Council of Europe, which is responsible for the European Convention on Human Rights (and for the court which polices it) has made respect for minority rights a condition of accession for countries in Eastern and Central Europe. Similarly, the European Community insisted on an end to anti-minority measures in Spain before that country was allowed to join, and the European Union has made it clear that Turkey's abuse of its Kurdish minorities is one of the most serious obstacles to Turkey becoming a member.
44. For a discussion of the difficulties attached to forming such interstate arrangements after secession has taken place, see M. Keating's 'Nations Without States: The Accommodation of Nationalism in the New State Order', paper presented to a Conference on 'Minority Nationalism in the New State Order', London, Ontario, 7–8 Nov. 1997, 10–11.

11

Myths and Misconceptions in the Study of Nationalism

ROGERS BRUBAKER

The resurgence of nationalism in Eastern Europe and elsewhere in the last decade has sparked—with only the shortest of lags—an even stronger resurgence in the study of nationalism. As a certifiably 'hot topic', nationalism has moved rapidly from the front pages to the journal pages, from the periphery—often the distant periphery—to the centre of numerous scholarly fields and subfields.[1] This new centrality is a mixed blessing. On the one hand, the robust demand for knowledge about—and 'fixes' for—nationalism brings new opportunities, resources, and attention to the field. On the other hand, the rapid expansion of the field has strengthened analytically primitive currents in the study of nationalism,[2] threatening to erode (or simply—given the volume of the new literature—to overwhelm) the analytical gains previously made in sophisticated works by Benedict Anderson, John Armstrong, John Breuilly, Ernest Gellner, Anthony Smith, and a number of other scholars.[3]

Borrowing Charles Tilly's phrase, this chapter addresses six 'pernicious postulates',[4] six myths and misconceptions that, newly strengthened by the dizzying expansion in the literature and quasi-literature on the subject, inform, and misinform, the study of ethnicity and nationalism. Although I draw illustrative empirical material mainly from post-Communist East Central Europe and the former Soviet Union, the theoretical debates I engage are central to the study of nationalism generally.[5]

I begin by addressing two opposed appraisals of the gravity and 'resolvability' of national conflicts. The first is the 'architectonic illusion'—the belief that the right 'grand architecture', the right territorial and institutional framework, can satisfy nationalist demands, quench nationalist passions, and

For comments and suggestions on earlier versions of this chapter I thank Zsuzsa Berend, Margit Feischmidt, Jon Fox, Mark Granovetter, John Hall, Victoria Koroteyeva, Peter Loewenberg, John Meyer, László Neményi, Margaret Somers, Peter Stamatov, David Stark, and Ronald Suny. An earlier version of this chapter has appeared in John Hall (ed.), *The State of the Nation: Ernest Gellner and the Theory of Nationalism* (Cambridge: Cambridge University Press, 1998) and is reprinted by permission of the publisher.

thereby resolve national conflicts. Most conceptions of grand architecture have involved the reorganization of political space along national lines, based on an alleged right of national self-determination or on the related 'principle of nationality'. Against this, I want to argue that nationalist conflicts are in principle, by their very nature, irresolvable, and that the search for an overall 'architectural' resolution of national conflicts is misguided.

Sharply opposed to the optimism of the first view is the dire pessimism of the second. This is the 'seething cauldron' view of ethnic and national conflicts. This gloom-and-doom perspective sees all of Eastern Europe—and many other world regions—as a seething cauldron of ethnic and national conflict, on the verge of boiling over into violence. More generally, it sees nationalism as *the* central problem in these regions, and sees national identities as strong and salient. Against this, I want to assert that ethno-national violence is neither as prevalent, nor as likely to occur, as is often assumed; and that national feeling is less strong, national identity less salient, and nationalist politics less central than is often assumed.

Next, I will address two opposed views of the sources and dynamics of resurgent nationalism. The first is the 'return of the repressed' perspective. This view sees national identities and national conflicts as deeply rooted in the pre-communist history of Eastern Europe, and as subsequently frozen or repressed by ruthlessly anti-national communist regimes. With the collapse of communism, these pre-communist national identities and nationalist conflicts have returned with redoubled force. Against this, I will stress the pervasive shaping and structuring of national identities and nationalist conflicts by communist regimes.

Categorically rejecting the primordialist understanding of nationhood that often accompanies the 'return of the repressed' view, and refusing to see national identity and nationalist conflicts as deeply encoded historically, is the 'élite manipulation' view. This perspective sees nationalism as the product of unscrupulous and manipulative élites, who are seen as cynically stirring up nationalist passions at will. While conceding, of course, that unscrupulous élites often do seek to stir up nationalist passions, I want to argue against this view that it is not always so easy for élites to stir up nationalist passions; and that it is mistaken to see nationalism in purely instrumental terms, to focus solely on the calculating stances of self-interested élites.

The fifth perspective is 'the realism of the group'. Based on a 'groupist' social ontology, this view sees nations and ethnic groups as real entities, as substantial, enduring, sharply bounded collectivities. It sees the social world, like a Modigliani painting (to borrow Ernest Gellner's image), as composed of externally bounded, internally homogeneous cultural blocs. Against this, I will argue that the 'Modiglianesque' vision of the social world is deeply problematic, that ethnic and national groups are not well conceived as externally sharply bounded, internally culturally homogeneous blocs.

Finally, I address the 'Manichean' view that there are, at bottom, only two kinds of nationalism, a good, civic kind and a bad, ethnic kind; and two corresponding understandings of nationhood, the good, civic conception, in which nationhood is seen as based on common citizenship, and the bad, ethnic conception, in which nationhood is seen as based on common ethnicity. Against this, I will argue that the distinction between civic and ethnic nationhood and nationalism is both normatively and analytically problematic.

I

I begin with the 'architectonic illusion'. This is the belief that if one gets the 'grand architecture' right—if one discovers and establishes the proper territorial and institutional framework—then one can conclusively satisfy legitimate nationalist demands and thereby resolve national conflicts. There have been many different conceptions of just what the proper grand architecture should look like. But most of these have appealed in one way or another to the idea of national self-determination or to the so-called principle of nationality.

The principle of national self-determination assigns moral agency and political authority to nations; it holds that nations are entitled to govern their own affairs and, in particular, to form their own states. The principle of nationality asserts that state and nation should be congruent; it thereby provides a powerful lever for evaluating, and redrawing, state boundaries, for legitimating, or delegitimating political frontiers according to a kind of 'correspondence theory' of justice.

These principles underlay, albeit imperfectly, the post-First World War territorial settlement in Central and Eastern Europe; the mid-twentieth century wave of decolonization in Asia and Africa; and the recent reorganization of political space in Eastern Europe and the former Soviet Union. In each of these cases, the period preceding the reorganization of political space along national lines was one of intensifying nationalist movements. In each case, the demands of these nationalist movements were viewed with sympathy by much of world public opinion. In each case, it was widely believed that a new 'grand architecture', involving the reorganization of political space along national lines, would satisfy the demands of these national movements and contribute to regional peace and stability by resolving national tensions.[6] Yet in each case, this expectation was disappointed. Political reconfiguration did not resolve national tensions but only reframed them, recast them in new (and in some cases more virulent) form.

I am not arguing that the reconfiguration of political space along ostensibly national lines in these cases was necessarily a bad thing (though I think in some cases—such as the former Yugoslavia—it was unfortunate). I am arguing, instead, against the idea that nationalism is a problem that can somehow be solved by 'correct' territorial and institutional arrangements; and, more specifically, against the idea that nationalist demands can be satisfied and national conflicts resolved by applying the principle of national self-determination or redrawing political boundaries according to the principle of nationality.

Today, of course, this argument is less likely to be advanced than it was a few years earlier. Several years after the last major reorganization of political space along national lines, it is all too evident that national conflicts have not been resolved, and that the most virulent conflicts have occurred after rather than before the reorganization of political space. But it is worth remembering that only a few years ago, a great deal of hope was invested in national self-determination. The prospect of the breakup of the Soviet Union and Yugoslavia was welcomed as a story of national liberation; the prevailing narrative was one of national imprisonment and liberation. The rising curve of enthusiasm for national self-determination, as communist regimes began to crumble, did not, to be sure, reach the apogee of 75 years earlier, when the first wholesale reorganization of previously multinational political space along national lines was undertaken. Yet the *fin de siècle* re-enchantment with national self-determination was substantial enough, incautious enough, and —in view of the disastrous sequel to the early twentieth-century experiment in national self-determination[7]—puzzling enough to give us pause.[8] Moreover, even if the re-enchantment has since yielded to a new disenchantment, even if yesterday's narrative of national imprisonment and liberation today seems one-sided, mischievous, or even downright pernicious, still the underlying way of thinking about nationalism that has historically accompanied appeals to the principle of national self-determination remains robustly entrenched.

The principle of national self-determination and the related principle of nationality are of course normative, not analytical principles; and I do not want to make here an argument in normative political theory.[9] But for a century and a half, the appeal to the principle of nationality or to an alleged right of national self-determination has been closely related to a particular—and I believe mistaken—account of the sources and dynamics of nationalism. And it is this account that I would like to dwell on for a moment.

This account is fundamentally a nation-centred understanding of nationalism. It posits the existence of nations as real entities whose tendency or *telos*—at least under modern social and political conditions—is to seek independent statehood. Nationalism, on this view, is thus nation-based, state-seeking activity.

If this understanding of nationalism were correct, then one might indeed expect the reorganization of political space along national lines to resolve national conflicts by fulfilling nationalist demands. The imagery here is that nationalism has a self-limiting political career. Fundamentally oriented towards independence, national movements in a sense transcend themselves, wither away in the very course of realizing their aims. When nationalist demands for statehood are fulfilled, the nationalist programme is satisfied; it exhausts itself in the attainment of its ends.

However, I do not think nationalism can be well understood as nation-based, state-seeking activity. In the first place, nationalism is not always, or essentially, state-seeking. To focus narrowly on state-seeking nationalist movements is to ignore the infinitely protean nature of nationalist politics; it is to ignore the manner in which the interests of a putative 'nation' can be seen as requiring many kinds of actions other than, or in addition to, formal independence; it is to be unprepared for the kinds of nationalist politics that can flourish *after* the reorganization of political space along national lines, *after* the breakup of multinational states into would-be nation-states. It is to be unprepared for the fact that nationalism was not only a *cause* but also a *consequence* of the breakup of old empires and the creation of new nation-states.

In the new or newly enlarged nation-states of interwar Central and Eastern Europe, and in the new nation-states of post-communist Eastern Europe today, several kinds of nationalism have flourished as a *result* of the reorganization of political space along ostensibly national lines. Here I would like to briefly characterize four such forms of non-state-seeking nationalism.

The first is what I call the 'nationalizing' nationalism of newly independent (or newly reconfigured) states. Nationalizing nationalisms involve claims made in the name of a 'core nation' or nationality, defined in ethno-cultural terms, and sharply distinguished from the citizenry as a whole. The core nation is understood as the legitimate 'owner' of the state, which is conceived as the state *of* and *for* the core nation. Despite having 'its own' state, however, the core nation is conceived as being in a weak cultural, economic, or demographic position within the state. This weak position is seen as a legacy of discrimination against the nation before it attained independence. And it is held to justify the 'remedial' or 'compensatory' project of using state power to promote the specific (and previously inadequately served) interests of the core nation. Examples of such nationalizing nationalisms abound in interwar Europe and the post-Communist present.[10]

Directly challenging these 'nationalizing' nationalisms are the transborder nationalisms of what I call 'external national homelands.' Homeland nationalisms are oriented to ethno-national kin who are residents and citizens of other states. Transborder homeland nationalism asserts a state's right—indeed its obligation—to monitor the condition, promote the welfare, support the activities and institutions, and protect the interests of 'its' ethno-national kin in other states. Such claims are typically made, and typically have greatest force and resonance, when the ethno-national kin in question are seen as threatened by the nationalizing policies and practices of the state in which they live.

Homeland nationalisms thus arise in direct opposition to and in dynamic interaction with nationalizing nationalisms. Prominent instances of homeland nationalism are furnished by Weimar (and in a very different mode) Nazi Germany, and by Russia today.[11]

The third characteristic form of nationalism found in the aftermath of the reorganization of political space along national lines is the nationalism of national minorities. Minority nationalist stances characteristically involve a self-understanding in specifically 'national' rather than merely 'ethnic' terms, a demand for state recognition of their distinct ethno-cultural nationality, and the assertion of certain collective, nationality-based cultural or political rights. Salient examples include Germans in many Eastern European countries in the interwar period and Hungarian and Russian minorities today.

The fourth form is a defensive, protective, national-populist nationalism that seeks to protect the national economy, language, mores, or cultural patrimony against alleged threats from outside. The bearers of such putative threats are diverse but can include foreign capital, transnational organizations, notably the IMF, immigrants, powerful foreign cultural influences, and so on. This kind of nationalism often claims to seek a 'third way' between capitalism and socialism, is often receptive to anti-Semitism, brands its political opponents as anti-national, 'un-Romanian,' 'un-Russian,' etc., is critical of the various ills of 'the West' and of 'modernity,' and tends to idealize an agrarian past. The social and economic dislocations accompanying market-oriented reforms —unemployment, inflation, tighter workplace discipline, etc.—create fertile soil for the use of such national populist idioms as a legitimation strategy by governments or as a mobilization strategy by oppositions.

Nationalism, then, should not be conceived as essentially or even as primarily state-seeking. Nor should it be understood as nation-based, that is as arising from the demands of nations, understood as real, substantial, bounded social entities. Nationhood is not an unambiguous social fact; it is a contestable—and often contested—political claim. Consequently, neither the principle of national self-determination nor the principle of nationality can provide an unambiguous guide to the reorganization of political space.

Claims to nationhood are often disputed—think, for example, historically, about the Macedonians, or about the dispute concerning whether interwar Czechoslovakia was one nation or two. Or, more recently, think of the Kurds, the Palestinians, the Québécois, and of a host of West European ethno-regional movements. And even when the status of nationhood itself is not disputed, the territorial or cultural boundaries of the putative nation are often contested, as is the manner in which nationhood ought to be construed for purposes of implementing the right of self-determination or of redrawing frontiers along national lines.

Given the very large number of more or less serious (and often conflicting) claims to nationhood, how are we to identify the national selves who are to enjoy the right or privilege of self-determination? And once we have identified these favoured national selves, how are we to determine their bounds and contours? This is not a theoretical quibble, but a question of the utmost practical import.

Take for example the case of Yugoslavia. Even if one could have agreed that the national selves who were to enjoy self-determination were the officially recognized constituent nations of Yugoslavia (but why not the Albanians? why not the Hungarians in Voivodina?), one still could not have avoided the question of how those national selves were to be construed. To put the question in its simplest form, supposing we agreed that self-determination was to be exercised by Serbs, Croats, and Muslims. How, then, were these self-determining units to be construed? Was the right of self-determination to be exercised by Serbia or by Serbs? By Croatia or by Croats? By Bosnia-Hercegovina or by Yugoslav Muslims? By territorial entities, that is, or by boundary-transcending ethno-cultural nations? Were all the inhabitants of the Croatian republic to enjoy a single right of self-determination? And similarly for all the inhabitants of the Serb republic, and of Bosnia-Hercegovina, by majority vote? Or rather, was self-determination to be exercised by the Croatian, Serb, and Muslim ethno-nations, whose populations spilled over republican borders? In practice, the international community opted for the former—but perhaps without realizing the tremendous difference between the two modes of construing self-determination for the same national units.[12] And the consequences were catastrophic.

There are of course many other examples of conflicting claims about how national selves should be construed. The negotiations concerning the post-First World War settlement furnished a whole catalogue of such conflicting claims, many involving a clash between historic-territorial and ethno-cultural versions of nationhood, with parties typically opportunistically advancing whichever claim would benefit them.

On a more philosophical level, we arrive here at the inescapable *antinomies of national self-determination*. Self-determination presupposes the prior determination of the unit—the national self—that is to enjoy the right of self-determination. But the identification and boundaries of this self cannot themselves be self-determined: they must be determined by others. Just as the boundaries of the demos that is presupposed by democratic institutions cannot themselves be democratically determined,[13] so too the boundaries of the national self that is presupposed by national self-determination cannot themselves be self-determined. Only in practice, the problem with national self-determination is more serious than with democracy. For in the routine functioning of democracy, the bounds of the demos are simply taken as given and unproblematic. But since national self-determination is precisely about setting the initial boundaries of the demos, there is no analog in the sphere of self-determination to the routine functioning of democracy within the frame of a taken-for-granted demos. Since the whole point of invoking national self-determination is to change unit boundaries, such boundaries cannot be taken for granted—especially given the pervasively contested, conflicting, and overlapping nature of claims to nationhood.

Against the architectonic illusion, then, against the illusion that nationalist conflicts are susceptible of fundamental resolution through national self-determination, I am asserting a kind of 'impossibility theorem'—that national conflicts are in principle irresolvable; that 'nation' belongs to the class of 'essentially contested' concepts; that chronic contestedness is therefore intrinsic to nationalist politics, part of the very nature of nationalist politics; and that the search for an overall 'architectural' resolution of national conflicts is misguided in principle, and often disastrous in practice.

In criticizing this naïvely optimistic view I should emphasize that I do not want to adopt a gloom-and-doom perspective. In fact the next myth I want to criticize is precisely the gloom-and-doom view of the region. My point is not to substitute a pessimistic for an optimistic reading, but rather to suggest that the search for solutions and resolutions of national conflicts—especially grand, 'architectonic,' isomorphic, 'one-size-fits-all' solutions and resolutions—is misguided. To assert the irresolvability of national conflicts is not to assert anything about their salience, intensity, or centrality. Indeed I believe, as I am about to argue, that their salience, intensity, and centrality are generally overstated. The search for some fundamental architectural resolution of national conflicts, then, is not only philosophically problematic and practically misguided; it is often simply unnecessary.

To criticize the search for solutions and resolutions of national conflicts is not to suggest that institutional design does not matter. On the contrary, it matters a great deal.[14] Clearly, institutional design can either exacerbate or ameliorate ethnic and national conflicts. But it cannot solve them. Rather, good institutional design can give political actors incentives to work around ethnic and national conflicts, to disregard them for certain purposes, to frame political rhetoric and political claims in non-ethnic or trans-ethnic terms. Moreover, institutional design is unlikely to have even these limited (but very important) effects if carried out in a grand, architectonic, one-size-fits-all mode. Good institutional design is more likely to be subverted than informed by grand architectural principles like the principle of national self-determination or the principle of nationality. Good institutional design has to be context-sensitive in a strong sense, that is, sensitive not only to the gross features of differing contexts but to finer details as well; it presupposes relatively 'thick' understandings of the local contexts in which it is to apply.[15]

In my view, national conflicts are seldom 'solved' or 'resolved'. Somewhat like conflicts between conflicting paradigms in a Kuhnian history of science, they are more likely to fade away, to lose their centrality and salience as ordinary people—and political entrepreneurs—turn to other concerns, or as a new generation grows up to whom old quarrels seem largely irrelevant. We need to devote more attention to studying how and why this happens —not only how and why politics can be pervasively, and relatively suddenly, 'nationalized', but also how and why it can be pervasively, and sometimes equally suddenly, 'denationalized'.

II

The second misconception that I want to discuss is in some ways the opposite of the first. If the architectonic illusion is characterized by the naïvely optimistic view that national conflicts are capable of a final resolution, the second misconception is characterized by a bleakly pessimistic appraisal of East European nationalism. I will call this the 'seething cauldron' view, since it sees the entire region as a seething cauldron of ethnic conflict, on the verge of boiling over into ethnic and nationalist violence, or, in another metaphorical idiom, as a tinder-box that a single careless spark could ignite into a catastrophic ethno-national inferno.[16]

This might also be called the 'orientalist' view of East European nationalism, since it often involves, at least implicitly, an overdrawn, if not downright caricatural, contrast between Western and Eastern Europe, built on a series of oppositions such as that between reason and passion, universalism and particularism, transnational integration and nationalist disintegration, civility and violence, modern tolerance and ancient hatreds, civic nationhood and ethnic nationalism.

Indisputably, there are important differences, conditioned by historical traditions and present economic, cultural, political, and ethno-demographic realities, between prevailing forms of nationhood and nationalism in Western Europe and Eastern Europe. Yet one must reject the complacent and self-congratulatory account of Western Europe that is implicit or explicit in this orientalist, 'seething cauldron' view of Eastern European nationalism. After all, the 'Europhoria' that surrounded discussions of European integration a few years ago was dissipated by the unforeseen (and partly nationalist) resistance to the Maastricht treaty; and nationalist and xenophobic parties have established a secure place in the political landscape of almost all Western European countries.

One must also reject the 'seething cauldron' account of Eastern Europe. It is this gloom-and-doom view of the East, rather than the paired complacent view of the West, that I address here. I focus on two problematic aspects of this account. The first concerns violence, the second the strength and salience of nationalism and national identities.

The violence in the region—in the former Yugoslavia, in Transcaucasia and the North Caucasus, in parts of Soviet Central Asia—has indeed been appalling. But the undifferentiated image of the region as a hotbed of ubiquitous, explosive, violent, or at least potentially violent ethnic and national conflict is quite misleading. Violence is neither as prevalent, nor as likely to occur in the region, as is generally believed. Journalists and scholars have focused on spectacular but atypical cases of violence (the former Yugoslavia) rather than on unspectacular but more typical cases of 'routine' ethnic and nationalist tensions, and they have tended to generalize from the atypical cases to the region as a whole. This case selection bias is one reason for the overemphasis on violence.[17]

Not only the actual incidence of violence, but also the danger of future violence is overestimated. Violence is often presented as an omnipresent possibility. 'If it happened in Yugoslavia'—so goes the argument—'it could happen anywhere.' I think this is mistaken. I have done some work, for example, on Hungarian minorities in neighbouring states, especially Romania and Slovakia. In this setting, several forms of nationalism are intertwined. The most important are the autonomy-seeking nationalism of the Hungarian minorities; the 'nation-building' or 'nationalizing' nationalisms of Slovakia and Romania; and the 'homeland' nationalism of Hungary, oriented to protecting the rights and interests of its co-ethnics in neighbouring states. Yet I think the danger of large-scale ethnic violence or nationalist war is minimal in this case. This is not because these national tensions can somehow be 'resolved.' I do not think they can be. These interlocking, mutually antagonistic nationalisms of national minority, nationalizing state, and external national homeland are intractable and are likely to persist as chronic tensions and conflicts. But their intractability should not be conflated with explosiveness or with a potential to engender large-scale violence.

If I am right about this, it raises the analytical question of what prevents these chronic, intractable, interlocking nationalist conflicts from escalating into violent confrontation. This neglected question of how to explain the absence or containment of violence, as political scientists James Fearon and David Laitin have recently argued,[18] is as important as the much more studied question of how to explain the occurrence of violence. In the case of Hungary and its neighbours, I would propose three reasons for the absence of violence.[19] The first is that Hungarians in the neighbouring states have enjoyed an accessible and relatively attractive 'exit' option—the possibility of emigrating to or working in Hungary. This has functioned as a 'safety valve' and has worked against the radicalization of ethno-national conflict, especially in Romania. Secondly, the embeddedness of national conflicts in regional processes of European integration has 'disciplined' central political élites, especially in the foreign policy domain. This has induced Hungary to limit its support for transborder co-ethnics to support for Hungarian culture and to scrupulously avoid inciting destabilizing political activity on the part of its co-ethnics. This is true even of the national-populist Antall government of the early 1990s, despite its strong rhetorical commitment to transborder co-ethnics. Third, the absence of credible narratives linking past ethno-national violence to present threat makes it difficult for radical, violence-oriented ethno-political entrepreneurs, whose stock in trade is fear, to succeed. By contrast, such narratives of danger and threat, linked to past violence, were strikingly evident in the former Yugoslavia before war broke out.[20]

Nor is this an isolated case. Estonia, for example, has been in the news a lot in recent years in connection with its bitterly contested citizenship laws and, more generally, in connection with the status of its large Russian minority. Rhetoric has been heated, indeed overheated: Russians (more frequently Russians in Russia than local Russians) have accused Estonia of apartheid and ethnic cleansing; Estonian nationalists have spoken of the Russian minority as colonists or illegal immigrants. Yet despite this overheated rhetoric, there is little fear of violence on the ground.[21]

It is not only violence that is overemphasized by the seething cauldron view. More generally, the strength, salience, and centrality of national feeling, national identity, and nationalist politics also tend to be overestimated. Consider for example nationalist mobilization. There have, of course, been dramatic, even spectacular, moments of high nationalist mobilization. One thinks, for example, of the 'human chain' across the Baltics in August 1989, or of the great crowds that filled the main squares of Yerevan, Tblisi, Berlin, Prague, and other cities in 1988–90. These searing moments, transmitted world-wide by television, are etched forever in our memories. But they have been the exception, not the rule. Moments of high mobilization—where they did occur—proved ephemeral; 'nation' was revealed to be a galvanizing category at one moment, but not at the next. On the whole, people have remained in their homes, not taken to the streets. In conspicuous contrast to interwar East Central Europe, demobilization and political passivity, rather than fevered mobilization, have characterized the political landscape. Much has been written on the strength of nationalist movements in the former Soviet Union; not enough has been written on their comparative weakness. And while the weakness of nationalism in certain regions (especially ex-Soviet Central Asia) has indeed been noted, too much attention has been given to variation across *space* in the intensity of nationalist mobilization, too little attention to variation over *time*. Declining curves of mobilization have been particularly neglected, although they are as common, as deserving of explanation, and as theoretically challenging as the more sexy ascending curves.

Even where national conflicts and national identity remain salient in the political sphere, they are not necessarily salient in everyday life. Nationalism may occur in the legislatures, in the press, in some branches of the state administration without occurring in the streets, or in the homes.[22] There is a loose coupling, or lack of congruence, between nationalist politics—which seems to run in a sphere of its own, unmoored from its putative constituencies—

and everyday life. People do not necessarily respond particularly energetically or warmly to the nationalist utterances of politicians who claim to speak in their name. This lukewarm responsiveness or even non-responsiveness to nationalist appeals of politicians is a legacy of a more general cynicism towards and distrust of politics and politicians. An 'us' versus 'them' distinction was indeed central to the way people understood politics under communism, and one might think this would be easily transposed into an exclusionary nationalism. Under certain circumstances, it may indeed be so transposed. In general, however, the 'us'–'them' distinction divided not one ethnic or national group from another, but 'the people' from 'the regime.' 'They'—representatives of the regime—were assuredly not 'us,' even when they claimed to speak in 'our' name (as they always did, of course, under communism). Nor did this change with the collapse of communism: deploying the idiom of ethno-nationalism (rather than that of class solidarity or socialist internationalism) is no guarantee that 'they' will be able to persuade 'us' that 'we' belong together, separated not by position in the mode of domination but by ethnic nationality from an external 'them.'

Nor are national identities in the region as strong as is often assumed. I return to this theme below; suffice it to observe here that, given the overwhelming evidence of contextual and situational shifts in self- and other-identification, one should be sceptical of the oft-repeated emphasis on the deep historical encoding of national identities in the region, and alert to the danger of over-historicization.[23]

Incipient but not insignificant cosmopolitan tendencies in the region, finally, have been obscured by the orientalist opposition between Western supra-nationalism and Eastern nationalism. Consider again Hungarians in Romania. It is no doubt true that, since the fall of Ceauşescu, the Hungarian-national element in their self-understanding has become more pronounced. The linguistic, cultural, religious, historical, and economic ties that link them to Hungary as *anyaország* or 'mother country' have become more palpable, more 'real'. But there is not necessarily an inverse relationship between national and cosmopolitan self-understandings. At the same time that they have become more aware of and concerned with their trans-state Hungarian nationality, they have also become more aware of and concerned with the wider European world.

Television has played an interestingly ambivalent role here. The establishment, relatively lavish financing, and diffusion from Hungary of Duna TV, a channel intended chiefly for Hungarians in the neighbouring states, has reinforced the Hungarian-national self-understanding of Transylvanian Hungarians. At the same time, however, the high prestige of French, German, and English-language channels (Eurosport, BBC, etc.)—widely available in Transylvania through cable and satellite systems—has probably had a certain (though admittedly hard to measure) de-nationalizing or trans-nationalizing effect.[24] An anecdote reveals the national ambivalence of television. Romanian authorities were distressed when they learned that a particular cable package was to include MTV. To them, this meant Magyar TV, i.e. the state television from Hungary. In fact, of course, it was the American music video channel that was at issue. And to the Transylvanian Hungarians, the American MTV was no doubt far more interesting than the Hungarian.

In sum, ethnic and nationalist conflict has been both less violent, and less salient, than many commentators have suggested; and where such conflict has occurred, it has often been chronic and low-level, a kind of 'background noise' occurring far from the focus of everyday life, rather than acute and explosive.

III

So far I have considered two overall appraisals of nationalist conflicts in the region, an optimistic view that sees them as resolvable through reorganizing political space along national lines, and a pessimistic view that sees them as deeply entrenched, pervasive, destabilizing, and on the verge of violent explosion.

I would now like to turn to two opposed accounts of the sources and dynamics of nationalist resurgence. The first of these is the 'return of the repressed' view. The gist of this account is that national identities and national conflicts were deeply rooted in the pre-communist history of Eastern Europe, but then frozen or repressed by ruthlessly anti-national communist regimes. With the collapse of communism, on this account, these pre-communist national identities and nationalist conflicts have returned with redoubled force.

This view can be expressed in (and often seems to draw at least implicitly on) a quasi-Freudian idiom. Lacking the rationally regulative ego of self-regulating civil society, the communist regimes repressed the primordial national id through a harshly punitive communist super-ego. With the collapse of the communist super-ego, the repressed ethno-national id returns in full force, wreaking vengeance, uncontrolled by the regulative ego. (The quasi-Freudian idiom makes clear the orientalist inflection of this view, and its close relation to the myth of the seething cauldron.)

Obviously, communist regimes of Eastern Europe and the Soviet Union did repress nationalism. But the 'return of the repressed view' mistakes the manner in which they did so. It suggests that these regimes repressed not only nationalism, but nationhood; that they were not only *anti-nationalist* but *anti-national*. It suggests further that a robust, primordial sense of nationhood survived in this period in spite of strenuous regime efforts to root it out in favour of internationalist and class loyalties and solidarities.

This view is fundamentally mistaken. Let me suggest why with a few words about the Soviet case.[25] To see late- and post-Soviet national struggles as the struggles of nations, of real, solidary groups who somehow survived despite Soviet attempts to crush them—to suggest that nations and nationalism flourish today *despite* the Soviet regime's ruthlessly anti-national policies—is to get things nearly backwards. To put the point somewhat too sharply: nationhood and nationalism flourish today largely *because of* the regime's policies. Although anti-national*ist*, those policies were anything but anti-*national*. Far from ruthlessly suppressing nationhood, the Soviet regime pervasively institutionalized it. The regime repressed *nationalism*, of course; but at the same time, it went further than any other state before or since in institutionalizing territorial *nationhood* and ethnic *nationality* as fundamental social categories. In doing so it inadvertently created a political field supremely conducive to nationalism.

The regime did this in two ways. On the one hand, it carved up the Soviet state into more than fifty national territories, each expressly defined as the homeland of and for a particular ethno-national group. The top-level national territories—those that are today the independent successor states—were defined as quasi-nation states, complete with their own territories, names, constitutions, legislatures, administrative staffs, cultural and scientific institutions, and so on.

On the other hand, the regime divided the citizenry into a set of exhaustive and mutually exclusive ethnic nationalities, over a hundred in all. Through this state classification system, ethnic nationality served not only as a *statistical category*, a fundamental unit of social accounting, but also, and more distinctively, as an *obligatory ascribed status*. It was assigned by the state at birth on the basis of descent. It was registered in personal identity documents. It was recorded in almost all bureaucratic encounters and official transactions. And it was used to control access to higher education and to certain desirable jobs, restricting the opportunities of some nationalities, especially Jews, and promoting others through preferential treatment policies for so-called 'titular' nationalities in 'their own' republics.

Long before Gorbachev, then, territorial nationhood and ethnic nationality were pervasively institutionalized social and cultural forms. These forms were by no means empty. They were scorned by Sovietologists—no doubt because the regime consistently and effectively repressed all signs of overt political nationalism, and sometimes even cultural nationalism. Yet the repression of nationalism went hand in hand with the establishment and consolidation of nationhood and nationality as fundamental cognitive and social forms.

Nationhood and nationality as institutionalized forms comprised a pervasive system of social classification, an organizing 'principle of vision and division' of the social world, to use Bourdieu's phrase. They comprised a standardized scheme of social accounting, an interpretive frame for public discussion, a dense organizational grid, a set of boundary-markers, a legitimate form for public and private identities. And when political space expanded under Gorbachev, these already pervasively institutionalized forms were readily politicized. They constituted elementary forms of political understanding, political rhetoric, political interest, and political identity. In the terms of Max Weber's 'switchman' metaphor, they determined the tracks, the cognitive frame, along which action was pushed by the dynamic of material and ideal interests. In so doing, they transformed the collapse of a regime into the disintegration of a state. And they continue to shape political understanding and political action in the successor states.

Similar points could be made about Yugoslavia.[26] In other states of East Central Europe, to be sure, the case is somewhat different; and there was not the same degree of public support for and pervasive institutionalization of national identities. However, even in these cases, communist regimes made various, albeit limited, accommodations to the sense of nationhood; and the repression of nationhood, especially in the post-Stalinist era, was not so consistent as is widely assumed.

In emphasizing the codification and pervasive institutionalization of nationhood and nationality by the Soviet and Yugoslav regimes, I am not making a claim about the strength or depth of the ethno-national identities thus institutionalized. It is important to distinguish between the *degree of institutionalization* of ethnic and national categories and the *psychological depth, substantiality, and practical potency* of such categorical identities. The former was unprecedentedly great in the Soviet Union, but the latter were highly variable, and in some cases minimal. At the limit—exemplified by some of the smaller officially recognized nationalities within the Russian Federation—strongly institutionalized categorical identities masked the near-complete absence of distinct cultural identities or distinct ethno-national *habitus*. In this limiting case, members of different 'groups' differed only in the official categorical ethno-national markers they bore; these categorical markers did not *represent* cultural or ethnic differences, but *replaced* them.[27] I do not mean to imply that this limiting case was the general one in the former Soviet Union. But the general point remains. A strongly institutionalized system of official ethno-national identities makes certain categories available for the public representation of social reality, the framing of political claims, and the organization of political action. This in itself is a fact of great significance. But it does not assure that these categories will have a significant, pervasively structuring role in framing perception or orienting action in everyday life. Institutionalized categorical group denominations cannot be taken as unproblematic indicators of 'real groups' or of strong 'identities'.

There is a version of the 'return of the repressed' argument to which I am more sympathetic. This is relevant especially in Yugoslavia, but also in parts of the former Soviet Union. The argument is that the tabuization of certain themes—in Yugoslavia the taboo preventing discussion of the fratricidal violence of the Second World War—prevented any kind of *Vergangenheitsbewaeltigung* (mastery of the past) of the sort that occurred in Germany. There was simply no way to publicly work through arguments about the massive wartime atrocities. This does not imply that discussing these openly would have resolved them: of course this would not have happened. Discussion would have engendered bitter conflicts. But still, the public discussion of these might have deprived them of some of their potency forty years later when they were resurrected in public in a situation of pervasive uncertainty and insecurity without any previous attempt to master the past discursively.

In any event, what 'returns' in the post-communist present is not something from the pre-communist past; it is something constituted in important ways by the communist past. In the Soviet case many national identities were first invented, imagined, and institutionalized under communism. But even elsewhere in Eastern Europe, where this was not true, the national phenomenon was constituted in part—if only negatively—by communism, by the suppression of civil society, by the suppression of a public sphere where past atrocities could have been, in part, discursively mastered.

IV

The 'return of the repressed' view often sees what returns as somehow primordial, or at least deeply rooted in the pre-communist history of the region. Hence the frequent reference to 'ancient hatreds'. Those who focus on unscrupulous and manipulative élites take the opposite view. Far from seeing nationalism as deeply rooted in primordial identities or ancient conflicts, they see it as stirred up in opportunistic and cynical fashion by unprincipled political élites. There is obviously much truth in this view. It is scarcely controversial to point out the opportunism and cynicism of political élites, or to underscore the crucial role of élites, whether cynical or sincere, in articulating national grievances and mobilizing people for nationalist conflict. And there are certain textbook-clear examples of cynically manipulative élites stirring up nationalist tensions and passions: perhaps Slobodan Milošević is the paradigmatic case—a pure example of a nationalist of convenience, rather than conviction. The élitist, instrumentalist focus of this view is also correct in its rejection of the view that contemporary nationalist politics is driven by deeply rooted national identities and ancient conflicts.

As a general account of the sources and dynamics of nationalism in the region, however, the élite manipulation view has at least three problematic implications. The first is that nationalism pays off as a political strategy; that it is therefore a rational strategy for opportunistic élites to adopt; and that it is relatively easy for manipulative élites to stir up nationalist passions in a politically profitable manner. The second is that if élite-instigated ethno-national mobilization could engender ethno-national war and mass violence in Yugoslavia, the same thing could happen elsewhere (in the strong version: anywhere). The third is that this élite-driven nationalism is essentially a politics of interest, and that it therefore must be explained in instrumental terms.

I think all three implications—or clusters of implications—are mistaken. To begin with, nationalism is not always a subjectively rational or objectively 'successful' political strategy. It is not always possible, let alone easy, to 'stir up nationalist passions'.[28] It is not always possible, let alone easy, to evoke the anxieties, the fears, the resentments, the perceptions and misperceptions, the self- and other-identifications, in short, the dispositions, the cast of mind against the background of which conspicuous and calculated nationalist stance-taking by élites can 'pay off' politically. Nor is it always possible, or easy, to sustain such a nationally 'primed' frame of mind, such propitiously 'nationalized' dispositions, once they have been successfully evoked.

The loosely related political stances or strategies we call 'nationalist' afford no generalized guarantee of political success, no generalized advantage over other political stances or strategies.[29] Investing in nationalism, *in general*, is no wiser than investing in any other political idiom or stance. At certain moments, to be sure, nationalist stances may yield higher returns. But it is hard to identify the boundaries of such moments *ex ante*. And once it is clear that such a moment has arrived, both politicians and analysts are likely to err by conceiving it in overgeneralized terms. The collapse of communist regimes—*a fortiori* those that ruled multi- or bi-national states—was such a moment. But how do we define this moment and its boundaries? I would argue that political entrepreneurs, closely monitoring other political entrepreneurs within bounded fields of comparison, and seeking a share of the windfall profits won by early investors in late-communist (or early post-communist) nationalism, have tended to overinvest in this (momentarily) successful strategy, just as analysts, monitoring other analysts (as well as politicians), and seeking a share of the windfall profits won by early analysts of late-communist (or early post-communist) nationalism, have similarly tended to overinvest in the study of nationalism in general, and in the study of élite manipulation in particular.[30]

The history of post-communism is short; but it is long enough to make it clear that nationalism is not always a winning strategy, even in the specifically post-communist setting. The record of electoral failure by nationalists —beginning with Lithuania in 1992 and including Hungary (1994), Ukraine (1994), Belarus (1994), Romania (1996) and others—is by now quite substantial.[31] The failure of one particular kind of nationalist appeal—the appeal to the need to protect transborder co-ethnics who are citizens and residents of other states—has been particularly striking. It is a source of chronic frustration to the Hungarian political élite, for example, how little the average Hungarian knows, or cares, about transborder Hungarians (in Romania, Slovakia, rump Yugoslavia, and Ukraine). What the average Hungarian 'knows' about them, he or she doesn't like: the 'fact' that the Hungarian government should be spending 'our' money on 'them', and the 'fact' that 'they' come to Hungary to take 'our' jobs. 'They' are certainly not recognized as 'us'; the most eloquent testimony to this is that Hungarians from Transylvania who come to work in Hungary are routinely called 'Romanians'.[32] Similarly, Russian politicians' attempts to mobilize on the issue of Russians stranded in the 'near abroad' have been conspicuously unsuccessful. The one organization specifically devoted to this theme—the Congress of Russian Communities (KOR)—failed even to clear the 5 per cent threshold in the December 1995 parliamentary elections.[33]

The second problematic implication is that if élite manipulation drove the former Yugoslavia into ethno-national barbarism, the same could happen elsewhere. I have already criticized the conclusion to this syllogism, arguing that large-scale violence between Hungarians and Romanians in Transylvania is unlikely despite intractable national tensions. Here I would like to challenge the premiss.

Élite manipulation was of course an important element in the unfolding Yugoslav catastrophe. But the élite manipulation thesis fails to specify the particular conditions that made key segments of the Yugoslav population especially *responsive* to élite manipulation as the state began to disintegrate; more generally, failing to account for the *differential success* of the mobilizing efforts and activities of élites, it over-predicts the severity and violence of ethnic conflict. In the Yugoslav case, a whole series of distinctive factors help explain why people were responsive to the cynical manipulations originating in Belgrade. These include the massive intercommunal violence during the Second World War; the narratives of that violence that, deprived of a public hearing, circulated in familial settings, especially in certain key regions such as the Serb-inhabited areas of Croatian Krajina; and the fear of the recurrence of that violence under conditions of rapid change in control over the means of state violence, especially when control over the means of state violence in Croatia was passing into the hands of a regime that incautiously (at best) employed certain symbols associated in the minds of Serbs with the murderous wartime Ustasha regime.[34] Of course politicians distorted the past. But these distortions could be perceived as resonant and relevant in certain regions of Yugoslavia in a way that has no close parallel elsewhere, except perhaps in the Armenian–Azerbaijani conflict. Such variation in *conditions of responsiveness* to inflammatory élite appeals remains untheorized by the élite manipulation approach.

The third problematic implication of the élite manipulation thesis is that nationalism is essentially a politics of interest, not a politics of identity, and that it therefore must be explained in instrumental terms, by focusing on the calculations of cynical, self-interested élites, not in primordial identitarian terms. We should not in fact have to choose between an instrumentalist and an identitarian approach to the study of nationalism. That this is a false opposition becomes clear when we think about the cognitive dimension of nationalism. Considered from a cognitive point of view, nationalism is a way of seeing the world, a way of *identifying interests*, or more precisely, a way of specifying interest-bearing units, of *identifying the relevant units in terms of which interests are conceived*. It furnishes a mode of vision and division of the world, to use Pierre Bourdieu's phrase, a mode of social counting and accounting. Thus it inherently links identity and interest—by *identifying how we are to calculate our interests*.

Of course 'interests' are central to nationalist politics, as to all politics, indeed to social life generally. The élite manipulation view errs not in focusing on interests, but in doing so too narrowly, focusing on the calculating pursuit of interests taken as unproblematically 'given' (above all politicians' interest in attaining or maintaining power), and ignoring broader questions about the *constitution* of interests, questions concerning the manner in which interests—and, more fundamentally, units construed as capable of having interests, such as 'nations', 'ethnic groups', and 'classes'—are identified and thereby constituted. Élite discourse often plays an important role in the constitution of interests, but again this is not something political or cultural élites can do at will by deploying a few manipulative tricks. The identification and constitution of interests—in national or other terms—is a complex process that cannot be reduced to élite manipulation.

V

My fifth target is the 'groupism' that still prevails in the study of ethnicity and nationalism. By groupism—or what I will also call the 'realism of the group' —I mean the social ontology that leads us to talk and write about ethnic groups and nations as real entities, as communities, as substantial, enduring, internally homogeneous and externally bounded collectivities.

A similar realism of the group long prevailed in many areas of sociology and kindred disciplines.[35] Yet in the last decade or so, at least four developments in social theory have combined to undermine the treatment of groups as real, substantial entities. The first is the growing interest in network forms, the flourishing of network theory, and the increasing use of network as an overall orienting image or metaphor in social theory. Second, there is the challenge posed by theories of rational action, with their relentless methodological individualism, to realist understandings of groupness. The third development is a shift from broadly structuralist to a variety of more 'constructivist' theoretical stances; while the former envisioned groups as enduring components of social structure, the latter see groupness as constructed, contingent, and fluctuating. Finally, an emergent post-modernist theoretical sensibility emphasizes the fragmentary, the ephemeral, and the erosion of fixed forms and clear boundaries. These developments are disparate, even contradictory. But they have converged in problematizing groupness, and in undermining axioms of stable group being.

Yet this movement away from the realism of the group in the social sciences has been uneven. It has been striking—to take just one example—in the study of class, especially in the study of the working class—a term that is hard to use today without quotation marks or some other distancing device. Indeed *the* working class—understood as a real entity or substantial community—has largely dissolved as an object of analysis. It has been challenged both by theoretical statements and by detailed empirical research in social history, labour history, and the history of popular discourse and mobilization. The study of class as a cultural and political idiom, as a mode of conflict, and as an underlying abstract dimension of economic structure remains vital; but it is no longer encumbered by an understanding of *classes* as real, enduring entities.

At the same time, an understanding of *ethnic groups* and *nations* as real entities continues to inform the study of ethnicity, nationhood, and nationalism. In our everyday talk and writing, we casually reify ethnic and national groups, speaking of 'the Serbs', 'the Croats', 'the Estonians', 'the Russians', 'the Hungarians', 'the Romanians', as if they were internally homogeneous, externally bounded groups, even unitary collective actors with common purposes. We represent the social and cultural world in terms reminiscent of a Modigliani painting as a multichrome mosaic of monochrome ethnic or cultural blocs.

I want to say a bit more about this Modiglianesque image of the social world. The metaphor I borrow from Ernest Gellner. Towards the end of *Nations and Nationalism*, Gellner invoked the contrasting painterly styles of Kokoschka and Modigliani—shreds and patches of colour and light in the former case, solid, sharply outlined blocs of colour in the latter—to characterize the passage from the cultural landscape of pre-national agrarian society to that of nationally and culturally homogenized industrial society.[36]

This is a striking image, but I think it is misleading. There are in fact two versions of the Modiglianization argument. The first—and this is Gellner's own argument—is the 'classical', nation-statist version. This is the argument that culture and polity gradually converge. Gellner was a master of compressed characterizations of vast, world-historical social transformations; and no doubt in very broad historical perspective one can speak of a substantial cultural homogenization of polities, and of a consequent convergence of cultural and political boundaries. There are, however, two problems with Gellner's account.

First, Gellner's stress on the homogenization functionally required by industrial society seems to me to be trebly misplaced: in over-emphasizing the degree of cultural homogeneity 'required' by industrial society; in side-stepping the problem, endemic in functionalist accounts, of explanation (to note that something may be 'required' or 'useful' for something else is not to explain its occurrence; no mechanism guarantees that what is 'required' will in fact be produced); and in neglecting the homogenizing pressures arising from interstate competition, mass military conscription, and mass nationalist public education in the classical age of the mass citizen army—pressures more powerful, in my view, than those arising from industrialism as such.[37]

Secondly, Gellner did not specify whether the homogenizing forces of industrial society are still at work, or whether late industrial society is no longer culturally homogenizing. A differentiated answer is required to this question. In certain respects—for example in the global diffusion of what is in many respects a single global material culture and dispositions associated with it—powerfully homogenizing forces are still at work. In other respects, however, this is not the case. Thus, for example, the very logic of advanced capitalist/late-industrialist/post-industrial society generates pressures for massive imports of immigrant labour, which tends to recreate a more Kokoschka-like cultural pattern.

It seems indisputable, however, that the homogenizing forces arising from militarized interstate competition in the classical age of the mass citizen army—at least in the advanced industrial world—peaked in the late nineteenth and early twentieth century. This was the maximally 'Modiglianesque' moment, I would argue: it was the 'high noon' of the citizen army, of the 'nation in arms,' of the highly assimilationist, homogenizing school systems that were linked in style and ideology to citizen armies, and of nation-states' claims to absolute internal sovereignty, claims that legitimated their attempts to 'nationalize' their own territories at will, even ruthlessly. With the passing of this maximally 'Modiglianesque' moment, there has been a certain relaxation in the homogenizing claims, aspirations, and practices of the state, at least in regions of the world (most strikingly in Western Europe) where states are no longer locked in fierce geopolitical and potentially military competition with one another.

But the classical, nation-statist version of the Modigliani-map argument is not the most current one. It is universally acknowledged today that culture and polity do not converge, that nearly all existing polities are in some sense 'multicultural'. Yet the multicultural landscapes of late modernity are themselves usually represented in Modiglianesque terms, in terms, that is, of juxtaposed, well-defined, monochrome blocs. I want to argue that this newer, 'post-national' (or, more precisely, post nation-state) version of the Modigliani map is as problematic as the older, classically 'nation-statist' version.

One might have thought that the mixed settlement patterns characteristic of most contemporary 'multicultural' polities would resist Modiglianesque representation. On this way of thinking, immigration-engendered ethnic heterogeneity, such as that of the United States, would be particularly refractory to representation in such terms; but so too would the intricately intermixed ethno-demographic landscape of Eastern Europe, and of East Central Europe in particular—a *locus classicus* of ethnically and nationally mixed settlement.

But this mistakes the nature—and the rhetorical power—of the Modigliani map. The spatial aspect of the representation—the image of continuous and homogeneous blocs situated next to, rather than interspersed with, one another—should not be interpreted too literally; it does not necessarily imply corresponding spatial characteristics of what is represented. The Modiglianesque representation of heterogeneity as the juxtaposition of homogeneous blocs does not presuppose that the blocs be territorially concentrated. The constituent blocs may be intermixed in space, for their 'blocness'—their boundedness and internal homogeneity—is conceptually located not in *physical* but in *social* and *cultural* space.[38] But the *conceptual* map is still groupist; it still sees the population as composed of definable, bounded, internally homogeneous blocs (for example, African-Americans, Native Americans, Latinos, Asian-Americans, and Euro-Americans, in the 'pentagonal' multiculturalist account of America[39]). The implicit if not explicit imagery is that of internally homogeneous, externally sharply bounded, though not necessary territorially concentrated, ethno-cultural blocs.

The fact of pervasive territorial intermixing, then, is not itself incompatible with the Modiglianesque representation of ethno-cultural heterogeneity. To challenge the Modigliani map, one must directly challenge the underlying groupist social ontology that informs most discussions of multiculturalism in North America (and indeed most discussions of ethnicity and nationalism throughout the world). There is by now an ample and sophisticated literature supporting such a challenge. As I noted above, moreover, a series of fundamental developments in social theory in recent decades have converged in problematizing assumptions of stable and bounded groupness. Yet these considerable theoretical and empirical resources have scarcely made a dent in the groupism that continues to prevail—that has indeed recently been strengthened—in theoretical and practical discussions of ethnicity and nationalism, sustained by the combined force of casually groupist ordinary language, parochial scholarly tradition (especially in ethnic and racial studies and area studies, but now also in the rapidly expanding sphere of nationalism studies), the institutionalization and codification of groups and group 'identities' in public policy, and the group-making, group-strengthening endeavours of ethno-political entrepreneurs.

The forces supporting—and strengthening—groupist social analysis are even stronger in Eastern Europe than in North America. The institutionalization and codification of ethnic and national groups, as noted above, went much further in multinational communist states than in North America. In Eastern Europe, moreover, the scholarly traditions associated with challenges to groupness—rational choice theory, network analysis, constructivism generally, and post-modernist emphases on the transient and fragmentary—have been much weaker than in North America. More fundamentally, Eastern Europe lacks the individualist traditions of North America, above all the fundamentally voluntarist conception of groupness originating in sectarian Protestantism but ramifying throughout social and political life, especially in the United States.

One might argue, moreover, that the prevailingly strongly groupist language of social analysis in Eastern Europe describes the ethno-national landscape of the region rather well. After all, this region has seen an enduring and conspicuous discrepancy between *national* boundaries—strongly maintained *within* and *against* states—and *state* boundaries. It has been the *locus classicus* of deeply sedimented, resilient, relatively stable ethno-national boundaries following, in much of the region, linguistic rather than political frontiers. The very forces that conspicuously hindered the Gellnerian convergence of culture and polity in the region, enabling ethno-national 'groups' to sustain boundaries that cut across political divisions, would seem to warrant a Modiglianesque representation.

There have indeed been impressive instances of sustained 'groupness' in the region—in particular, of the maintenance of group boundaries and strengthening of group identities against the homogenizing, assimilationist pressures and practices of nationalizing states. One notable instance is that of Poles in Eastern Prussia in the late nineteenth and early twentieth century. One cannot generalize, however, from this case to the region as a whole—or even to other settings involving Poles and Germans. In other nearby settings, the boundaries between Poles and Germans proved quite weak and unstable, and a great deal of assimilation occurred in both directions. The maintenance and strengthening of national boundaries in this instance must be seen as reflecting particular circumstantial forces and factors, not as somehow emanating from some properties putatively intrinsic to 'Poles' as such. Groupness was strengthened in dynamic, interactive, organized response (involving a highly developed agricultural co-operative movement, credit associations, land-purchase organizations, school strikes, and strong support from the Catholic church) to the harshly assimilative practices of the Prussian/German state. It was sustained by a strong basis in the Catholic church (and by religiously as well as ethno-linguistically sustained endogamy) in a region where linguistic and religious cleavages coincided (in regions where

Catholic Germans encountered Poles, national boundaries were much weaker). Groupness in this case was thus a product of politics and collective action, not a stable underlying basis for these.[40]

In other cases boundaries are much weaker. Consider for example late- and post-Soviet Ukraine. As we have noted above, the Soviet regime pervasively institutionalized nationhood and nationality as fundamental social categories. A key expression (and instrument) of that institutionalized scheme was the census, which recorded the self-identified ethno-cultural nationality (*natsional'nost'*) of every person. At the time of the 1989 census, some 11.4 million residents of Ukraine identified their nationality as Russian. But the precision suggested by this census data, even when rounded to the nearest hundred thousand, is entirely spurious. The very categories 'Russian' and 'Ukrainian', as designators of putatively distinct ethno-cultural nationalities, are deeply problematic in the Ukrainian context, where rates of intermarriage have been extremely high, and where nearly 2 million of those designating their ethnic nationality as Ukrainian in the 1989 census admitted to not speaking Ukrainian as their native language *or* as a second language they could 'freely command'—a figure many consider to be greatly underestimated. One should therefore be sceptical of the illusion of bounded groupness created by the census, with its exhaustive and mutually exclusive categories. One can imagine circumstances in which a self-conscious ethnically Russian minority might emerge in Ukraine, but such a 'group' cannot be taken as given or deduced from the census.[41]

The boundary between Hungarians and Romanians in Transylvania is certainly sharper than that between Russians and Ukrainians in Ukraine. Even in Transylvania, however, group boundaries are considerably more porous and ambiguous than is widely assumed. The language of everyday life, to be sure, is rigorously categorical, dividing the population into mutually exclusive ethno-national categories, and making no allowance for mixed or ambiguous forms. But this categorical code, important though it is as a *constituent element* of social relations, should not be taken for a *faithful description* of them. Reinforced by ethno-political entrepreneurs on both sides, the categorical code obscures as much as it reveals about ethno-national identifications, masking the fluidity and ambiguity that arise from mixed marriages, from bilingualism, from migration, from Hungarian children attending Romanian-language schools, from intergenerational assimilation (in both directions), and from sheer indifference to the claims of ethno-cultural nationality.

'Groupness' and 'boundedness' must thus be taken as *variable*, as *emergent properties* of particular structural or conjunctural settings; they cannot properly be taken as given or axiomatic. Comparative studies of ethnicity and nationalism provide abundant support for this point, but it remains inadequately appreciated outside this specialized research tradition. The point needs to be emphasized today more than ever, for the unreflectively groupist language that prevails in everyday life, journalism, politics, and much social research as well—the habit of speaking without qualification of 'Hungarians' and 'Romanians', for example, as if they were sharply bounded, internally homogeneous 'groups'—not only weakens social analysis but undermines the possibilities for liberal politics in the region.

VI

Finally, I want to discuss the 'Manichean' view that there are two kinds of nationalism, a good, civic kind and a bad, ethnic kind; and two corresponding understandings of nationhood, the good, civic conception, in which nationhood is seen as based on common citizenship, and the bad, ethnic conception, in which nationhood is seen as based on common ethnicity. This is often connected to an Orientalist conception of East European nationalism, for in general civic nationalism is seen as characteristic of Western Europe, ethnic nationalism as characteristic of Eastern Europe. But the civic–ethnic distinction is also used within regions, sometimes in an ideological mode, to distinguish one's own good, legitimate civic nationalism from the illegitimate ethnic nationalism of one's neighbours, and sometimes in a scholarly or quasi-scholarly mode, to characterize and classify different forms of nationalism and modes of national self-understanding. Today the distinction is often used to frame discussions of the new states of Eastern Europe and the former Soviet Union, and to 'keep score' on contemporary processes of nation- and state-building in the region; it provides a handy—all too handy, in my view—tool for classifying incipient processes of state- and nation-building as civic or ethnic.

By labelling this a Manichean view, I caricature it, of course, but not too violently. In its more nuanced forms, the distinction certainly has some-analytical and normative merit. I myself have used a related (though not identical) distinction between state-centred and ethno-cultural understandings of nationhood in my own previous work. Still, I think the distinction between civic and ethnic nationalism, especially in the rather simplistic form in which it is usually applied, is both analytically and normatively problematic.[42]

One way of highlighting the analytical weakness of the Manichean view is by noting its uncertainty over how to conceptualize the cultural dimension of nationhood and nationalism. Roughly speaking, there are two very different ways of mapping culture onto the civic–ethnic distinction:

- On the one hand, ethnic nationalism may be interpreted narrowly, as involving an emphasis on descent, and, ultimately, on race, on biology. In this case, there is very little ethnic nationalism around, for on this view an emphasis on common culture, without any marked emphasis on common descent, has to be coded as a species of civic nationalism. But the category of civic nationalism then becomes too heterogeneous to be useful, while that of ethnic nationalism is underpopulated.

- On the other hand, ethnic nationalism may be interpreted broadly, as ethno-*cultural*, while civic nationalism may be interpreted narrowly, as involving an acultural conception of citizenship, a sharp separation of citizenship from cultural as well as ethnic nationality. But in this case, the problem is just the opposite: civic nationalism gets defined out of existence, and virtually all nationalisms would be coded as ethnic or cultural. Even the paradigmatic cases of civic nationalism—France and America—cease to count as civic nationalism, since they have a crucial cultural component. (Interestingly, two recent books argue for the existence of an American cultural nationality: American nationhood, they argue, is not purely political, founded on an idea; it is cultural; America is a nation-state founded on a common, and distinctive, American culture[43].)

The normative weakness of the distinction similarly pivots on the ambiguous place of culture:

- If ethnic is interpreted broadly as ethno-cultural, then the blanket normative condemnation of ethnic nationalism is problematic, for in certain circumstances it is easy to have normative sympathy for the defensive power of ethno-cultural nationalism (e.g. for that of Poland during the time of partition, for that of the Baltic nations under Soviet rule, indeed for minority cultures everywhere, whose nationalism cannot assume a civic form, though it need not, of course, be 'ethnic' in the narrow, biologically based sense).
- If culture, however, is classified with civic nationhood and nationalism, then many nationalizing 'civic' nationalisms, more or less suffused with cultural chauvinism, and seeking to reduce or (at the limit) eradicate cultural heterogeneity within a state, although indifferent to ethnicity in the sense of descent as such, are normatively ambiguous at best.

From a normative point of view, the joining of state power to nationalist or nationalizing practices should always be cause for concern. A sceptical stance towards statist nationalizing nationalisms (not to be equated with a blanket condemnation of them) is more adequate, and more supple, than the conceptually muddled blanket embrace of civic (and condemnation of ethnic) nationalism. The policies and practices of nationalizing states may be assimilationist, in a variety of modalities ranging from benign—or not so benign—neglect of ethnic or cultural differences to harsh or even coercive attempts to eradicate such differences. On the other hand, nationalizing policies and practices may be dissimilationist—premised on, even constitutive of, fundamental differences between groups. The assimilationist stances are not necessarily 'civic' in any normatively robust sense, while the dissimilationist stances are not necessarily 'ethnic' in the narrow sense (not necessarily premised on descent-based group difference). Both assimilationist and dissimilationist nationalizing nationalisms warrant normative scepticism, though our normative evaluation of them will depend heavily on rich contextual knowledge—knowledge that cannot adequately be captured, even in simplified form, by an impoverished and ambiguous coding of them as 'civic' or 'ethnic'.

From an analytical point of view, a more useful (though of course closely related) distinction can be drawn between *state-framed* and *counter-state* understandings of nationhood and forms of nationalism. In the former, 'nation' is conceived as congruent with the state, as institutionally and territorially framed by the state; in the latter, it is conceived in opposition to the territorial and institutional frame of some existing state or states. This distinction can do the analytical work that is expected of the civic–ethnic distinction without the attendant confusions.

Clearly, there is not necessarily anything 'civic'—in the normatively robust sense of that term—about state-framed nationhood or nationalism. It is the state—not citizenship—that is the cardinal point of reference; and the state that frames the nation need not be democratic, let alone robustly so. Moreover, the notion of state-framed nationhood or nationalism can accommodate linguistic, cultural, and even ethnic aspects of nationhood and nationalism in so far as these are (as they often are in fact) framed, mediated, and shaped by the state.[44] Escaping the constricting definitional antithesis between civic and ethnic or ethno-cultural nationalism, we can see that state-framed nationalisms are often imbued with a strong cultural content and may (though need not) be ethnicized is well.[45]

Counter-state nationalisms, on the other hand, need not be specifically ethnic; nationhood conceived in opposition to an existing state need not be conceived in ethnic terms, or even, more loosely, in ethno-cultural terms. Quite apart from the difference, mentioned above, between narrowly ethnic and broadly ethno-cultural understandings of nationhood, counter-state definitions of nation may be based on territory, on historic provincial privileges, on distinct political histories prior to incorporation into a larger state, and so on. These are all cases of counter-state but non-ethnic definitions of nationhood—of nation defined in opposition to the institutional and territorial framework of an existing state or states but without reference to a distinct ethnic or ethno-cultural collectivity. Moreover, whether the counter-state nation in question is defined in ethnic or ethno-cultural terms or in some other fashion, counter-state nationalisms may partake of 'civic' qualities; indeed demandingly participatory counter-state nationalist movements may provide a particularly rich setting for the cultivation, display, and exercise of participatory and thereby in some sense 'civic' virtue—which the conventional civic–ethnic antithesis definitionally—but misleadingly—associates with 'civic' and denies to 'ethnic' nations and nationalisms.

CONCLUSION

The 'pernicious postulates' I have discussed—some directly opposed to others—do not add up to a single theory of nationalism. Nor have I sought to construct such a theory in my critique of these postulates. The search for 'a' or 'the' theory of nationalism—like the search for 'a' or 'the' solution to nationalist conflicts—is in my view misguided: for the theoretical problems associated with nationhood and nationalism, like the practical political problems, are multiform and varied, and not susceptible of resolution through a single theoretical (or practical) approach. What I have sought to provide, then, is not a comprehensive theory of nationalism, but a series of pointers away from a set of analytical clichés, theoretical dead-ends, and misguided practical stances towards more promising ways of thinking about, writing about, and coping practically with nationalism and national conflicts.

NOTES

1. A partial listing of these would include international relations and security studies (as the end of the Cold War has fostered new understandings of 'security' and 'insecurity'); political science (as the study of nationalism has spread from its traditional home in comparative politics into more theoretically ambitious, self-consciously 'scientific' areas of political science); rational choice theory (in sociology as well as political science); anthropology (as it has increasingly taken complex, 'modern' societies as its object); sociology (especially with the 'cultural turn' in comparative, historical, and political sociology); ethnic studies (with a partial convergence between the literatures on ethnicity and on nationalism); cultural studies; comparative literature; art history; women's studies; musicology; and a variety of area-studies fields including, in a spectacular instance of scholarly *perestroika*, post-Soviet and East European studies.
2. In the post-Soviet field, this has happened as academic entrepreneurs, in search of windfall profits, have entered the field, unburdened by any but the most minimal acquaintance with the comparative and theoretical literature of the field, to say nothing of the wider theoretical and empirical literature of the social sciences, and hastily converting their intellectual capital from forms suddenly devalued by the end of the Cold War and the collapse of the Soviet regime into newly revalued forms, for example, in the sub-field of 'security studies', from a weapons-oriented understanding of security and insecurity to one centred on ethnic and national conflict. In other fields, far removed from the traditional disciplinary loci for the study of nationalism (cultural studies, musicology,

comparative literature, etc.), the historical and social scientific literature on nationalism has been appropriated in a highly selective way.

3. For a sampling of that literature, see B. Anderson, *Imagined Communities: Reflections on the Origin and Spread of Nationalism* (London: Verso, 1983 (2nd edn. 1991)); J. Armstrong, *Nations Before Nationalism* (Chapel Hill, NC: University of North Carolina Press, 1982); J. Breuilly, *Nationalism and the State* (Chicago: University of Chicago Press, 1985); E. Gellner, *Nations and Nationalism* (Ithaca, NY: Cornell University Press, 1983); and A. D. Smith, *The Ethnic Origins of Nations* (Oxford: Blackwell, 1986).
4. C. Tilly, *Big Structures, Large Processes, Huge Comparisons* (New York : Russell Sage Foundation, 1984).
5. Apart from the fact that my own recent work has concerned nationalism in this region, there are good analytical reasons for focusing on this region. Nowhere—for reasons suggested in n. 2—is the theoretical primitivism in the study of nationalism more striking than in the literature (and quasi-literature) on this region. Nowhere, moreover, do the myths and misconceptions I address have more superficial plausibility than in this region.
6. It is an uncomfortable truth that, around the time of the 1938 Munich agreement, the dismemberment of Czechoslovakia through the separation of the Sudeten German lands from the rest of the country was presented and justified in Britain—and not only in Germany—in the name of national self-determination. See A. J. P. Taylor, *The Origins of the Second World War* (London: Hamish Hamilton, 1961), ch. 8; M. Kovács, 'A nemzeti önredelkezés csapdája' ['The Trap of National Self-Determination'], *Népszabadság*, 12 Aug. 1995.
7. For a classic, albeit highly compressed, statement of the sequel, see the epilogue to A. J. P. Taylor, *The Habsburg Monarchy* (Chicago: University of Chicago Press, 1976), 252 ff.; for a more extended, though still splendidly concise, account, see J. Rothschild, *East Central Europe between the Two World Wars* (Seattle and London: University of Washington Press, 1974), especially ch. 1. It is problematic, to be sure, to assign responsibility for the disastrous developments in Central Europe in the two decades following the First World War to the principle of national self-determination—not least because the principle was applied so selectively in the post-War settlement. One could argue that it was not so much the application of the principle as the failure to apply it more consistently—for example, by allowing the peaceful accession of rump Austria to Germany—that proved disastrous.
8. See Kovács, 'A nemzeti önredelkezés csapdája'.
9. For sophisticated recent discussions from the perspective of normative political theory, see Y. Tamir, *Liberal Nationalism* (Princeton: Princeton University Press, 1993); W. Kymlicka, *Multicultural Citizenship* (Oxford: Clarendon Press, 1995); and D. Miller, *On Nationality* (Oxford: Clarendon Press, 1995).
10. For an analysis of inter-war Poland as a nationalizing state, with some concluding reflections on nationalizing states today, see ch. 4 of my *Nationalism Reframed: Nationhood and the National Question in the New Europe* (Cambridge: Cambridge University Press, 1996).
11. For a comparison of Weimar German and contemporary Russian homeland nationalism, see ch. 5 of *Nationalism Reframed.*

12. See *inter alia* Susan Woodward, *Balkan Tragedy* (Washington: Brookings Institution, 1995), 209 ff.; Kovács, 'A nemzeti önredelkezés csapdája'.
13. As Robert Dahl put it, 'We cannot solve the problem of the proper scope and domain of democratic units from within democratic theory. Like the majority principle, the democratic principle presupposes a proper unit. The criteria of the democratic process presuppose the rightfulness of the unit itself.' See for a thorough exploration of this point R. Dahl, *Democracy and its Critics* (New Haven and London: Yale University Press, 1989), 147–8, 193–209; the quotation is from p. 207.
14. For penetrating analysis of institutional design and ethnic conflict, see D. L. Horowitz, *Ethnic Groups in Conflict* (Berkeley: University of California Press, 1985), and id., *A Democratic South Africa? Constitutional Engineering in a Divided Society* (Berkeley: University of California Press, 1991).
15. For an eloquent contextualist plea for the 'adjustment of claims to circumstances', see M. Walzer, 'The New Tribalism', *Dissent* (Spring 1992), 164–71. To argue that good institutional design must be context-sensitive in a strong sense does not mean that generalizing analysis of the workings of different types of institutions—say, for example, different types of electoral systems—is inappropriate. Horowitz undertakes such generalizing analysis, but it is a generalizing analysis of the very different effects that 'the same' electoral system can have in differing contexts. And Horowitz's most sustained discussion of institutional design—in *A Democratic South Africa*—is densely contextual in my sense, blending relatively 'thick' description of a particular context with generalizing arguments about the effects of particular institutions in a variety of settings.
16. Although I limit my remarks to Eastern Europe here, the gloom-and-doom view of putatively explosive ethnic nationalism has considerably wider currency. It is even used in the USA, for example, to link multiculturalism to 'Balkanization' and attendant bloodshed. Critical though I am of many multiculturalist pieties (see for example Section 5), I find the argument of a 'slippery slope' leading from the follies of multiculturalism *à l'américaine* to ethnic warfare just plain silly.
17. J. D. Fearon and D. Laitin, 'Explaining Interethnic Cooperation', *American Political Science Review*, 90/4 (1996), 715–35.
18. Ibid.
19. I should emphasize that this is a relative, not an absolute, absence of nationalist violence. There was one serious incident of violent clashes between Hungarians and Romanians, in Tirgu Mures in the spring of 1990, but this did not trigger further violence. Other forms of violence—notably violent attacks on Gypsies in Romania and other East European countries—have been quite serious; my attention here is limited to relations between Hungarians and majority nationalities in states neighbouring Hungary.
20. Fearon and Laitin ('Explaining Interethnic Cooperation') correctly caution against explaining ethnic violence by appealing to narratives of 'loss, blame, and threat', arguing that such narratives characterize non-violent forms of ethnic conflict as well. But not all such narratives are equal, or equally likely to be connected to violence. There is an important difference, in particular, between memories and threats of death and physical violence on the one hand and narratives of loss,

blame, and threat in general on the other. Credible narratives of loss, blame, and threat are ubiquitous; credible narratives linking memories of past mass violence to threats of future mass violence are not. What was distinctive about the Yugoslav situation—and in my view centrally connected to the violence there—was the availability of plausible, and for some key actors, compelling narratives linking the occurrence of large-scale violence, in particular mass killings, in the past to the threatened recurrence of such violence in the present.

21. David Laitin, personal communication.
22. In Estonia and Latvia, for example, the clash between the claims of the newly independent nationalizing states and those of their Russian and Russophone minorities, strongly amplified from the outside by the homeland-nationalist claims of Russia to 'protect' Baltic Russians, has remained intense and intractable at the level of high politics. But there has been little popular nationalist mobilization in the last few years on the part of majority nationalities or on the part of the Russian and Russian-speaking minorities (on the relative political passivity of Russians, see N. Melvin, *Russians Beyond Russia* (London: Royal Institute of International Affairs, 1995)).
23. There is, of course, a parallel danger of under-historicization. I address this below in my discussion of the failure of 'élite manipulation' accounts to explain or systematically address the historically conditioned differential resonance of appeals made by manipulative or opportunistic nationalist politicians. (To the extent that historically conditioned differences in responsiveness to inflammatory nationalist rhetoric are addressed at all in the 'élitist' literature, they are addressed in ad hoc fashion, relegated to the category of 'other factors' or to an under-theorized residual 'context'.)
24. Both the Hungarian Duna-TV and the various West European channels have high prestige among Transylvanian Hungarians. Romanian state television, by contrast, has very low prestige, although a new private Romanian channel self-consciously 'Western' in style, is widely watched.
25. For a fuller version of this argument, see ch. 2 of my *Nationalism Reframed.*
26. See V. Vujacic and V. Zaslavsky, 'The Causes of Disintegration in the USSR and Yugoslavia', *Telos*, 88 (1991), 120–40.
27. In Bourdieuian terms, two sets of persons might share exactly the same habitus (or, more sociologically, the same distributions of habitus); they might look at the world in the same way, speak the same language, dress in the same manner, consume the same goods, etc; yet they still might exist as two 'groups' because of public categorical recognition.
28. The expression itself is problematic; presuming that nationalist passions are always already there to be 'stirred up', it glosses over the difficulties involved in what might be called the 'work of nationalization'.
29. For a sophisticated argument to the contrary, see J. Rothschild, *Ethnopolitics* (New York: Columbia University Press, 1981), 41–66, esp. 64–5.
30. In another sense, to be sure, analysts have underinvested in the study of nationalism; or, their investments have been short- rather than long-term. In search of a quick pay-off, they have underinvested in the long-term study of nationalism, but overinvested in quick discussions and in 'bidding up' the significance of the phenomenon of nationalism.

31. One should not replace a global overestimation of the power of nationalist political appeals with a global underestimation. The 'return of the left' does *not* mean that nationalism is no longer a viable political option in the region. The return of a 'left' far more 'monetarist', far more acceptable to the IMF in some instances, than anything the preceding 'right' government undertook—may well be followed by the return of the 'return of the right'. Moreover, the 'left'—think of the Communists in Russia—is quite as capable of nationalism as the 'right'—if these labels mean anything at all, which is doubtful. Nationalism had no fixed location on the political spectrum back when it made sense to speak of a political 'spectrum'; still less does it have any such fixed location today.
32. This is not, of course, peculiar to Hungary: 'Germans' from Kazakhstan who resettle in Germany are called 'Russians', as are Jews from Russia (or elsewhere in the former Soviet Union) who resettle in Israel.
33. The lack of electoral success of appeals to the protection of Russians outside Russia does not mean that this theme will disappear from Russian political discourse. Even if such appeals are unprofitable in the arena of domestic political competition, they may be useful in international contexts. I have developed this argument in 'Homeland Nationalism in Weimar Germany and "Weimar Russia"', ch. 5 of my *Nationalism Reframed.*
34. For a more detailed statement of this argument, see ibid. 72 f.
35. The argument of this and the next paragraph is drawn from, and developed more fully in, 'Rethinking Nationhood: Nation as Institutionalized Form, Practical Category, Contingent Event', ibid. 13 ff.
36. Gellner, *Nations and Nationalism*, 139–40.
37. Gellner of course did devote considerable attention to education, but he saw mass 'exo-education' as arising from the logic of industrial society, not from the logic of interstate competition in the age of mass warfare. See ibid., ch. 3.
38. Even mixed settlement patterns, though, are often imagined in mosaic-like terms as composites of bounded and homogeneous units. 'Heterogeneity', in this mode of imagining it, is a distribution of homogeneous units. Heterogeneity is still conceptualized in groupist terms. Sometimes this finds literal representation on maps—as for example when maps of ethnic 'diversity' or 'mixing' are represented as juxtaposed solid-colour patches. How to represent ethnic heterogeneity on a two-dimensional map is a difficult—and philosophically interesting—question. Certainly, though, the simple juxtaposition of solid-colour fields is often quite misleading, suggesting a much greater degree of local homogeneity than in fact exists, and relegating heterogeneity to a higher-level unit. That is, such maps imply that provinces (for example) are heterogeneous, but smaller regions and villages are not; and this implication is often mistaken.
39. For critical discussions of conceptions of this multicultural pentagon, see D. Hollinger, *Post-Ethnic America* (New York: Basic Books, 1995) and M. Lind, *The Next American Nation* (New York: Free Press, 1995).
40. For a general statement of this point, see C. Calhoun, 'The Problem of Identity in Collective Action', in Joan Huber (ed.), *Macro-Micro Linkages in Sociology* (Newbury Park, Calif.: Sage, 1991), 59.
41. The data on nationality and language are from Gosudarstvennyi Komitet po Statistike, *Natsional'nyi Sostav Naseleniia SSSR* (Moscow: Finansy i Statistika, 1991),78–9.

42. For a critique of the ethnic–civic dichotomy from the point of view of political theory, see Bernard Yack, 'The Myth of the Civic Nation', *Critical Review*, 10/2 (Spring 1996), 193–211.
43. See Hollinger, *Post-Ethnic America*, and Lind, *The Next American Nation*.
44. France may again be cited as a paradigmatic instance of state-framed nationhood. Culture is indeed constitutive (not—as I argued in *Citizenship and Nationhood in France and Germany*—simply expressive) of French nationhood; but this is pervasively state-framed culture, not culture conceived as prior to and independent of the territorial and institutional frame of the state.
45. Again, in this case, we would be talking about a *statist* ethnicization of nationhood, not some kind of pre-state or extra-state ethnicity. 'Ethnicity' and 'culture' thus may be found in state-framed nationalism, but only in so far as they themselves are state-framed or state-'caged' (to use Michael Mann's phrase). There is no opposition between the statist component—which refers to the framing—and ethnicity or culture.

SELECT BIBLIOGRAPHY

Adamson, I. (1974), *Cruthin: The Ancient Kindred* (Newtownards, NI: Nos-mada Books).

Akenson, D. H. (1991), *God's People: Covenant and Land in South Africa, Israel, and Ulster* (Montreal and Kingston: McGill-Queen's University Press).

Alesina, A. and Spolaore, E. (1995), 'On the Number and Size of Nations', National Bureau of Economic Research, Working Paper No. 5050, March 1995.

Anderson, B. (1983), *Imagined Communities: Reflections on the Origin and Spread of Nationalism* (London and New York: Verso).

Andrew, E. (1988), *Shylock's Rights: A Grammar of Lockian Claims* (Toronto: University of Toronto Press).

Appiah, K. A. (1996), 'Cosmopolitan Patriots', in J. Cohen (ed.), *For Love of Country* (Boston: Beacon Press).

Arend, A. C. and Beck, R. (1993), *International Law and the Use of Force: Beyond the U.N. Charter* (New York: Routledge).

Armstrong, J. (1982), *Nations Before Nationalism* (Chapel Hill, NC: University of North Carolina Press).

Attanasio, J. B. (1991), 'The Rights of Ethnic Minorities: The Emerging Mosaic', *Notre Dame Law Review*, 66: 1205–08.

Barber, B. R. (1996), 'Constitutional Faith', in Cohen (ed.), *For Love of Country*.

Baron, S. (1985), *Ethnic Minority Rights: Some Older and New Trends*, the Tenth Sacks Lecture, 26 May 1983 (Oxford: Oxford Centre for Postgraduate Hebrew Studies).

Barry, Brian (1989), *Democracy, Power, and Justice* (Oxford: Clarendon Press).

Bauhn, P. (1995), *Nationalism and Morality* (Lund: Lund University Press).

Beiner, R. S. (1992), *What's The Matter with Liberalism?* (Berkeley: University of California Press).

—— (1998), *Philosophy in a Time of Lost Spirit: Essays on Contemporary Theory* (Toronto: University of Toronto Press).

Beitz, C. (1989), *Political Equality* (Princeton: Princeton University Press).

Bennet, C. (1995), *Yugoslavia's Bloody Collapse: Causes, Course and Consequences* (New York: New York University Press).

Beran, H. (1984), 'A Liberal Theory of Secession', *Political Studies*, 32: 21–31.

Berat, L. (1990), *Walvis Bay: Decolonization and International Law* (New Haven, Conn.: Yale University Press).

Berg, J. (1991), 'The Right to Self-Determination', *Public Affairs Quarterly*, 5: 211–25.

Berlin, I. (1992), 'The Bent Twig', in H. Hardy (ed.), *The Crooked Timber of Humanity* (New York: Vintage Books).

Bernier, J. (1997), 'Liberalism, Secession, and the Problem of Internal Minorities', paper presented to the American Political Science Association, Washington, August 1997.

Bin Mohamad, M. (1970), *The Malay Dilemma* (Singapore: Donald Moore).

Binder, G. (1993), 'The Case for Self-Determination', *Stanford Journal of International Law*, 29: 223–70.

Birch, A. H. (1984), 'Another Liberal Theory of Secession', *Political Studies*, 32: 596–602.

Bremmer, I. and Taras, R. (1997), *New States, New Politics: Building the Post-Soviet Nations* (Cambridge: Cambridge University Press).

Breuilly, J. (1985), *Nationalism and the State* (Chicago: University of Chicago Press).

Brighouse, H. (1998), 'Against Nationalism' in J. Couture, K. Nielsen, and M. Seymour (eds.), *Rethinking Nationalism* (Calgary: University of Calgary Press).

Brilmayer, Lea (1991), 'Secession and Self-Determination: A Territorial Interpretation', *Yale Journal of International Law*, 16: 177–202.

Brubaker, R. (1992), *Citizenship and Nationhood in France and Germany* (Cambridge, Mass.: Harvard University Press).

—— (1995), 'Aftermaths of Empire and the Unmixing of Peoples: Historical and Comparative Perspectives', *Ethnic and Racial Studies*, 18/2: 189–218.

—— (1996), *Nationalism Reframed: Nationhood and the National Question in the New Europe* (Cambridge: Cambridge University Press).

Buchanan, Allen (1989), 'Assessing the Communitarian Critique of Liberalism', *Ethics*, 99: 852–82.

—— (1991), *Secession: The Morality of Political Divorce from Fort Sumter to Lithuania and Quebec* (Boulder, Colo.: Westview Press).

—— (1992), 'Self-Determination and the Right to Secede', *Journal of International Affairs*, 45: 347–65.

—— (1993), 'The Role of Collective Rights in the Theory of Indigenous Peoples' Rights', *Transnational Law and Contemporary Problems*, 3: 90–108.

—— (1996), 'What's So Special About Nations?', in Couture, Nielsen, and Seymour (eds.), *Rethinking Nationalism*.

—— (1997), 'Theories of Secession', *Philosophy and Public Affairs*, 26/1: 30–61.

—— (1997), 'Secession, Self-Determination, and the Rule of International Law', in J. McMahan and R. McKim (eds.), *The Morality of Nationalism* (Oxford: Oxford University Press).

Buchheit, L. (1978), *Secession: The Legitimacy of Self-Determination* (New Haven, Conn.: Yale University Press).

Bugajski, J. (1995), *Ethnic Politics in Eastern Europe* (London: M. E. Sharpe).

Burleigh, M. and Wippermann, W. (1991), *The Racial State: Germany 1933–1945* (Cambridge: Cambridge University Press).

Cairns, Alan (1995), 'The Legacy of the Referendum: Who are We Now?', paper prepared for a post-referendum panel organized by the Centre for Constitutional Studies, University of Alberta.

Calhoun, Craig (1991), 'The Problem of Identity in Collective Action', in Joan Huber (ed.), *Macro-Micro Linkages in Sociology* (Newbury Park, Calif: Sage).

Caney, S., George, D., and Jones, P. (eds.) (1996), *National Rights, International Obligations* (Boulder, Colo.: Westview Press).

Cassese, A. (1979), 'Political Self-Determination: Old Concepts and New Developments', in A. Cassese (ed.), *UN Law/Fundamental Rights: Two Topics in International Law* (Alphenaanden Rijn, Neths.: Sijthoff and Noordhoff).

Chazan, Naomi (ed.) (1991), *Irredentism and International Politics* (Boulder, Colo.: Lynne Rienner).

Chen, L.-C. (1991), 'Self-Determination and World Public Order', *Notre Dame Law Review*, 66: 1287–97.

Christiano, T. (1990), 'Freedom, Consensus, and Equality in Collective Decision-Making', *Ethics*, 101: 151–81.

—— (1996), *The Rule of the Many* (Boulder, Colo.: Westview Press).

Cohen, G. A. (1988), *History, Labour and Freedom* (Oxford: Clarendon Press).

Conference on Security and Co-operation in Europe (1990), *Document of the Copenhagen Meeting of the Conference on the Human Dimension, 29 June 1990*, 29 I.L.M., 1305–24.

Connor, Walker (1984), *The National Question in Marxist-Leninist Theory and Strategy* (Princeton: Princeton University Press).

—— (1994), *Ethnonationalism: The Quest for Understanding* (Princeton: Princeton University Press).

—— (1997), 'From a Theory of Relative Economic Deprivation Toward a Theory of Relative Political Deprivation', paper presented to a Conference on 'Minority Nationalism and the New State Order', London, Ont., 7–8 November 1997.

Copp, D. (1997), 'Democracy and Communal Self-Determination', in McMahan and McKim (eds.), *The Morality of Nationalism.*

Crawford, J. (1979), *The Creation of States in International Law* (Oxford: Clarendon Press).

Crnobrnja, M. (1994), *The Yugoslav Drama* (Montreal and Kingston: McGill-Queen's University Press).

Crowther, W. (1993), 'Exploring Political Culture: A Comparative Analysis of Romania and Moldova', unpub. paper, University of North Carolina at Greensboro, NC.

Daes, E. A. (1993), 'Consideration of the Right of Indigenous Peoples to Self-Determination', *Transnational Law and Contemporary Problems*, 3: 1–11.

Dahl, R. (1989), *Democracy and its Critics* (New Haven, Conn. and London: Yale University Press).

Dawes, W. D. (1991), *The Territorial Dimension of Judaism* (Minneapolis: Fortress Press).

De George, R. T. (1991), 'The Myth of the Right of Collective Self-Determination', in Twining (ed.), *Issues of Self-Determination.*

Denitch, B. (1996), *Ethnic Nationalism: The Tragic Death of Yugoslavia*, rev. edn. (Minneapolis: University of Minnesota Press).

De Silva, C. R. (1987), *Sri Lanka: A History* (New Delhi: Vikas Publishing House).

De Zayas, A. (1986), *A Terrible Revenge: The Ethnic Cleansing of the East European Germans, 1944–1950* (New York: St Martin's Press).

Djilas, M. (1991), *The Contested Country* (Cambridge, Mass.: Harvard University Press).

Donnelly, D. K. (1996), 'State and Substates in a Free World: A Theory of National Self-Determination', *Nationalism and Ethnic Politics*, 2/2: 286–311.

Dworkin, R. (1981), 'What is Equality? part 1: Equality of Welfare', and 'What is Equality? part 2: Equality of Resources', *Philosophy and Public Affairs*, 10/4: 283–345.

—— (1984), 'Rights as Trumps', in J. Waldron (ed.), *Theories of Rights* (Oxford: Oxford University Press).

—— (1987), 'What is Equality? part 4: Political Equality', *University of San Francisco Law Review*, 22/1: 1–30.

Eastwood Jr., L. S. (1993), 'Secession: State Practice and International Law After the Dissolution of the Soviet Union and Yugoslavia', *Duke Journal of Comparative and International Law*, 3: 299–349.

Elazar, D. (1994), *Federalism and the Way to Peace* (Queen's University, Kingston: Institute of Intergovernmental Affairs).

Elster, J. (1988), 'Introduction', in J. Elster and R. Slagstad (eds.), *Constitutionalism and Democracy* (Cambridge: Cambridge University Press).

Emerson, Rupert (1960), *From Empire to Nation* (Cambridge, Mass.: Harvard University Press).

—— (1964), *Self-Determination Revisited in an Era of Decolonization* (Harvard University Center for International Affairs, Occasional Papers in International Affairs, No. 9).

—— (1971), 'Self-Determination', *American Journal of International Law*, 65/3: 459–75.

Etzioni, A. (1992–3), 'The Evils of Self-Determination', *Foreign Policy*, 89: 21–35.

Falkowski, J. E. (1991), 'Secessionary Self-Determination: A Jeffersonian Perspective', *Boston University International Law Journal*, 9: 209–42.

Fearon, J. D. and Laitin, D. (1996), 'Explaining Interethnic Cooperation', *American Political Science Review*, 90/4: 715–35.

Franck, T. M. (1992), 'The Emerging Right to Democratic Governance', *American Journal of International Law*, 86: 46–91.

French, S. and Gutmann, A. (1974), 'The Principle of National Self-Determination', in V. Held, S. Morgenbesser, and T. Nagel (eds.), *Philosophy, Morality and International Affairs* (New York: Oxford University Press).

Gauthier, D. (1994), 'Breaking Up: An Essay on Secession', *Canadian Journal of Philosophy*, 24: 357–72.

Gellner, Ernest (1965), 'Nationalism' in *Thought and Change* (Chicago: University of Chicago Press).

—— (1983), *Nations and Nationalism* (Ithaca, NY: Cornell University Press).

—— (1996), 'Do Nations Have Navels?', *Nations and Nationalism*, 2/3: 366–70.

Gibson, J. L. and Duch, R. M. (1991), 'Attitudes toward Jews and the Soviet Political Culture', *Journal of Soviet Nationalities*, 2: 77–117.

Glendon, M. (1991), *Rights Talk: The Impoverishment of Political Discourse* (New York: Free Press).

Graff, J. A. (1994), 'Human Rights, Peoples and Self-Determination', in J. Baker (ed.), *Group Rights* (Toronto: University of Toronto Press).

Grand Council of the Crees (1995), *Sovereign Injustice: Forcible Inclusion of the James Bay Cree and Cree Territory Into a Sovereign Quebec* (Grand Council of the Crees).

Gross, L. (1948), 'The Peace of Westphalia', *American Journal of International Law*, 42: 20–41.

Halberstam, M. (1989), 'Self-Determination in the Arab–Israeli Conflict: Meaning, Myth and Politics', *New York University Journal of International Law and Politics*, 21: 465–87.

Halperin, M. and Lomasney K. (1993), 'Toward a Global "Guarantee Clause"', *Journal of Democracy*, 4: 60–9.

—— and Sheffer, D. J. (1992), *Self-Determination in the New World Order* (Washington: Carnegie Endowment for International Peace).

Hannum, H. (1990), *Autonomy, Sovereignty, and Self-Determination: The Accommodation of Conflicting Rights* (Philadelphia: University of Pennsylvania Press).

—— (1991), 'Contemporary Developments in the International Protection of the Rights of Minorities', *Notre Dame Law Review*, 66: 1431–48.

—— (n.d.), 'Self-Determination, Yugoslavia, and Europe: Old Wine in New Bottles?', unpub. paper.

Hardin, R. (1995), *One for All: The Logic of Group Conflict* (Princeton: Princeton University Press).

Harpes, J.-P. (ed.) (forthcoming), *Nouvelles voies de la démocratie* (Luxembourg: Presses du parlement européen).

Hayden, R. M. (1992), 'Constitutional Nationalism in the Former Yugoslav Republics', *Slavic Review*, 51: 654–73.

—— (1995), 'Constitutional Nationalism and the Wars in Yugoslavia', paper prepared for the Conference on 'Post-Communism and Ethnic Mobilization', Cornell University, 21–3 April 1995.

Hehir, J. B. (1995), 'Intervention: From Theories to Cases', *Ethics and International Affairs*, 9: 1–13.

Helsinki Watch (1988), *Destroying Ethnic Identity: The Kurds of Turkey* (New York: Helsinki Watch).

Heraclides, A. (1990), 'Secessionist Minorities and External Involvement', *International Organization*, 44: 341–78.

—— (1991), *The Self-Determination of Minorities in International Politics* (London: Frank Cass).

—— (1992), 'Secession, Self-Determination and Non-intervention: In Quest of a Normative Synthesis', *Journal of International Affairs*, 45: 399–420.

Higgins, R. (1963), *The Development of International Law through the Political Organs of the United Nations* (Oxford: Oxford University Press).

Hirschman, A. O. (1970), *Exit, Voice and Loyalty* (Cambridge, Mass.: Harvard University Press).

Hobsbawm, E. J. (1990), *Nations and Nationalism Since 1780* (Cambridge: Cambridge University Press).

—— (1996), 'Ethnicity and Nationalism in Europe Today', in Gopal Balakrishnan (ed.), *Mapping the Nation* (London and New York: Verso).

Hollinger, D. (1995), *Post-Ethnic America* (New York: Basic Books).

Holmes, S. (1988), 'Gag Rules or the Politics of Omission' in J. Elster and R. Slagstad (eds.), *Constitutionalism and Democracy* (Cambridge: Cambridge University Press).

Horowitz, Donald, L. (1985), *Ethnic Groups in Conflict* (Berkeley: University of California Press).

—— (1990), 'Making Moderation Pay: The Comparative Politics of Ethnic Conflict Management', in J. V. Montville (ed.), *Conflict and Peacemaking in Multiethnic States* (Lexington, Mass.: Lexington Books).

—— (1991), 'Irredentas and Secessions: Adjacent Phenomena, Neglected Connections', in N. Chazan (ed.), *Irredentism and International Politics* (Boulder: Lynne Rienner).

—— (1991), *A Democratic South Africa? Constitutional Engineering in a Divided Society* (Berkeley: University of California Press).

—— (1992), 'A Harvest of Hostility: Ethnic Conflict and Self-Determination After the Cold War', *Defence Intelligence Journal*, 1: 137–63.

Howard, R. (1995), *Human Rights and the Search for Community* (Boulder, Colo.: Westview Press).

Howse, R. and Knop, K. (1993), 'Federalism, Secession, and the Limits of Ethnic Accommodation: A Canadian Perspective', *New Europe Law Review*, 1: 269–320.

Human Rights Watch/Helsinki (1994), *Denying Ethnic Identity: The Macedonians of Greece* (New York: Human Rights Watch/Helsinki).

Huttenbach, H. (1993), 'Post-Factum Diplomacy: Bonn's Revisionist Apologia for Its Policy of Recognizing Croatia', Association for the Study of Nationalities, *Analysis of Current Events*, 5: 1–3.

Jennings, Ivor (1956), *The Approach to Self-Government* (Cambridge: Cambridge University Press).

Kampelman, M. M. (1993), 'Secession and the Right of Self-Determination: An Urgent Need to Harmonize Principle with Pragmatism', *Washington Quarterly*, 16: 5–12.

Kaufman, C. (1996), 'Possible and Impossible Solutions to Ethnic Civil Wars', *International Security*, 20: 136–75.

Kaufman, S. (1994–5), 'The Irresistible Force and the Imperceptible Object: The Yugoslav Breakup and Western Policy', *Security Studies*, 4: 281–329.

Keating, M. (1996), *Nations Against the State: The New Politics of Nationalism in Quebec, Catalonia and Scotland* (Basingstoke: Macmillan).

—— (1997), 'Nations Without States: The Accommodation of Nationalism in the New State Order', paper presented to a Conference on 'Minority Nationalism in the New State Order', London, Ont. 7–8 November 1997.

Kedourie, E. (1960), *Nationalism* (London: Hutchinson).

Kingsbury, B. (1992), 'Claims by Non-State Groups in International Law', *Cornell International Law Journal*, 25: 481–530.

—— (1992), 'Self-Determination and "Indigenous Peoples"', in *Proceedings of the American Society of International Law*, 86th Annual Meeting: 383–94.

—— (1995), 'Indigenous Peoples as an International Legal Concept', in R. H. Barnes *et al.* (eds.), *Indigenous Peoples of Asia* (Ann Arbor, Mich.: Association for Asian Studies).

Kirby, M. (1993), 'The Peoples' Right to Self-Determination', *New Zealand Law Journal* (Sept.), 341–4.

Kolodner, E. (1994), 'The Future of the Right to Self-Determination', *Connecticut Journal of International Law*, 10: 153–67.

Kolstoe, P. (1995), *Russians in the Former Soviet Republics* (Bloomington, Ind.: Indiana University Press).

Kovács, M. (1995), 'A nemzeti önredelkezés csapdája' ['The Trap of National Self-Determination'], *Népszabadság*, 12 Aug.

Kreyenbroek, P. G. and Sperl, S. (eds.) (1992), *The Kurds: A Contemporary Overview* (London: Routledge).

Kuper, L. (1981), *Genocide: Its Political Uses in the Twentieth Century* (New Haven, Conn.: Yale University Press).

Kymlicka, Will (1995), *Multicultural Citizenship: A Liberal Theory of Minority Rights* (Oxford: Clarendon Press).

Ladas, S. P. (1932), *The Exchange of Minorities: Bulgaria, Greece and Turkey* (New York: Macmillan).

Laforest, G. (1995), *De l'Urgence* (Montreal: Boréal).

Laitin, D. (1995), 'Ethnic Cleansing, Liberal Style', MacArthur Foundation Program in Transnational Security, Working Papers Series, M.I.T. Center for International Studies and Harvard Center for International Affairs.

Landis, J. B. (1973), 'Racial Attitudes of Africans and Indians in Guyana', *Social and Economic Studies*, 22: 427–39.

Lapidoth, R. (1994), 'Autonomy: Potential and Limitations', *International Journal on Group Rights*, 1: 269–90.

Lemarchand, R. (1986), 'Ethnic Violence in Tropical Africa', in J. F. Stack, Jr. (ed.), *The Primordial Challenge: Ethnicity in the Contemporary World* (New York: Greenwood Press).

Levesque, R. (1968), *An Option for Quebec* (Toronto: McClelland and Stewart).

Levine, A. (1998), 'Just Nationalism: The Future of an Illusion', in Couture, Nielsen, and Seymour (eds.), *Rethinking Nationalism.*

Levinson, S. (1995), 'Is Liberal Nationalism an Oxymoron?', *Ethics*, 105: 626–45.

Lichtenberg, J. (1981), 'National Boundaries and Moral Boundaries: A Cosmopolitan View', in Peter G. Brown and Henry Shue (eds.), *Boundaries: National Autonomy and Its Limits* (Totowa, NJ: Rowman and Littlefield).

Lijphart, A. (1977), *Democracy in Plural Societies* (New Haven, Conn.: Yale University Press).

Lind, M. (1994), 'In Defense of Liberal Nationalism', *Foreign Affairs*, 73/3: 87–99.

—— (1995), *The Next American Nation* (New York: Free Press).

Lustick, I. (1995), 'What Gives a People Rights to a Land?', *Queen's Quarterly*, 102/4: 53–68.

MacCormick, N. (1991), 'Is Nationalism Philosophically Credible?', in W. Twining (ed.), *Issues of Self-Determination* (Aberdeen: Aberdeen University Press).

McCorquodale, R. (1992), 'Self-Determination Beyond the Colonial Context and Its Potential Impact on Africa', *African Journal of International and Comparative Law*, 4: 592–608.

McDowall, D. (1992), *The Kurds: A Nation Denied* (London: Minority Rights Group).

McGarry, J. (1998), 'Demographic Engineering: The State-Directed Movement of Ethnic Groups as a Technique of Conflict Regulation', *Ethnic and Racial Studies*, 21/4.

—— and O'Leary, B. (1993), 'Introduction: The Macro-Political Regulation of Ethnic Conflict', in J. McGarry and B. O'Leary (eds.), *The Politics of Ethnic Conflict Regulation* (London and New York: Routledge).

—— —— (1995), *Explaining Northern Ireland: Broken Images* (Oxford: Blackwell).

Maine, H. S. (1931), *Ancient Law* (London: Oxford University Press).

Margalit, A. and Raz, J. (1990), 'National Self-Determination', *Journal of Philosophy*, 87: 439–61.

Marrus, M. (1985), *The Unwanted: European Refugees in the Twentieth Century* (New York: Oxford University Press).

Masalha, N. (1992), *Expulsion of the Palestinians: The Concept of 'Transfer' in Zionist Political Thought 1882–1948* (Washington, DC: Institute for Palestine Studies).
Maxwell, M. (1992), 'Normative Aspects of Secession and Supranationalism', paper presented to the Annual Meeting of the American Political Science Association.
Melvin, N. (1995), *Russians Beyond Russia* (London: Royal Institute of National Affairs).
Michalska, A. (1991), 'Rights of Peoples to Self-Determination in International Law', in W. Twining (ed.), *Issues of Self-Determination* (Aberdeen: University of Aberdeen Press).
Mill, J. S. (1873), 'A Few Words on Non-Intervention', in his *Dissertations and Discussions,* iii (New York: Henry Holt).
—— (1951), 'Considerations on Representative Government', in Mill, *Utilitarianism, Liberty, and Representative Government* (New York: E. P. Dutton (originally pub. 1861)).
Miller, David (1988), 'The Ethical Significance of Nationality', *Ethics*, 98: 647–62.
—— (1993), 'In Defence of Nationality', *Journal of Applied Philosophy*, 10: 3–16.
—— (1995), *On Nationality* (Oxford: Clarendon Press).
—— (1996), 'On Nationality', *Nations and Nationalism*, 2/3: 409–21.
—— (1998), 'The Limits of Cosmopolitan Justice', in D. R. Mapel and T. Nardin (eds.), *The Constitution of International Society: Diverse Ethical Perspectives* (Princeton: Princeton University Press).
—— (forthcoming), 'Justice and Global Inequality', in A. Hurrell and N. Woods (eds.), *Inequality in World Politics* (Oxford: Oxford University Press).
Moore, Margaret (1996), 'Miller's Ode to National Homogeneity', *Nations and Nationalism*, 2/3: 423–9.
—— (1997), 'On National Self-Determination', *Political Studies*, 45/5: 900–13.
—— (forthcoming), 'The Limits of Liberal Nationalism', in Brendan O'Leary and George Schopflin (eds.), *Understanding Nationalism* (London: Edgar Allen).
Nagel, J. (1980), 'The Conditions of Ethnic Separatism', *Ethnicity*, 7: 279–97.
Nanda, V. P. (1992), 'Ethnic Conflict in Fiji and International Human Rights Law', *Cornell International Law Journal*, 25: 565–77.
Nickel, James (1995), 'What is Wrong with Ethnic Cleansing?', *Journal of Social Philosophy*, 26/1: 5–15.
Nielsen, Kai (1993), 'Secession: The Case of Quebec', *Journal of Applied Philosophy*, 10: 29–43.
—— (1996–7), 'Cultural Nationalism, Neither Ethnic nor Civic', *Philosophical Forum*, 28/1–2: 42–52.
Norman, W. (1994), 'Toward a Philosophy of Federalism', in Judith Baker (ed.), *Group Rights* (Toronto: University of Toronto Press).
—— (1995), 'The Ideology of Shared Values', in J. Carens (ed.), *Is Quebec Nationalism Just?* (Montreal and Kingston: McGill-Queen's University Press).
—— (1998), 'Démocratie et secession', in J.-P. Harpes (ed.), *Nouvelles voies de la democratie* (Luxembourg: Presses du parlement europeen).
Nussbaum, M. (1996), 'Patriotism and Cosmopolitanism', in J. Cohen (ed.), *For Love of Country* (Boston: Beacon Press), 3–17.
Ofuatey-Kodjoe, W. (1977), *The Principles of Self-Determination in International Law* (New York: Nellen).

O'Leary, B. (1997), 'On the Nature of Nationalism', *British Journal of Political Science*, 27: 191–222.

—— and McGarry, J. (1993), *The Politics of Antagonism: Understanding Northern Ireland* (London: Athlone).

—— Lyne, T., Marshall, J., and Rowthorn, B. (1993), *Northern Ireland: Sharing Authority* (London: Institute for Public Policy Research).

Pellet, A. (1992), 'The Opinions of the Badinter Arbitration Committee: A Second Breath for the Self-Determination of Peoples', *European Journal of International Law*, 3: 178–85.

Pentzopoulos, D. (1962), *The Balkan Exchange of Minorities and its Impact upon Greece* (Paris: Mouton).

Petropulos, J. A. (1976), 'The Compulsory Exchange of Populations: Greek-Turkish Peacemaking, 1922–1930', *Byzantine and Modern Greek Studies*, 2: 135–60.

Pflanze, O. (1966), 'Characteristics of Nationalism in Europe: 1848–1871', *Review of Politics*, 28: 129–43.

Philpott, Daniel (1995), 'In Defence of Self-Determination', *Ethics*, 105/2: 352–85.

Pogge, T. (1992), 'Cosmopolitanism and Sovereignty', *Ethics*, 103: 48–75.

Premdas, R. R. (1990), 'Secessionist Movements in Comparative Perspective', in R. R. Premdas, S. W. R. de A. Samarasinghe, and A. P. Anderson (eds.), *Secessionist Movements in Comparative Perspective* (London: Pinter).

Rawls, J. (1971), *A Theory of Justice* (Cambridge, Mass.: Harvard University Press).

Raz, J. (1986), *The Morality of Freedom* (Oxford: Clarendon Press).

Roemer, J. (1985), 'Equality of Talent', *Economics and Philosophy*, 1/2.

Rothschild, J. (1974), *East Central Europe between the Two World Wars* (Seattle and London: University of Washington Press).

—— (1981), *Ethnopolitics* (New York: Columbia University Press).

Said, E. and Hitchens, C. (1988) (eds.), *Blaming the Victims* (London: Verso).

Sandel, M. J. (1982), *Liberalism and the Limits of Justice* (Cambridge: Cambridge University Press).

Schuman, H., Steeh, C., and Bobo, L. (1985), *Racial Attitudes in America* (Cambridge, Mass.: Harvard University Press).

Seton-Watson, H. (1977), *Nations and States; An Enquiry into the Origins of Nations and the Politics of Nationalism* (London: Methuen).

Simmons, A. J. (1979), *Moral Principles and Political Obligations* (Princeton: Princeton University Press).

Smith, A. D. (1971), *Theories of Nationalism* (London: Duckworth).

—— (1986), *The Ethnic Origins of Nations* (Oxford: Blackwell).

—— (1996), 'The Nation: Real or Imagined?', *Nations and Nationalism*, 2/3: 358–65.

Sniderman, P. M. and Piazza, T. (1993), *The Scar of Race* (Cambridge, Mass.: Harvard University Press).

Stannard, David, E. (1993), *American Holocaust* (New York: Oxford University Press).

Steiner, H. (1996), 'Territorial Justice', in S. Caney, D. George, and P. Jones (eds.), *National Rights, International Obligations* (Boulder, Colo.: Westview Press).

Steinhardt, R. G. (n.d.) 'International Law and Self-Determination', unpub. paper, Atlantic Council Project on Individual Rights, Group Rights, National Sovereignty, and International Law, 41–3.

Strengthening Democratic Institutions Project (1992), *Fact Sheet on Ethnic and Regional Conflicts in the Russian Federation* (Cambridge, Mass.: Strengthening Democratic Institutions Project, Harvard University, Sept. 1992).

Sunstein, Cass (1991), 'Constitutionalism and Secession', *University of Chicago Law Review*, 58/2: 633–70.

Tamir, Yael (1991), 'The Right to National Self-Determination', *Social Research*, 58: 565–90.

—— (1993), *Liberal Nationalism* (Princeton: Princeton University Press).

Taylor, A. J. P. (1961), *The Origins of the Second World War* (London: Hamish Hamilton).

—— (1976), *The Habsburg Monarchy* (Chicago: University of Chicago Press).

Taylor, C. (1992), 'The Politics of Recognition', in A. Gutmann (ed.), *Multiculturalism and the 'Politics of Recognition'* (Princeton: Princeton University Press).

—— (1993), 'Alternative Futures', in G. Laforest (ed.), *Reconciling the Solitudes: Essays on Canadian Federalism and Nationalism* (Montreal and Kingston: McGill-Queen's University Press).

Thornberry, P. (1989), 'Self-Determination, Minorities, Human Rights: A Review of International Instruments', *International and Comparative Law Quarterly*, 38: 867–89.

—— (1991), *Minorities and Human Rights Law* (London: Minority Rights Group).

Tilly, C. (1984), *Big Structures, Large Processes, Huge Comparisons* (New York: Russell Sage Foundation).

Tishkov, V. A. (1993), 'Nationalities and Conflicting Ethnicity in Post-Communist Russia', Conflict Management Group, Working Papers on Ethnic Conflict Management in the Former Soviet Union (Cambridge, Mass., April).

UNESCO (1960), 'UNESCO Convention against Discrimination in Education', *United Nations Treaty Series*, 429.

UNITED NATIONS (1951), 'International Convention on the Prevention and Punishment of the Crime of Genocide', *United Nations Treaty Series*, 277.

—— (1993), *Declaration on the Rights of Persons Belonging to National or Ethnic, Religious and Linguistic Minorities*, United Nations General Assembly, A/RES/47/135, 3 February, 1993 (adopted 18 Dec. 1992).

Vujacic, V. and Zaslavsky, V., 'The Causes of Disintegration in the USSR and Yugoslavia', *Telos*, 88: 120–40.

Waldron, Jeremy (1992), 'Minority Cultures and the Cosmopolitan Option', *University of Michigan Law Reform*, 25: 751–93.

Walzer, M. (1977), *Just and Unjust Wars* (New York: Basic Books).

—— (1992), 'The New Tribalism', *Dissent* (Spring), 164–71.

Weil, F. D. (1985), 'The Variable Effects of Education on Liberal Attitudes: A Comparative Historical Analysis of Anti-Semitism Using Public Opinion Survey Data', *American Sociological Review*, 50: 458–74.

Wellman, C. H. (1995), 'A Defence of Secession and Political Self-Determination', *Philosophy and Public Affairs*, 24/2: 142–71.

Winthrop, J. (1964), 'Reasons to be Considered, and Objections with Answers', repr. in Edmund, S. Morgan (ed.), *The Founding of Massachusetts: Historians and the Sources* (Indianapolis: Bobbs-Merrill).

Wood, J. (1981), 'Secession: A Comparative Analytic Framework', *Canadian Journal of Political Science*, 14: 107–34.

Woodward, S. (1995), *Balkan Tragedy* (Washington: Brookings Institution).

Wright, R. (1992), *Stolen Continents: The 'New World' Through Indian Eyes* (Harmondsworth: Penguin).

Yack, B. (1995), 'Reconciling Liberalism and Nationalism', *Political Theory*, 23/1: 166–82.

—— (1996), 'The Myth of the Civic Nation', *Critical Review*, 10/2: 193–211.

Young, R. (1994), 'How Do Peaceful Secessions Happen?', *Canadian Journal of Political Science*, 26/4: 773–92.

Zaslavsky, V. (1992), 'The Evolution of Separatism in Soviet Society under Gorbachev', in G. W. Lapidus, V. Zaslavsky, and P. Goldman (eds.), *From Union to Commonwealth: Nationalism and Separatism in the Soviet Republics* (Cambridge: Cambridge University Press).

INDEX

Aaland Islands Treaty 203
absolutism 163, 166, 168
accommodation 205, 217, 221–2, 226–8
Acton, Lord 159
administrative borders 135–41, 150–1, 154
Africa 10, 14, 70, 84, 104, 138, 151, 186–7, 194, 203, 218, 235
Albania 145, 181, 183–4, 199
alienation 4, 109–10, 120–1, 139, 170, 201
America 80, 84, 96, 105, 127, 142, 146–7, 189, 215, 254, 256–8
Anderson, Benedict 1, 233
Anglo-Irish Agreement 227
apartheid 201, 243
arbitration 63, 86–7, 94, 97–8, 111, 192, 199–200
architectonic illusion and national conflict 7, 233–41
Armenia 140–1, 184, 250
Armstrong, John 233
Asia 84, 138, 186, 218, 235
assimilation 37, 44, 49, 140, 253, 255–6, 258–9
association, freedom of 5, 17, 35, 38–9, 45
atrocities 80, 88, 91–2, 190, 248
attachment to land 68, 105, 143–4
Austria-Hungary 87, 96
Austrian State Treaty 203
Austro-Italian Treaty 203
authority, political 25–7, 34, 42, 53, 65–6, 68–9, 235
autonomy:
  choice theory 37
  collective 174, 220
  equality 130
  federal 86, 89
  individual 16–19, 35, 38–9, 115, 117, 126–7, 197–8, 216, 223
  liberal 34
  minority 53, 55, 141
  moral 81, 83
  national 242
  political 7, 36–7, 42, 44–5, 47, 49, 65–6, 69–70, 75, 79, 82–3, 85, 103–6, 119
  regional 204–5, 225–6
  rights 206
  secession and 135–6, 173
  self-determination and 2, 5, 10, 12, 150
Azerbaijan 140–1, 188, 222, 250

Badinter Arbitration Committee 139, 192, 199–200
Baltic States 25, 29, 68, 111, 181, 187–9, 219, 222, 243, 258
Bangladesh 1, 14, 26, 87, 111, 185, 187, 190, 199, 201
Barry, Brian 134
Basques 1, 49, 69, 74, 84, 105, 113, 191, 226
Bauhn, Per 198
Beiner, Ronald 11, 158–74
Belgium 113, 192
Beran, Harry 170
Berlin, Isaiah 159
Biafra 187–9, 192, 199
blackmail 95–7
Blair, Tony 171
Bosnia 72, 79–80, 83, 87–8, 91–2, 97, 116, 138–9, 151, 153, 182, 189–90, 192–3, 195, 199, 219, 221, 223, 239
Bossi, Umberto 160
boundaries:
  ethnic groups 182
  fixed 1, 72, 75, 129, 205
  groupism 251–2, 254–7
  internal 193
  language of rights and 162
  multiethnic 160
  pluralism 219, 221, 225
  political 20, 22–4, 30, 182–7, 190
  reorganization 42, 53, 192–3, 234–8, 245
  secession and 134–6
  self-determination and 201
  social 234
  territory 149, 153
Bourdieu, Pierre 246, 251
Breuilly, John 233
Brighouse, Harry 109, 126
Brubaker, Rogers 7–8, 12, 221, 226, 233–60

Buchanan, Allen:
Beiner on 169–72
democracy and secession 14–30
Horowitz on 198
McGarry on 216
Miller on 62–3, 68, 73
Moore on 135
Nielsen on 103–4, 108–31
Norman on 34–5, 37–8, 41, 50–2
Philpott on 80, 90
theories of secession 4–6, 10
Bulgaria 181, 218

Canada 11, 43, 62, 67, 69, 71, 105–6, 114, 116, 124, 127, 135, 139, 152, 164, 167–8, 171, 174, 192, 220, 223, 226–7
Cassese, Antonio 204
Catalans 1, 49, 62, 66, 69, 104–5, 152, 191, 220
Caucasus 181, 188, 241
Ceausescu, N. 244
Central Asia 181, 188, 241, 243
centralization 217, 225–6
de- 19, 103, 108, 110, 119–20, 171, 221, 225–7
Chechnya 116, 182, 187–8, 222
Chile 106–7
China 43, 160, 184
choice theory 5, 7–8, 35, 37–45, 47, 49–51, 53, 55
chosen people and divine rights 145–7, 150
citizenship 12, 39, 42, 106–7, 137, 139–40, 194, 205, 221, 235, 243, 257–9
civic nationalism 12, 235, 257–60
claim:
to nationhood 238
political 182
to secession 24, 29, 46, 63–7, 69, 71, 73, 75, 168, 171, 185–6, 192
to self-determination 11, 82, 84–92, 98–9, 173, 199–200, 218
to territory 5, 41, 142–3, 149–50
classification, national 246–7, 254–5
clauses, secession 40–1, 45, 48, 50–6, 93, 95, 100
clean break illusion 190–2
colonialism 3–4, 6, 15, 45, 80, 82–7, 89–91, 96, 106, 136, 138, 146, 151, 158–9, 186, 194, 201, 235
communism 1, 234, 236–7, 244–5, 247–9, 255
communitarianism 137, 158, 161, 171
community 7, 39, 65–6, 68, 73–5, 104–6, 170–1, 193–7
compensation 74, 83
competition 227, 253
concessions 97, 183, 195
conflict 2–3, 7–8, 26, 36, 39–40, 42, 49, 70–1, 74, 137, 147, 149, 151, 153, 169, 182, 186–7, 189, 191–3, 195–200, 202, 204–6, 215–17, 221, 224, 226, 233–6, 239–42, 245, 248, 260
Congress of Russian Communities 250
Connor, Walker 4, 140
consensus 22, 85, 95, 200–1, 220
consent 25, 35, 38, 46, 67, 94, 188–9, 202
consociation 195–6, 226–7
constitutionalism 9, 21, 24, 40–1, 45–50, 53, 55, 63, 81, 84–5, 89, 93–100, 115, 171
constructivism 252, 255
Copenhagen Agreement (1990) 27–9, 203
Copp, David 16–17, 19–20, 24–5
Corsica 49, 205
cosmopolitanism 109, 127, 244
Council of Europe 204
Croatia 26, 88, 91–3, 138–9, 151, 153, 174, 189–90, 192–3, 199, 205, 217–18, 221, 223–4, 239, 250
Croats 79, 91, 97, 153, 193, 203, 219, 221, 239
culture:
alienation 183
diversity 74–5, 122
efficiency and 147–50
encompassing 104–5, 107, 110, 124–7
ethnic 38–9, 195–6
majority 218, 221
minority 203
nationalism 65–7, 103–9, 215, 217, 238–9, 253
preservation 3, 7, 36–7, 41, 72, 80, 201
right to secede 82, 96
rights 224
secession 12
suppression 63, 69–71, 166, 169
survival 111
territory 136–7, 144
Curzon, Lord 222
Czech Republic 79, 171, 181, 223–4
Czechoslovakia 1, 219–20, 238

decision-making 2, 5, 17–24, 30, 43, 63–4, 68, 134, 172–3, 203
democracy:
autonomy and 79, 81–2
ethics and 35, 43, 45, 47–8
exclusion and 195

liberal nationalism and 103–4, 107, 110, 112–13, 115
politics and 199, 204–6
secession and 5, 14–30, 37–9
self-determination and 6, 10–11, 83, 86, 88–9, 94–6, 239–40
territory and 134, 137–8
democratization 10–11, 14–16, 25, 28, 204
demonstration effects of self-determination 4
Denmark 11, 106, 113–14, 116
descent 12, 246, 257–9
Dewey, John 131
discrimination 6, 37, 41, 74, 80, 111–13, 118, 123, 125, 187, 198, 201–2, 206, 216, 237
dissenters 151–2
dissolution 187–90, 192, 222
'distinct society' 139–40
divorce analogy of self-determination 38, 46, 49, 67, 82, 93, 191
domination 136, 138–40, 153, 191, 195–6, 221, 224, 227, 244
domino secessions 188, 222
Dworkin, Ronald 52, 165

East Timor 42, 166–8
efficiency 144, 147–50
elections 48, 53–5, 83, 87, 89, 151, 195–6, 204, 249–50
élite manipulation 5, 234, 248–51
empowerment 91, 95, 97
entitlement 1, 3, 134, 141, 143–5, 149, 158, 160, 166–7, 201, 204, 206, 235
equality 23–4, 36, 42, 71, 110, 117, 126, 142, 144, 217, 225–6
Eritrea 92, 187, 190, 192, 199
Estonia 187, 193, 219, 221, 226, 243
ethics of secession 3, 5, 7–8, 34–56, 135–6, 227
Ethiopia 1, 183, 187, 192, 199
ethnic cleansing 70, 72, 152, 190, 206, 243
ethnic groups 105–6, 114, 118, 136–9, 141, 170, 181–201, 246–7, 251–7
ethnic nationalism 12, 106–8, 235, 257–60
ethnicity 2–3, 5, 9, 12, 82
Europe 10, 14, 79, 91, 93, 95, 158–9, 181, 186, 189, 195, 200, 202, 205, 221–4, 227, 233–5, 237–8, 241, 243, 245, 247–8, 253–5, 257
European Community 88, 93, 174
European Union 139, 227
exchange, population 72, 190
exclusion 195–6, 203, 206, 244
exit 10, 22, 24, 93, 242
exploitation 6, 41, 51, 69, 130
expression, freedom of 17, 165

Fearon, James 242
federalism 36, 39, 48, 53, 95, 106, 119–20, 139–40, 153, 171–2, 192–3, 196, 201, 206, 226
Finland 106, 203
First Nations 105–8, 127, 140, 142, 146
Flanders 1, 49
Flemish 104, 107
foreign policy 81, 85, 88, 242
fragmentation 14, 62, 115, 160, 170, 187, 192
France 106, 124, 205, 215, 258
Franck, Thomas M. 204
Franco (Bahamonde), Francisco 226
Freud, Sigmund 245

Galston, William 161
Gandhi, Mohandas 83
Gauthier, D. 74
Gellner, Ernest 4, 7, 62, 90, 91, 159, 233, 234, 252–3, 255
generalizability 104, 116, 125, 137, 149–51, 181
genocide 6, 166, 191, 199, 201, 216, 221
Genocide Convention (1951) 203
geographical residence 65, 82, 104
Georgia 187, 222
Germany 54, 65, 88–91, 93, 107, 138, 145, 174, 181, 189, 205, 218, 238, 248, 255–6
gerrymandering 141, 219
Glendon, Mary Ann 161, 162
globalization 227, 253
good, political 162, 167–8, 170–1
Gorbachev, Mikhail 181, 188, 246–7
government:
as agent 123, 126, 135
central 53, 185–90, 226
democracy 14–15, 27–30
just 52
overthrow 28–9
post-secession 220–4
see also self-government
Graff, James A. 145
Greece 145, 217, 218
grievances 25, 80, 82–3, 86, 90, 96, 99, 167
groupism and nationalism 234, 251–7

Halperin, Morton H. 204–5
Hannum, Hurst 204

hatred, ancient 241, 248
Hegel, F. W. 110
heterogeneity 70, 160, 184, 191–3, 199, 216–17, 219–20, 224, 228, 254, 258
Hirschman, Albert O. 10, 21, 22
historical roots 65, 68–9, 96, 104–7, 109, 127, 149, 198, 201, 215
history:
  national 215
  territory and 3, 137–8, 141, 145, 149–50, 154
Hobsbawm, Eric 160
homeland 3–4, 237–8, 242, 246
homogeneity 19, 23–4, 65–6, 69–72, 91, 151–3, 160, 183, 190–1, 199, 206, 216–17, 219, 234, 251–5, 257
Horowitz, Donald L. 4–5, 7, 9–10, 39, 42, 70, 138, 174, 181–206
human rights 6, 14, 17, 25, 27–30, 70–2, 85, 87–9, 92–3, 106–7, 110–13, 116, 118, 120, 126, 129–30, 153, 164, 191, 201, 216
humanitarianism 41, 87, 89, 93
Hume, David 161
Hungarians 199, 219, 238, 242, 244–5, 250, 256–7
Hungary 184, 221, 242, 245, 249–50
Hussein, Saddam 79, 83

Ibo 188–9, 192, 199
Iceland 3, 11, 68, 113–14, 116, 160, 223–4
ideal theory 113, 118, 130–2
identity:
  collective 23, 135, 150–2, 197–8, 254–6
  distinct 140, 171
  dual 66–7, 152, 154, 220, 222, 227
  ethnic 105, 137–8, 160, 199
  minority 136, 217
  national 2–7, 12, 37, 39, 49, 62–3, 65, 69, 71–2, 74–5, 106, 108–10, 124, 134, 160, 170, 234, 241, 243–5, 247–8, 251
  political 169
  Russian 188
  secession and 224–5
  self 110, 120, 125–6
  self-determination 82–3
  separatist 95–6
immigrants 44, 65, 105–8, 143, 191, 201, 243, 253–4
impartiality 86–8, 98
incentives 9, 22, 36–7, 42, 44, 63, 84–5, 94, 116, 118, 129, 190
independence:
  attempt 184
  colonial 75, 79–80, 82–7, 90–6, 136, 158–9
  indigenousness and 202
  majority 15–16
  minority 14, 173, 185
  nationalism 236–7
  outright 154
  pluralism 217–22, 225–7
  political 3, 49, 62, 66, 69
  territory 192, 194
Independence to Colonial Countries and Peoples, Declaration Granting of (UN 1960) 84
indeterminacy 2, 134–5
India 83, 160, 184–5, 192–3, 196, 199
indigenousness 141–5, 149–50, 201–2, 224
individualism 162–6
Indonesia 42, 166
injustice:
  democracy 15, 25
  ethics 37, 40–5, 48, 53
  intervention and 87
  minority 74
  nationalism and 115, 117–18, 130–1
  pluralism 216
  right to secede 111–14, 135
  right to self-determination 80, 83, 90, 96, 99
  rights language 169
  self-determination and 4–6, 198
  territory 140, 142
institutions:
  democratic 22–3
  electoral 196
  ethics 50–2, 55–6
  minorities and 151
  moral reasoning 8–9, 24, 44–50
  nationalism and 127–8, 130, 233, 235–6, 240, 246–7, 254–6, 259
  secession and ethics 35, 38
  self-determination and 7, 81–2, 84–5, 88, 92, 94, 98–9
  state and secession 224–6, 228
instrumental value of democracy 17–18, 23
integration 105, 191, 196, 215, 226, 241–2
interest, national 20, 250–1
intermingled population 66, 72, 105, 120, 152–4, 182, 192, 254
international relations 26, 89
intervention 27–9, 64, 87–90, 92–3, 100, 227
  non- 71, 173

intrinsic value of democracy 17–18, 20, 23
invasion 63, 106, 116
Iraq 1, 42–3, 49, 79, 83, 87, 111, 166–7
Ireland 1, 72, 74, 84, 113, 135, 143–4, 146–7, 151, 217–19, 224–5
irredentism 91, 182–6, 193, 224–5
Israel 1, 49, 71, 120, 145–8, 201, 224
Italy 106, 160, 167, 203

Japan 160
Jennings, Ivor 2
Jews 145–6, 246
Jinnah, Mohammed 83
jurisdictional units 134–5, 140, 144, 149
just-cause theory 5–6, 8, 35, 38, 41–5, 47, 50–6
justice 2, 25, 27, 30, 51, 53, 135, 161–2
 distributive 7, 12, 35, 43, 65, 73–5, 80, 83, 86, 94
 see also injustice
justification:
 for democracy 15–17, 19–21, 23–4
 of power 26–7
 for secession 1, 5, 19, 37, 63–5, 70, 74, 96–7, 112, 116, 131, 169–70, 172, 198
 for self-determination 80, 82
 for territory 135, 141, 143, 145–51, 154

Kant, Immanuel 197
Kashmir 1, 88, 184, 218
Kazakhstan 187, 193, 219
Kedourie, Elie 6, 159, 169
Kokoschka, Oskar 252, 253
Kosovo 183–4, 199
Kuhn, Thomas 240
Kurds 1, 42, 66, 79, 83, 87, 105, 111, 166–7, 217–18, 238
Kymlicka, Will 37, 126, 198

Laitin, David 242
language 3, 36–7, 66–7, 71–2, 82, 96, 104, 106–7, 124–5, 136, 138, 142, 202–3, 215, 218–19, 221, 224–5, 238, 255–6, 259
 of rights 11, 158–74
Lapps 105–6
last resort, secession as 25, 39, 86–8, 90–1, 94, 96
Latin America 10, 14
Latvia 54, 219, 221, 226
law, international:
 colonialism 218
 democracy and 14–16, 21, 24–8, 30
 ethics and 35–6, 40, 44–7, 49–50
 nationalism 111, 114–15, 119, 128–30
 politics and 189–90, 197, 200–6
 rights language 174
 self-determination and 1–3, 8–10, 182
 self-determination in practice 81, 84–93, 98–100
 territory 136
leadership 184–5, 188, 195–6
legalization of self-determination 84, 86, 88–91, 98–9
legitimacy:
 of nationalism 158–60
 political 24–30
 of secession 5–6, 15, 35, 37–8, 41, 46, 51–2, 73, 115, 173–4, 192–3, 216, 218
 of self-determination 84
Lessing, Doris 108
levelling function of rights language 165–6
Levine, Andrew 109
liberal democracy:
 ethics 45
 nationalism and 103–4, 107–8, 110, 112–19, 122, 129–31
 philosophy 79–80, 83, 85–6
 rights language 161
 secession 11–12, 35, 37, 40, 43
liberal nationalism and secession 103–32
liberalism 2, 5, 52, 72, 86, 94–5, 125
 pluralism 215–16, 223–4, 228
 rights language 158–9, 161, 164, 169–70, 173
 secession and 34–6, 39, 41
 territory 137, 150
liberty 34, 150–1, 236
Lithuania 93, 224, 249
Locke, John 6, 144, 147, 148

Maastricht Treaty 241
MacCormick, Neil 197
Macedonia 145, 189, 238
McGarry, John 4, 7, 10, 12, 215–28
MacIntyre, Alasdair 161
Madison, James 196
Magyars 141, 220, 221–2
Maine, Henry Sumner 194
majority:
 democratic 17–18
 ethnic 219–20
 minority relations 10–12, 45, 67–8, 116, 215–17, 221–2, 227
 numbers 70
 preference to secede 37, 41, 80, 111, 115, 172
 right to secede 15–16, 19, 21–3

majority (*cont.*):
rights language 159, 166
self-determination 2–3
super- 6, 53–5, 64, 83, 86, 94, 97
territory 136, 150–1, 154
Malaysia 143, 183, 192, 219
Manichean view of nationalism 235, 257–60
Margalit, A. 39, 170, 172–3, 174, 197, 199
marginalization 142
Mazzini, G. 159
Meciar, Vladimir 221
migration 143–4, 149, 191, 222, 225
Mill, J. S. 52, 80, 151, 159
Miller, David 7, 9, 11, 62–75, 104, 122, 169, 171, 173, 197
Milosevic, Slobodan 248
minorities:
dissenters and 151–2, 154
distributive justice 73–5
ethics 42–4, 47, 49
ethnic 194
ethnic and pluralism 218–21
identity 136, 217
language rights 170, 173
majority relations 10–12, 45, 67–8, 116, 215–17, 221–2, 227
nation-states 65, 67
national 4, 12, 35–9, 53, 55, 106–8, 112–14, 118, 238
numbers 69–72
problems of 199–200, 224–8
rights 65, 80, 83, 88, 92, 94–6, 99, 107–8, 115, 120, 142, 153, 200–6, 297–8
secession 14, 21, 217
self-determination 62
stranded 79, 91, 97
territory 134, 138–40
veto 21, 30
mobilization 3–5, 7, 36, 42, 219, 222–4, 243, 248–50
Modigliani, Amedeo 234, 252–5
Moldova 187, 222
Moore, Margaret 1–12, 134–54, 172, 174
moral rights:
language of 158, 160–2, 164–9
to secession 128–30
to self-determination 80–4, 95–6, 99, 172–4
morality 4–10, 16, 34, 40, 45–7, 49–50, 52, 54–5, 128, 137, 140, 147, 160, 171, 198
More, Thomas 147
movements:
democracy 14–15
ethics of secession 35, 37–40, 42, 44, 46, 49–51, 53, 55
national 70, 113, 118, 235, 237–8, 243
pluralism and 216–19, 224–5
politics and 202, 298
politics and self-determination 181–91
rights language 159
self-determination 5–8, 10–12
self-determination in practice 79, 81, 83, 85–6, 90–1, 98–9
territory and secession 139–40
multiculturalism 253–4
multiethnicity 55, 136, 159–60, 195–6, 198, 201–2, 215
multinationalism 1, 35, 45, 49, 53, 103, 108, 110, 116, 119–20, 159, 167–8, 171, 215, 217, 225–7, 236–7, 255
Muslims 79, 83, 91, 97, 151, 153, 239

Nagorno-Karabagh 182, 184, 222–3
nation-building 37, 40, 42, 151, 218, 242, 257
nation-states:
ethics 40, 55
nationalism 105, 107–8, 110, 114, 116, 119–20, 129, 235, 237–8, 246, 252–3, 258–9
nationality 63, 65, 70
rights language 159–60, 167, 170
self-determination 10
territory 138
US as 215
national pluralism 215–28
national self-determination:
ethnic and democratic 150–4
rhetoric of rights 158–74
territory 134, 137, 141–50
theory 5, 7–8, 35–7, 39, 41–2, 44–5, 47, 49–51, 55
nationalism:
ethnic 223
myths and misconceptions 233–60
rights language 158–9, 161, 163–72, 174
secession and liberal 103–32
self-determination 1–2, 7–8, 117, 119–21, 234–6, 238–40
territory 138–41, 151
nationality:
nationalism and 118, 120–7
secession and principles of 62–75
nationalization 221–2, 225–6, 237–8, 241–2, 244, 249, 253, 255, 258–9

nationhood 234–5, 238, 240–1, 245–7, 252, 256–60
Nehru, Jawaharlal 83
network analysis 251, 255
Nielsen, Kai 7, 9, 11–12, 38, 103–32, 134, 223, 224
Nigeria 188–9, 192, 195, 199
no-fault secession 38, 41
Norman, Wayne 4–5, 6, 8, 34–56, 95, 97, 166
normative theory 1, 4–5, 7–9, 12, 26–7, 35–43, 48, 55, 115, 117–18, 128–9, 131, 159–60, 170, 222, 227, 236, 257–9
Norway 11, 106, 113–14, 223

obligations 25–7, 65, 73, 104–5
occupancy, first 142, 202, 216
Ogaden 183–4
Organization of African Unity 190
orientalism 241, 244–5, 257

Pakistan 87, 111, 184–5, 187, 192–3, 199
Palestine 1, 120, 146–8, 201, 218, 238
Paris Peace Accord (1919) 3, 136
participation, political 17–19, 21–3, 25, 81–2
partition 152, 168, 191–3
Peres, Shimon 148
philosophy, political 4–5, 7, 9, 17, 25–7, 34–6, 39, 41–2, 47, 71, 80, 100, 158, 163, 165, 168–9, 182, 197–200, 216
Philpott, Daniel 4–7, 9–11, 16–19, 23–5, 38, 43, 79–100, 134–5, 172–4, 216, 218
Pinochet, Ugarte 107
plebiscitary right to secession 15–22, 24–5, 29–30
plebiscite 3, 10, 86, 94, 134, 150, 172, 216
pluralism 24, 123–4, 126, 193–7, 199
  secession and 215–28
Poland 145, 218, 255, 258
politics:
  democratic 18–23
  ethnic 39
  national 237, 243–4, 246–51
  nationalism 260
  secessionist 44, 48–9, 51, 55, 100
  self-determination 38, 181–7, 182
polynationalism 127
post-modernism 252, 255
power:
  political 26–7
  relations 48, 137, 185, 195–6, 203, 221, 226, 258
practice, self-determination in 79–100
primary right theory 5, 41, 111–12, 114–16, 118–19, 121–2, 127–32, 134–5
procedures for secession 6, 9, 12, 24, 45, 48–9, 50–3, 55, 63–4, 81, 94, 96–9
property rights 35, 68, 147–8
protection of minorities 173, 200, 203, 221, 224–5, 237, 242, 249
prudence 173–4
Prussia 255–6

Quebec 1, 11–12, 49, 62, 64, 67, 71–2, 79, 88, 90, 92, 94, 96, 98, 105–7, 114, 116, 124, 126, 135, 139–40, 152, 163–4, 167–8, 172–4, 217–18, 220, 223–4, 226–7, 238

Racial Discrimination, Convention on the Elimination of All Forms of (1961) 203
rational choice theory 251, 255
Rawls, John 22, 39, 47, 52, 125, 161
Raz, J. 39, 170, 172–3, 174, 197, 199
rebellion 221–3
reciprocal secessions 188–9
recognition 26–8, 30, 46, 66, 86–90, 93, 122, 136, 140, 150, 152–4, 173–4, 189–90, 201, 204–6, 215, 224, 238
referenda 48, 52–5, 64–5, 96–7, 134–5, 140, 149, 152, 218, 220, 223
refugees 41, 44
regionalism 65, 97, 184, 193, 198, 205
religion 3, 137, 141, 145–7, 149, 154, 185, 219, 255
remedial right theory 6, 15, 25, 29–30, 41, 110–12, 114–15, 118, 121–2, 135
representation 17, 19, 43, 55, 81–3
repressed, return of the, and conflict 234, 245–8
resources 20, 74–5, 112–13, 149
respect, equal 2, 12, 16, 19–21, 23, 30, 103, 108–9, 121–3, 130, 200, 204, 215, 223, 228
rhetoric 163–6, 169
right to secession:
  democracy 15, 28, 30
  ethics 35–7, 40–1, 44, 46, 48, 50–2
  justice 135–6
  nationalism 108, 110–12, 114–15, 117, 121
  nationality 63, 75
  pluralism 216
  politics 197–8, 200

right to secession (*cont.*):
presumptive 34, 43, 103, 110, 135
rights language 165, 169, 171–3
self-determination and 1, 4–6, 8–11
right to self-determination 1, 3, 7
ethics 35
nationalism 115, 118, 239
pluralism 216
politics 193, 201–2
in practice 80–1, 86, 93–9
rights language 163, 165, 170–4
territory 139, 145, 151, 154
rights:
collective 5, 7, 162–5, 198, 222, 238
definition 165
ethnic 200
individual 18, 171, 173, 215, 228
land 141–5
language and self-determination 158–74
minority 39, 42–4, 138, 153, 193, 197, 200–6, 297–8
see also human rights
Rights of Indigenous Peoples, Declaration on the (UN) 142, 201–2
Rights of Minorities, Declaration on the (UN) 203
Romania 141, 224, 242, 244–5, 249–50, 256–7
Rousseau, J.-J. 44, 47, 52, 81
Russia 181, 188, 192–4, 219–22, 226, 238, 243, 250, 256
Rwanda 80, 87

Sandel, Michael 161–2
scope of distributive justice 73
Scotland 11, 49, 64, 67, 69, 113–14, 116, 124, 152, 205, 220, 223–4
secession:
pluralism and 215–28
politics and 182–90, 192–3, 196–206
theory 25, 63–5, 113, 127–9, 171
Security Council (UN) 86–90, 93, 99
'seething cauldron' and conflict 234, 241–5
Selassie, Haile 187
self, national 238–9
self-definition 7, 109–10, 120–3
self-government:
autonomy 81–3
democracy 15, 17–20, 23
nationalism 103–6, 108, 110, 112, 115–16, 119–23, 127, 235
pluralism 219, 226
politics 197
rights language 172–3
self-determination 10
territory 135, 137, 140, 150
separatism 12, 83–4, 88, 90–2, 94–9, 114, 185–90, 201, 205, 223, 225–6
Serbia 88, 116, 138–9, 153, 184, 189, 199, 239
Serbs 79, 83, 91, 97, 145, 151, 153, 181, 193, 199, 219, 221, 239, 250
Sheffer, David J. 204–5
short-circuiting function of rights language 165–8
Simmons, John A. 25
Singapore 91, 219
Sinhalese 143, 195, 202
Slovakia 79, 92, 96, 98, 181, 184, 199, 220–2, 242, 250
Slovenia 64, 88, 92–3, 138, 153, 174, 189, 203, 219, 223
Smith, Anthony 233
Somalia 49, 87, 183–4, 187, 189
South Africa 14, 27, 143, 146–7, 201
sovereignty:
democracy as 15, 17
legitimacy 42
nation 194–5
nationalism and 110–11, 119, 127, 253
population and 204–6
rights 174
self-determination and 63, 65, 85–6, 89–91, 93–4, 98–9
territory and 135–6, 140, 152–3
units of 4
Soviet Union 1, 10–11, 14, 29, 53–4, 68, 79, 85, 87, 92–3, 104, 116, 140–1, 160, 181, 187–90, 200, 219, 222, 235–6, 243, 245–8, 256–8
Spain 62, 66, 69, 74, 113, 152, 220
Sri Lanka 1, 143, 187, 191, 195, 202, 218
stability 12, 22, 30, 40, 91, 94, 119, 139, 182, 185–7, 219, 222, 235, 245
state 27, 39–40, 47–8, 63, 87–8, 98–9, 111, 215, 236–7, 259
state-building 87, 89, 93, 257
stigmatization 183–4
strategic behaviour and democracy 21–4, 30
subordination 6, 14, 42, 44, 63, 82–3, 91, 94, 96, 99, 105, 108, 118–19, 169, 173, 189, 191, 198–9, 204
Sudan 1, 183, 185, 190
Sunstein, Cass 95
support 28, 53, 185–7, 217–20, 224–6
supra-state partnerships 217, 227
survival 111, 166, 198

Sweden 11, 106, 113–14, 203
Switzerland 119, 226

Taiwan 183–4
Tamir, Yael 170
Tanzania 138, 191
Taylor, Charles 161
television, role of, and nationalism 244–5
territory:
democracy and 25, 28–9
dimension of self-determination 134–54
ethics and 36–7, 41–2, 44–5, 49, 54
nationalism and 104–5, 110, 114–17, 119–20, 127, 129, 233, 235–6, 238–9, 246, 253–4, 259
nationality and 62–5, 67–9, 72, 75
pluralism and 215–18, 222, 225, 227
politics and self-determination 181–2, 184–98, 201–4
rights 141–5, 147–50
rights language and 170, 172
self-determination 2–5, 6–7
threat:
as right to secession 80, 82, 86, 90, 96, 99
of secession 21, 30, 38, 42, 54–5, 95, 97, 118–19
of violence 243
Tibetans 42, 201
Tilly, Charles 233
Tito (Josip Broz) 138
titular nationality 194, 246
transborder groups 4, 54, 185, 193, 205, 217, 225, 237, 242–3, 249–50
Transylvania 66, 184, 243, 250, 256
treaties 202–3
trumping function of rights language 165
Turkey 1, 42, 65–6, 181, 217, 224
Tyroleans 106, 203

Ukraine 181, 219, 221–2, 224, 227, 249–50, 256
Ulster Scots 146–7
UNESCO Convention against Discrimination in Education (1960) 203
United Kingdom of Great Britain and Northern Ireland 11, 43, 113–14, 116, 124, 135, 171, 189, 205, 215, 219–20, 225
United Nations (UN) 9, 36, 84–7, 92–3, 99, 114, 139, 142, 200, 202–3
Charter 136, 193
unity 40, 95, 217–18, 226
universalism of claims 167, 169–70
use of land and rights 148–9

vanity secessions 52–5, 95, 99, 166
Versailles Treaty 200, 202
victimization 86, 96
violence 42–3, 54, 79–81, 83, 91, 99, 112–14, 116, 218, 221–3, 234, 241–3, 245, 249–50

Waldron, Jeremy 122, 126–7
Wales 64, 69, 105, 113–14, 205
Walzer, M. 80
war 42, 54, 79, 83, 88, 91–2, 99, 183, 186, 188–90, 193, 198–9, 201, 205, 242, 249
Weber, Max 247
Wellman, C. H. 75
Westphalia, Peace of (1648) 89–90, 202, 227
Wilson, Woodrow 2–3, 80, 85, 136, 194, 202
Winthrop, John 147, 148
Wittgenstein, Ludwig 124, 165
World Court 86–8

Yack, Bernard 169, 171
Yeltsin, Boris 188
Yugoslavia 1, 11, 64, 71, 83, 88, 104, 120, 138–9, 145, 151, 153, 173–4, 181, 189–92, 194, 199–201, 205, 219, 235–6, 239, 241–3, 247–50

Zaire 49, 80, 191, 199
Zangwell, Israel 148